PITTSBURGH RISING

Pitts

EDWARD K. MULLER
& ROB RUCK

FROM FRONTIER TOWN T

burgh Rising

O STEEL CITY, 1750–1920

UNIVERSITY OF PITTSBURGH PRESS

Published by the University of Pittsburgh Press, Pittsburgh, Pa., 15260
Copyright © 2023, University of Pittsburgh Press
All rights reserved
Manufactured in the United States of America
Printed on acid-free paper
10 9 8 7 6 5 4 3 2 1

Cataloging-in-Publication data is available from the Library of Congress

ISBN 13: 978-0-8229-4772-1
ISBN 10: 0-8229-4772-2

Cover art: Hayley Lever, *Allegheny River*, Pittsburgh, ca. 1923. Oil on canvas,
20 x 24 inches. Westmoreland Museum of American Art.
Cover design: Joel W. Coggins

FOR KATE AND MAGGIE

CONTENTS

PITTSBURGH RISING

INTRODUCTION

CATHECASSA BLACKHOOF IS LARGELY FORGOTTEN IN PITTSBURGH, except for a roughly cut stone marker in Schenley Park. But his life intersected with James Smith, Mike Fink, James O'Hara, and the men and women who forged the city from the 1750s into the early nineteenth century. The warrior fought against George Washington during General Braddock's 1755 campaign to dislodge the French, and later clashed with US forces driving indigenous people from land they once roamed. After their defeat at Fallen Timbers in 1794, he acknowledged US supremacy. A year later he signed the Treaty of Greenville that conceded native claims to western lands and encouraged the Shawnee to coexist with "white people." When the republic failed to deliver on its promises, he implored President Thomas Jefferson to stand by its word. Blackhoof, who remained the principal leader of the Shawnee until his death in 1831 at the age of 109, was sadly disappointed by Jefferson's response. Though he resisted efforts to push the Shawnee across the Mississippi River, Blackhoof believed that continued warfare was futile. His attempt to coexist was a path not taken. Smith, Fink, and O'Hara had little interest in accommodating indigenous people, whom most white people feared and many loathed. Instead, they created Pittsburgh in their own image.

Thomas Mellon, Martin Delany, Margaret Carnegie, William Frank, Miranda Hollander, and thousands like them came to Pittsburgh in the first half of the nineteenth century knowing little of the people who had first lived in the region. They hoped to improve their prospects; only some succeeded. Following the Civil War, waves of immigrants from southern, central, and eastern Europe arrived. So did wayfarers from the Eastern Seaboard and African Americans from southeastern states. Many came to tap the opportunities the rapidly industrializing region offered in its mines, mills, and factories. George and Elena Kracha, Palmira and Agostino Carlino, Mamie and William Tinker, and other émigrés added new ethnic, religious, and racial pieces to the cultural mosaic established by earlier migrants.[1] More men came at first because Pittsburgh's economy offered women fewer opportunities. Over time those who stayed made choices about where to live, whom to marry, what religious and social groups to join, whether to vote, and when to take their protests into the streets. Their decisions and those of their children and grandchildren propelled Pittsburgh into the twentieth century. They built the city and surrounding towns and defended their way of life during the Revolutionary War, the Civil War, and World War I. But they also fought with each other as they endeavored to establish themselves in the region.[2]

Rapid industrial growth and a surging population created a dynamic, ever-changing urban economy and neighborhoods where people sometimes thrived but often struggled. Some came equipped with skilled trades, such as puddler James Davis of Welsh ancestry, or with education, such as Isaac Frank, the son of German Jews. Boys like Andrew Carnegie and Henry Oliver tapped their social connections in Allegheny City's Scottish immigrant community, while philanthropist Kate McKnight benefited from her family's lineage and ample wealth. They for the most part achieved considerable status and forged remarkable careers. Others without such advantages, such as Miranda Hollander and Mike Dobrejcak, settled here as unskilled, disposable workers in factories, mills, and mines or joined the ranks of domestic servants and day laborers in construction and hauling where low wages, insecure employment, and dangerous conditions circumscribed life.[3]

Class and cultural differences divided these diverse immigrants and native-born Pittsburghers between the shop floor and managerial offices, and thwarted efforts by unskilled and skilled workers to seek common ground. Ethnic, religious, and racial solidarities provided some comfort and mutual assistance but also sparked animosity. None carried a heavier burden of difference and discrimination than the Delanys and Tinkers, whose African American heritage visibly distinguished them. Irish, Italian, and southern and eastern European Catholic immigrants also felt the sting of perceived racial differences for a generation or longer. Through the eyes of management, Kracha's son-in-law Mikhail "Mike" Dobrejcak, was just a "Hunky."[4] It did not matter that he learned English and became a citizen; Mike never escaped the limitations and injustices of unskilled millwork. Instead of entering the mills, Italian immigrant Agostino Carlino's sons carried on their father's stonework and, as second-generation ethnics, participated more fully in American life, speaking English, gaining education, and purchasing homes. Similarly, German Jew William Frank's sons achieved success in business and the professions.[5] So did William Tinker's son Carl, who became a pharmacist, one of the few professions open to African Americans in the city. Though their names were not affixed to downtown skyscrapers or corporations, these immigrants' tenacity and that of their sons and daughters shaped Pittsburgh's emerging narrative.

Pittsburgh began as a remote colonial outpost on the North American frontier in the 1750s. Nearly a century and a half later it was a national powerhouse. The eighteenth century's wars of empire, initiated by England and France, periodically enveloped southwestern Pennsylvania. These conflicts brought faraway rivalries to the succession of forts and villages at the forks of the Ohio River. Native Americans, the first people to rove through the region, were prominent actors in these imperial struggles and their aftermath. They bore the brunt of European expansion, which took their land and dismissed their humanity. Once stewards of the backwoods, most indigenous people would abandon the territory.

With the conclusion of the American Revolution and the formation of the United States, the frontier town of Pittsburgh at the confluence of the three rivers—the Allegheny, Monongahela, and Ohio—became the lynchpin for trade and migration between Philadelphia and Baltimore to the east and settlements rising in the Ohio Valley to the west. Insulated from more advanced eastern competitors by the seemingly endless ridges of the Allegheny Mountains, Pittsburgh grew into a modestly sized city with aspirations of becoming the mid-continent's commercial emporium. By the middle of the nineteenth century, however, western settlement had inexorably moved to and beyond the Mississippi River Valley, where newer cities—Louisville, Cincinnati, and St. Louis—more easily serviced the receding frontier. The rapid development of railroads further eroded the natural advantages of the city's location at the headwaters of the Ohio River. Both freight and passengers could now bypass Pittsburgh as they journeyed westward.

As these commercial roles declined, manufacturers partnered with market-savvy, financially resourceful merchants to exploit nearby coalfields and develop nascent glass and iron industries. Demand for munitions during the Civil War and a burgeoning railroad market for rails and equipment transformed the once commercial city into a center for iron manufacturing. With the shift from iron to steel after 1880, several small partnerships evolved into modern industrial corporations led by entrepreneurs who were as innovative as they were aggressive. The likes of Andrew Carnegie, B. F. Jones, Henry Oliver, Henry Clay Frick, and George Westinghouse boosted Pittsburgh and southwestern Pennsylvania to national leadership in mass-produced steel, railroad equipment, coke, and machinery. Local investors and venture capitalists, notably but not only the Mellons, developed the capacity to underwrite new products such as aluminum and plate glass. They backed the costly transition to vertically integrated production. The latter entailed controlling primary resources such as coal and iron ore, engaging in each phase of production, and marketing finished goods under one corporate umbrella. The financiers also underwrote buyouts of competitors and engineered mergers to form ever-larger corporations that reverberated throughout the country and crossed borders. With its population surpassing a million before World War I, the Pittsburgh industrial region ranked among the nation's half-dozen largest metropolitan areas. But its rapid growth came at a steep cost for many.

Pittsburgh's industrialists, bankers, and professionals heartily embraced a private enterprise, free market ideology stressing individual initiative and responsibility. Many were Scottish and Scotch-Irish Presbyterians who believed that the accumulation of wealth and power was a sign of their favorable predestination by God. Business leaders saw only a limited role for government and favored leaving the economy to the operation of market forces. They considered individuals largely responsible for their own welfare. Men and women whose wealth derived from commercial and professional pursuits or family inheritance exercised substantial power and authority. Sharing family connections, neighborhoods, churches, clubs, and political affiliations, they forged a cohesive class identity. Protestants dominated the city's upper class, while Catholics like Daniel Rooney and Jews like Isaac Frank who succeeded in Pittsburgh's business and professional arenas built separate social spheres.[6] As the region grew, the elite class became more varied in composition but remained self-consciously distinct from the socially diverse working and middle classes who comprised the bulk of the population. The wealthy enjoyed considerable control over the business and political life of the city, though their hegemony was weakening by 1900.[7]

The power and perspective of the upper class did not go unchallenged. Mass production, new waves of immigrants, and feeble governmental responses to public needs fomented dissatisfaction and conflict, even bloodshed. As owners' and workers' interests diverged in the first half of the nineteenth century, workers' protests, strikes, and violence punctuated peaceful, though fragile, labor relations. Skilled craftsmen eventually gained a measure of power on the shop floor by leveraging their unity and knowledge of production. But between the Civil War and World War I, mechanization in factories and mills, along with the increasing scale of production, shattered skilled workers' traditional craft practices and power. In spontaneous work stoppages, organized labor actions, and at the polls, Pittsburgh workers protested their deteriorating wages, working conditions, and status. Girls and women took axes to the doors of textile factory compounds in 1848. The entire community angrily protested the use of the state militia to suppress railroad protesters in 1877, and the Monongahela River turned red with the blood of Pinkerton detectives and mill workers in Homestead in 1892. But manufacturers, with the support of the upper class, the state's police power, and the courts, usually prevailed. The arc bent toward justice in the workplace, but very slowly.[8]

Remarkable diversity along ethnic, religious, and racial lines further fragmented the region's social cohesion. Those divisions both incited conflict among different groups of working people and fueled opposition to upper-class rule. Long-standing animosities between Protestants and Catholics turned vicious at times and exacerbated underlying citizen distrust of civic leaders. Enmity among ethnic groups and between skilled and unskilled workers frequently disrupted labor's unity in their episodic challenges to manufacturers. As industry decentralized, spreading along the rivers beyond the original urban core, and improved transportation facilitated residential suburbanization, Pittsburgh's classes and cultures grew farther apart. This spatial separation, reinforced by western Pennsylvania's hilly topography and rivers, splintered the region into dozens of small, autonomous civil divisions, triggering its legendary fragmentation.[9] The uneven distribution of public services, such as water, sewers, street paving, and lighting, underscored stark political and class inequalities. Environmental and health problems especially burdened industrial neighborhoods and mill towns.[10] These inequities provoked sporadic political mobilization to bring about more satisfactory conditions for underserved communities.

Pittsburgh's neighborhoods and the region's small towns forged strong identities based on class, ethnicity, race, and place. They also encountered powerful centralizing counterforces. Huge corporations, such as the Carnegie Steel Company with its sprawling network of plants, mines, railroads, and Minnesota ore reserves, centralized operations and set new standards for industrial efficiency and output. In response, labor groped toward overcoming its internal divisions in order to field commensurate organizational power. Similarly, Pittsburgh's rapid growth, especially the annexation of the

South Side in 1872 and Allegheny City in 1906, cried out for a central government authority that could manage citywide infrastructure. A budding cohort of professional managers in business and government added to the separation of, and friction among, classes and local communities. These large, centralized institutions with growing bureaucracies threatened community control over schools and governance, even churches and charities. These forces contributed to a pervasive and almost innate distrust of outside authority that can be traced as far back as the "Whiskey Rebels" in the 1790s.

In sync with the nation's free market, individualistic, and political economy, Pittsburgh became a leading industrial metropolis. A few individuals grew unimaginably wealthy, and the city's East End, where Westinghouse, H. J. Heinz, Frick, the Mellon brothers, and other industrial magnates lived, became one of the most affluent neighborhoods in the country during the late 1800s. A comfortable middle class also emerged, but the largest share of the population lived with neither a secure nor adequate income. Mike Dobrejcak and steel laborers across the region feared the destitution that frequently accompanied workplace injury, illness, or layoffs. Clustered in neighborhoods fouled by a degraded environment, they lived in ramshackle dwellings and crowded tenements. Women like Elena Kracha and Mary Dobrejcak suffered the consequences of industrial capitalism as much as men. Largely excluded from the workplace, they were tasked with keeping the family healthy, bearing and rearing the children, and supplementing household income by taking on piecework or taking in boarders. Providing a bed and food for single men who labored in the mills, washing their clothes, and offering them a semblance of family life were the only ways many families survived, but added to women's already strenuous familial duties. In the struggle to remain afloat, the Carlinos and other immigrant, low-income families often depended on churches, charitable groups, and a marginally responsive government to ameliorate their situation. Voluntary philanthropic and reform efforts, occasionally supported by local and state government, experienced modest success. But whenever environmental, housing, and health reform proposals impinged on the conduct of business, they faltered in the face of powerful forces that privileged industrial growth and the assumed rights of private property.[11] Consequently, the problems associated with treacherous workplace conditions, poverty, and severely polluted air, water, and land challenged civic leaders throughout the twentieth century.

While economic and social inequalities diminished for European immigrants' children and grandchildren, racial discrimination stifled African Americans' prospects. Having fled slavery, Martin Delany and other African

Americans in antebellum Pittsburgh formed a small, viable, and free community, only to have the 1850 Fugitive Slave Law tear it apart. They slowly rebuilt their community after the Civil War. Beginning in the 1890s, a new wave of black migrants began making their way to the city. Those who came with education and expertise, like Cumberland Posey Sr. and Robert L. Vann, redefined African American success in business and journalism. But among them were many poorly educated, unskilled, rural southern folk. Tensions arose between long-term black residents and these impoverished migrants. The latter in particular suffered discrimination in employment and segregation in housing that made it difficult to escape poverty and find a reason to remain in Pittsburgh, which contributed to higher residential turnover for African Americans than most other émigrés to the city.

The centralization of corporate and financial power under the control of the city's elite, whose skyscraping headquarters downtown bore their names, increasingly distanced them from the working-class communities spread throughout the city and region. A growing rancor and distrust across the widening class divide aggravated the municipal fragmentation already hindering the cooperation necessary to resolve metropolitan issues. In short, the rapacious industrial capitalism that carried Pittsburgh to the front ranks of American industrial metropolises came at a terrible cost. It left the city and region economically and socially imbalanced, environmentally degraded, and racially divided, challenges that defined the region for the next century.

Ironically, this rapacious phase of industrial capitalism was already changing by World War I. With reformers, local government, and labor organizations nibbling at upper-class prerogatives, the elite's grip was eroding. A handful of powerful national corporations wrested ownership of the iron and steel industry away from them.[12] Carnegie Steel's demise exemplified this shift. Though the company was Pittsburgh's premier industrial corporation at the end of the nineteenth century, it and nearly two dozen other local iron and steel companies merged in 1901 to form the U.S. Steel Corporation. The industrial behemoth, the largest company on the planet, was headquartered more than three hundred miles away in New York City. During the twentieth century large national organizations with priorities that had little to do with Pittsburgh replaced other corporate decision makers. The process was uneven and slower than in several, often smaller, industrial cities, but no less painful when Pittsburgh corporations and banks were gobbled up. Of course, Pittsburgh businesses were not just victims of the nationalizing process. Some corporate and financial powers, including Alcoa, Gulf Oil, Heinz, Westinghouse, and Mellon Bank, had been investing and expanding into national and international markets as early as 1920 and did so even more aggressively after World War II. By then corporate Pittsburgh's branch plants, satellite offices, and investments in real estate developments were scattered from coast to coast.

The pre–World War I industrial metropolis was the product of more than 150 years of innovation, cooperation, and conflict. Those decades set the foundation on which Pittsburgh and the region—its citizens as much as its business leaders and their companies—would navigate the twentieth century. In terms of economic and population growth, Pittsburgh was at the top of its game, but the twentieth century was not kind to the city or the region. Increasing competition from other metropolitan areas, the Great Depression, and an overspecialized industrial base diminished the region's growth rate. Fear of long-term economic decline after World War II fostered a new, coordinated relationship between Pittsburgh's corporate leaders and local government officials to finally confront the region's persistent problems and diversify its economy. Despite significant success, especially in addressing air and water pollution, and national acclaim for its redevelopment program known as Renaissance I, Pittsburgh remained overly concentrated in its capital-intensive, pre–World War I industries and vulnerable to the harsh effects of globalization. At the same time, civic leaders cavalierly overlooked the damaging effects of urban redevelopment on low-income residents.

During the 1970s and 1980s overspecialization and globalization's irresistible pressure devastated much of the region's economic base, forcing it to turn away from its traditional industries. Unthinkable plant closures, the departure of iconic corporations, massive unemployment, racial strife, and steep population loss stimulated aggressive, partially successful redevelopment programs. But redevelopment and the shift to medicine, education, and high tech left a trail of winners and losers across southwestern Pennsylvania. Highly educated technology workers and professionals thrived, while former industrial and unskilled, low-wage workers floundered, many leaving the region forever. They held on to their emotional ties and clutched Terrible Towels as the Steel City became the City of Champions, but they could no longer support themselves in their hometown as industry contracted and their livelihoods crumbled.[13]

Still, Pittsburgh and southwestern Pennsylvania endured the twentieth century's tribulations. Pittsburgh's prospects for the twentieth-first century look decidedly more favorable than they have for more than half a century. Many attribute this persistence and transformation to the resilience and roguishness forged by the workers, entrepreneurs, and their families in the cauldron of the nineteenth century's rugged, impressive, and unsympathetic industrialization. Others point to the financial resources of its legacy foundations, the innovative impacts of its research universities, and the increasingly attractive amenities of its recuperating environment. These positive attributes can be traced in one way or another back to its formative years. This book spans the creation of Pittsburgh through World War I.

ONE

ON THE FRONTIER

ON JULY 3, 1755, AS JAMES SMITH AND ARNOLD VIGORAS RODE WEST through the Allegheny Mountains, they were fired on from a blind of bushes set off from the trail. Hit twice, Vigoras died before he struck the ground. Unscathed but thrown from his horse, Smith was seized by his captors, two Delaware and a Caughnawaga. While one of the assailants scalped Vigoras, another asked the Pennsylvanian in English if there were other white men nearby. He answered that he knew of none, and without deliberation the three warriors and their eighteen-year-old prisoner set off north through the mountains, running at what for Smith was a punishing pace. They did not stop until they had covered fifteen miles and passed the night without a fire, the first night of four years that Smith spent among indigenous people west of the Alleghenies.

Geopolitics and a respite from romance had brought the young man to western Pennsylvania. "I had fallen violently in love with a young lady," Smith recalled, "possessed of a large share of both beauty and virtue."[1] But in May 1755 Smith joined General Edward Braddock's campaign against the French, leaving his sweetheart in central Pennsylvania. Smith reckoned he would be back in her embrace by summer's end. He was as wrong in this as were the British forces who expected their march to the headwaters of the Ohio River would meet with quick success.

While Smith desired only a summer's adventure, the British sought control over the immense expanse of land west of the mountains. Their expedition aimed to seize Fort Duquesne, a French stockade recently erected on the triangle of land at the confluence of the Allegheny and Monongahela Rivers. There, at the future site of Pittsburgh, the British challenged the French for access to the vast heartland of North America.

Pittsburgh emerged as a military and pioneer outpost during the long and violent struggle in which Native Americans, Europeans, and colonists fought with and against each other to command the region. James Smith played a part in each of these overlapping conflicts. In the first, Britain wrested control of North America from France. In the second, the British and their colonial allies squashed indigenous resistance. In the third, the British, now with considerable indigenous support, tried to suppress their rebellious colonies. This time they lost. The fourth conflict determined whether Virginia or Pennsylvania would oversee the Ohio River Valley.

The unlikely winners in these clashes were colonists who joined the successful national liberation movement of 1776 and, in its wake, made Pittsburgh their home. These struggles left a lasting imprint, defining the region's economy and altering its ecosystem. They influenced the city's architecture and planning, as well as its languages, religions, and sports. And as they learned to distrust distant governments' willingness to protect them and offer them stability, the colonists developed a combative, antiauthoritarian localism, a political culture which has echoes in the present. Later waves of immigrants added their own legacies to the "city at the Point" as Pittsburgh has often been called.[2]

IMPERIAL CLAIMS

During the half-century before James Smith arrived in the Ohio River Valley, three aspiring empires—France, Britain, and Iroquoia—fought over the region. Resorting to force rather than reason or law, each tried to impose its authority over the sparsely populated territory. Each failed, but their imperial ambitions swept western Pennsylvania into the century-long "Great War for Empire" between France and England. Conflict at the headwaters of the Ohio River reignited that global confrontation, which was waged in Europe, India, the Philippines, and the Caribbean, as well as in Canada and west of the Appalachian Mountains. Known as the Seven Years' War (1756–1763), this conflict cost France its North American colonies and left Britain poised for global hegemony. While few at the time could have found the region on a map, the first blows of war were struck there.

James Smith, whose Scotch-Irish family had emigrated from the Isle of

Skye to Ulster and then Pennsylvania, had little sense of the geopolitical drama unfolding in the summer of 1755.³ He had scant knowledge of the waterways linking France's Canadian possessions to its foothold in New Orleans, or that the road he was carving through the mountains led to what Europeans perceived as North America's last great uninhabited and unexplored domain. Smith knew only that he was hungry, tired, and scared. Just the day before he had been working with three hundred Pennsylvanians hired by his brother-in-law to cut a wagon road from Fort Loudon in Franklin County west to the Youghiogheny River. Their path would carry provisions for General Braddock's force of 1,400 British regulars and 450 Virginians marching north from Maryland to confront the French.

Smith and Arnold Vigoras were checking on supply wagons when they were ambushed by indigenous scouts supporting the French at Fort Duquesne. When they didn't return to camp, a party of twelve men searched for them. They found Vigoras's body, but not his hair, and Smith's horse and hat, but not the youth. After small bands attacked the road company that night and the next day, thirty of them quit and headed home. No further efforts were made to find Smith.

The morning after Smith's capture, the warriors shared their meager breakfast with him, scrupulously dividing a few ounces of moldy biscuit and roasted groundhog served cold. They then trekked fifty miles, through thickets of mountain laurel and across a series of hills, until they reached the Loyalhanna Creek on the western slopes of Laurel Mountain. When Smith's captors uttered several long yells, which he became familiar with as the "scalp halloo" announcing that a scalp or prisoner had been taken, a party nearby answered with musket fire.

Once in camp Smith hungrily accepted their offer of turkey and venison. The next morning the combined parties headed toward Fort Duquesne. Reaching the fort, Smith stood numbly on the banks of the Allegheny River as the French greeted the warriors by firing muskets and detonating artillery pieces, all the while shouting in tongues foreign to him. Warriors bivouacked by the fort came racing toward them. Dressed in breechcloths and painted in what Smith considered the most hideous hues of vermilion, black, brown, and blue, they formed two rows. Smith realized that he had to run their gauntlet to reach the safety of the fort. Despite being flogged repeatedly, Smith had almost made it to the end of the line when he was knocked to the ground. As he tried to rise, a warrior tossed sand into his eyes, blinding him. "They continued to beat me most intolerably, until I was at length insensible," he wrote in his journal. "Before I lost my senses, I remember my wishing them to strike the fatal blow, for I thought they intended to kill me, but apprehended that they were too long about it."⁴

Smith awoke to find a French doctor hovering over him. The doctor opened a vein in his arm to bleed him and washed his wounds with brandy. Officers interrogated him about the road, threatening him with torture if he failed to answer truthfully. When the English-speaking Delaware who had captured Smith visited him in the infirmary, Smith asked if he had offended them so that they had cause to beat him "so unmercifully." The Delaware responded that Smith had been treated in customary fashion, but that from here on he "would be well used." To Smith's chagrin, that meant he wouldn't remain with the French but go with his captors after they and their French allies met Braddock's forces on the field of battle, a confrontation expected within days.[5]

European claims to western Pennsylvania were tenuous. England asserted its right to rule by virtue of John Cabot's voyage to North America in 1497. From a ship off the North Atlantic coast, the explorer claimed all lands stretching west to the Pacific Ocean. France countered in 1669, when Robert de La Salle and Louis Joliet, wintering on the shores of Lake Erie, declared possession of the lake and the "unoccupied territory" adjoining it. After reaching the spot where the Mississippi River empties into the Gulf of Mexico, La Salle expanded French pretensions, proclaiming sovereignty over all the land drained by the river. However, neither European power questioned its right to make such assertions or considered indigenous peoples' stewardship of the region.

By then the English monarch Charles II had granted the upper Ohio River Valley to William Penn to pay a debt owed the Quaker's father. The Province of Pennsylvania would extend to the west and north of the Delaware River, but its exact western boundary was not set. As Pennsylvania's proprietor, Penn exercised great latitude in shaping the colony. Mindful of the abuse Quakers had suffered in England and Massachusetts, he designated it as a religious refuge for them and other Christians. With no established church or religious taxes, Pennsylvania attracted a mix of immigrants that Penn envisioned living together in a colonial utopia.

Penn dealt honestly with native people. Seeking to coexist peacefully, he pledged not to take their lands without consent. As historian Daniel Richter wrote, "Infused with its Founder's personal vision and the Quaker values of many early colonists, Pennsylvania enjoyed remarkably peaceful relationships with its Native neighbors for more than half a century."[6] Penn considered them the "true lords of the soil."[7] Some colonists east of the Alleghenies grew close to indigenous people, eating and drinking with them, conducting trade, and even paying rent to farm their land. But this era of amity did not last.

After William Penn returned to England in 1701, his sons, who displayed few of their father's scruples, contrived to sell native lands in the eastern part of the colony to settle debts.[8] Harmony was even more fleeting in western Pennsylvania where both colonists and Native Americans committed massacres. As the influx of settlers seeking land grew, discord prevailed. So did Euro-American fears and anxieties.[9]

By the time James Smith was captured, the European presence along the Atlantic Seaboard had shaken indigenous life to its core. Even before many Europeans ventured across the Alleghenies, traders, settlers, and the microbes they carried had altered native culture and the landscape.[10] Europeans exchanged guns, powder, bullets, and other goods for furs and pelts, especially beaver. Firearms made conflict among native peoples deadlier, while the slaughter of beavers wiped the animal out in some locales, altering the ecological balance their dams sustained. Europeans then began seizing land for farming and animal husbandry. These sedentary farming practices introduced notions of private ownership alien to Native Americans who saw the land as a resource to be used but not owned. They chose to migrate with the season, minimizing impact on forests and meadows.[11]

The headwaters of the Ohio became a virtual no-man's land. European diseases coursed through the native population, striking as tribes were taking up arms against each other. "Never again in North America," historian Richard White argued, "would Indians fight each other on this scale or with this ferocity." War and disease bolstered European colonial power at the expense of Native Americans. Meanwhile, losses from epidemic and war were so catastrophic that tribes adopted prisoners taken in battle to replace those who had died. That kept James Smith and thousands of others alive.[12]

The Iroquois ruled western Pennsylvania by right of conquest from their homeland in the Mohawk Valley and Finger Lakes (present-day upstate New York). They stood in the way of French penetration from Canada and the Great Lakes and blocked British access via the Mohawk Valley. The Cherokee and Catawba made migration through the southern mountains almost as difficult. Nor was western Pennsylvania worth enough to risk tribal wrath. Other than pelts, the area was too far from the coast to market whatever goods it might produce.[13]

The Iroquois confederation known as the League of Five Nations was well positioned because the headwaters of the Hudson, Delaware, and Susquehanna Rivers lay within Iroquoia. These rivers and their tributary streams constituted the primary transportation grid for trade and travel. After all but wiping out the Erie in 1653, the Iroquois used western Pennsylvania as a hunting ground and demilitarized buffer zone between themselves and other tribes. Few dwelt there, nor did the region seem to matter—until the eighteenth century.

In the early 1700s settlers and land speculators along the Eastern Seaboard began squeezing the tribes living there. No longer able to freely range over the land, bands of Lenni Lenape, Seneca, and Shawnee crossed the Alleghenies. With the region hardly inhabited, a multi-tribal mix of Native Americans set up seasonal camps along the rivers. English and French traders lived among them, summering with tribes and exchanging metalware, guns, and alcohol for skins and furs. They brought packhorses loaded with trade goods over mountain trails and returned with beaver, fox, bear, and deer pelts.

Neither England nor France paid much attention to the disputed expanse between the Appalachians and the Mississippi River until the 1740s. By then the French had reason to fear that English influence over the tribes would undermine their fledgling North American empire. Unable to compete with better-made, less expensive British trade goods, they felt compelled to act when England claimed dominion over the Iroquois.

New France at mid-century consisted of Canada and Louisiana connected by a 1,500-mile artery of lakes and rivers. A Frenchman could leave Quebec and travel along the St. Lawrence River, across Lake Ontario and Lake Erie, down French Creek to the Allegheny River, from there to the Ohio, and finally float the Mississippi to New Orleans. He might portage on occasion or wait for rain to make the rivers navigable, but this watery highway was then state of the art. It offered better access to the interior than the mountain trails that the British trod.[14]

The Iroquois, however, saw the headwaters of the Ohio River as their fiefdom and recognized no claims to the land but their own. In 1744 they negotiated a treaty in Lancaster, Pennsylvania, with the Virginia Colony. The Virginians walked away four hundred pounds poorer but contending that the Iroquois had sold them all the land within the province "to the setting sun," including the Ohio River Valley. The Iroquois, on reflection, said they had understood the treaty to extend only as far west as the ridge of the Allegheny Mountains. That disagreement remained a sore spot for decades, until the sheer force of European arms and settlement made it moot.[15]

George Croghan, a Dublin-born immigrant known as the "King of the Traders," built a small empire in the region and became the Pennsylvania colony's de facto representative to Native Americans. From his headquarters where Pine Creek empties into the Allegheny (today the town of Etna) a few miles upriver from Fort Duquesne, Croghan's twenty-five-man operation included a boatyard, one hundred packhorses, and trading posts as far away as Lake Erie. In the spring of 1748 Croghan gathered delegations of Delaware, Shawnee, and Wyandot at Logstown, an indigenous town along the Ohio River. There Pennsylvania and Virginia presented a thousand pounds of powder, lead, and goods to the tribes, strengthening their ties to the colonies. Courted by the French and the British, Native Americans made tactical alliances with both. They welcomed the acquisition of copper kettles, textiles, steel knives, and muskets but recognized that rum caused grief and muskets required repair, powder, and lead available only from Europeans. Still, they realized that Europeans coveted the territory.

Fearing that loss of the Ohio River Valley would cost them Canada and Louisiana, France wagered it could impose its will on the region. Instead of relying on Native American allies to block the British, the French would occupy the region. Their gamble would cost them New France. In June 1749 Pierre Joseph Celeron de Blainville led twenty French soldiers and two hundred indigenous warriors to the Ohio River on a mission to reclaim the region and solidify ties with its inhabitants.[16] Paddling the St. Lawrence to Lake Erie, Celeron's flotilla portaged to Lake Chautauqua and made for the Allegheny River. Heading downstream to the Ohio, they nailed the French royal arms to trees and buried lead markers stating their claims to the region. Celeron warned the Native Americans he encountered that if they did not ally with his king, English settlers would push them west out of their lands. While willing to accept Celeron's presents and mindful of British incursions, the Native Americans rejected French sovereignty. Celeron buried the markers without the Native Americans present because he feared they would remove them. Nor would Native Americans forsake English traders, on whom they depended for firearms. Celeron accomplished little; his journal reveals misgivings that his forces were more the intimidated than the intimidators.

Indigenous people, as a matter of self-interest, did not bar British traders from the region. After making clear to Virginians that the Lancaster treaty of 1744 had not surrendered their land west of the Alleghenies, the Iroquois allowed them to build two forts along the Ohio River and settle to its south. They expected that Virginia's presence would fend off the French and assure a steady stream of trade goods.

The long war for empire between France and England remained quiet until France appointed Marquis Duquesne as governor of New France in 1752. His mandate was to arrest English advances in the region. Reshaping New France's pathetic military forces into a more formidable presence, Duquesne sent an expedition to construct forts from Presque Isle at Lake Erie to the headwaters of the Ohio. It was the largest display of force yet in western Pennsylvania. Native Americans dared not confront the expedition, and many worked for it as porters or hunters. But an outright challenge was not necessary. French forces crumbled on their own as scurvy, dysentery, and desertion incapacitated almost two-thirds of its 2,300 soldiers, stopping them long before they reached the Ohio.[17] Plans to build Fort Duquesne were postponed, but the expedition alarmed the Iroquois, who warned the French not to advance beyond Lake Ontario. France ignored their demands, however, and the Iroquois waited to see how the English would respond.

In 1753 Virginia governor Robert Dinwiddie countered, sending twenty-three-year-old George Washington to the headwaters of the Ohio to demand France leave western Pennsylvania. Washington had more than Virginia and Crown interests in mind as he appraised the region. Land speculation was how many acquired wealth in the colonies and his relations, Lawrence and Augustine Washington, had joined the Ohio Company, which successfully petitioned Dinwiddie and George II to grant them an enormous tract across the Alleghenies.[18]

By late November 1753 Washington reached the confluence of the Allegheny and Monongahela Rivers. Standing near where James Smith would wait for Braddock's army to free him, Washington noted in his journal that a fort at the "Land in the Fork" would command three rivers. Washington then went overland to deliver his message to the French at Fort Le Boeuf. The French scoffed at Washington's ultimatum. Over supper in which wine "gave a Licence to their Tongues to reveal their Sentiments more freely," French officers said they would soon possess the Ohio River Valley. Conceding that Britain could draw on greater resources and numbers, they reasoned British forces would respond too slowly to block them.[19] Britain's North American presence dwarfed that of France. While British colonial subjects numbered two million, New France counted only 150,000, and British commercial and naval superiority would be unstoppable in a protracted struggle. But the French believed that British colonial rivalries undercut their concerted action, while they could mobilize with greater speed and impact. Their native allies certainly could.

On his return Washington delivered the French response along with his expedition journal to Governor Dinwiddie. His description of France's growing presence in western Pennsylvania coursed through the transatlantic press, sounding alarms about French intentions. It also made the young Virginian a public figure. Courting native allegiances, Virginia promised the Iroquois it would build a "strong house" at the forks of the Ohio, where they could obtain superior goods and protection from the French.[20]

Virginia soon dispatched a small contingent of workmen and soldiers to the site to build Fort Prince George, more a garrison than a fort, before France beat them to it. When superior French forces arrived in mid-April

1754, the Virginians struck their colors and surrendered the post. The peaceful handover was no harbinger of the bloody war to come. By the time Washington returned in May, the French had built Fort Duquesne on the triangular piece of land where the Allegheny and Monongahela Rivers converged to form the Ohio River. The rivers protected two of its sides and a twelve-foot-wide stockade of earth and logs defended the third.

Fort Duquesne's daunting presence caused British traders and native allies to evacuate posts and villages along the rivers. But Washington, believing reinforcements would allow him to seize Fort Duquesne, was undeterred. Advancing to the Great Meadow, east of Chestnut Ridge, he struck the first blows in the Seven Years' War. On May 28, 1754, Washington and Tanacharison, an Iroquois chieftain, surprised French forces encamped north of the meadow. Coulon de Jumonville, the French commander, was reading a warning to the British to leave "French territory," when he was shot in the head and then scalped. French casualties were ten dead and twenty-one captured; Washington lost one man. Though the Seven Years' War did not officially commence for another two years, this ambush was the first direct combat between the European powers.

French charges of an unprovoked assassination circulated in Europe. Native Americans, believing that the restoration of British influence was imminent, began moving to Fort Necessity, Washington's camp at the Great Meadow. They were gone by July 4 when an overwhelming French and indigenous force compelled Washington's surrender.[21] Dismayed by Washington's lack of prowess as a warrior, the Iroquois no longer challenged the French and instructed those under their authority to "stand neutral."[22]

Washington unwittingly confessed to Jumonville's assassination when he signed a rain-splotched document of surrender, written in French and haltingly translated to him. News of the defeat caused little stir in Virginia, where many saw Washington's expedition as a speculative land grab. Benjamin Franklin, however, took French advances seriously. On May 9, 1754, he published his now-famous cartoon of a snake cut into thirteen pieces with the caption warning "Join or Die."

By then the Iroquois perceived both the English and French as dubious allies, but they needed to align with one or the other to obtain firearms essential to self-defense. Their goal was not so much to help either side win as to counter threats to their own autonomy. But their strategy wasn't working. "We don't know what you Christians, English and French together, intend," the Iroquois complained. "We are so hemmed in by both, that we have hardly a hunting place left."[23] With the prevailing winds shifting toward New France, many tribes switched sides or sought neutrality. However, neither the British military nor Virginia's governor Dinwiddie were willing to surrender control over the Ohio River Valley.

General Edward Braddock, recently appointed commander in chief of Britain's North American forces, arrived in Virginia in February 1755 with orders to take Fort Duquesne. Plagued by supply logistics, he demanded that a road be built across Pennsylvania's Allegheny Mountains to connect with forces marching through Virginia and Maryland. That road led to James Smith's imprisonment.

Although an experienced officer, Braddock was unprepared for the style of combat or the terrain he encountered. As he advanced, warriors from Canada and the Great Lakes reinforced Fort Duquesne. Because the garrison was vulnerable to cannon fire from the nearby hilltops, the French sought to waylay Braddock, whose army crept within ten miles of the fort in early July, days after Smith's capture. His captors told him that Braddock's army, marching in close order, would be surrounded, and as his informant put it, they would "shoot um down all one pigeon."[24] That's what happened.

On July 9 Smith was roused by a commotion. Using a staff, he climbed atop the fort's wall and watched indigenous warriors and French troops departing. Counting only four hundred in the war party, Smith was "in high hopes that I would soon see them flying before the British troops, and that General Braddock would take the fort and rescue me." But that afternoon he heard what he dolefully concluded was the "voice of Joy and triumph" in French, a language he did not speak.[25]

The attackers encountered Braddock's vanguard on the banks of the Monongahela River where a town would later bear his name. While French regulars held firm, their allies enveloped the English along their flanks. Braddock's advance guard retreated, jamming against the main body of troops. Almost half were killed or wounded, many by their own fire. Braddock, who had four horses shot out from under him, was among the victims. George Washington, his aide-de-camp, lost two mounts but was unscathed.

Though forewarned, Braddock had ignored his indigenous allies' counsel and dismissed the acumen of his opponents. The Iroquois chief Scarouady remarked that Braddock "looked upon us as dogs, and would never hear anything what was said to him. We often endeavored to advise him of the danger he was in with his Soldiers; but he never appeared pleased with us and that was the reason that a great many of our Warriors left him."[26] Benjamin Franklin recounted that when he warned Braddock of ambush, the commander in chief "smil'ed at my Ignorance, and reply'd 'These Savages may indeed be a formidable Enemy to your raw American Militia; but upon the King's regular and disciplin'd Troops, Sir, it is impossible they should make any Impression.'"[27]

By day's end Smith slumped against Fort Duquesne's ramparts as the victors, preceded by choruses of scalp halloos, arrived. At sundown a party returned with a dozen prisoners. They were stripped, their faces blackened, and hands bound. Taken to the riverbank across from the fort, the captives were tied to stakes and burned to death. Smith watched as a man was branded with irons until his doleful screams and tormentors' shrieks became too much to bear.

Braddock's defeat left the frontier in French hands. Despite Governor Dinwiddie's exhortations to launch another attack, British troops hastily retired to winter quarters. British forces met with defeat elsewhere and settlers retreated to a string of settlements extending south to the Carolinas. Many warriors, emboldened by Braddock's defeat, believed an alliance with the French would push the British off the continent, allowing them to reclaim their lands. They could deal with the French later.

While the charred remains of the men captured in Braddock's rout smoldered, James Smith awaited his fate. The French treated him graciously before handing him over to his captors. Unable to hike great distances, Smith was taken by canoe upriver to the present-day site of Kittanning. After convalescing, he traveled west to a town on the Muskingum River. Smith believed he would die there. The next day warriors came for him. One pulled Smith's hair out, leaving just a patch of it on the crown of his head. He then cut all but three locks of hair. Wrapping two with beaded garters, he braided the third with silver broaches. As Smith sat, dreading a horrible ritual sacrifice, holes were bored in his nose and ears through which rings and jewels were attached. They ordered him to strip and don a breechcloth. Afterward they painted his body and put a band of wampum around his neck and silver clasps around his wrists and right arm.

A chief led Smith through the town as people came running. Following an oration he could not understand, three young women took him into the river until he was waist deep. When they indicated that he should submerge, Smith lost all hope and resisted efforts to dunk him. Meanwhile, the crowd howled with mirth. Finally, one woman managed a few words of English, "No hurt you," and Smith surrendered. "I gave myself up to their ladyships, who were as good as their word; for though they plunged me under water, and washed and rubbed me severely, yet I could not say they hurt me much."[28]

After his baptism Smith was taken to the council house and dressed in a ruffled shirt, beaded leggings, garters adorned with porcupine quills, and moccasins. His head and face were painted, and red feathers tied to his locks. He was seated on a bearskin and given a pipe, tomahawk, and polecat skin pouch containing tobacco, flint, and steel. "My son," the sachem intoned, "you are now flesh of our flesh, and bone of our bone." By this ceremony "every drop of white blood was washed out of your veins." Smith realized that he had been adopted to take the place of a great man who had been killed and would be treated with the same love and support accorded any of the chieftain's people. Initially skeptical, he later wrote that "since that time I have found that there was much sincerity in said speech—for from that day I never knew them to make any distinction between me and themselves in any respect whatever until I left them."[29]

Smith's preconceptions of Native Americans derived from a childhood on the frontier, where settlers perceived them as savages who lived like animals. He had witnessed acts of brutality at Fort Duquesne and lacked any sense of the inner workings of indigenous society. The account of his four-year sojourn, published forty years later, is a revealing portrait of their lives. The first misconception that Smith overcame was that indigenous people lived in poverty despite their bountiful habitat. Europeans were awed by the potential of the land: while Europe seemed overcrowded and short of animal life, North America appeared devoid of people but teeming with game, fish, and fowl. Though wood was scarce in Europe, colonists delighted in bountiful forests. A poor servant in the New World possessing only fifty acres of land could have a fire bigger than that of an English nobleman, Francis Higginson wrote in 1630.[30] Most of all, colonists were dazzled by the limitless expanses of what they considered unoccupied land stretching west. Amid such promise, wrote another observer, the Indians live like "our Beggers in England."[31] Some of Smith's experiences confirmed that view. He and his new relations endured bouts of desperate hunger when game became scarce and winter reserves gave out. Most colonists saw their privation as due to improvidence and their failure to store enough food to last the winter.

Smith often noted the untapped potential of the region's virgin land but realized that Native Americans were not poor so much as responding to different motivations. European society rested on owning land and maximizing its agricultural and commercial potential. Native Americans emphasized neither. Land was held in common, if at all; amassing goods and wealth was an alien concept. Though villages cultivated corn and vegetables, there was little farming and less commerce. The bulk of their food came from the forests, rivers, and skies, not from domesticated animals or cultivation. Nor were they driven to maximize production.

Native Americans sorely disappointed Europeans by refusing to become like them spiritually or materially. To Europeans their disinclination to exploit the land's bounty was incomprehensible. Accordingly colonists characterized indigenous people as less than human and argued that their "inhumanity" forfeited their rights to the land. If Native Americans would not conform to European notions of land use, they would push them away or eliminate them altogether.

Native society was a multi-tribal mix of wayfarers living in small groups that coalesced and dispersed as the seasons and political needs dictated. Most inhabitants of western Pennsylvania had arrived after the 1720s, migrating after encroachment on their eastern homelands. They also came because the region was largely devoid of people but not game. Consequently the region attracted a diverse mix of migrants, just as Pittsburgh would time and time again. Their overall numbers were relatively small. The biggest population clusters were small towns, often seasonal in nature. In the 1750s the Delaware, Shawnee, Miami, and Wyandot could send between 1,500 and 2,000 warriors into battle.[32]

Indigenous people took advantage of what each season offered and migrated accordingly.[33] Smith traveled a circuit with small bands bonded by kinship. Owning little that could not be easily replaced or carried by a person, horse, or canoe, they broke camp in hours and traveled long distances with astonishing facility. Smith soon learned how well they understood their world. Their intimate sense of the forest and its rhythms was the basis of a hunting-and-gathering economy. With few tools, they made much from their surroundings. They knew where to find wild apples, plums, potatoes, and hickory nuts and when to congregate at spots where migrating fowl could be easily killed. They tapped salt licks and made sugar from maple trees. They turned skins and furs into clothes, bedding, and pouches to carry bear fat and maize. Smith marveled that they could make canoes and lodgings with no more than knives and hatchets. He rode the rivers in birch bark vessels, which were thirty-five feet long, four feet wide, and three feet deep, yet light enough that four men could carry one for miles across hilly portages. He wintered along a stream emptying into Lake Erie and, despite the harshness of the season, found his quarters more than adequate.

Yet as soon as their winter home was built, Smith and his family experienced severe food shortages. He struggled with their feast-or-famine approach. After a hunt, food was consumed liberally. Yet there was often nothing to eat. Then, Smith recounts, "I began to conclude that if I had anything that would banish pinching hunger, and keep soul and body together I would be content."[34] Smith was struck by their egalitarianism, especially in times of want. When hunters returned with two small turkeys during a brush with starvation, the scant provisions were divided "with the greatest equity and justice" among the twenty-one hungry people in the band.

But their desire for trade goods led Native Americans to accumulate skins to trade, introducing notions of prices and equivalent relations between pelts and trade goods. Widening their hunting grounds to secure pelts intensified tribal conflict and fueled an arms race. Before long, killing animals for trade devastated beaver, bison, wild turkey, and passenger pigeon populations.

As they schooled him about their world, Smith realized their knowledge of it was far more advanced than that of colonials and the British. So was their sense of backwoods warfare. "They are not an ignorant or stupid sort of people, or they would not have been such fatal enemies," he observed. "When they came into our country they outwitted us—and when we sent armies into their country, they out-generaled, and beat us with inferior force."[35] Many believed they could drive the Europeans back across the sea. "White people," Smith wrote, "appeared to them like fools," unable to guard against surprise. British and Americans would need to learn how to defend against their way of war and bring their greater numbers into play to prevail.

Smith's experiences were not atypical. Though most white people taken in battle were killed, hundreds came to know native life from the inside. As full and equal members of the tribe adopted to take the place of those killed by disease and warfare, they enjoyed the benefits of tribal society. Children were sometimes dunked as a punishment but rarely struck, and women, unlike their colonial sisters, exerted political clout. When treaties released these "prisoners," Native Americans expressed great sorrow at their departure. Many captives did not want to leave; others fled back to the tribe. That was also true for those escaping slavery.

Despite internalizing indigenous ways, Smith wanted to return to his home in central Pennsylvania. He, an ailing older native brother, and his young son were near starvation one winter. On their own, they depended on Smith's improved skills to pull them through. While hunting, he despaired of finding any game and concluded that if he did not take off for Pennsylvania, he would starve. He was ten miles into his escape when he came upon the tracks of a buffalo. Hunting it down, Smith made a fire and ate some barely cooked meat. Then, rather than escape, Smith packed as much meat as he could carry, secured the rest against wolves, and returned to his family. He could not desert them.

In April 1759 the same threesome paddled from Detroit to an indigenous town north of Montreal. There Smith heard of a ship at Montreal holding Englishmen to be exchanged for French prisoners. Slipping away, he stole aboard the ship and turned himself in. The vessel, however, never sailed because the British had bottled up the St. Lawrence River. After four months in a Montreal prison, Smith was taken to the French fort at Crown Point and exchanged for prisoners held by the British. By early 1760 he was back home in Conococheague. His sweetheart had wed days before his return.

THE BRITISH RETURN

By then an expedition led by Brigadier General John Forbes had regained control of the headwaters of the Ohio.[36] Forbes learned from Braddock's fiasco. During the summer of 1758 he mustered a force of 6,000, including Royal Americans, Scottish Highlanders, Pennsylvanians, and 1,500 Virginians. They moved cautiously across Pennsylvania to Fort Duquesne, where the French counted on several hundred native allies. Most of them were asleep near Fort Duquesne on September 13 when an advance party of 800 men under Major James Grant crept atop the hill overlooking the fort (near present-day Grant Street). Believing it was lightly defended, Grant inexplicably ordered his pipers and drummers to sound reveille in the early morning, squandering his chance of surprise. French forces exceeded Grant's estimates and their awakened allies raced up the riverbanks until they outflanked his men. The English lost 300 in the rout, including Grant, who was captured.

But French forces had been deteriorating. Resupply via Canada was no longer possible, given the distance involved and the looming onset of winter, and many of their indigenous allies had left. Realizing that Fort Duquesne could not withstand artillery bombardment, its commander, Francois de Ligneris, preemptively attacked Forbes's forces at Loyalhanna in October near present-day Ligonier. He hoped to force them into winter quarters, delaying an attack on Fort Duquesne until the spring. But the battle was a draw, and more native allies departed. In Forbes the warriors encountered a more capable foe than Braddock. Smith was told that American riflemen at Loyalhanna had finally learned how to fight. "The Indians said if it was only the red-coats they had to do with, they could soon subdue them, but they could not withstand *Afhalecoa*, or the Great Knife, which was the name they gave the Virginians."[37]

As winter approached, Forbes decided to put off an attack until spring. But a captured British renegade under threat of death revealed that French forces were but half the one thousand men that Forbes thought were there and that their native auxiliaries had disappeared. Forbes immediately advanced. De Ligneris, unable to forestall an attack, sent his artillery down the Ohio, fled with his men, and torched Fort Duquesne. When British troops reached its smoldering ruins, they were greeted by a number of heads severed from the bodies of Grant's men killed two months earlier.[38]

Forbes wrote Prime Minister William Pitt, who had revitalized England's flagging war effort against France, announcing he had renamed the settlement Pittsborough in his honor. The newly built Fort Pitt bolstered British efforts to control the Ohio River, defend the frontier, and forge tribal alliances. But with the French as close as Venango and the threat of tribes swooping down from the Great Lakes, it was isolated and far from secure. Forbes, ailing from the bloody flux (dysentery), left for Philadelphia in December. Carried most of the way on a litter, he died in March.

European combat in North America diminished after 1760, a prelude to the cessation of hostilities in the Great War for Empire in February 1763. France ceded Canada and its territory east of the Mississippi to England, except for New Orleans and Louisiana, which it gave to its ally Spain to compensate for her loss of Florida to Britain. Native Americans, however, fought on. Unlike the French, this was their home. Their way of life required access to large wilderness tracts, which British-American agriculture and notions of private property foreclosed. Their seminomadic lifestyle disappeared from the headwaters of the Ohio, but before leaving the valley, Native Americans joined Pontiac's Rebellion in 1763. They continued to terrorize settlers across western Pennsylvania until 1795. No matter how hard they fought, though, they could not dislodge the beachhead settlers had established at Pittsburgh.

Native Americans and colonists stood in the way of fulfilling William Pitt's vision of British hegemony over the Ohio River Valley. Pennsylvania's renunciation of claims to the land west of the Alleghenies in 1758 had briefly recognized Native Americans as its legal owners. But while the British tried to discourage settlement and regulated trade, they failed to do either. After the French withdrew, native life was in upheaval. Fearing reprisals, many headed west, while others congregated at Fort Pitt, an irregularly shaped pentagon covering eight acres on the floodplain between the rivers, to trade with the British. With its stockade walls and moat, Fort Pitt was the most impressive fortification on Britain's western flank and its intermediary with native fur traders. It was also Britain's base for frontier operations. Realizing that trade and security went hand in hand, British commander in chief Jeffrey Amherst tried to prohibit the sale of rum and reduced ammunition sales in 1762. Traders easily circumvented his edicts.

Maintaining good relations was costly. The British wearied of wining and dining Native Americans, who expected that they would be received and fed as guests whenever they came to Fort Pitt, as would any stranger among their people. They also expected presents to keep the peace and for releasing white people who lived among them. But Amherst, who viewed the British as conquerors, considered the Native Americans inconsequential now that the French had withdrawn.[39]

Reduction in British largesse and their failure to help during a famine and epidemic in 1762 aggravated Native Americans.[40] But the principal problem was the growing British presence at Fort Pitt. While the tribes wanted the British to fulfill their 1758 promise to quit the Ohio River Valley, the British had no intention of leaving. Neither did traders along the Allegheny and Youghiogheny Rivers, or squatters and hunters who defied prohibitions against settlement and hunting. Their numbers increased, and a cluster of cabins and huts housed roughly 150 people around Fort Pitt. Though these ramshackle dwellings were destroyed in 1763 to prevent their use as cover for attacks, the village quickly re-formed. Colonel John Campbell brought some order to it by surveying a four-block street plan centered along the Monongahela River, encompassing today's Stanwix and Market Streets from Fort Pitt Boulevard to the Boulevard of the Allies.

Native Americans were incensed when word of the 1763 treaty ending the Great War for Empire reached them. France had transferred rights to their lands to the British without indigenous consent. Within months the Ohio River Valley witnessed the most significant indigenous uprising in British North American history. News of France's withdrawal, Fort Pitt's captain Simon Ecuyer wrote, came as a "thunderclap" to Native Americans. George Croghan described them as driven almost to despair.[41] Word that England would take over Canada brought rebellion closer, and wampum belts circulated from Canada to the Carolinas. These belts of beaded shells signified that tribal councils backed an uprising to drive the British back across the mountains.

In May 1763 Odawa leader Pontiac attacked Fort Detroit while warriors struck across the frontier. Every fort west of Erie was hit, and raiding parties crossed the mountains, assaulting homesteads as far east as the Cumberland Valley. Many settlers fled, but not all made good on their escape. Perhaps two thousand Native Americans and as many white people lost their lives. Six hundred white people died on the Pennsylvania frontier alone, and most British traders in the Ohio River Valley were killed or chased away.

British posts at Venango, Le Boeuf, and Presque Isle were overrun; a family was slaughtered at a farm on the Youghiogheny; and soldiers were killed nearby. Fort Pitt was not among the rebellion's early targets. Ecuyer, in charge of its two-hundred-man detachment, brought civilians into the fort and burned surrounding dwellings. In late June a band of Delaware came to the fort and traded lies with him. The Delaware claimed that an attack by western tribes was imminent and offered to guarantee safe passage east. Ecuyer countered by asserting that a large army was marching toward Fort Pitt to smash the rebellion.

When the Delaware returned on July 26, with neither marauding indigenous warriors nor British relief having appeared, Ecuyer stood firm. Fort Pitt would not be abandoned. According to some accounts, Ecuyer gave the Delaware several blankets from the fort's smallpox hospital when they left, spreading disease among them.[42] The Delaware besieged Fort Pitt for over a week but inflicted little damage. Colonel Henry Bouquet was dispatched from Philadelphia to relieve the fort and reached Bushy Run fifteen miles east of Pittsburgh. When Native Americans attacked, Bouquet suffered heavy losses. Feigning to retreat the next morning, Bouquet lured them into the open, where they were defeated, swinging momentum back to the British.

The following year British forces, including James Smith and the militia unit he led, marched into the Ohio River Valley. Smith realized that success required adopting his foes' way of fighting. They painted their "faces red and black, like Indian warriors," he explained. "I taught them the Indian discipline, as I knew no other at that time."[43] His men, known as the Black Boys because most of them lived in or near Black's Town in the Conococheague Valley, defended settlers against indigenous raids and launched violent reprisals of their own.

Pontiac's Rebellion was not defeated so much as it was frustrated by the overwhelming strength of British and colonial forces. An end to hostilities was negotiated, and by 1765 many Native Americans accepted the British as semipermanent paternal figures east of the Mississippi in lieu of the French. But the British, ambivalent about that role, displayed neither the adroitness with which the French had acted in that capacity, nor the willingness to underwrite native allegiances and frontier security. Native Americans remained, albeit in smaller numbers, after their defeat. Many aligned with the British during the American Revolution, again picking the losing side. In 1794, after the decisive battle at Fallen Timbers (in present-day northwestern Ohio), their presence in the Ohio River Valley was mostly over.

If one way of life was in eclipse, another was ascending. Pontiac's defeat opened the region to settlement. While the Proclamation of 1763 banned settlers west of the Appalachian divide and reserved the region as a native hunting ground, the British were incapable of policing it. Too many settlers, land speculators, and traders wanted in. The British grip on the frontier had never been secure and squatters ignored Crown edicts. Nor did the colonial government in Philadelphia exercise authority in western Pennsylvania. As early as 1760 Colonel Henry Bouquet complained that the Monongahela River Valley was overrun by vagabonds masquerading as hunters. Though the 1763 uprising had convinced most settlers to evacuate, they returned in force after the fighting had stopped. Troops swept the region, chasing settlers away and burning their huts, but within months there were twice as many as before. Squatters dismissed the ban as a "contrivance of the

Gentlemen and Merchants of Philadelphia" seeking to control the land for themselves.[44]

The Royal Proclamation of 1763 sought to appease Native Americans west of the mountains, declaring "that the several nations or tribes of Indians, with whom we are connected, and who live under our protection, should not be molested or disturbed in the possession of such parts of our dominions and territories as, not having been ceded to, or purchased by us, are reserved to them."[45] To police it, ten thousand British regulars were dispatched to the colonies and the Sugar Act and Stamp Act were enacted to help pay for them. Neither the troops nor the taxes were well received. The ban on westward migration was particularly galling because the French defeat and the failure of Pontiac's Rebellion made land on the other side of the Appalachians more accessible than ever.

Settlers along the frontier not only ignored warnings to leave, they often abused indigenous people hunting there. Because Pennsylvania had not mustered a military force to defend settlers across the Alleghenies, those seeking land and security formed local militias. James Smith's Black Boys were among them. Often unruly, motivated by fear and the desire for revenge, these militias not only defended their homes and families but slaughtered indigenous children and women, took scalps, and desecrated corpses. By the 1750s, historian James Merrell concluded, "Penn's Woods became an abattoir."[46]

In 1768 the Crown wearied of policing the region and abandoned efforts to regulate trade and trans-Appalachian settlement. It surrendered authority to the colonies, leaving indigenous inhabitants vulnerable. The Iroquois, acknowledging that they could not stem the incoming tide of colonists, sold much of their remaining land. As the British abandoned western outposts, Fort Pitt was downsized and portions sold as building materials.[47]

Pennsylvania began selling the property it purchased from the Iroquois. However, as land-hungry settlers and speculators grabbed titles, they found that much of the land was already occupied by squatters. The squatters' titles were "tomahawk claims," whereby a man asserted ownership by tomahawk slashes in trees to show his right of possession. In the past officials had not recognized claims based solely on physical possession of property and its improvement. This time squatters prevailed, and tomahawk claims were usually validated.

Settlers from eastern Pennsylvania, Virginia, and Maryland traveled along roads that Braddock and Forbes had once trod. Some wanted only enough land to support their families; others dreamed of vast estates. In either case land was the lure. By some estimates the population exploded from about five thousand people in 1770 to seventy-five thousand in 1790 when a census was commissioned.[48] As Native Americans departed the region and the Ohio country opened to exploitation, a new conflict erupted. This one did not pit traditional antagonists against each other—the British, French, and Native Americans—but Pennsylvania and Virginia.

PITTSBURGH, VIRGINIA?

If not for the Revolution, Pittsburgh might have become a part of Virginia or the capital of a new colony, Vandalia. Virginia based its claim to southwestern Pennsylvania on the London Company's 1609 royal charter, which granted a swath of land extending from sea to sea. Although the Company's charter was revoked in 1624, the vacant land within it reverting to the Crown, Virginia maintained that it controlled land not subsequently granted by the king to another colony. Though Virginia's assertion was dubious, Pennsylvania's claim was weakened by its ambiguous western and southern boundaries. Pennsylvania's 1681 charter vaguely defined its demarcation with Maryland. Virginia argued that Penn's charter, which extended five degrees west of the Delaware River, followed the curves of the river and stopped at Laurel Mountain. Pennsylvania countered that its border continued past Pittsburgh. Most inhabitants in the disputed area favored Virginia, which offered cheaper land and larger holdings. But as long as they could obtain land and title to it, those flooding the region cared little whether they were Virginians or Pennsylvanians.

The British presence muted intercolonial squabbles, limiting settlement to those with permits until the 1768 Fort Stanwix Treaty. In 1772, after the British reduced their presence and the Earl of Dunmore became Virginia's governor, the dispute flared. Dunmore, like George Washington, wanted to speculate in western land. Furthermore, he saw control over the region as the fulcrum for asserting Virginia's influence farther west.

Dunmore came to Pittsburgh in 1773 to meet with Dr. John Connolly, an ex-military man. Afterward Connolly announced that Dunmore had appointed him commander of Pittsburgh's militia. Pennsylvania's local officials, operating out of Hanna's Town near present-day Greensburg, responded by jailing Connolly. Freed a week later, Connolly assembled an armed force and took over Fort Pitt. Renaming it Fort Dunmore, he claimed legal authority over Pittsburgh. Throughout the rest of 1774 Pennsylvania and Virginia jockeyed for control. They came to blows several times with the Virginians getting in the best licks, but more serious trouble began when Dunmore provoked war with the Shawnee. In the spring of 1774 spats over hunters and settlers in Shawnee territory escalated. Raids panicked the frontier, and settlers fled across the Alleghenies or retreated to hastily built fortifications. Pennsylvania rangers patrolled from Ligonier to Pittsburgh, but this was Virginia's conflict. Its victory left Virginia with an imposing military presence in southwestern Pennsylvania.

Rebuffing Pennsylvania overtures, Dunmore argued that Pennsylvania had forfeited its claims by allowing France to occupy the region. The accusation hit a nerve because Pennsylvania had failed to protect the area and rationalized inaction by questioning the westward extent of its jurisdiction. Dunmore, emboldened by success in what was dubbed Dunmore's War, rejected a generous settlement that would have made the Monongahela River the line of demarcation. He declared he would obey nothing less than a royal edict to relinquish control.

After Dunmore's War Virginia began implementing its county court system, encountering little protest from settlers. Soon a far greater struggle, the American Revolution, overshadowed the intercolonial conflict and simmering hostilities with Native Americans. When Dunmore and Connolly threw their lot in with England, and revolutionary partisans discovered that Connolly was sounding out Native Americans and settlers to back the British, they imprisoned him. Freed, rearrested, and released again, Connolly fled and met Dunmore on a British man-of-war in the Chesapeake Bay, where they made plans to seize Fort Pitt. Their scheme collapsed when revolutionaries captured Connolly near Pennsylvania's border. Neither he nor Dunmore threatened Pittsburgh again.

Both Virginia and Pennsylvania heeded the Continental Congress directive to unite against the British. The region split into de facto spheres of influence with Virginia supporters controlling Pittsburgh and the Monongahela Valley and Pennsylvania adherents running Westmoreland County. In 1783 Pennsylvania and Virginia formed a joint commission to set the boundary of western Pennsylvania, extinguishing the disputes embroiling the region. With the survey completed the next year, Pennsylvania made concessions along its southern border and in return pushed its border farther west than it had ever claimed. As part of the deal Pennsylvania recognized more than 1,100 land titles covering over six hundred thousand acres which Virginia had issued. The crucial question of which state had jurisdiction at the forks of the Ohio was settled.[49]

A third force, of indeterminate strength, sought a radically different future, and in the summer of 1776 petitioned the Continental Congress to create a new state extending from the Alleghenies into Ohio and southward to the Cumberland Gap. These secessionists contended that rule by a distant government in Philadelphia or Williamsburg was impractical. Stressing their revolutionary credentials, the proponents of Westsylvania, as the new state would be named, objected to arbitrary subjugation.

Westsylvania was reminiscent of an earlier effort to create a colony anchored in western Pennsylvania. At the 1754 Albany Congress, Benjamin Franklin had proposed two new colonies, one in the upper Ohio River Valley, another south of Lake Erie.[50] After Forbes's victory, there was talk of creating Pittsylvania, a Pittsburgh-centered colony extending into the Ohio country. Traders seeking compensation for losses during Pontiac's Rebellion sought royal land concessions from the Monongahela River south. Joined by the Ohio Company's principal figures, they proposed a new royal colony, Vandalia, which might have included southwestern Pennsylvania.

But 1776 ended talk of new royal colonies. Though the question of western lands came before the Continental Congress, Pennsylvania refused to adjust its borders. When settlers rejected Pennsylvania's authority and refused to pay taxes, authorities called efforts to organize a new state treasonous. Some residents voted with their feet, migrating west. Others lost interest in secession after the native threat waned and they began benefiting from new trade routes. Though neither a new colony nor state came about, such an entity might have made Pittsburgh its capital and then become more of a force in the early nineteenth century than it ever became as the westernmost and often neglected end of Pennsylvania.

PITTSBURGH AND THE REVOLUTION

Almost two weeks passed before word of the April 19, 1775, battle at Lexington crossed the mountains and ended squabbles over colonial jurisdiction. Though the region was hardly of one voice in seeking independence, those meeting at a Pittsburgh tavern embraced the rebels and formed a militia to support their cause. Raising a liberty pole, partisans kindled a bonfire around which they drank and fired rifles in celebration until dawn.[51] Much of the frontier's rebellious spirit was based on a desire to be free of government from afar, be it from London, Philadelphia, or Williamsburg.

James Smith joined the fight before 1776. After returning from captivity, he married Anne Wilson, with whom he fathered seven children. Despite empathy for the Native Americans with whom he had lived for four years, Smith was hardly sanguine about the prospects of peace along the frontier. Determined to defend family and neighbors from danger, whether from Native Americans or the British, he led his band of frontier irregulars now known as Smith's Black Boys. In 1765 they took up arms against the British in what some later called the first skirmish between British and colonial forces. While their animus against native people was strong, so was their scorn for Britain's feeble efforts to subdue indigenous warriors and push them farther west to allow for white settlement.[52] When a train of George Croghan's packhorses carrying gun powder for trade with Native Americans came through the Conococheague Valley in 1765, Smith remonstrated that resupplying Native Americans "would be a kind of murder . . . trading at the expense of the blood and treasure of the frontiers." The traders, he said, laughed at them. Rather than rely on British authorities, Smith gathered his Black Boys and ambushed the caravan on Sidelong Hill east of Bedford. Cutting the packhorses down, they burnt the goods.[53] After a detachment of soldiers from Fort Loudon arrested several men for attacking the traders, Smith mustered three hundred followers and began capturing British soldiers. When he had twice as many captives as the British, Smith exchanged prisoners.

Four years later Smith took on British authority again. After several frontiersmen were imprisoned for destroying goods intended for Native Americans, the Black Boys marched on Fort Bedford. Arriving before dawn, they rushed in to free their comrades as soon as soldiers opened the gates. "This," Smith remarked, "was the first British fort in America that was taken by what they called the American rebels."[54] They blockaded trade with Native Americans until a final peace was proclaimed.

Later that year, strangers accosted Smith, calling him by name as he surveyed land along the Youghiogheny River. They subdued him, but not before one assailant died. Smith, who denied he had shot the man, was jailed in Carlisle to prevent his rescue. The Black Boys marched to free him anyway, but Smith persuaded them to withdraw, reasoning that breaking out of the jail would undercut his claim of innocence. Acquitted four months later, he returned to his home on Jacob's Creek, a branch of the Youghiogheny. When independence was declared, Smith represented Westmoreland County at Pennsylvania's first constitutional convention.[55]

While not a significant front during the Revolution, Pittsburgh was central to the embryonic nation's defense of its western flank. Like James Smith, most people on the frontier were more concerned with thwarting native attacks than fighting Redcoats back east. Pittsburgh enjoyed relative security through 1777, but when relations with native inhabitants deteriorated, the region was on its own. Many innocents were slaughtered by both sides. Smith, whose Black Boys had harassed the British in the East, returned to bolster frontier defenses. Despite Cornwallis's surrender at Yorktown on October 19, 1781, clashes with Native Americans continued. Even after the Crown relinquished claims to land west of the Alleghenies in the 1783 treaty ending the war, indigenous people held on for several years. Resistance eventually crumbled, and soon western Pennsylvania was no longer theirs to roam.

What did it mean that neither France, the Iroquois, England, nor Virginia gained sway over what became Pittsburgh, and that Pennsylvania and the United States did? Besides not becoming French-speaking, what paths were not followed, what values or ways of life lost, what dilemmas avoided? If France had triumphed, would Native Americans in the Ohio River Valley have gained time to reach accommodations with the Europeans? Could they have recovered from the catastrophic population losses and social disarray incurred after exposure to Europeans? If able to stabilize, might they have built upon a century of French–indigenous interactions that differed from British–indigenous relations?

The French had far less interest in settling and developing western Pennsylvania than the British. They often lived among indigenous people, taking wives and learning their languages, without seeking to change them or occupy their land so much as obtain access to furs and assistance against the British. Moreover, France's principal North American ventures were in Quebec and New Orleans. The Ohio country connected these cities and that mattered more than possessing and exploiting the region. Such disinterest could have been salutary, giving Native Americans a chance to negotiate a healthier relationship with France. If native stewardship had endured, fewer people and less development might have spared the ecosystem the trauma of unregulated capitalism.

If Britain had thwarted independence, the impact would have been less consequential for Pittsburgh's emergence as a Gateway to the West. Virginia, of all the losers in the fight for western Pennsylvania, had the greatest chance of winning. If the region's fate had been determined by majority sentiment or force, the Old Dominion would have triumphed. Settlers looked to Virginia for leadership in subduing Native Americans, not to Pennsylvania, which hesitated to fund frontier defense and equivocated whether the area fell within its boundaries. Only Pennsylvania's proprietors, who saw the revenues at stake in the sale of land, consistently claimed the area.

Had Virginia won, Pittsburgh would not have been part of Pennsylvania, which historian Henry Adams, the great-grandson and grandson of presidents, called "the only true democratic community then existing in the eastern States." Instead of belonging to the new republic's most democratic state, Pittsburgh would have been the western frontier of a state stamped by slavery and top-down political rule.[56] Pennsylvania's Pittsburgh saw slavery wither away; Virginia's Pittsburgh would have given slavery a second wind regionally and possibly altered the nation's balance of power. Although Philadelphia often dominated the state, representative democracy took hold in Pittsburgh more than it would have in Virginia's county-dominated politics. A quarrelsome, local political culture emerged as settlers learned not to rely on distant governments for protection and stability, a viewpoint that persisted long past the eighteenth century. Pennsylvania's influence also stamped the place names, architecture, language, and foodways of Pittsburgh. But most of all, Pittsburgh defined its future as a free labor economy within a relatively democratic state.

Though he lived with Native Americans for four years, when James Smith and his Caughnawaga brothers walked through forests or paddled Ohio Valley rivers, they did not always see the same vista. Both Native Americans and white people encountered hilly topography, thick forests, and plentiful animal life. They each knew that the forests and animals were sources of shelter and sustenance. Smith marveled at indigenous people's skills as naturalists and their ability to secure nourishment, shelter, and clothing from their world, but he also saw western Pennsylvania's commercial possibilities. He constantly appraised the land's potential for crops; described its diversity of bottomlands, meadows, glades, and prairies; inventoried its mix of hardwoods; and noted its access to water.

Standing atop the eastern ridges that bordered southwestern Pennsylvania, Smith surveyed the hills and valleys spread out before him. Hilltops of roughly similar heights were what remained of the Appalachian Plateau that once covered the region. Over centuries water and gravity had carved out valleys. Creeks, racing streams, and quiet rivers left both narrow and wide valleys and rolling hills. Dense forests offered an array of deciduous hardwoods and coniferous trees that provided settlers with the materials of everyday life. Oak, walnut, hickory, cherry, wild apple, sugar maple, and pine offered shelter, fuel, and building materials, along with nuts, fruit, maple sugar, and habitat for game. Deer, bison, elk, bear, and beaver were plentiful, as were panthers, wildcats, rattlesnakes, and copperheads. The forests yielded ginseng, a valuable root that became one of the region's early exports. Its skies were filled with quail, partridge, turkeys, and pigeons. Trout, catfish, sturgeon, pike, bass, turtles, and eels swam in its rivers and lakes.[57]

Awed by the region's potential, Smith did not realize that far greater wealth lay beneath the surface. Though he found fossils in streambeds and made his way through swamps, he did not know that a vast inland sea had once submerged the region, or that the layers of sand and vegetation left behind had become sandstone and coal. He made no mention of the outcroppings of coal exposed by eroded hillsides and along riverbanks that gave evidence of the great seam underlying western Pennsylvania. He knew nothing of the iron deposits that figured in Pittsburgh's first smelters nor of the gas fields near the city. Smith might have seen "Seneca oil," the freefloating petroleum found on streams and used by Native Americans for medicinal purposes, but he did not understand its future value.

Smith did understand the importance of fast-moving streams and rivers for water mills and the utility of sandstone and limestone for fertilizer and building materials. He traveled on those rivers and lakes and realized that Pittsburgh could become a jumping-off point for western exploration. But he did not envision that the land at the forks and its access to the Ohio River Valley, coal, and other resources would allow a city to emerge as an epicenter of global industrialization and the core of a densely peopled part of North America. Nor could James Smith have anticipated the tradeoffs that outcome would demand—clear-cutting forests, gashing mountains to procure coal, and fouling rivers and streams.

TWO

FRONTIER CITY

ON AUGUST 2, 1794, AN ANGRY CROWD OF SEVEN THOUSAND MEN AND women gathered outside Pittsburgh, ready to sack the fledgling town of fewer than a thousand people. Upset by the federal government's efforts to tax distilled whiskey, they had answered the summons of local militia units to assemble at Braddock's Field, eight miles outside town. There these rural rebels vowed to make Pittsburgh pay for their ire. Hugh Henry Brackenridge rode out to the assembly with the Pittsburgh militia hoping to pacify the "whiskey boys." "The whole country was [an] inflammable mass," he wrote. "It required but the least touch of fire to inflame it. . . . The common talk of the country was they were coming to take Pittsburgh." Some spoke of plundering it, others of burning it down. Castigating the town's alleged sinfulness, the rebels argued that the biblical "Sodom had been burnt by fire from heaven," but Pittsburgh, "this second Sodom should be burned with fire from earth."[1] Clad in hunting shirts with bandannas around their heads, men fired guns into the air, threatening to guillotine their enemies and seize Fort Fayette, the garrison defending Pittsburgh. "The idea of the people at the time," Brackenridge concluded, "was that law was dissolved and that the people themselves, in their collective capacity, were the only tribunal." The

Scottish-born spokesman for Pittsburgh feared for his life, as did many who remained in town, burying their valuables and papers.[2]

But Pittsburgh escaped the wrath of its rural neighbors. The Whiskey Rebellion, fueled by southwestern Pennsylvania's displeasure with rule from afar, did not lead to secession. It fizzled and most of those at Braddock's Field made their peace with federal authority or moved west. Just as the American Revolution had stifled dreams of a new western republic in the 1770s, the failure of the Whiskey Rebellion crushed a similar vision of independence. Had it succeeded, Pittsburgh might have become the capital of a new republic or at least a new American state. Instead, the rebellion was the last gasp of its frontier economy. Within three decades a fluid and rough frontier gave way to a more structured, stratified society. Commercial agriculture supplanted the hardscrabble, subsistence farming that many supplemented with hunting. The rebellion's collapse and pacification of Native Americans opened the Ohio River Valley to migration and vaulted Pittsburgh from a frontier outpost into the Gateway to the West. Merchants and entrepreneurs harnessed the enormous commercial and industrial potential that its location and mix of human and natural resources offered. But just a few years after the *Niles' Register* predicted that Pittsburgh would "probably become the greatest manufacturing town in the world," depression shrouded the city.[3]

REBELLION IN THE WEST

The Whiskey Rebellion not only threatened Pittsburgh with destruction, it brought the nation to the brink of civil war between East and West. Although the insurgency engulfed much of the frontier, southwestern Pennsylvania was its flashpoint. More than a protest against taxing distilled whiskey, the insurrection vented the frustrations of people upset by a precipitous decline in their prospects.[4] Against a backdrop of rural isolation and deprivation, they contended with an economy in which a few had become quite successful while many had lost ground. That disparity made the whiskey tax especially volatile.

Those in the backcountry were a self-reliant group, for whom peace and order were a long time coming. They prized autonomy but rarely tasted prosperity, and the threat of attack from indigenous warriors lingered. Carving out clearings to plant crops, they tended livestock and built single-room cabins measuring about sixteen by eighteen feet, with a loft for sleeping and storage. They did their best to make their homes warm and comfortable without the goods and services available in towns, subsisting on what they grew, raised, hunted, and foraged.[5]

Survival was difficult on one's own. Widows and widowers often remarried, if not for love but because marriage was a practical way to deal with daily demands, especially if they had children. Fertility was high in the backwoods, with rough estimates from the 1790 census suggesting an average of six children per family, not counting the many lost in childbirth or infancy.[6] Men became jacks-of-all-trades. They farmed, cared for animals, smoked meat, and learned tanning and blacksmithing. But as Elizabeth and Solon Buck, early chroniclers of the region, wrote, "Undoubtedly the member of the frontier family who did the hardest work was the housewife and mother."[7] Women also worked the fields, foraged in surrounding forests, and tended to gardens. They not only made food, but candles, bedding, poultices, herbal cures, and clothing. They treated illness and injuries and educated their children as best they could. Consequently, women achieved a functional equality with men in the backwoods. That was harder to attain for women in Pittsburgh, where they had few opportunities to earn money outside the home.[8] Functional equality, however, was not matched by their legal standing, which accorded women less respect. Under English common law, on which Pennsylvania law was based, married women had no rights to property other than what they brought to the marriage. Any property or income built during marriage belonged to their husbands.[9]

By 1800 southwestern Pennsylvania counted ninety-three thousand inhabitants, almost triple the number at the close of the Revolution in 1783. Most had settled on small farms or in market towns where they sought self-sufficiency and security. But the yeoman ideal of agricultural independence was difficult to attain. The yeoman farmer, a landowner with good prospects, had not disappeared; about a third of all households held that status. But the "dependent classes" of tenant farmers, rural wage laborers, and the poor—those without land or marketable skills—already outnumbered them.[10] Without land, they were reduced to working someone else's property as a tenant or wage laborer or moving on. In some locales landlessness stigmatized three-fifths of the population, an unattractive status in a society prizing independence.[11]

Families squatting on land without legal title were hit the hardest. Surviving French and native raiders, many had cleared and worked the land for years, believing that their efforts to improve property conferred some degree of rights to it. These "tomahawk claims" had been customarily respected and vigorously defended, and if a squatter's circumstances had improved, he could secure legal ownership by paying a purchase price. But that was no longer the case.[12]

As the frontier advanced west, a more stratified community took shape, and squatters were driven off their land or reduced to tenancy. They had endured the worst the frontier could offer, but now that it was tamed, the gains they expected were not materializing.[13] Especially galling was the growing number of large, often absentee landowners. Men like John Neville, the former Continental Army brigadier general whose Bower Hill estate was appointed with European furnishings, were the clear winners in this new society. There were far more losers, those like William Miller, a struggling farmer from Peters Creek who fought in the Revolution but now sought to leave for Kentucky to try again.

The whiskey tax ignited this explosive mix. Like their counterparts elsewhere on the frontier, many viewed federal and state government skeptically. They had two particular grievances: the threat of native attack and restricted access to the Mississippi River. Though the national government was spending over 80 percent of its operating budget fighting Native Americans, westerners didn't feel enough was being done. Since 1784 the government had failed to negotiate a treaty with Spain to allow Americans to freely navigate the Mississippi. Few frontier commodities were valuable enough to haul east over the mountains, making access to the Mississippi vital to market their goods.[14]

Many felt neglected by government and resented speculators grabbing the land they wanted. "Anyone who bothered to notice," historian Thomas Slaughter argued, "could have perceived the creation of a truly desperate populace, a growing body of frustrated men with little to lose."[15] President George Washington, no stranger to western Pennsylvania, was keenly aware of its alienation. But his priority was not alleviating western discontent so much as preventing that rage from fueling a movement for secession that could tear the fragile country apart. Washington feared frontier resistance becoming entangled with renewed British and Spanish challenges for sovereignty over North America. Hypersensitive to rhetoric smacking of secession, he vowed to come down hard on tax protesters.[16]

In 1791 the Internal Revenue Act had levied duties on imported spirits and domestically distilled liquor. Secretary of the Treasury Alexander Hamilton hoped the excise would stabilize the republic's finances and enable government to pay off the state debts it had assumed.[17] But neither Washington nor Hamilton appreciated the role that whiskey played in the frontier's cash-poor, barter economy. Its main drink and only viable export, whiskey was used where cash was in short supply and comprised part of farmworkers' wages. Farmers unable to ship surplus grain down the Mississippi or send bulky goods to eastern markets, could distill grain into whiskey. The excise now taxed this vital commodity.[18]

Washington and Hamilton dismissed the excise's disproportionate impact on rural families and less competitive distillers. Penalizing tenant farmers who distilled grain to raise cash to pay rent, the tax also hurt laborers who, after receiving bushels of rye as partial payment, went to distillers to transform their wages into cash or drink. For those already struggling to subsist, the excise was intolerable.[19]

A closely-knit group of commercial distillers leveraged their political connections to corner the market. This "whiskey junto" included John Neville, his son Presley, son-in-law Isaac Craig, and Abraham Kirkpatrick. Presley Neville was a state legislator and large landowner with an estate within sight of his father's home. Craig, the army's deputy quartermaster, owned a distillery, and Kirkpatrick grew and distilled large quantities of grain that he sold to the army, the junto's biggest buyer. They were committed to enforcing the excise, and when the whiskey rebels targeted them, Washington made western Pennsylvania a test of federal resolve.[20]

Anyone familiar with the frontier knew that reaction to the tax would come quickly. Though Pennsylvania had taxed whiskey since 1756, the law had never been enforced. Drawing on a tradition of tax resistance in the British Isles, locals bloodied those who tried to collect it with ritualized violence. During the 1780s bands of men blackened their faces as James Smith's Black Boys had done years earlier, dressed in women's clothes, and confronted tax collectors. They humiliated the excise men, often tarring and feathering them. Most resigned their commission and fled. If their tormentors were brought to trial, they usually escaped with light judicial admonitions.

Washington and Hamilton should have expected trouble on the frontier, where opposition to a whiskey excise was universal. But they were adamant about enforcing it, especially in western Pennsylvania. Defiance that close to the federal seat of power in Philadelphia could not go unchecked. Moreover, Washington had won his spurs there, taking part in the opening salvos of the French and Indian War and surviving the rout of British forces which occurred at the same spot near the Monongahela River where the whiskey rebels gathered almost forty years later. The region signified profit and power to Washington. Accumulating massive landholdings, often with little regard for the interests of others or the letter of the law, he controlled sixty-three thousand acres west of the mountains and was one of western Pennsylvania's biggest absentee landowners. Washington brooked no opposition to his claims, especially if the land in question was choice. Where there were squatters or rival claimants to property he wanted, he tried to evict them or went to court. According to Thomas Slaughter, many locals considered Washington little more than a "rapacious speculator and grasping landlord."[21]

Their disdain was mutual. Enamored with the land, Washington scorned its inhabitants, whom he deemed too foreign and less than fervent in their support of the republic. Their lack of patriotism worried him, for he believed the West was a vital buffer against British and Spanish threats, crucial to

America's economic future and his own fiscal well-being. Against that back-drop, Washington saw the threat of western secession as tantamount to treason.[22]

Collecting taxes was a low priority in 1793, when on top of European intrigues, yellow fever devastated Philadelphia. Government operations all but ceased as townspeople fled. The following summer, the federal govern-ment resolved to enforce its whiskey tax. Marshall David Lenox arrived in Pittsburgh on July 14 with summonses requiring sixty distillers to appear in a Philadelphia court for not complying with the law. After spending the eve-ning with Brackenridge, he set out with John Neville, who supervised local excise collection, to serve warrants. He didn't realize that Neville's presence would inflame the furor of an already sensitive citizenry.

At midday they came to the home of William Miller, a farmer from Pe-ters Creek, several miles outside Pittsburgh. Miller, like Neville, had fought for the republic and campaigned against indigenous people. But unlike Nev-ille, who had since prospered, Miller had struggled and intended to head farther west in the fall. The summons horrified Miller, ordering him to "set aside all manner of business and excuses" and appear in Philadelphia.

"I felt myself mad with passion," Miller later told Brackenridge. "I thought 250 dollars would ruin me; and to have to go [to] the federal court in Phila-delphia would keep me from going to Kentucky." That Neville dared to ac-company Lenox infuriated Miller. "I felt my blood boil at seeing General Neville along to pilot the sheriff to my very door," he explained, especially since Neville had once opposed the whiskey tax himself. "When old Gra-ham, the excise man, was catched and had his hair cut off [in 1783], I heard General Neville himself say they ought to have cut off the ears of the old rascal." Miller reckoned that Neville had sold out after assuming the office of regional excise collector, for which he received a yearly salary of $450 and 1 percent of the taxes he collected.[23]

As Lenox and Miller argued, an angry, somewhat intoxicated crowd of about forty men wielding pitchforks and muskets appeared. They had been harvesting nearby fields and, as was customary, drinking as they worked. When told that Miller was being hauled off to Philadelphia, they ran to his home. Finding Miller free, they allowed Lenox and Neville to leave. After the two had ridden away, a shot rang out. "I believe they meant to hit them," Miller said. The men made their escape, Lenox to Pittsburgh and Neville to his Bower Hill mansion ten miles from town.[24]

The Mingo Creek militia, in which Miller commanded a company, was meeting that day to muster troops to fight Native Americans. The mainstay of frontier defense, militias were locally organized squads to which all free white men between the ages of eighteen and fifty-three belonged. Run democratically, militias mustered regularly, mixing debate with camaraderie. Outraged by the summons, Mingo Creek's militia resolved to capture Lenox. They believed their defiance would thwart the tax.

Thirty men, including Miller, marched to Neville's house, where they thought Lenox was hiding. They confronted Neville, who ordered them to leave and began shooting. William Miller's nephew Oliver was fatally wounded in the first salvo. The poorly armed militia retreated after men enslaved by Neville opened fire from their cabins in his and their defense. Though enslaved, they hardly trusted the militia. If able to escape, they often sought refuge among Native Americans. The next day, a much larger militia force returned intent on vengeance. Although Neville requested reinforcements, only Major James Kirkpatrick with ten soldiers from Pittsburgh came to his defense. They were badly outnumbered by militiamen, who set siege to Bower Hill. After parading in a show of strength, the militia demanded Neville's surrender. Kirkpatrick, who had already snuck Neville away, agreed to let the militia search the premises, but refused to remove his men, fearing Bower Hill's destruction.

When the militia torched Neville's outbuildings, shooting broke out. Thinking that a cease-fire had been called, James McFarlane, a Revolutionary War veteran commanding the militia, walked into the open to negotiate. Immediately struck by a shot to his groin, he died within minutes. The militia resumed firing and did not stop until the soldiers surrendered. At least one other militiaman died, and several on both sides were wounded.[25] Neville's plantation was destroyed except for the smokehouse, which was spared after Neville's enslaved workers pleaded that they would starve without its provisions.

Slavery was not widespread in the region, but Neville, his son Presley, and son-in-law Isaac Craig were its three largest slave owners, owning thirty-five in all. Only large operations with cash crops like theirs found slavery profitable. A few wealthy persons, especially in Pittsburgh, kept household slaves as status symbols, but Pennsylvania had passed a gradual abolition law in 1780. A child born to an enslaved woman after March 1780 had the status of an indentured servant until becoming free at age twenty-eight. By 1800 few remained in bondage in Allegheny County. The number of free African Americans, however, was rising.[26]

The bloody encounter at Neville's plantation was a turning point. Western Pennsylvania had a long tradition of "hating out" individuals refusing to conform to community norms. Most people thought a show of force would, as it had in the past, compel widespread resistance to the whiskey excise.

The government, however, saw the shoot-out as the stirrings of a movement for secession and refused to back down. Nor would Washington and Hamilton allow local democratic societies to seize the initiative.

These extra-legal assemblies had met in western Pennsylvania since the summer of 1791. They condemned the government's foot-dragging in opening the Mississippi River to navigation and compared the excise to the Stamp and Sugar Acts. Denouncing elites and office holders who manipulated their position for private gain, they embraced the rhetoric of French revolutionaries. Meeting in Pittsburgh on April 19, 1794, delegates declared, "Our minds feel this with so much indignity, that we are almost ready to wish for a state of revolution and the guillotine of France for a short space in order to inflict punishment on the miscreants that enervate and disgrace our government."[27]

Days after torching John Neville's home, the militants intercepted letters by Presley Neville, town officials, and Fort Fayette's commander bitterly condemning them. An angry circular called for the militias to assemble at Braddock's Field on August 1 as a prelude to marching on Pittsburgh, taking the fort, and seizing the letter writers. It was a call to arms. The Braddock's Field circular asked every citizen to "express his sentiments not by his words but by his actions." They should come armed to the rendezvous with four days' provisions. "Here, sir," it stated, "is an expedition proposed in which you will have an opportunity of displaying your military talents and of rendering service to your country."[28]

Pittsburghers panicked. Although its residents were poorer on average than country folk due to the number of laborers, widows, servants, and freed black people living there, Pittsburgh was perceived as possessing greater wealth, influence, and power. Rural people resented its higher standard of living and the amenities that some enjoyed in town, where one could buy snuff, dry goods, chintzes, coffee, chocolates, and goods from Europe and the West Indies.[29] Moreover, they saw Pittsburgh as the center of excise enforcement with its leading citizens the beneficiaries. The Nevilles and their associates, who had town houses as well as country estates, attracted special ire.[30] Cash-poor country folks pegged Pittsburgh shopkeepers as avaricious and underhanded. Several were heard to say in the days leading up to the Braddock's Field muster that they would have the goods available in Pittsburgh's stores for less in a few days.[31] The day of the assembly, a lone horseman galloped through town waving a tomahawk and shouting, "This is not all that I want; it is not the excise law only that must go down, [but] your high offices and salaries." Brackenridge, noting crowds of women on the hills overlooking the town, presumed they were waiting their chance to share in the spoils by plundering Pittsburgh.[32]

As country women spoke of humbling the town's fine ladies and sales of gunpowder and flint soared, the specter of a rural horde ransacking and burning the town inspired self-preservation. At a quickly convened town meeting, a committee from Washington, Pennsylvania, the region's second-biggest town, offered a way out. They argued that catastrophe could be averted by banishing those made "obnoxious" by their letters, joining the assembly at Braddock's Field, and convincing rural militias that they stood with them.[33]

Desperate to save themselves, Pittsburghers resolved to persuade the rebels that they too opposed the excise. They would "put on a mask of being with the people and join them at Braddock's Field," Brackenridge explained, for "if they [the militias] came, most assuredly lives would be taken and the town laid to ashes. . . . There was no man so destitute of sense as not to see the instant propriety of the measure."[34]

Brackenridge nervously led Pittsburgh's delegation to the rendezvous, where his anxieties worsened. That Brackenridge championed the town was startling, but no more surprising than him being there in the first place. Born in Scotland in 1748, Brackenridge had immigrated with his family to York County, Pennsylvania, as a boy. Working his way through Princeton, he served in the Continental Army as a chaplain and studied law before arriving in Pittsburgh in 1781. He saw himself as a democratic idealist and man of letters.[35]

There was nobody else in Pittsburgh as cultured or consequential in shaping the town. By the time he rode out to Braddock's Field, Brackenridge had won state financing for improved eastward transportation; started the *Pittsburgh Gazette*, the first newspaper west of the Allegheny Mountains; and incorporated the Pittsburgh Academy, which later became the University of Pittsburgh. A champion for the region, he initiated legislation creating Allegheny County in 1788. Adamantly opposing western secession, Brackenridge backed adoption of the federal constitution and delivered the principal oration celebrating its impending ratification in June 1788 to a crowd of 1,500 on the slopes of Grant's Hill.[36] He berated its opponents as "frogs of the marsh, local demagogues, insidious declaimers" whose swampy habitat would soon dry up. But federalism was unpopular in the West, and many thought Brackenridge too obliging to national authority. He regained some favor by opposing the whiskey tax in the *Pittsburgh Gazette* and defending men who had defied the excise. He also represented squatters whom George Washington wanted to evict from land he owned.[37]

The Pittsburghers riding out to Braddock's Field hoped to ingratiate themselves with the rebels. Castigating the excise, they belittled its supporters. Brackenridge sensed that some militiamen were ambivalent about sacking Pittsburgh and had been intimidated into coming to Braddock's Field. "Every man was afraid of the opinion of another," he noted, keeping his thoughts to himself out of fear of becoming a target. But most seemed eager to march on Pittsburgh, seeking western independence and access to land.[38]

Rebel leaders, uncertain about their goals, hesitated as the reality of confronting federal authority set in. The prospects of attacking Fort Fayette were sobering. When asked about the possibility of seizing it, Brackenridge nonchalantly replied: "No doubt of it." When asked if the loss would be great, he replied, "Not at all; not above a thousand killed and five hundred wounded." The longer they talked, and the more Pittsburghers proclaimed their solidarity, the less inclined the rebels were to pillage Pittsburgh. After confirming that Pittsburgh had banished the letter writers who had offended them, they abandoned plans to seize the fort and destroy the town. Instead, they would march en masse to Pittsburgh to show their resolve.

Brackenridge dispatched messengers alerting townspeople, who brought casks of whiskey, buckets of water, and baskets of refreshments to the plains east of town to greet the men marching their way. Many other "whiskey boys" simply went home. Brackenridge led the procession, taking a route that avoided Fort Fayette. Once there he helped bring water and whiskey to the rebels. "I thought it better to be employed in extinguishing the fire of their thirst than of my house," he remarked. Townspeople tried to mollify the rebels and escort them peacefully out of town as quickly as possible. They were, for the most part, successful.[39]

Shaken but not shattered, Pittsburgh escaped harm. The rebels dispersed, believing their show of force would block enforcement of the excise. But another army was already forming, one that would march on Pittsburgh led by George Washington. On August 4 US Supreme Court justice James Wilson declared that western Pennsylvania was in rebellion. Amnesty was offered to those complying with the law, and moderates were winning out over militants, but neither Washington, Hamilton, nor a rebel faction welcomed a peaceful resolution. Washington sought a decisive display of force to reaffirm federal resolve. With the excise inflaming three other states and the Northwest Territories, he was determined to prevent the movement from jeopardizing the republic. Unrepentant rebels meanwhile continued to terrorize their enemies.[40]

Brackenridge seized on the offer of amnesty and campaigned for it. At a key August meeting at Parkinson's Ferry, moderates prevailed. Delegates petitioned Congress to repeal the tax but stopped short of committing themselves to complete compliance. The eastern press, however, still attacked Pittsburgh's sansculottes, denouncing their lower-class and foreign origins, while Hamilton penned screeds under the pseudonym of Tully branding the rebels as treasonous anarchists.[41]

Washington prepared for war on the West, assembling an invading force of nearly thirteen thousand. On September 11 local referendums asked citizens to take an oath of submission. Some areas unanimously declared their loyalty, but in locales where many lacked land and class divisions were widening, resistance continued. These protestations of fealty were too late to stop the troops marching on Pittsburgh.[42] With no insurgents to fight, the troops satisfied themselves by arresting several hundred suspected rebels and intimidating others. One roundup netted 150 men as they slept. The soldiers, who did not permit their prisoners to dress before marching them through the night, held them in muddy pens for ten days in the rain. No distinction was made between men suspected of insurrection and those who were only potential witnesses. The more rebellious the area, the harsher the crackdown, with Mingo Creek feeling the worst of the invaders' wrath. The most outspoken rebels, along with another two thousand people, had fled westward before the army arrived. Many never returned. William Miller, the first farmer served with a summons, was among them. Others waited until Washington's army left before emerging from the forest.[43]

Brackenridge's intervention saved Pittsburgh from the torch and averted a possible battle with federal forces, but he was vilified by both sides afterward. After defending himself against accusations of treason, Brackenridge was appointed to Pennsylvania's supreme court in 1799 and left town. But the insurrection left him less than sanguine about the state of democracy and culture west of the mountains.

In late November the twenty men still detained left for Philadelphia, the seat of federal government. They arrived on Christmas day, walking the entire way. Paraded before large, demonstrative crowds, the men—by then in wretched condition—spent months in jail awaiting trial. These unfortunates had not been major players in the rebellion; most were landless laborers or failing landowners. Only two were convicted of treason, and Washington pardoned both. Federal power prevailed, but it did not address the visceral distrust of government that many in the hinterlands felt. Nor did it alleviate their sense of victimization at the hands of Native Americans, landowners like the Nevilles, and government from afar. And though Pittsburgh would drive the regional economy, hostility to better-educated and inscrutable townsmen like Brackenridge lingered. These attitudes never completely went away.

AFTER THE REBELLION

Revolution did not sweep the region, yanking it out of the union and dispossessing its propertied classes. Instead, pacification of native people, army spending, and opening the Mississippi River kept Pittsburgh and the countryside within the nation. The very day a US Supreme Court justice declared western Pennsylvania in rebellion, one of the causes of its anxiety was removed. In the Battle of Fallen Timbers, General Anthony Wayne routed a force of Miami and Shawnee. Afterward the Native American presence in the Northwest Territories dwindled.

By then army spending had stimulated the local economy. Gathering in Pittsburgh, Wayne's forces trained for a year before heading west. Their need for food, whiskey, transportation, and supplies benefited farmers, boatbuilders, teamsters, and artisans. Ironically, the military's economic impact did more to alleviate western discontent than its use of force.[44] In 1795 Pinkney's Treaty with Spain removed another grievance by allowing US citizens to freely navigate the Mississippi and conduct business in New Orleans. Pittsburgh's markets expanded and produce flowed down the Ohio to the Mississippi, even into the Caribbean.[45]

Small distillers continued to fail and western residents still grumbled about taxes, but whiskey was no longer central to their rural economy. In 1802, after Thomas Jefferson became president, the excise was repealed and memories of insurrection faded.[46] A year later, as the Louisiana Purchase pushed the republic's center of gravity west, the frontier swept past Pittsburgh. But the path to that new western frontier started at the Point. Pittsburgh was no longer a rustic military outpost on the nation's periphery. Sitting at the headwaters of the Ohio River, it became the biggest, most important city west of the mountains. As military contracting slowed, regional trade and outfitting west-bound migrants shaped its future.

Though neither Mike Fink nor James O'Hara was in Pittsburgh in 1794 when rebels threatened the town, they personified Pittsburgh's changing turn-of-the-century economy. According to legend, Fink was half-horse, half-alligator, and could outfight, outdrink, outshoot, and outpole anybody on the river from Pittsburgh to New Orleans. He was born in a cabin outside Fort Pitt in 1770, two years before O'Hara arrived in Pittsburgh. By then O'Hara had acquired a classical education, military training, and a taste for business that, along with substantial family connections, propelled him into Pittsburgh's elite. Fink became known as the "King of the Keelboatmen," O'Hara as Pittsburgh's "Napoleon of industry." Each took part in taming the frontier, but only O'Hara adapted as its economy gave way to commerce and industry. Those changes were less to Fink's liking. He chased the frontier west, enlarging his legend and dying along the way.

Both Fink and O'Hara entered Pittsburgh's fur trade, which flourished before the Revolution. Native Americans annually harvested a quarter of a million deer skins and thousands of beaver, fox, cougar, raccoon, bear, and mink pelts, which they exchanged for rum, ammunition, metalware, and blankets shipped from Philadelphia. Though far smaller than Canada's fur trade, Pennsylvania's trade surpassed that of the southern colonies.[47] But only a few prospered in Pittsburgh as intermediaries with native people; the surest path to financial success was filling the military's needs for food, fodder, and logistical support as it subdued the tribes. The army, especially expeditions launched from Pittsburgh, drove the economy. Buying farm produce; enriching James O'Hara; and employing Mike Fink, scouts, hunters, teamsters, and boatmen, it injected cash into an area starved for it.[48]

Born in County Mayo, Ireland, in 1752, John O'Hara entered a Jesuit seminary in Paris. Thereafter he was commissioned in the Coldstream Guards when his uncle, the Lord of Tyrawley and the regiment's field marshal, interceded. Later Tyrawley secured O'Hara employment with a Liverpool maritime broker, where he received a grounding in trade, finance, and risk taking.[49] Sailing for Philadelphia in 1772, he became an agent for a firm trading for furs. On his first western foray O'Hara met George Washington, who encouraged him to acquire as much land as possible around Fort Pitt. Trading beads, garments, lead, powder, tobacco, and metalware for pelts and furs, O'Hara learned native dialects and mastered trading's intricacies. After receiving an inheritance from Lord Tyrawley, he partnered with a rival company.[50]

O'Hara gained an intimate knowledge of the region. He sided with Pennsylvania against Virginia in their territorial disputes and joined the Continental Army, whose Committee of Safety directed him to gather powder and ammunition. Raising and equipping a company of sixty-five men at a personal cost of $2,000, he led them into combat. As Fort Pitt's quartermaster, O'Hara not only outfitted the garrison but traded and speculated on the side. He took boatloads of powder and lead to forts down the Mississippi, returning with provisions and livestock. Cornering the salt market, he charged what some considered extortionate prices.

After the war O'Hara briefly worked in Philadelphia, where he married Mary Carson, an innkeeper's daughter. They moved to Pittsburgh, living in a log house O'Hara built along the Allegheny River in the Officers' Orchard (present-day Penn Avenue below Sixth Street).[51] While provisioning the western army and trading for furs, he operated a general store. With the military constantly campaigning and needing goods to give as gifts in treaty negotiations, O'Hara did better helping pacify Native Americans than he ever had trading with them.[52]

Well connected, O'Hara knew how to acquire what the army needed. His wheeling and dealing diversified when he became its paymaster. Arriving at distant posts to pay troops for months of service, he then sold them goods and liquor he had brought with him, returning to Pittsburgh with almost as much cash as he had taken to pay out.[53] In April 1792 President Washington appointed O'Hara as quartermaster general of the army. Hiring scores of blacksmiths, carpenters, wheelwrights, and mechanics, he oversaw construction of western outposts, complete with granaries and magazines, and assembled flotillas to transport troops and goods. An indispensable part of the military establishment, he played a key role in General Wayne's pacification campaign and was present when the treaty concluding hostilities was signed in 1795.[54]

Leaving active duty, O'Hara contracted with the military to supply flour, liquor, candles, soap, and herds of cattle. He finally stopped working for the government in 1800 because his other ventures demanded that he spend more time in Pittsburgh and less trekking along the frontier.[55] Adhering to Washington's advice to acquire as much land as possible around Pittsburgh, O'Hara became a leading property holder. The O'Haras left Officers' Orchard for a frame house in Clapboard Row alongside Pittsburgh's upper crust near the Monongahela River. Adding to his holdings, he bought 160 lots in Pittsburgh and across the river in Allegheny, then a separate town. Anticipating growth patterns, O'Hara focused on riverfront property. He also owned large tracts scattered throughout five counties and the Northwest Territories.[56]

Mike Fink undoubtedly knew O'Hara. Growing up in Pittsburgh, he would have heard of O'Hara's escapades and recognized him as one of the town's leading citizens. Fink, his four brothers, and a sister probably shopped at O'Hara's general store, seasoned their venison with his salt, drank his beer, and worked for his commercial empire. Fink and O'Hara both served in the 1794 campaign that pacified the Ohio Valley. O'Hara in turn likely knew the Finks, a family of German descent who had arrived in Pittsburgh before him and lived outside the fort. When O'Hara returned after the Revolution, Fink already stood out from his peers. As big as most grown men by the age of thirteen, he was assigned a porthole when Fort Pitt was under attack and accompanied rangers on forays against Native Americans. Fink, who like most of his peers loathed Native Americans, collected more than a few scalps. But after the Native Americans were defeated, he and other scouts were unemployed. Unwilling to settle down and accustomed to the rough and tumble, he became a boatman.

GATEWAY TO THE WEST

After the battle of Fallen Timbers, Pittsburgh's economy surged as it became the jumping-off point for settlers heading west.[57] Now that the Native American presence had been erased, more migrants arrived. Some stayed in western Pennsylvania, but even more headed downriver to the Ohio Country and the District of Kentucky. By 1794 as many as thirteen thousand people passed through each year. Outfitted locally, they waited for weeks aboard flatboats or in makeshift shelters until the rivers were high enough to travel. After arriving in the West, they depended on Pittsburgh to maintain contact and trade with the East.[58]

Pittsburgh became the principal entrepôt connecting the new frontier with the Atlantic Seaboard. Pittsburgh merchants sent eastern merchandise, regional goods, and locally manufactured products downstream to Ohio Valley towns and as far as New Orleans. In turn they dispatched regional and valley products eastward. The Allegheny River and its tributaries, the Kiskiminetas and French Creek, provided entrée to northwestern Pennsylvania and western New York. The Monongahela and Youghiogheny Rivers tapped southwestern Pennsylvania and northern Virginia (later West Virginia). Flatboats and keelboats floated white pine and hemlock, potash, coal, pig iron, whiskey, agricultural goods, and flour to Pittsburgh and returned with goods for local markets.[59] O'Hara catered to these migrants. So did scores of merchants and specialized shops, who sold groceries, supplies, and West Indian goods. Both farmers and manufacturers profited from this trade with newly settled territories.[60]

Transportation linkages complemented the waterways. The road James Smith helped carve through the mountains in 1755 for General Forbes became a crucial land artery connecting Pittsburgh to Philadelphia. The firm of Bayton, Wharton, and Morgan sent trains of packhorses, each capable of carrying two hundred pounds of goods over the mountains, to service the trade, built boats in Pittsburgh, and employed three hundred men in forays down the Ohio. Hugh Henry Brackenridge helped persuade the state to improve the road, increasing two-way trade. Soon Conestoga wagons sent packhorses to pasture and completed the 297-mile trip from Philadelphia to Pittsburgh in three weeks. By the 1820s as many as four thousand wagons made the trek annually, their teamsters adding to Pittsburgh's boisterous, transient ambience.[61]

So did boatmen. Before widespread adoption of steamboats in the 1820s, flatboats and keelboats dominated river transport. Flatboats carried tens of thousands of migrants and all their earthly goods downriver, but they were one-way vessels. Unable to go against the current, these floating arks, sometimes piloted by farmers taking goods to market, were disassembled at their destination, their lumber sold for reuse. Keelboat men, the rivers' rowdiest professionals, scorned the crude and cumbersome flatboats, because keelboats could return upriver. They were lighter and tapered at both ends with a long oar serving as a rudder. Built on three-inch keels, they were able to navigate shallow waters. Sixty to eighty feet long and eight to ten feet wide in the beam, fitted with a cabin, mast, and sails, keelboats were designed for continued use. A cleated running board ran down both sides of the boat, allowing men like Mike Fink to muscle the boat with or against the current by using a long pole that touched the river's bottom.

Both merchants and rivermen took risks. A third of all crafts were lost to snags, whirlpools, sandbars, ice, treacherous currents, rocks, or piracy. Nor

did the cargo's arrival downriver guarantee a profit. It was difficult to antici-
pate what prices commodities would fetch, and sometimes just as hard to
receive payment. Zadok Cramer, whose *Navigator* and *Almanacks* were popular guides to the river, estimated in 1814 that "nine out of ten lose rather
than gain by the trip." While no tally was kept of fatalities on the river, it
was likely high.[62]

Contemporaries described keelboat men as rough, profane, and unedu-
cated men who braved hardships with stoicism and nonchalance. They could
pole a boat upstream from New Orleans to Pittsburgh in four months, aver-
aging fifteen miles a day. On the river crews competed to see whose boat
was the fastest. In taverns from the Monongahela wharf to New Orleans,
they tried to outlie, outdrink, and out-gamble each other. When races and
other pastimes were not enough to resolve matters of manly supremacy,
they fought brawls involving each boat's champion or entire crews.[63]

For a quarter of a century Mike Fink wore a red feather in his cap signi-
fying he was his boat's champion. Fink rebuffed all challenging his status as
King of the Mississippi, another of his nicknames. Morgan Neville, who
grew up with Fink, described him as having perfectly symmetrical propor-
tions and Herculean powers. With dark skin that made him appear to be
mixed-race, raven black hair, and blue-gray eyes, Fink dressed in the red
flannel shirt, blue fringed vest, and moccasins favored by rivermen, topped
off with a leather cap.[64] In one of the many accounts lionizing Fink, he
boasted: "I'm a land-screamer—I'm a water-dog—I'm a snapping turkle
[sic]—I can lick five times my own weight in wild-cats. I can use up Injens
by the cord. . . . I can out-run, out-dance, out-jump, out-dive, out-drink,
out-holler, and out-lick, any white things in the shape o'human that's ever
put foot within two thousand miles o' the big Massassip."[65]

Fink's legend began in waterfront taverns and spread as settlers passed
through Pittsburgh on their way downriver. Morgan Neville first wrote
about Fink in 1828 in a ladies' book, as these handsome volumes sold as
presents to young women were called. Davy Crockett, or perhaps his editors, burnished these stories in *Davy Crockett's Almanacks*, paperbacks mixing tall tales and practical information about the West. Scores of writers
added to Fink's quasi-biographical history in magazines, newspapers, travel
books, and histories before the Civil War. A century later Walt Disney revived Mike Fink's legend in a motion picture in which Fink bedeviled Crockett before they joined forces to fight together in the Battle for New Orleans
and advance the nation's Manifest Destiny.[66] The Fink that emerged in these
tales was often a violent man who casually abused his wife, black people,
and Native Americans.

Mike Fink might have been a salt river roarer chock-full of fight and able
to best varmints and villains alike, but he couldn't defeat the steamboat.[67] By

1815 nine steamboats had been christened in Pittsburgh. They would push keelboats and men like Fink off the rivers in the 1820s. Rather than adapt, he followed the frontier, heading up the Missouri and Yellowstone Rivers to trap game. Fink died there, probably in 1823, although the more than a hundred accounts of his death place his demise as occurring between 1823 and 1860. In one version Mike, perhaps "corned too heavy," missed shooting the tin cup atop a man's head, and struck him dead instead. In this account, the man's friend shot Fink down in return, and Fink was buried at the mouth of the Yellowstone River. By the time Fink left Pittsburgh, the primitive outpost in which he had been born had become "the great emporium of western commerce." A gathering and distribution hub for the region and the lynchpin in a growing national trade, Pittsburgh was also establishing a formidable manufacturing presence.[68]

INDUSTRIAL OPPORTUNITIES

Men like O'Hara, who made their fortunes in commerce, diversified. Merchants became de facto bankers, accepting barter, loaning money, and buying land warrants from Revolutionary War veterans. Their capital and initiative fueled Pittsburgh's industrialization. Some manufacturing, especially flour mills, whiskey stills, and sawmills, took place in the countryside. Artisans, including boot and shoemakers, hatters, weavers, tailors, furniture makers, and blacksmiths set up shops in the city to make goods on a small scale for local markets. Pittsburgh was also becoming a transportation hub and the source of commodities for emerging western markets. Wagonmakers, wheelwrights, saddlers, harness-makers, coopers, and boatbuilders serviced the wagon traffic through the Alleghenies and migrants who congregated on the waterfront eager to head downriver. Merchant manufacturers, meanwhile, built iron foundries, naileries, steam engine works, and glassworks to supply western demand.

Pittsburgh also benefited from global politics. In retaliation for Britain and France seizing vessels flying the American flag, impressing seamen, and blocking access to Caribbean ports, President Jefferson imposed nonimportation and trade embargo acts in 1807. Shielded from foreign competition, Pittsburgh manufacturing thrived. Production swelled even more during the 1812 war with Britain.[69] By the time it ended three years later, Pittsburgh was the largest manufacturing city west of the mountains. The *Niles' Register* pronounced that Pittsburgh would become a great city. Others called it America's Birmingham.[70]

Commerce was O'Hara's springboard into manufacturing. He knew what people needed and began making those commodities, bypassing eastern manufacturers. O'Hara's first success came in 1796 when he found an inexpensive way to bring salt to Pittsburgh. While contracting for the army in upstate New York, he chanced on the Onondaga salt springs. The logistics were daunting, but O'Hara built ships for the Great Lakes, improved roads, and executed portages few thought possible to sell salt for half the price of that packed through the mountains. Trade reached twelve thousand barrels a year by 1809, before rival saltworks opened on the Allegheny and Kiskiminetas Rivers.[71]

By then O'Hara had helped create a major local industry: glass. Because it was expensive to convey glass safely across the mountains, whoever manufactured it in Pittsburgh could tap a lucrative market for windows and bottles. O'Hara and Major Isaac Craig, who had been O'Hara's deputy quartermaster, lured Peter William Eichbaum, the peripatetic descendant of generations of German glass cutters, to construct the nation's first coal-powered glassworks. Eichbaum told them to dig twenty-five tons of clay and let it to ripen until he arrived. O'Hara built his glassworks at the foot of Coal Hill, which loomed three hundred feet above the Monongahela River, opposite the Point. Coal dug atop the hill, later renamed Mt. Washington, hurtled down chutes to the works.[72]

The works blew its first glass bottle in February 1798 at a cost, O'Hara wryly noted, of $30,000. Before long, highly skilled glassworkers were making window glass, pickling jars, apothecary bottles, pocket flasks, and clock faces. The company produced glassware 25 percent cheaper than eastern imports and sold its wares as far away as Natchez, but encountered high start-up costs, shortages of acceptable raw materials, and labor problems. O'Hara clashed with artisan glassblowers over wages and working conditions but couldn't function without them. When the glassworks, which housed employees in a compound by the factory, became profitable, his venture became one of Pittsburgh's most celebrated manufacturing accomplishments. In 1808 Benjamin Bakewell opened a flint glass factory facing the Monongahela wharf across the river. It became famous for its craftsmanship, and Pittsburgh glassware was sold throughout the Mississippi River Valley and on the Atlantic coast.[73]

O'Hara built a brewery on the Monongahela in McKeesport before shifting production to a plant in the remains of Fort Duquesne at the Point. It turned barley, wheat, and corn into bottles, casks, and barrels of beer and porter sold as far away as New Orleans.[74] O'Hara also operated a sawmill, tannery, and gristmill, and cashed in on the city's emergence as the Gateway to the West by building boats, for which O'Hara and other boatbuilders hired a small army of carpenters, joiners, rope makers, sailmakers, and mechanics. Vital to transportation, his boats worked local rivers, plied lucrative but precarious Caribbean waters, and sailed for Liverpool and Marseilles.[75]

In 1804 O'Hara launched a 350-ton brig from his Pittsburgh shipyard. A year later he sent the *General Butler* downstream to Natchez with a load of glass and his son, William, aboard. But after taking on cargo for Liverpool in Natchez, it was captured by a Spanish schooner off Havana and never returned.[76] That did not deter local shipbuilders. Keeping pace with the needs of producers and western migrants, they built a score of ocean-going vessels during the early 1800s and hundreds of flatboats and keelboats.

O'Hara enjoyed a golden touch with most of his ventures but failed in the industry for which Pittsburgh became fabled. Iron had been packed over the mountains to Pittsburgh until 1790 when a furnace was built along Jacobs Creek, Fayette County, where James Smith had once lived. A handful of blast furnaces initiated production, using charcoal made from surrounding forests and limestone and iron ore mined nearby. While Pittsburgh would not have a blast furnace for decades, its forges, foundries, and a rolling mill turned pig iron, blooms, and bars made in rural shops into pots, stove plates, tools, and cannon balls. By 1815 iron goods, Pittsburgh's most important manufactured product, accounted for over a quarter of the value of its manufactured goods. O'Hara took over an idled furnace near Ligonier after its owner failed to make good on a debt, but couldn't make a go of it and ceased operations.[77]

While he is remembered as Pittsburgh's Napoleon of industry, O'Hara's greater legacy was the land he amassed. Some of it became public space decades later, including land for the Carnegie Museum and Library, the School for the Blind, and Schenley Park. O'Hara was the template for Thomas Mellon, Andrew Carnegie, and other Pittsburghers who wielded even greater wealth and influence in the city and beyond.

For two centuries Pittsburgh manufacturing roared whenever the nation went to war. The War of 1812 was no exception. Although Britain won most of the battles and domestic dissent provoked a secession crisis, Pittsburgh prospered. In 1814 the federal government constructed the Allegheny Arsenal in Lawrenceville to house its western armory. Local products were in demand after the British blockade of New Orleans reoriented trade up the Mississippi and through the city, while the region's farmers supplied American forces in the Northwest Territories. By war's end, Pittsburgh had become a key manufacturing hub with a growing market footprint.[78] A speculative boom after the war convinced most people that the city's expansion would continue unchecked. They were mistaken.[79]

THE URBAN FRONTIER

Like its economy, Pittsburgh faced the rivers. The 1790 census recorded only 376 residents in the small frontier town. Within twenty-five years the population swelled to an estimated 8,000, most residing in the pie-shaped 250 acres bound by the Allegheny and Monongahela Rivers and Grant's Hill. People began calling it "the triangle." Another 600 people lived across the river in Allegheny City and a smaller number in the newly laid-out town of Birmingham on the floodplain across the Monongahela. But the 1819 depression whittled Pittsburgh's population down to 7,248 inhabitants by 1820.

The Monongahela waterfront became Pittsburgh's center of gravity. The sloping mudflat from Water Street to the river's edge was a noisy, chaotic, commercial maelstrom. Congested with travelers, merchants, hustlers, teams of horses, and tons of freight, the wharf was the nexus for goods sold right off boats or consigned for distant markets. Teamsters searched for their loads, families secured passage aboard flatboats, and shippers negotiated rates. During low water, boats packed with goods lay tied to the shore. For weeks, even months, thousands of migrants with all their worldly possessions waited on the riverbanks for the ice pack to break up in the spring or high water to return in the fall, so that they could continue their journey.[80]

The city spread out from the wharf. Surveyors Colonel George Wood and Thomas Vickroy designed a street plan in 1784, orienting it to the Monongahela River with Water Street running along the wharf. They incorporated Colonel John Campbell's 1764 four-square-block layout within a larger gridiron extending from West Street near Fort Pitt to Grant Street toward the east. Like Philadelphia, the model for many American town plans, Wood and Vickroy established Market Street perpendicular to the waterfront, running northward for five blocks where it bisected a public square, known as the Diamond (present-day Market Square). Because the Allegheny River ran at an acute angle toward their confluence, the surveyors plotted a second grid oriented to the Allegheny. It was only two blocks deep with Penn and Liberty Avenues paralleling the river. The two gridirons met at Liberty Avenue, creating odd street angles that would frustrate traffic and traffic engineers for years to come.[81]

Whether from the rivers, wharf, or atop Mount Washington, visitors in 1820 saw a low skyline of two- and three-story buildings punctuated by church steeples and the county courthouse spire on the Diamond. Merchant storerooms clustered on Water Street near the wharf, and the city built public markets along Market Street at Water and Second Streets, now the Boulevard of the Allies, and on the Diamond. Stores, workshops, and more than nine hundred brick and wooden houses, along with gardens and stables, were scattered across the triangle. Manufactories appeared along the riverbanks away from the wharf and across the rivers in Allegheny and Birmingham. Travelers remarked that smoke from coal-burning businesses and homes shrouded the city and darkened its buildings.

Limited public services and infrastructure reflected the prevailing outlook that individuals were largely responsible for satisfying their own needs.

The small municipal government's primary role was promoting economic growth. That view, propounded by a patrician mercantile elite, shaped a profit-oriented, privately organized, and fragmented city. Schools were private entities, churches offered charity to those in need of food, and voluntary groups provided firefighting service. Newspapers announced local happenings and allowed merchants and shippers to track commodity prices in distant markets. Private social organizations such as the Mechanical Society, Freemasons, and Hibernians responded to the interests of a segmented population.

Town government, geared to supporting the city's economic aspirations, limited itself to concern for streets, public markets, the wharf, and protecting property. The state legislature established Pittsburgh as the county seat in 1788 and granted it borough status six years later. Initially a town meeting oversaw governance, with citizens electing two burgesses.[82] When growth made town meetings unwieldy, a revised 1804 charter provided for an annually elected, unpaid council of thirteen members. This council regulated public markets, created a night watch, haphazardly oversaw privy vaults, set minimal taxes and fines, and maintained four public wells. Most people drew water from private wells or vendors selling water from the rivers. The council supervised street improvements, which were usually paid for by abutting property owners. Many streets remained unpaved, and life was made difficult by poorly drained storm- and wastewater, ponds, damp ground, and annual floods. Streets were often muddy and during droughts intolerably dusty. Horse dung, trash, and roaming pigs and dogs added to the stench. In these aspects Pittsburgh was typical of other newly settled North American cities.

Pittsburgh and its neighbors across the rivers and to the east constituted an emerging urban complex connected by roads, ferries, and privately owned wooden toll bridges erected in 1818 and 1819 to span the rivers. By then some Pittsburghers looked back nostalgically to what they believed had been a simpler, more egalitarian time before the "rankling thorns of envy" pricked their social conscience. The *Pittsburgh Directory* described the "castes of society, graduated and divided with as much regard to rank and dignity as the most scrupulous Hindoos maintain."[83] Members of James O'Hara's Pittsburgh sat side by side in the pews of the First Presbyterian Church and in the meetings of cultural, scientific, and employers' societies, and on the board of the Bank of Pennsylvania. Not long removed from the town vilified by visitors as dirty, dismal, and "damned without the benefit of clergy," they aspired to greater gentility and the social swirl of more established elites in Philadelphia and Baltimore.[84]

At the same time Mike Fink's ilk elbowed and shoved their way in crowded taverns, cheap inns, brothels, and workshops near the waterfront.

This cohort thought less about civic refinement than daily survival. Strikes by journeymen shoemakers seeking higher wages foreshadowed frequent, sometimes epic, labor struggles later in the century. Though John O'Hara's and Mike Fink's worlds often intersected, they diverged as commerce gained momentum and class divisions widened.[85]

The speculative economy and flux of frontier life heightened social separation. No group typified this budding class conflict more than the floating proletariat of boatmen who worked throughout the Ohio River Valley. They were a "thoughtless, profligate, and degenerate" lot according to the Western Navigation and Bible Tract Society, which distributed pamphlets titled *The Happy Waterman* and *The Drunkard's Looking Glass* to steer them back to sobriety and religion.[86] Along with teamsters, carters, day laborers, stevedores, French Canadians, freed black people, and runaway indentured servants, they belonged to an insecure and boisterous working class whose existence was defined by hard work, economic insecurity, and danger. Less rooted in Pittsburgh than O'Hara's peers or the skilled craftsmen who worked in shipyards, glassworks, and artisan shops, these men passed through Pittsburgh, gravitating to the waterfront where many sought work or a way out of town. Their transient and precarious lifestyles undercut a stronger sense of solidarity and concerted action.[87]

ECONOMIC COLLAPSE

The War of 1812 boom proved short-lived and demand for Pittsburgh's products fell drastically when it ended. A national depression began along the Eastern Seaboard in 1815, pulling Pittsburgh into its first depression. That December a committee appraising its economy found a 14 percent across-the-board decrease in manufacturing; by 1819 manufacturing employment and the value of goods had declined a whopping two-thirds. James O'Hara died that year.[88]

With access to easy credit drying up, western settlement slackened while British manufacturers, free of war-induced barriers to trade, counterattacked by dumping goods abroad. A member explained to the British House of Commons in 1816 that dumping, while causing immediate losses, would "stifle in the cradle those rising manufactures in the United States which the war has forced into existence contrary to the usual course of nature." Making matters worse, agricultural prices dropped as European commodities flooded the market.[89]

The city's production of iron, steam engines, textiles, and glass fell precipitously. The clamor of workshops, foundries, and factories stilled; the thick clouds of smoke Zadok Cramer had noted in his 1814 edition of the *Navigator* thinned. While merchants and manufacturers suspended or curtailed operations, workers confronted the specter of debtor's prison. During six weeks in 1819, 115 people were imprisoned because they couldn't pay their debts. Two-thirds of them owed less than ten dollars. More people left the city than arrived, and as depression deepened, many concluded that Pittsburgh's future would never be as glorious as its past.[90]

Compounding Pittsburgh's woes, alternative avenues of transportation threatened the geographic advantages that had made it the Gateway to the West. The federal government opened the toll-free National Road from Maryland to Wheeling, crossing the Monongahela at Brownsville and by-passing Pittsburgh. New York state began construction of the Erie Canal to connect New York City to Lake Erie at Buffalo, and Maryland merchants proposed a canal along the Potomac River to Cumberland and then on to the Ohio River south of Pittsburgh. These alternative routes threatened to divert migrants, travelers, and trade to other cities. Two decades of rapid growth had come to an end, and the future was worrisome, if not grim. For the city to recover, it would need to adapt.

THREE

FRACTURES IN THE COMMERCIAL CITY

MIRANDA HOLLANDER RAISED AN AXE HIGH IN THE AIR AND HACKED AT the Penn Cotton Factory door. The angry throng of striking cotton mill workers surrounding her cheered as the last barrier keeping them from the mill splintered. Earlier that morning the crowd of two thousand had hurled gobs of mud, rocks, and insults at the handful of factory operatives daring to report to work. Breaching the factory's outer fences, they overwhelmed a sheriff's posse. Not content with their victory over the police, those assembled—mostly young women and girls—now wanted to enter the mill and shut it down so that someday they could go back to work under conditions more of their choosing.[1]

It was July 31, 1848. In February protesters took to the street in Paris, Palermo, and Berlin to battle for social and political emancipation. In Brussels Karl Marx finished *The Communist Manifesto* and sent it to London for publication. Closer to Pittsburgh, activists convened in Seneca Falls, New York, to place women's rights on the nation's agenda. Miranda Hollander was probably unaware of revolution in Europe, had never read Marx, nor likely knew about Seneca Falls. Nonetheless she joined an upsurge by the disenfranchised who made 1848 a year of global upheaval.

Miranda had gathered with coworkers and supporters before dawn outside the Allegheny City factory. Their goal, shutting the mill down, would prevent it from circumventing a law mandating a ten-hour workday for textile employees. The *Pittsburgh Daily Gazette* (hereafter the *Gazette*) described the factory girls storming the gates as a mob of infuriated Amazons. The *Pittsburgh Morning Post* (hereafter the *Post*) countered that Hollander and her fellow protesters were striking a blow for the rights of labor. They were both correct. Miranda Hollander was angry and did riot, but she was not simply consumed by rage. She sought a semblance of control over her working life and the chance to redefine her place in Pittsburgh. The strikers' fury reflected how industrialization was changing Pittsburgh.[2]

By mid-century Pittsburgh was no longer a small city defined principally by its commercial position at the headwaters of the Ohio. Along with Allegheny City and boroughs on the south shore of the Monongahela River and to the east, Pittsburgh was an urban complex of eighty thousand residents, one of the nation's largest. Its economic center of gravity was shifting to manufacturing with scores of textile factories, glassworks, iron rolling mills, and foundries, along with hundreds of workshops, hugging the riverbanks. Pittsburgh, no longer Gateway to the West, was becoming the Iron City.

Miranda Hollander and those laboring in these shops and factories belonged to an emerging working class. During the 1840s as thousands of Irish Catholics, Germans, and African Americans flooded a city where most people were native-born white people or immigrants from the British Isles, ethno-religious friction unsettled neighborhoods and workplaces. While most people cheered the factory girls on, Joe Barker and his adherents raged against Irish Catholic immigrants. Standing atop a soapbox in the Strip District, a working-class neighborhood along the Allegheny River, Barker berated the Sisters of Mercy as whores and the Catholic Church as a whorehouse in weekly harangues that often ended in violence. Within a year Barker would be sworn in as Pittsburgh's mayor. While Barker spoke for nativist white people alarmed by immigration, Martin Delany defended Pittsburgh's black community. Organizing "slavenappings" to free enslaved black people passing through town, Delany vowed to defend his family and neighbors in Little Hayti from white vigilantes. Frederick Douglass said of Delany, "I thank God for making me a man, but Delany thanks Him for making him a *black* man."[3]

This motley cast of working people was not solely responsible for Pittsburgh's transformation. A powerful, self-confident elite also emerged, embracing a shared worldview reinforced by family connections and wealth.[4] That elite, historian John Ingham argued, embodied the Presbyterian, Scotch-Irish culture that imprinted the city with the "moral fiber of strict no-nonsense Calvinism."[5] Their relentless drive to accumulate and prosper spearheaded Pittsburgh's ascent. Few personified the city's economic rise or that Scotch-Irish culture more than Thomas Mellon and Andrew Carnegie, who arrived as boys but left as economic moguls. Pittsburgh's expansion, industrial trajectory, and formidable elite were hardly unmitigated blessings. By mid-century coal dust and smoke hung over the city, and cholera had repeatedly ravished it. Fragmented by neighborhood, class, nationality, religion, and race, Pittsburghers confronted a complex of social problems, most of which were of their own making.

THE ECONOMY IN TRANSITION

Rocked by depression after the War of 1812, Pittsburgh fought to retain its role as Gateway to the West.[6] But as the frontier moved into the Mississippi Valley and the Great Lakes, Cincinnati, St. Louis, Buffalo, and eventually Chicago were better positioned to serve new settlements. Meanwhile, the National Road, the Erie Canal, the Chesapeake and Ohio Canal, and Ohio Canal systems bypassed Pittsburgh and connected western cities to New York and Baltimore. These canals, usually built along rivers, were cheaper, safer to navigate, accommodated larger loads, and offered longer traveling seasons.

Civic leaders, trying to preserve their commercial position, lobbied the state to upgrade transportation and pressed Congress to impose tariffs on foreign goods.[7] They pushed for a turnpike, a canal, and improved river navigation. Completed in 1820, the turnpike provided an alternative to the National Road, which connected Baltimore to the Ohio River at Wheeling. Constructed over parts of the old Forbes Road, it cut the five-to-seven-day trip from Philadelphia to Pittsburgh almost in half.[8] Pennsylvania's Main Line Canal used locks and an inclined plane portage railroad to carry boats across the mountains via the Juniata, Conemaugh, and Allegheny River Valleys. Opened in 1834, the canal never effectively competed with the Erie Canal, but its economic impact was enormous. The Main Line Canal transported pig iron, agricultural goods, furniture, and merchandise to and from Pittsburgh until the railroads abruptly captured its business in the 1850s.

While turnpikes and canals vastly improved transportation with the East, steamboats revamped western travel. Moving large loads faster and far more inexpensively than keelboats and flatboats, they steamed upstream almost as easily as downriver. When prosperity returned in the mid-1820s, steamboats jammed the Monongahela wharf. During high water, shallow-draft boats went up the Allegheny to Franklin, sometimes as far as Warren. Other vessels plied the Monongahela, where locks and dams extended the navigation season.[9] In 1837 alone 1,810 steamboats arrived from western ports, and by mid-century the estimated tonnage of goods shipped via Pittsburgh reached 380,000. To local boosters the wharf was a "beautiful" cacophony of stacked goods, scurrying shippers, and deafening noise.[10] Despite these improvements, Pittsburgh lost its geographic advantage to western cities.

By the time Miranda Hollander became a factory girl, Pittsburgh had regained its predepression footing. No longer the principal outfitters and middlemen for farmers, manufacturers and merchants repositioned the city and diversified its economy with an emphasis on iron making.[11] When compared to British and eastern ironworks in 1826, Pittsburgh's eight foundries and six rolling mills were small, technologically backward and relied on blast furnaces scattered in the mountains well east of the city for pig iron. But iron manufacturing, which accounted for nearly half of the value of goods produced, was on the rise.[12]

With two dozen rolling mills and more than thirty foundries by mid-century, iron eclipsed other manufacturing. As iron and textile production swelled, plants with more than fifty employees became common. Roughly 40 percent of all industrial hands worked in textile mills, ironworks, foundries, and rolling mills. Iron makers had not yet integrated blast furnaces into their operations or begun producing railroad rails, which was emerging as the industry's biggest market. Merchant partners provided the capital required to expand production and to market goods. Forges refined pig iron into wrought iron bars for blacksmiths and wheelwrights, while the rolling mills turned bars and blooms into plates, nails, wire, and rods. A few entrepreneurs made small batches of blister or crucible steel from which plows and springs were fashioned, but Pittsburgh's reputation was as a center for iron production, not steel.[13]

The glass industry was also growing. Taking advantage of good sand, inexpensive fuel, and access to markets, glassmakers made window glass, bottles, and tableware. In the late 1820s they began pressing glass mechanically, hastening production, standardizing wares, and slashing costs. By 1840 there were fifteen local glassworks, most on the south shore of the Monongahela River, and another dozen in small towns downriver. Textile mills would enter their twilight within a decade, but iron and glass were on the cusp of even greater advances. Pittsburgh's gateway role had vanished, giving way to an industrial future.[14]

THE WORKING CLASSES

Industrialization did more than revamp Pittsburgh's economic landscape and propel manufacturers into the elite class; it brought thousands of men and women and more than a few children into workshops and mills. Many were immigrants, who comprised half the city's population at mid-century, including an astonishing 70 percent of industrial male workers. That workforce had expanded from fewer than two thousand in 1815 to over thirteen thousand in 1850.[15] But as Pittsburgh became more of a working-class and foreign-born city, it became less homogenous and cohesive.

Industrialization begat a divided working class. At times the difficulties and insecurities of daily life prompted many to share a sense of commonality and articulate a distinctive class agenda. Most workers resented the industrial discipline driving production. Autonomous, free-thinking craftsmen saw their skills devalued as employers replaced them with low-cost workers who endured long hours under close supervision. Because wages lagged the cost of living, many lived in squalor, undernourished and vulnerable to disease. Industrialization fouled the air they breathed and the rivers from which they drank. Clouds of smoke hung over the city. Though not yet described as the "blackest, dirtiest, grimiest city in the United States," Pittsburgh was on its way to such an opprobrium.[16]

Working people were rarely a presence in the electoral arena. Twelve-hour shifts six days a week left little time to participate in democratic processes. Most foreign-born were not yet eligible to vote, and many native-born were denied the franchise due to property qualifications that lasted into the 1830s. Still others—itinerant laborers on the canal and rivers—floated in and out of town without establishing a stake in the city.[17]

Earlier in the century artisans' wages were higher and their prospects for advancement better than in the East. Perhaps half of these craftsmen were self-employed, and many journeymen expected to ultimately own their own shops.[18] But upward mobility declined as the size of the marketplace and the spread of wholesaling increased the capital required to establish a business. Iron, glass, and textile factories replaced many smaller, more intimate workshops. Completing an apprenticeship and serving as a journeyman no longer assured opening a shop of one's own.[19]

The gap in wealth between the well-heeled and poorly shod, who brushed against each other in the street, became a chasm. In a letter to the *Post* during an ironworkers' walkout in 1850, "Vox Populi" complained that while employers lolled on lounges in princely mansions, puffing Havanas and scheming how "they can grind" their workers even lower, ironworkers endured long days in unbearable heat. "Enlightened people," Vox Populi pointed out, know that an old ironworker is a rarity. "A Puddler" added that his mates wanted nothing more than their rights as citizens not to be "constrained by the iron hand of oppression to submit to the terms that arristocratic [sic] Capitalists would wish to impose upon them."[20] Craftsmen watched their standing deteriorate while less-skilled workers, whose existence had been precarious even during Mike Fink's heyday, condemned their jobs as wage slavery. But fault lines among immigrant, native-born, and a growing African American community, undercut their incipient class solidarity. These tensions reappeared whenever Pittsburgh's makeup changed. Though the city was well on its way to becoming the epicenter of an industrializing nation, social fallout was already considerable.

THE 1848 TEXTILE STRIKE

When Charles Dickens visited Pittsburgh in 1842, he was unsurprised that working conditions were grim. Women operated steam-driven machines in dimly lit Allegheny City textile factories, while children tended to a myriad of tasks to mass-produce cotton yarn, sheets, and batting. Though better off than domestic servants, these women and children were vulnerable and made much less than male mechanics and artisans.[21] The local industry had ridden a roller coaster since Englishman Samuel Haslam began making cotton cloth in 1803. By 1848 Pittsburgh's seven mills were enjoying unprecedented prosperity, ranking behind only iron and glass in importance to the local industrial economy. But manufacturers were preoccupied with a disgruntled workforce that had not shared in the industry's bounty.[22]

By mid-century women and girls far outnumbered men and boys in textile mills. Though employers reckoned that females would be docile workers, they were mistaken. Female cotton workers blocked pay cuts in 1843, parading in the streets with a banner demanding "Two dollars a day and roast beef."[23] They struck again for five weeks in 1845 in their first, albeit unsuccessful, effort to win the ten-hour workday. Though not yet organized into a trade union, these female operatives acted with a sense of purpose and understanding of the past.[24] They had ample cause for dissatisfaction. In 1837 ten days of hearings about local working-class life by a Pennsylvania Senate investigating committee indicted the factory system. Falling wages and the rising cost of food and coal coupled with unsteady work had pushed many to despair.[25] Housing was in scant supply, quarters cramped, and rents high. Scottish-born physician Dr. L. Callaghan described families crammed into tiny, densely packed dwellings, suffering in "ill-ventilated rooms and cellars, among the poorest of the poor, in old frame houses where the atmosphere is peculiarly bad, highly impregnated with putrid miasma, arising from the offal of a crowded and miserable population."[26]

They were especially helpless during epidemics. If Miranda Hollander was sixteen years old in 1848, she had survived cholera outbreaks in 1832, 1833, and 1834. Additional epidemics followed in 1849, 1850, 1854, and 1855. A *Gazette* editorial in the summer of 1837 noted that "people are so pressed together, and families crowded upon families" that it "would seem as if the first breath of Cholera must precipitate them by scores into the grave."[27] However, working people, who died disproportionately from cholera and other ailments, were blamed for their own demise. According to better-off contemporaries, drinking and folly were what killed workers. During the 1833 outbreak a commentator postulated that every death could be "traced directly to some imprudence of the sufferer or to dissolute habits."[28]

Work was highly regimented, supervision capricious and authoritarian. Textile workers averaged six-day, seventy-two-hour workweeks. Miranda went to work at 5:00 a.m. in the summer and stayed until 7:00 or 7:30 p.m. She saw daylight only on Sundays, during two brief meal breaks, and for a few minutes each evening. In the winter Miranda lived even more in the dark. Twelve-year-old Andy Carnegie, who arrived in Allegheny City with his family during the summer of 1848, found work as a bobbin boy paying $1.20 a week in fellow Scotsman William Blackstock's factory. "The hours hung heavily upon me," he confessed, "and in the work itself I took no pleasure."[29] The preservative oil for bobbins nauseated him, and fears that the boiler might explode kept him awake at night.

Arriving five minutes late cost a worker one-fourth of her daily wage; repeated tardiness meant dismissal. Carelessness by a child or woman prompted slaps or the strap.[30] A thirteen-year-old told the committee that foremen often pulled his ears, once until they bled, because he didn't have the strength for a particular task.[31] "I have seen poor innocent females," another child testified, "beat over the shoulder by a rope with knots on the end, until their backs were black and blue."[32]

Females, a fifth of whom were under five years old, made up two-thirds of the workforce.[33] A Philadelphia doctor described girls entering the mills in good health who became pale and sickly, bothered by headaches, nervous stomachs, and irregular menstrual cycles.[34] Children, Dr. Callaghan testified, have their constitutions "utterly and irreparably destroyed for life. . . . They never acquire that buoyancy and hilarity of spirits, common to children of their age. . . . They are early attacked with rickets . . . and the child is rendered disabled."[35] Machines mangled hands and fingers. Tuberculosis, skin diseases, eye strain, and nervous disorders were frequent companions.

Because they started work so young, no more than one in three workers under eighteen was literate. Once they entered the mill, their education was over.[36] In a republic dependent on the virtue and intelligence of its members, the committee concluded, it was better to "forego pecuniary advantages" than allow so many children to become "the miserable victims of an oppressive system, and to grow up in ignorance and vice, alike disgraceful to themselves and dangerous to the community."[37]

There's no way of knowing how long Miranda Hollander had been working in the mills by 1848 or even how old she was. She left few traces in the historical record. At the trial following the riot, she was described as a pretty, young girl, the sole support of her widowed mother, two younger brothers, and a kid sister. Her landlady and neighbors swore that Miranda was a "peaceable and well-disposed" girl. But like hundreds of mill workers, she was anything but happy about her lot in life.[38] That's why she and other workers stood outside the Penn Factory before dawn on a summer morning. Refusing to comply with the new state law mandating a ten-hour workday, six local mills had shut down on July 1. Acting on its own, the Penn Factory announced that it would resume production on July 31, but only with workers who had signed agreements waiving their right to shorter workdays. Miranda and her peers were determined to prevent that from happening.

After some New England states passed statutes limiting the workday, Pennsylvania joined them in March 1848. Capping workdays at ten hours and workweeks at sixty hours, it also banned labor by children under twelve. But the law had loopholes. Adults signing waivers could work more than ten hours, and a parent or guardian could sign for minors over fourteen.[39] Local manufacturers conceded that children under twelve should not work in their factories but opposed limiting older employees' hours. Instead they offered to reduce wages in exchange for fewer hours, a pay cut of about one-sixth. But a reduction in already paltry wages was out of the question for most factory operatives. For Miranda Hollander, who was supporting several dependents, reduced pay would mean calamity.[40]

At the Penn Factory a crowd of several hundred hissed and screamed "white slaves" at the forty or so employees who reported to work under the old system on July 31, 1848. The strikers' ranks quadrupled by mid-morning, and some hurled potatoes, eggs, rocks, and mud over the factory fence. Allegheny City police, intimidated by the throng, called for the county sheriff's posse.[41] Instead of calming those gathered outside the factory, the posse's presence enraged it. Jeering and cursing the mostly Irish contingent of Pittsburgh police, a few men confronted the sheriff and told him that it was wrong to bring in outsiders to settle the dispute. But ethnic tensions were otherwise muted during the protests.[42]

When the girls who had reported to work taunted the protesters from second-story windows and threw bobbins at them, protesters rushed the fence. Owner Robert Kennedy then ordered his chief engineer to release hot steam into the factory yard, thinking the noise might force them back. Instead, the steam sprayed hot water, vapor, and mud on the crowd, burning a small girl. As word of her scalding spread, Kennedy came to the gate with a double-barreled gun. He took aim at those standing before him, but according to the *Post*, "not one flinched."[43] A few girls renewed their assault with axes. Breaking the gates open, they charged into the yard, followed by the men. When Miranda Hollander shattered the factory door, they surged inside. The posse, with the help of a few protesters, led those who had reported for work out a back door to escape the crowd's wrath. Triumphant women and children celebrated by tossing the fleeing workers' dinners and whatever else they could find out the windows. They pushed and struck Kennedy and a few policemen before leaving of their own accord.

Textile operatives met at the Allegheny Market House that night and appointed a committee of two men and two women from each factory to negotiate with the owners. But manufacturers refused to meet, claiming the committee included individuals not working in the mills. The factory girls rallied again a few days later at Pittsburgh's Diamond Market House, where an assembly of artisans, mechanics, and citizens backed the strike. Men did most of the talking, and press accounts downplayed the role that women and girls played, making no mention of what Hollander and her female comrades had to say, with one exception. A journalist noted that "among the most devoted advocates" of the protests was "a young and strikingly beautiful girl" referred to as "The Unknown." She was described as "the master spirit among the girls—directing all their movements." More enamored with her looks than anything she said, he compared her to Joan of Arc. "She is a pale, dark-eyed girl, with flowing tresses, delicate features and an expression of peculiar intelligence, dignity and self-possession. Her figure is correspondingly good." Other girls shared The Unknown's commitment, including a fifteen-year-old who refused to let her friends post her $300 bond, and awaited trial in jail as a protest.[44]

The operatives were not the only ones organizing. Mill owners sought prosecution and waged a campaign to convince the public that the strikers were breaking the law and destroying the economy. Unless mills elsewhere also cut hours, manufacturers asserted that they would go under if they alone followed the new law. The *Gazette* argued that a prolonged turnout would impoverish the girls, injure employers, prevent new factories from being built, and cause those already there to leave. Besides, the paper added, many of the girls would gladly go to work if not for "the triumph of mob spirit."[45] These laborers, it opined, did not perceive how closely bound by Providence they were to their owners. "Their interests are identical—the prosperity of one is the prosperity of the other."[46] The paper claimed that workers had sacrificed $35,000 in wages during the strike's first six weeks and cost $150,000 in local trade. "All this is irretrievably lost to the community, to say nothing of the privation and suffering felt by many families thrown out of employment." It claimed that idle capital, missed profits, and alienated customers had injured the city and besmirched its reputation as a reliable center of manufacturing and trade.[47]

The *Post*, more supportive of the factory girls, agreed that proprietors had experienced great loss, but argued that the factory operatives suffered even more. "We encourage the strike. It is a strike for social and political rights, and we hope for the success of the weaker party." These "working people have but little to lose, and much to gain. The transition may be painful, but the ultimate result will no doubt be beneficial."[48] Noting that ironworkers, glassworkers, and craftsmen backed the operatives, the *Post* warned that should another attempt to resume production under the old system occur, "a general riot will be the result."[49]

Momentum began shifting to the employers, but when the Allegheny Cotton Factory announced it would resume production on August 7, no girls answered the morning bell. Owners and foremen tried running the plant themselves before giving up at midday. The *Post* ridiculed: "The Five Hour System: Something New in Factory Operations."[50] When three other factories tried opening two days later, crowds stoned the returning girls, some of whom turned away. But overall the strikers were more restrained than before. As operatives grew desperate to return to work, their solidarity crumbled, and more resumed work. Still, they struck again over wages and working conditions in September and the mills remained partially shuttered until early 1849.

Public attention turned to the courts, where on January 15, 1849, twelve men and five women, including Miranda Hollander, were tried on multiple counts of riot.[51] Mill owners hired as prosecutors Charles Shaler, who had presided over the Court of Common Pleas for more than a decade, and his young partner, Edwin Stanton, Abraham Lincoln's future secretary of war. Though Shaler had supported the operatives prior to the riot, he now condemned them as no better than a desperate mob. The rule of law, he argued, was the issue before the court, not the ten-hour day.[52]

Defense attorneys, who volunteered their services, asserted that owners had violated the operatives' social rights and provoked their outburst by releasing steam at them.[53] Mexican War hero Colonel Samuel Black led the defense and made an impassioned plea for Miranda. Citing witnesses who called her virtuous, peaceable, and hard-working, Black protested that she was guilty of nothing more than seeking the law's protection. For that, should she be fined fifty dollars, imprisoned for three months, and made to pay court costs? "Be it so," Black declared. "The widow suffers! What of that? It is a widow's business to suffer. Let her take a crust the less and drink water instead of milk, or if need be let her drink of the abundance of her tears. The children can go shoeless to the street and supperless to bed. Frost and famine for the orphan is a goodly portion."[54]

Black cast defendants as sympathetic victims, a portrayal many found believable. But not presiding judge Benjamin Patton, an unflinching advocate of law and order.[55] He noted that the court would "rejoice to see the hours of toil and labor reduced . . . so that the operatives in our factories might have more time for recreation, and for moral and intellectual improvement." That aim was "demanded by the spirit of the age and must sooner or later be conceded."[56] However, these goals could not defy the law. After nine hours the jury returned with convictions for thirteen of the seventeen defendants, including all five girls.[57]

Though convicted, they apparently did not pay their fines or serve their sentences. At least seven of the thirteen jumped bail. Court records do not reveal the imposition of sentences, suggesting that the others may also have left town. Like many working people, they moved on. The case attracted attention well beyond Pittsburgh, earning the city a reputation as inhospitable to working people. Though overblown, Pittsburgh's reputation as a strife-ridden city lingered long after the textile industry left town.[58]

A year after the riots the Reverend W. D. Howard told his Second Presbyterian Church congregation that God's goodness was manifested in the textile industry's prosperity, while the cholera epidemic afflicting Pittsburgh was punishment for the rebellion by the textile girls against "order, property, [and] virtue."[59] His sermon fell on deaf ears. In March 1850 a hundred women armed with stones and sticks invaded the Graff, Lindsay, and Company iron rolling mill on the South Side during a work stoppage by puddlers. They chased away scab workers who had been brought from the East to break their husbands' and neighbors' strike. Two years later women and children walked out of the Eagle and Hope textile mills in protest. By then textile production was in decline, unable to compete with New England factories that dwarfed Pittsburgh's mills. Iron- and metalworking now dominated the industrial landscape.[60]

TWO SCOTTISH IMMIGRANTS

There's no evidence that Andrew Carnegie's father, Will, was at the gates of the Penn Factory on July 31, 1848, or that he took part in later protests. His presence, though, would have been unsurprising. Carnegie was no stranger to agitation. He had witnessed and perhaps engaged in vigilante action against textile factories in Dunfermline, the Scottish town where he lived before coming to Pittsburgh that summer. A veteran radical committed to egalitarianism, Carnegie presided over a society of handloom weavers and championed the movement to secure a political charter in Great Britain.[61] But by the time Carnegie arrived in Allegheny City with his family, the forty-four-year-old damask weaver was a broken man. The fire sustaining his activism had died.

The Carnegies were among the 188,000 emigrants from the British Isles who arrived in the United States in 1848, the most yet in a single year. Many of them, fiercely proud working people, stoked labor clashes. Others like Thomas Mellon, who had arrived earlier, rejected working-class life to pursue the entrepreneurial opportunities of industrializing Pittsburgh. They heeded Minister W. D. Howard and his colleagues in Protestant pulpits who urged congregants to grow wealthy and join Pittsburgh's elite. Their scorn for people like Miranda Hollander widened a class divide that embroiled Pittsburgh for decades to come.[62]

Joining the "flitting," as Scots called the immigration to America, had not been easy for Will Carnegie. A third-generation weaver, he wove damask goods valued as much for their artistry as their utility. Damask weavers, who created fabrics for table linens and upholstery, were artisans on par with jewelers and cabinet makers. Will prospered, married Margaret Morrison in 1834, fathered a son Andrew in 1835, then a daughter and another son.[63] But Dunfermline was not immune to global economic currents. Cheaper, mass-produced cotton goods and a depression in the 1840s reduced many weavers to beggary.[64] Will dismissed his apprentice and sold all but one of his four looms. They moved to a smaller cottage, and Margaret opened a shop selling foodstuffs and assisted her brother in shoemaking. Their year-old daughter Ann died in 1841, a year when more people in Dunfermline died from disease and hunger than ever before.[65] The handloom weaver's day was done. Will tramped the Scottish countryside seeking work, but refused to enter the factories or mines, which to a craftsman signified personal degradation.[66]

Margaret Morrison Carnegie was not at the Penn Factory riot either. Her family, well known for leading radical struggles, had been shoemakers for three generations. Her father had organized the town's skilled craftsmen into the Political Union in the late 1820s and collaborated closely with English radical William Cobbett. By the late 1840s, with both economic and political tides turning and Will mired in his own depression, Margaret sought a way out of town.[67] Her younger sister Anne Aitkin, who had left in 1840, wrote Margaret: "This country's far better for the working man than the old, & there is room enough & to spare, notwithstanding the thousands that flock into her borders. As for myself, I like it much better than at home, for in fact you seem to breathe a freer atmosphere here."[68]

In the spring of 1848 the Carnegies sold their household possessions at a public auction, took a steamer to Glasgow, and boarded the *Wiscasset* for their fifty-day voyage to New York City.[69] Agents there steered them to Pittsburgh via the Hudson River, the Erie Canal, Lake Erie, and the Ohio and Erie Canal, an arduous three-week trip. Tired and virtually penniless on arrival, they lived rent-free in two small rooms Margaret's sister provided in Allegheny City. They gazed on poverty at least as oppressive as the destitution they had left behind in Dunfermline.

Will Carnegie bought a loom and wove simpler, coarser products than he had in Dunfermline. He peddled them door-to-door, but his son recalled, "the returns were meager in the extreme."[70] Margaret fell back on old skills, working in her sister's grocery store and stitching shoe leather at home with the aid of five-year-old Tom. Though Will left Dunfermline to stay out of the factory, he entered one in Pittsburgh to watch over Andy, who worked as a bobbin boy.[71] Father and son reflected two different immigrant fortunes. Though Andy's life became the classic tale of rags to riches, his father, biographer Joseph Wall concluded, "remained the same defeated and disillusioned man that had left Dunfermline."[72] Andy wrote his uncle that while he sometimes thought he would like to be back in Scotland, poverty would likely have been his lot there. "But here, I can surely do something better," and if not, "it will be my own fault, for anyone can get along in this country."[73]

If anyone rivaled the success that made Andrew Carnegie an American icon, it was another boy with Scottish roots. Thomas Mellon's father, Andrew, brought his family to western Pennsylvania in 1818, thirty years before Will Carnegie. Unlike Will, Andrew was not giving up on a failing craft or fleeing hunger. He came because he thought he could make his good life even better.[74] Thomas was five when his family left its twenty-three-acre farm in County Tyrone, Ireland, to join his grandfather Archibald, who had left first in 1816. By then Scotch-Irish migrants like the Mellons and Scots like the Carnegies made up a sizable portion of the region's population, shaping its culture and values. Scots alone comprised a quarter of Allegheny County in 1790; by the 1820s their presence was even larger.[75]

The Mellons sailed to Baltimore via New Brunswick, Canada, a trip of fourteen weeks. After a day in quarantine, they set off by Conestoga wagon for western Pennsylvania, a journey of three more weeks.[76] They bought a farm and moved into a rough two-room cabin on Duff's Hill in Poverty Point, near today's Murrysville. Their farm was seven times larger than the one they had left behind and lightly taxed. "The prospect before us now was greatly superior to that we had left behind," Thomas Mellon recounted. Still, he reflected, "we were to experience hard times and encounter a mountain of labor and privation which few others would have overcome."[77]

In 1819 a year after their arrival, the boom accompanying the War of 1812 ended. When the bubble burst, the Mellon farm was not worth half what they owed on it and paying the mortgage appeared hopeless. Mellon attributed his family's ability to overcome these obstacles and thrive to their individual strengths and the collective character of the Scotch-Irish. During the fifteen years he lived at Poverty Point, there "were implanted in my nature those root principles of right and duty, tenacity of purpose, patient industry and perseverance in well doing which have accompanied me through life."[78]

The Scotch-Irish and Scots attained considerable power in Pittsburgh.

With their Calvinistic emphasis on predestination, Presbyterians viewed secular success as evidence of divine selection. Their identification of material wealth with god's favor spurred them to work ever harder. Though their lives seemed devoid of aesthetic pleasures and joy, they stamped Pittsburgh with their hard-working, self-reliant, and austere ethic. No one better personified their dour Presbyterian emphasis on accumulating material wealth than Thomas Mellon.[79]

In 1823 he walked to Pittsburgh "to see the wonders I had heard related of it." Only ten years old, he was entrusted with a packhorse and a bag of rye to sell to pay for his trip. Stopping along the way, Mellon sat on a hillside overlooking the East Liberty Valley, not realizing the site would become his home. Below him stood a few homes, a steam mill, and a store surrounded by a meadow and orchard. Wheat and cornfields extended west to the Strip District. In the city Thomas marveled at a cotton factory, iron mills, and river traffic. He then returned home.[80]

Andrew Mellon expected his son to become a farmer. When Thomas was seventeen, his father went to Greensburg to sign an agreement by which his son would take over a farm. But while cutting wood that morning, Thomas realized that "all my air castles and bright fancies of acquiring knowledge and wealth or distinction were [about to be] wrecked and ruined." Throwing down his axe, he ran ten miles to town to stop his father from closing the deal. "This decision was the turning point of my life."[81]

A few years later Mellon returned to Pittsburgh, the region's educational, legal, and commercial hub. He attended Western University, which Hugh Henry Brackenridge had founded as the Pittsburgh Academy in 1787 and which became the University of Pittsburgh in 1904. Afterward he studied law with Charles Shaler, who would prosecute the textile workers.[82] While in college, Mellon parleyed money he saved from teaching and a $200 gift from his father into $700 by investing in small judgments, mechanic's liens, and debts. After graduation, he practiced law and continued to speculate in debts and real estate. By 1843 Mellon had accumulated the considerable sum of $12,000 and regarded Pittsburgh as an economic vista full of opportunity.[83]

At mid-century merchants and manufacturers were often indistinguishable in their business interests. Many of the latter depended on merchants for capital to operate. The American Iron Works, which became the Jones & Laughlin Steel Company, owed its name not to the iron manufacturers who started it but to Benjamin Jones and James Laughlin, the merchants backing its expansion. By mid-century, historian John Ingham observed, these older mercantile elements had merged with newer manufacturing interests to create a "strong, tightly knit local aristocracy."[84] They capitalized on the region's location, resources, and labor.

Scotch-Irish and Scottish Presbyterians, who were the core of this elite, defined its consciousness. They dominated mercantile activity and gained the social approval of their native-born peers in a place called Presbyterian Valley.[85] Members of Pittsburgh's elite, overwhelmingly Presbyterian and Episcopalian, lived close to each other in older downtown wards. They worshipped, danced, and played together, intermarrying and building fortunes. Tied together by economic self-interest, social class, and religion, they exercised considerable sway over city affairs.[86]

Pittsburgh's upper class had its roots in the mercantile families of the 1820s. Though Thomas Mellon and Andrew Carnegie were not initially part of this privileged group, they became exemplars of its emerging capitalist mentality. Distinctively Scotch-Irish and Scottish in sensibility and values, the elite also included English and Welsh businessmen and entrepreneurs who shared their motivations and goals. But their mentality did not go unchallenged. From time to time Miranda Hollander and other working people defied them, both at the point of production and in their neighborhoods.[87]

IMMIGRANT PITTSBURGH

Early in the century Pittsburgh's working classes shared Scottish, Scotch-Irish, English, and native-born backgrounds with the region's elite. But during the 1840s an influx of Irish and German immigrants remade the working classes, and the city's population more than doubled. The immigrants' presence was felt in crowded, ethnically diverse, industrial neighborhoods and workplaces. Catholicism became an institutional and spiritual rival to Protestant denominations and questions of religion and nationality infused local politics. While class differences fueled labor conflicts, religion and nationality introduced new social and cultural discord. Some of these tensions had crossed the Atlantic in the immigrants' cultural baggage. Others began here.

Some Germans and Irish came early to Pittsburgh, working as servants, artisans, and shopkeepers along the frontier. A German church was founded in 1782, while Irish Catholics joined English coreligionists to form a parish in 1808. Immigration surged after 1830, and by mid-century 17,000 Irish and 10,500 Germans comprised a third of the population.[88] Gaelic and German languages and Catholic and Lutheran faiths tested native-born white people's tolerance of people who were different from them. But the immigrants' centrality to the labor force meant they could not be ignored. Irish and Germans accounted for half of the city's male workers in 1850, dominating particular industries and trades.[89]

They were not cut from the same cloth as earlier émigrés in terms of religion, financial status, and occupation. The great divide for the Irish was the potato famine, which began in 1845. On the eve of the famine nearly a third of Ireland was already among "the worst fed, the worst clothed, and the worst housed in Europe." The blight decimating potato crops in 1845 and 1846 and the cholera and fevers that followed savaged Ireland, driving many to leave.[90] The Irish who immigrated to Pittsburgh before the famine were no strangers to hardship, but they were not fleeing "the smell of the grave" that traumatized the island during the famine. Those who had left earlier, like the Mellons, were more likely to have been Ulster Protestants, for whom migration was a choice to improve their situation. Though many left because mechanization undermined their crafts, these Irish Protestants were better prepared for American life than those who left later. They were also more likely to have come as families and speak English.[91]

Those fleeing the famine were usually Catholics, a quarter of whom spoke only Gaelic. Communally oriented and often fatalistic, most were rural folk with little industrial experience.[92] In Pittsburgh they worked on the waterfront and rivers, in boatyards, or as laborers and servants. Only 11 percent became artisans, clerks, or shopkeepers. Penniless and lacking marketable skills, a majority of men had only their physical labor to sell and were frequently without work.[93] Irish women fared no better. Half of them, mostly girls and single young women, toiled as domestic servants, primarily at downtown hotels, inns, and boardinghouses or in the homes of native-born Protestants. Many of the rest were seamstresses and washerwomen. Only a few escaped low-paying, poorly regarded occupations to clerk or run boardinghouses and stores.[94] To survive on meager incomes, the Irish sought housing outside the business district. Many lived as, or took in, boarders, and depended on their children to contribute to the family income.

The fairly well-off, mostly Ulster Presbyterians resided downtown and clustered around St. Paul's Cathedral at Grant Street and Fifth Avenue. The rest settled in poorer, heavily Irish Catholic neighborhoods of day laborers on the Hill overlooking the city's downtown or near factories along the river in the Strip. Housing there was ramshackle, services minimal. Thickly populated with almost equal numbers of Irish, Germans, and native-born white people, the Strip witnessed brawls on election day, St. Patrick's Day, and July 12 Orangemen's Parades.[95]

German immigration did not provoke as much nativist backlash as the Irish. Some had left their homeland to find work, others to practice Lutheranism or escape the fallout of the failed revolutions of 1848. Those arriving during the 1830s were skilled workers who often fit easily into the economy. But during the 1840s a greater number of German peasants, farmers, artisans, and shopkeepers, not so well equipped financially or occupationally, joined them.[96] Most settled near factories and workshops, especially in Birmingham, which became the South Side, and Deutschtown, a neighborhood in the eastern portion of Allegheny City. Two-fifths of all household heads worked as day laborers on the wharf, at construction sites, or in factories. But unlike the Irish, almost as many were skilled tradesmen, working as shoemakers, tailors, and bakers.[97]

By 1850 Pittsburgh's foreign-born and their children were in the majority, a demographic balance that unsettled the native-born and prevailed until the 1930s. Consequently, immigrants and their children were the core of the workforce, especially in unskilled and semiskilled positions, which employed about two-thirds of Irish and almost half of German men. In contrast, about three-fourths of native-born white men held skilled or white-collar jobs.[98]

As immigrants swelled the population of Pittsburgh and adjacent towns to eighty thousand, new neighborhoods formed around factories and workshops. Housing was scarce, overcrowding common. Because most residents could not afford to ride a horse-drawn omnibus, much less own a horse, these were walking communities. People lived close to where they worked, often along the floodplains.[99] The hills and rivers imposed topographic borders that sheltered inward-looking neighborhoods, reinforced by immigrants seeking the comfort of living among fellow émigrés. Thus ethnic groups dominated a few neighborhoods. Many others were ethnically diverse, though solidly working class.

The Pennsylvania Main Line Canal's turning basins spawned concentrations of factories and workshops in both Allegheny City and Pittsburgh. Many working there settled nearby, with development spreading eastward from the canal's terminus near Eleventh Street into the Strip and to Lawrenceville and the Allegheny Arsenal. With the triangle below Grant Street becoming a dense mix of commerce, workshops, and dwellings, people seeking more affordable lodgings moved into the lower Hill and uptown along Forbes and Fifth Avenues.

Allegheny City, nearly half the size of Pittsburgh, and the three small communities comprising present-day South Side, with more than seven thousand residents, were separate jurisdictions at that time but linked to Pittsburgh. Though toll bridges and ferries crossed the rivers, people held strong municipal and neighborhood loyalties. Work tied many to their communities. So did sporting rivalries with neighborhood rowing clubs contesting for bragging rights and purses. Pittsburgh's attempts to annex Allegheny City were not viewed favorably, and many living there rarely crossed the river. Will Carnegie disapproved of young Andy working as a telegraph messenger boy across the river in Pittsburgh, fearing "there would be dangers to encounter" if his son left their Scottish enclave in Allegheny City.[100]

Pittsburgh's spatial expansion prompted the city council to divide the city into four wards in 1833 and add five more after annexing Bayardstown (the Strip) and Pitt Township immediately to the east. Ward representation deepened a sense of fragmentation as people competed for better services. The provision of street paving, lighting with coal-gas lamps, water, and sewers routinely favored wealthier wards, pitting those older wards against newer, more working-class districts.

Water was a critical issue, especially when cholera ravished the city. In 1828 the City of Pittsburgh built its first waterworks, pumping water from the Allegheny River to a reservoir on Grant's Hill from which gravity distributed it. The network of pipes was expanded in the 1840s to address population growth and the terrible fire of 1845. That year a small fire in a wooden shed blazed out of control, burning fifty acres and one thousand buildings downtown along the Monongahela River. Volunteer fire companies were helpless as wind and flammable coal dust ignited wood-frame structures. Remarkably, only two people died. Sanitary conditions were far deadlier. Private well water often became polluted, and public water was not treated. Households disposed of solid waste and wastewater in cesspools and backyard privies, while garbage and animal waste accumulated in the streets. The first underground sewers to remove stormwater were constructed in the late 1840s, but a cleaner, healthier urban environment was not on the horizon.[101]

Although industrialization, immigration, population growth, and the city's geographical expansion created public health and infrastructure challenges, local government emphasized individual rather than collective responsibility. The city and surrounding municipalities reluctantly addressed the problems, unwilling to pay to adequately tackle public health problems, particularly for residents with marginal resources. The failure of government exacerbated tensions over class, ethnicity, and religion, fraying the city's social fabric. And nothing strained public cohesion more than rampant anti-Catholicism.

ANTI-CATHOLICISM

In 1841 Pittsburgh's vicar general Michael O'Connor wrote to his superiors in Rome that "prejudice against the Catholic religion is greater here than in any other part of the United States that I have visited."[102] A decade later the embattled O'Connor, now a bishop, told the directors of the Association for the Propagation of the Faith in Paris that matters had worsened. "During the past two or three years, we have suffered persecution here which is without comparison in a civilized nation."[103] Torch-lit processions, cross burnings, street preachers, and newspaper editors incited anti-Catholic nativists, who beat priests and vandalized churches. In 1851 fire destroyed St. Paul's Cathedral, the Catholic community's primary place of worship.

Earlier generations, fearing indigenous people, denied their humanity and drove them from the region. While native-born white Protestants considered Irish Catholics as less than human, pushing them out was not an option. Many viewed Catholicism as an undemocratic, socially regressive, and immoral ideology conniving to undermine America. They decried its role in defeating European revolutions in 1848, efforts to school Catholic children separately, and notions of papal and priestly allegiance. Nor did Protestants welcome a rival in their institutional and spiritual stronghold. For them, Catholic immigrants evoked the specter of poverty, crime, superstition, and immorality.[104] These tensions worsened during the 1840s as Catholics, many of them foreign-born, grew to an estimated quarter of Pittsburgh's population, aggravating Protestant workers' insecurities over their jobs.[105]

During the 1840s native-born white workers embraced a network of quasi-secret fraternal lodges and mutual insurance societies that sustained an increasingly hostile, nativist movement. Members of the Order of United American Mechanics (OUAM) and the United Sons of America believed that Irish newcomers were undermining their wages and social status. OUAM supporters not only voted en masse for Protestant standard-bearers, their gangs joined native-born workers battling Irish workers on the waterfront. By the early 1850s they made the anti-immigrant Know Nothing Party a formidable local force.[106]

Ethnic and religious antagonisms pervaded Pittsburgh's working classes. Joe Barker, the son of a Methodist preacher, began haranguing crowds as large as two thousand people on Sundays in the Strip and twice weekly from the Market House on what was then called the Diamond and later Market Square. Among those listening to the clean-shaven demagogue in a cape, white scarf, and stovepipe hat were men thrown out of work by slumping glass and iron factories. Appealing to their frustrations, Barker excoriated Catholic partisans as men who would "tear down the stars and stripes and put them under the spout of a holy-water pot."[107]

Barker, a former street commissioner and toll collector on a bridge over the Allegheny River, condemned foreigners, Masons, politicians, intemperance, slavery, and, most of all, Catholicism during his frequent "street services." Standing on the steps of St. Paul's Cathedral in the fall of 1849, he railed against the Catholic Church as hundreds listened. The Sisters of Mercy, he shouted, were whores, the priests whoremasters, and the Catholic Church no more than a whorehouse. The Pope and Bishop Michael O'Connor, the tall, thin street preacher exclaimed, were "mahogany-headed-sons-of-bitches." Before long, Barker's vilification engendered the desired response, an assault on Catholics. When it was over, Barker was arrested for the sixth time that year for disturbing the peace and inciting a riot.[108]

He soon found himself in front of Judge Benjamin Patton, who had presided over the textile riot trial. Patton was unmoved by defense claims that Barker was simply practicing his right to free speech, following in the footsteps of Patrick Henry and Thomas Jefferson. He condemned Barker for using "the most horribly obscene language that was perhaps ever uttered by a public speaker before a public assemblage in any part of the civilized world." But Patton was hardly urging greater tolerance. Reflecting community sentiments, he professed, "We yield to no one in sincere and ardent wishes of the continued progress and ascendancy of the Protestant religion, and if seriously assailed or threatened with the hand of violence or usurped power, we would be among the first to stand forth in its defense."[109]

The jury deliberated through the night before returning a guilty verdict. When the packed courtroom cleared without incident, the still defiant Barker addressed an immense crowd from the Court House steps. "Judge Patton made a threat two weeks ago of what he would do if I was thrown into his power," Barker proclaimed. "Now let him touch me if he dares. I'll hang him to a lamp post if he lays a finger on me." The crowd roared its approbation. Patton, undeterred, sentenced Barker to a year's imprisonment and a $250 fine.[110]

Portrayed as an imprisoned martyr for Protestantism and free speech, Barker's notoriety soared. When Mayor John Herron declined to seek reelection, Barker entered the January 1850 election and, though confined to the county jail, won the three-way race. On election night the "Barker Boys" paraded by torchlight to the county jail. A few days later their champion was allowed out of the jail so that he could be sworn in—by Judge Patton. Afterward Barker returned to jail until a pardon from the governor arrived.[111]

Barker's voters tended to be unskilled laborers and property-less artisans. As mayor he was their advocate, personally checking market scales and confiscating butter and other commodities if their weights were false and delivering them to the poorhouse. He prosecuted those who cornered the market on produce to drive up prices. An advocate of moral reform as well as intolerance, Barker closed brothels, banned prizefighting, enforced the Sabbath ban on drinking, and instituted the ten-hour workday for some city employees.[112] But his administration became a circus, and he was repeatedly arrested on charges ranging from abduction to assault and battery. Defeated for reelection, Barker's street preaching became ever-more obscene and provocative. But accusations that Bishop O'Connor had raped a nun and other fabrications did not revive his political career.[113] On his way home from a meeting about the Civil War, Barker slipped while crossing the railroad tracks and was decapitated by a train.[114]

If Barker's anti-Catholic tirades were vulgar and offensive, a more genteel attack resonated among better-off Protestants. Unconcerned about immigrants driving down wages, they feared Catholicism's growing institutional presence and electoral power, and blamed immigrant Catholics for social disorder. With six parishes, the Catholic Church's brick and mortar presence of a seminary, a hospital, a newspaper, orphanages, and an educational system worried them. It also maintained an active, fervent presence with missions, revivals, and itinerant preaching. That zeal ran smack against a larger, more evangelical Protestant establishment. With over seventy churches, three newspapers, and a network of preachers, ministers, and reform societies, Presbyterian-dominated Protestantism had little tolerance for Catholicism. Some dubbed Pittsburgh the Belfast of America. Bishop O'Connor was convinced that Protestant vitriol derived from the numerous "Orange Irishmen" in the city. They relentlessly persecuted Catholics, he said, and did so shamelessly.[115]

In the 1850s Pittsburgh voters joined a national flirtation with the Know Nothings, a nativist party seeking to extend the requirements for naturalization to twenty-one years and exclude Catholics from public office. By then earlier immigrants had finished their five-year naturalization residency and were voting disproportionately for Democratic candidates.[116] Even "respectable" Pittsburghers saw Catholics and immigrants as fueling crime and poverty. The *Gazette* published lists of those arrested in Allegheny City in March 1855, noting that only twenty-two "white" Americans had been arrested versus 76 foreigners. The *Post* added that while fifty-four "white" Americans used the services of the Fourth Street soup house, 351 foreigners had helped themselves to free meals.[117] The Irish and the Germans, regardless of religion, were seen as intemperate Sabbath breakers. But after peaking in 1854 and 1855, the Know Nothings' electoral clout rapidly disintegrated. Nevertheless, Bishop O'Connor reflected, these attacks had left Catholic Pittsburgh "dispersed, beaten, discouraged without the means to unite."[118] None of this encouraged class solidarity. In the years after the Civil War, a more mature industrial Pittsburgh witnessed an even greater working-class challenge to Pittsburgh's elites. This time, class mattered more than religion or ethnicity.

EARLY BLACK PITTSBURGH

Like Irish and German immigrants, black migrants encountered resistance from white, native-born Protestants. But while the former evinced considerable strength by the late nineteenth century, the black community, despite its early vitality, waned after mid-century. When nineteen-year-old

Martin Delany arrived in Pittsburgh in 1831, about five hundred African Americans lived there. Looking for a sign of their presence, he saw a barber pole in front of John Vashon's shop on Third Avenue. That was enough for Delany, who made Pittsburgh his home for the next quarter-century. He became a catalyst to a more visible, vibrant, and assertive black community. But in 1850, after passage of the Fugitive Slave Law provoked a mass exodus to Canada, black Pittsburgh crumbled.

Originally enslaved on a Virginia tobacco farm, Delany's maternal grandfather, Shango Peace, gained his freedom. His free-born daughter Pati married Samuel Delany, a carpenter in Charles Town, a Shenandoah Valley town. Though Samuel was enslaved, their five children were free because of Pati's status.[119] Denied admission to school, Martin was befriended by a New England peddler who gave him a primer, which the family used to learn to read and write. When a sheriff issued a summons for violating a state law forbidding black people from being educated, Pati and the children fled across the border to Chambersburg, Pennsylvania, where Martin attended school. After stints on a farm and the Pennsylvania Main Canal, he left for Pittsburgh in July 1831.[120]

Like Thomas Mellon, Delany came to Pittsburgh on foot, walking 150 miles through the mountains.[121] His first night there, he met men unlike any he had ever encountered. Educated and intent on working for the race, they offered the newcomer entrée to Pittsburgh's small black community and became his mentors. John Vashon gave Delany access to his library and a place to lodge. Lewis Woodson, a Quaker-educated minister who had recently arrived in town, was intent on opening a school. Like Vashon, he ran a barbershop downtown. So did John Peck, who partnered with Vashon to form a benevolent society. As barbers catering to a white clientele, they were well-connected men.[122]

A War of 1812 veteran, Vashon owned a public bathhouse and was the local agent for William Lloyd Garrison's antislavery newspaper, *The Liberator*. While staying with John Vashon, Delany shared a bed with his son, George, Oberlin College's first black graduate. John Peck's son David, one of the country's first African Americans to gain a medical degree, also broke educational barriers. Their cultural and political energy enveloped Delany. In turn he became black Pittsburgh's best-known leader and was regarded as the father of black nationalism.[123]

Slavery never sunk deep roots in western Pennsylvania. Its slave population peaked in 1790 when 880 people, most living outside Pittsburgh, were held by 362 families. Most slave owners kept only one or two people in bondage. By 1820 there were no enslaved people in the city and few left in its environs.[124] This had little to do with moral repugnance to servitude; slavery simply did not make economic sense because of the small size of farms and their diversified crops.[125] Moreover, the state assembly had voted in 1780 to gradually abolish slavery. Children born to enslaved women after March 1, 1780, were accorded the status of an indentured servant until the age of twenty-eight, when they became free.[126]

In contrast, the region's free black population soared from 145 in 1790 to 940 in 1800 and 3,739 in 1820. By 1830, 473 free black people lived in Pittsburgh; twenty years later they constituted nearly 4 percent of the city.[127] They built their own churches, benefit societies, educational groups, and activist organizations. Three months after Delany arrived, citizens meeting at Vashon's home organized the African Education Society and the Anti-Slavery Society. The latter was the first west of the Alleghenies. Several white people, including Dr. Edward Gazzam and Eagle Cotton Mill owner and minister Charles Avery, were charter members. Delany plunged into these reform efforts, embracing their goals of education, sobriety, and freedom.[128]

Pittsburgh's educational possibilities far exceeded Delany's expectations. He shared a room and the search for an African heritage with Molliston Madison Clark, a twenty-five-year-old student at nearby Jefferson College. Together, they explored Egyptian, African, and Haitian history and formed the Theban Literary Society. Its name affirmed their search for black civilization at a time when the legitimacy of black culture was routinely discounted.[129]

Delany worked alongside African Americans on the waterfront, but he wanted to become a doctor. After persuading Dr. Andrew McDowell to informally apprentice him, Delany prepared poultices and emetics, scrubbed instruments, and accompanied the doctor on rounds. At night he read anatomy and sometimes answered McDowell's calls, learning how to set broken bones, suture wounds, and bleed patients. When dwindling resources interrupted his studies, he heeded McDowell's suggestion to become a doctor's assistant and advertise his services as a cupper, bleeder, and leecher.[130]

Though Delany's family joined him in Pittsburgh, Martin's commitment to antislavery took him away from home. In 1839, despite warnings from friends, he ventured into the South, traveling down the Ohio River aboard *The Buckeye State*. Delany knew some of the ship's waiters, stewards, and firemen from working on the waterfront. South of Louisville, he watched men who had been sold to sugar and cotton plantations brought on board. After traveling through Mississippi, Louisiana, and Texas, he resolved to work to abolish slavery and gain equality for northern black people. Delany later turned his trip into a novel in which a black man traveling through the South organized a slave rebellion. During the Civil War, Delany tried to do just that.[131]

By the 1840s as Pittsburgh's black population quadrupled, a self-conscious, assertive, and cohesive black community emerged. A majority of the new arrivals had fled bondage in Virginia, Maryland, and Washington, DC. Marrying free people of color, these runaways were embraced by the black community, which resolved to free any enslaved African Americans brought through Pittsburgh.[132] Close to the Mason-Dixon Line, Pittsburgh became a haven for fugitives, and its Philanthropic Society emerged as the core of black resistance and self-help. A benevolent society, it was part of a black underground that liberated the enslaved. Delany was secretary of its executive committee.[133] Several Underground Railroad routes, some created as early as 1815, connected in Pittsburgh with lines running north along the Allegheny River to Erie and Buffalo and west to Cleveland and the Western Reserve.[134] African Americans working at downtown hotels, restaurants, and on the wharves alerted the Society's underground arm as soon as any black people arrived. It quickly mobilized a "slavenap" party to carry them off. According to one account, the society sent 269 people it freed to Canada in a single year.[135]

But African Americans were less integrated into the city's political, cultural, and educational life than European immigrants. While no laws or codes explicitly limited African Americans, custom nonetheless dictated where they could dine, shop, or sleep. Race also regulated access to work. The best "black" jobs were as barbers, waiters, porters, and coachmen. A far greater number labored as laundresses, teamsters, dockworkers, garbagemen, and janitors.[136] Marginality deepened their sense of solidarity. If divided by their socioeconomic prospects, black Pittsburghers were united by opposition to slavery in the South and racial restrictions in the North.[137]

Pittsburgh experienced few racially motivated attacks. When it did, Vashon, Peck, and Woodson, who tended to the mayor, judges, and other white leaders in their barber chairs, reached out to secure their support. The Duquesne Greys, a white militia, helped disperse a white mob in Little Hayti. When another attack left a child dead and several tenements pulled down, the mayor and Delany jointly appointed an interracial force to arrest the rioters. After John Vashon's home was attacked, Delany told the authorities that if they idly stood by, black Pittsburghers would protect themselves with arms if necessary.[138]

Vashon, Peck, Woodson, and Delany were indefatigable advocates, speaking, writing, and agitating against slavery and anything smacking of second-class citizenship. They prioritized education and the vote. Pittsburgh's public schools denied black children access and made no provisions for educating them. Consequently, the black community created its own schools while simultaneously fighting for their children's inclusion in the public system. In 1837 the Miller Street School opened on the Hill and taught black youth, but its abysmal quality made it a long-standing grievance in black Pittsburgh.

When Pennsylvania's 1837 constitution disenfranchised black males, Delany helped draft the call for a convention seeking to regain the vote. Held locally at the African Methodist Episcopal Church, delegates also resolved to create a newspaper speaking for black Pennsylvanians.[139] In 1843 Delany began publishing the *Mystery*, a four-page weekly costing two cents.[140] Traveling widely, lecturing with uncommon militancy, and critiquing racism from the podium or in the *Mystery*, Delany pushed the boundaries of black behavior. He boarded white-only stagecoaches and forced open the doors to Harvard College's medical school. At trials determining whether African Americans were fugitives, he testified that he knew the people in question to be free prior to their alleged enslavement. While not the only citizen testing racial toleration and integration's limits, Delany was the most vociferous.[141]

But in September 1850 Congress passed the Fugitive Slave Law, shattering northern communities where runaways had found sanctuary and lived free. The infamous law devastated black Pittsburgh.[142] Strengthening slave owners' ability to capture runaways, it allowed slave catchers to seize *any* African American, free or enslaved, without recourse to due process. Those accused of fleeing slavery were denied jury trials and the right to testify. Instead, special commissioners determined their status. The law made free black people vulnerable to kidnapping, while anyone—black or white—allegedly helping someone elude capture faced substantial penalties.

The exodus from Pittsburgh began overnight. "This iniquitous law . . . has come upon them like a mighty and resistless avalanche," lamented the *Gazette*, "burying their hopes and sweeping away the last vestige of confidence and trust in the protection and justice of the American Government." Both free-born and fugitive were threatened. Over one hundred men left for Canada within days of the law's enactment, twice that number soon after. Women and children, many born free, followed later. One hotel lost its entire staff of waiters as labor shortages hit downtown establishments and the waterfront. Although there is no way of knowing how many African Americans left because of the Fugitive Slave Law, the 1860 census reveals a substantial drop of over eight hundred since 1850, a decline of 40 percent, at a time when the urban area's combined population climbed by 23 percent.[143]

White and black Pittsburghers denounced the law as "iniquitous and unconstitutional." The mayor, a congressman, and Delany addressed a protest held in Allegheny City's market house. When Delany warned that if a slave catcher "should enter my dwelling, one of us must perish," the mostly white audience thundered its approval. Black crowds kept confronting slave owners and liberating slaves, but their defiance could not stem the flight of African Americans from Pittsburgh or prevent damage to the black community. In some ways that community was never again as focused or empowered.[144]

Delany left Pittsburgh too, but not for Canada. Instead, he sought admission to Harvard's medical school, which had recently accepted two African Americans sponsored by a colonization society with the understanding that they would practice in Liberia. Delany was another matter, and when white students protested his presence, Harvard caved. Delany returned home, upset that New England abolitionists had not rallied to his defense.[145]

Practicing medicine without a degree, he wrote and lectured about race and slavery and presided over Pittsburgh's annual August First celebrations marking the end of slavery in the British West Indies. When the Fugitive Slave Law was not repealed and new measures further restricted free black people's rights in the North, Delany's frustration deepened. By 1852 he concluded that the future for African Americans lay not in the United States or in Africa, but in emigration to Central and South America. After arguing this in a pamphlet, Delany tried to put his words into practice.[146]

Nevertheless, he ended up in Canada, not Central America. In February 1856 the Delanys left for Chatham, a Thames River town in Ontario. Black expatriates, many from Pittsburgh, comprised over half of its four thousand residents. After settling into the community, Delany's enthusiasm for emigration waned. When Lincoln called for emancipation, he recommitted to a domestic solution to slavery and racism. Traveling the Midwest, he implored African Americans to enlist in the Union army. Many returned from Canada to do so, including his oldest child, Toussaint, who at the age of eighteen enlisted in the all-black Massachusetts Fifty-Fourth Regiment.[147]

Black Pittsburgh's commitment to the Union grew stronger and the Hannibal Guards and other local companies mobilized. At least a dozen men left to join Toussaint in the ranks of the Massachusetts Fifty-Fourth and Fifty-Fifth Volunteer Infantry Regiments. Delany's Pittsburgh days, however, were behind him. He remained a significant and controversial figure until his death in 1885 but figured less in Pittsburgh politics.[148]

Sent into a tailspin by the Fugitive Slave Law, Pittsburgh's black community recovered some momentum during the war. Two grievances that had festered since the 1830s were resolved in its aftermath. The Fifteenth Amendment enfranchised black men in 1869, while in 1875 Pittsburgh integrated public education.[149] But it took decades to recover from the Fugitive Slave Act. A larger and more dynamic black community would reemerge in Pittsburgh, but not until later in the century.

In the decades following the 1819 depression, Pittsburgh and surrounding communities underwent a transition from the gateway to North America's heartland to an industrially based economy. The iron firms, their entrepreneurial leaders, and highly skilled workers faced burgeoning markets, cyclical downturns, and stiff competition. But they built a foundation that allowed them to navigate coming economic challenges. Meanwhile, European immigrants and black migrants arrived to labor in the mills, factories, workshops, and wharves and fill unskilled jobs. Along with industrialization and these diverse newcomers came class conflicts; ethnic, religious, and racial divisions; and environmental and health problems. Churches, ethnic organizations, and political parties grappled with, and often exacerbated, these divisions and problems. They and the small and reactive municipal governments had little success in resolving them. As the city became more socially stratified and partisan, its formerly small-town intimacy was lost. Even larger upheavals were on the horizon.

Fig. 1. Catehecassa Blackhoof stone marker. The Shawnee warrior, now largely
forgotten, fought for decades against British and US forces trying to drive
indigenous people from the region. Courtesy of Scott Smith.

Mike Fink, the Ohio Boatman.

Fig. 2. Mike Fink became a legendary figure, described as half-horse, half-alligator, and able to outfight, outdrink, outshoot, and out-pole anybody on the river from Pittsburgh to New Orleans. Courtesy of Carnegie Library of Pittsburgh.

Fig. 3. Hugh Henry Brackenridge, a Scottish-born lawyer, talked the Whiskey
Rebels out of burning Pittsburgh and helped found the *Pittsburgh Gazette*, a
forerunner of the *Pittsburgh Post-Gazette*; the Pittsburgh Academy, forerunner of the University of Pittsburgh; and Allegheny County. Courtesy of
Carnegie Library of Pittsburgh.

COPR. DETROIT PUBLISHING CO.

71510 LAKE AND PANTHER HOLLOW FROM ACROSS RAVINE, PITTSBURGH, PA.

Fig. 4. Schenley Bridge and Pond. James O'Hara left a substantial expanse of land to his granddaughter Mary Schenley, who donated a section of it to the city in 1889 to create its first public park. Courtesy of Carnegie Library of Pittsburgh.

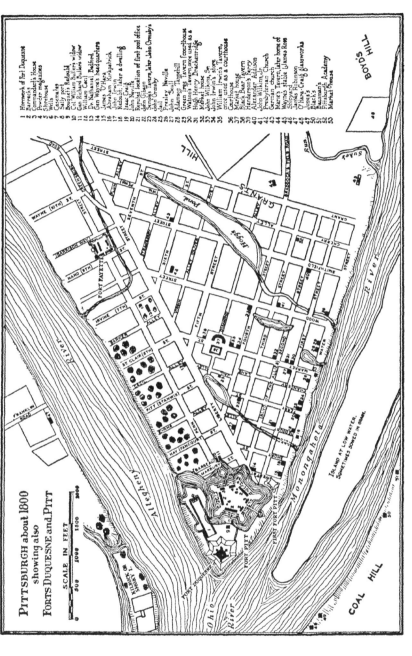

Fig. 5. The Woods-Vickroy Plan of Pittsburgh, 1784, laid out the street pattern for the new town and ultimately downtown, which in its orientation to both the Monongahela and Allegheny rivers has created traffic nightmares ever since. Courtesy of Archives Services Center, University of Pittsburgh.

1864 · Pomroy's Express – a passenger packet on the Allegheny

Fig. 6. The keelboat replaced the one-way rafts that carried cargo and settlers down the Ohio and Mississippi Rivers to ports south because it was built to be poled upstream by rough and rowdy boatmen like Mike Fink. Courtesy of Carnegie Library of Pittsburgh.

JOSEPH BARKER
Mayor of Pittsburgh
1850

Fig. 7. Joe Barker, who stood atop a soapbox in the Strip District berating the Sisters of Mercy as whores and the Catholic Church as a whorehouse in weekly harangues that ended in violence, was elected as Pittsburgh's mayor in 1850. Courtesy of Carnegie Library of Pittsburgh.

Fig. 8. Martin Delany. Frederick Douglass said of Martin Delany, "I thank God for
making me a man, but Delany thanks Him for making him a *black* man."
Courtesy of Carnegie Library of Pittsburgh.

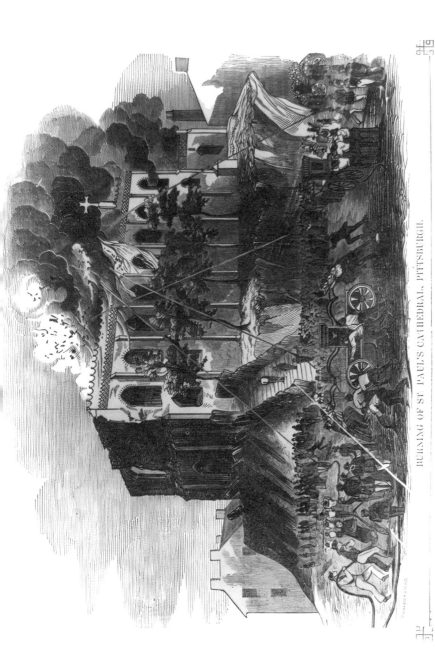

BURNING OF ST. PAUL'S CATHEDRAL, PITTSBURGH.

Fig. 9. Burning of St. Paul's Cathedral, Pittsburgh. Torch-lit processions, cross burnings, street preachers, and newspaper editors incited anti-Catholic nativists, who beat priests, vandalized churches, and in 1851 set fire to St. Paul's Cathedral, the Catholic community's primary place of worship. Courtesy of the Library of Congress.

On July 31, 1848, an angry throng of striking cotton workers gathered before dawn at Penn Cotton. They cheered as Miranda Hollander raised an axe high in the air and chopped downward against the Penn Cotton Factory door. Their goal was to prevent the mills from circumventing a law mandating a ten hour workday for textile employees.

Fig. 10. Textile workers protest. Thousands of girls and women, some as young as five years old, worked for twelve hours a day or longer in textile factories in Allegheny City. Courtesy of Bill Yund.

Fig. 11. 1877 Railroad strike wreckage. On Saturday, July 21, 1877, state militia arriving from Philadelphia dispersed workers who had shut down Pittsburgh's railroads in a dispute over wage cuts. The militia's assault turned a peaceful strike into a rampage that riveted the nation's attention on Pittsburgh. Courtesy Carnegie Library of Pittsburgh.

Fig. 12. Breakfast Room at the Clayton Mansion. H. C. Frick hosted frequent poker games for a few friends of similar wealth and industrial stature in the breakfast room of his Point Breeze estate, which was outfitted with products of their businesses, such as aluminum, electricity, and plate glass. Courtesy of The Frick Collection/Frick Art Reference Library Archives.

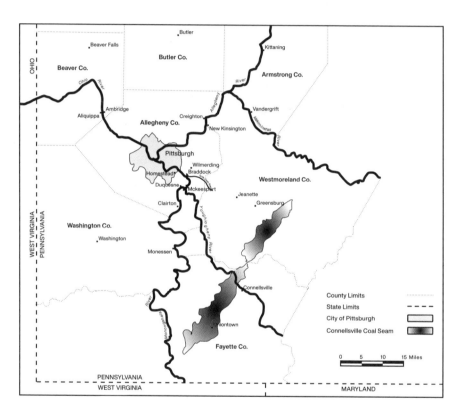

Fig. 13. Map 2 of the region. Map depicting the Pittsburgh Metropolitan Area, ca. 1920, shows that due to industry, the outline of the twentieth-century region had already been established long before suburban development filled it in. Courtesy of University of Pittsburgh Press.

Fig. 14. The shop floor at Westinghouse illustrates the crowded, poorly lit, and particle-filled air typical of the new mass-production factories of the turn-of-the-century era. Courtesy of the Heinz History Center, Library & Archives.

Vol. XXXVI.—No. 1854.
Copyright, 1892, by Harper & Brothers.
All Rights Reserved.

NEW YORK, SATURDAY, JULY 16, 1892.

TEN CENTS A COPY.
FOUR DOLLARS A YEAR.

THE HOMESTEAD RIOT.—Drawn by W. P. Snyder after a Photograph by Dabbs, Pittsburg.—[See Page 678.]
THE PINKERTON MEN LEAVING THE BARGES AFTER THE SURRENDER.

Fig. 15. During the Homestead lockout, initiated by Andrew Carnegie and H. C.
Frick, barges packed with three hundred armed Pinkerton guards came up
the Monongahela River on July 6, 1892, to escort strikebreakers into the
steelworks. The river ran red, and almost a dozen Pinkertons and workers
died. Cover, *Harper's Magazine*, July 16, 1892. Courtesy of the Rivers of Steel
National Heritage Area.

Fig. 16. H. J. Heinz and other companies employed large numbers of young women in repetitive, poorly paid tasks for long hours, such as these women who are filling and capping mustard jars. Courtesy of the Heinz History Center, Library and Archives.

Fig. 17. While working at the Homestead Steel Works, these Russian steelworkers found some semblance of community in the homes where they boarded. Photo by Lewis W. Hine. Courtesy of the George Eastman Museum.

FOUR

THE IRON CITY

PITTSBURGH WAS BURNING—FROM THE UNION DEPOT ON THE EDGE OF downtown for three miles up the railroad tracks running along the Allegheny River. Over 1,200 freight cars, 150 locomotives and passenger cars, and two score buildings smoldered as crowds sought vengeance for the deaths of at least twenty from their ranks the day before. That Saturday afternoon, July 21, 1877, six hundred state militia arrived from Philadelphia and dispersed striking workers who had shut down Pittsburgh's railyards. Their assault turned a peaceful strike into a rampage that riveted the nation's attention on Pittsburgh.

As dawn approached on Sunday morning, the state militia huddled inside the Pennsylvania Railroad roundhouse, choking on smoke from the fires consuming Pittsburgh. They had spent the night without food or sleep, besieged by a grief-stricken crowd, huddled inside the cavernous building where locomotives were pivoted to change directions. Several soldiers had been wounded. During the night they repulsed an effort to use a captured artillery piece against their sanctuary, killing or wounding eleven of their assailants. At midnight men and boys rammed flaming cars of coal and oil against the sand house, an adjoining building. By dawn smoke from burning cars and the larger conflagration made it impossible to stay there any longer.[1]

Early Sunday morning, the troops marched four abreast out of the roundhouse. Their objective in coming to Pittsburgh, to end a walkout by railroad workers, was no longer as critical as getting out alive. The day before state militiamen had easily overwhelmed striking railroad workers and their supporters, a mix of iron- and glassworkers, unemployed laborers, women, and children, whose stones and taunts were no match for bayonets and rifles. Sunday's skirmish would not be so one-sided. Snipers atop buildings and in alleyways shot at the soldiers as they headed down Penn Avenue. The troops returned fire and another score of Pittsburghers and a few soldiers soon lay dead or dying. Abandoning their mission of breaking the strike, the troops fought their way to safety.

As news of the carnage spread, headlines across the nation warned that madness, anarchy, and revolution had engulfed the land. President Rutherford B. Hayes, alerted to the clash that evening at his summer residence, convened his cabinet. The republic, many feared, was poised on the abyss.[2] But peace returned as strikers and citizens restored order on their own. Pittsburghers extinguished the fires and mourned their dead. When troops returned a week later, they encountered little resistance. But Pittsburgh did not go back to work. Instead, the strike spread to iron and steel mills, workshops, and nearby mines. Soon most of the region, like much of the country, was on strike.

The Great Strike, as it became known, had begun on July 16 when railroad workers walked out at Camden Junction near Baltimore and in Martinsburg, West Virginia. Within days these incidents snowballed into the country's first nationwide labor conflict. Unprecedented in scope, the Great Strike appeared to many like revolution or the apocalypse. But the 1877 uprising should have come as no surprise in Pittsburgh or elsewhere in industrial America. The financial panic that began in 1873 had morphed into a full-scale depression. Starvation stalked the land, and the railroad strikes were the catalyst that turned frustration and despair into defiance and riot. Nowhere was the outburst more cataclysmic than in Pittsburgh. Nowhere was greater damage done, more people killed, or the violence more widely publicized. These days of rage, the deadliest single clash in Pittsburgh since the eighteenth century, had been in the making since the Pennsylvania Railroad rolled into town in 1852. Pittsburgh's convulsions were the downside of its transformation into an industrial city.

Though the insurrection surpassed prior clashes between labor and capital in Pittsburgh, 1877 was about much more than polarization along class lines. It signified the extent to which working people, manufacturers, and the middle classes had collaborated in making Pittsburgh into the nation's

Iron City. Class antagonisms erupted frequently, but mostly within the context of negotiations between labor and capital. Though hardly coequals in this social web, Pittsburgh's workers possessed considerable power, more than they ever had before or would have again until the 1930s. The strike and riots of 1877 were not a revolution as much as an upsurge by desperate working people backed by much of their community. As long as their foe was the Pennsylvania Railroad Company (PRR), the very incarnation of an unbridled monopoly encroaching on local rights, workers could count on support that transcended class. The railroad had spurred Pittsburgh's transformation into the Iron City, but it was also a source of its discontents. The strike foreshadowed even more strife as mechanization and mass production eroded the power of skilled craftsmen and deepened inequality across society.

ANDY CARNEGIE

By the summer of 1877 Andrew Carnegie was ten years gone from Pittsburgh and in the employ of the Pennsylvania Railroad. Ensconced with his mother in a suite at the Windsor Hotel on New York's Fifth Avenue, Carnegie returned often to Pittsburgh and kept abreast of his mills there via telegraph. A major force in shaping Pittsburgh during the last quarter of the century, he was no longer of that world.

As a twelve-year-old immigrant, Andy Carnegie hated working in an Allegheny City textile factory and was grateful for the respite from the shop floor that office work upstairs offered. In the spring of 1849, when his uncle told him a telegraph office in Pittsburgh was looking for a messenger boy, Andy leaped at the chance. The telegraph and the railroad were the vanguard of the communications and transportation revolutions driving industrialization. O'Reilly's Telegraph Company maintained communications with the East Coast, making it indispensable to the railroad. Carnegie, grasping the opportunities his position offered, memorized the layout of city streets, business locations, and the faces of prominent businessmen. Charming his way to the edges of power, Andy knew not only businessmen but their business. Soon the senior messenger boy, he delegated tasks and persuaded the boys, mostly Scottish immigrants like himself, Robert Pitcairn and Henry Oliver, to pool and evenly divide their bonus money from trips outside the central district. Picking up telegraphing, Andy began spelling regular operators, and soon became one himself. He even learned how to interpret messages without transcribing a transmission's dots and dashes, a skill few achieved.[3]

While his father sunk into apathy as his craft became obsolete, Andy was excited about his future and that of his adopted country. Believing that the United States was destined to spread the American dream across the continent, he read voraciously and organized a debating society. Meanwhile, he flattered prospective employers, including Tom Scott, the PRR's new Western Division superintendent, who made Carnegie his personal operator and took to calling him "my boy, Andy."[4] Scott gave the seventeen-year-old full rein to develop, and his boy Andy seized the chance. If Scott were unreachable when a message arrived regarding an accident or serious delays on the eastern line, Carnegie telegraphed orders he thought Scott would give and tapped his boss's name to authorize the message. "'Death or Westminster Abbey' flashed across my mind," Carnegie later wrote. But Scott approved of his gamble and delighted in regaling colleagues about "my boy's" boldness.[5]

Andy learned how the railroads and other businesses operated and became privy to information allowing him to assess their prospects. Scott soon became his patron as well as his mentor. Tipping his protégé to an investment opportunity in the Adams Express Company, Scott loaned Andy the money to purchase stock. When Andy received his first dividend check, he wrote, "It gave me the first penny of revenue from capital—something that I had not worked for with the sweat of my brow. 'Eureka!' I cried. 'Here's the goose that lays the golden eggs.'" That investment was the first of several enabling Carnegie to profit from other people's sweat.[6]

When Scott was promoted to general superintendent in January 1858 and moved to Altoona, he brought Andy along as his secretary. Soon after their arrival a company blacksmith Carnegie had befriended approached him as he walked to his hotel after work. The man said that maintenance workers were planning to strike and revealed their identities. Carnegie immediately told Scott, who fired the men before they could act. In just a few years Carnegie had forsaken his father and grandfather's craftsmen's ideals.[7] As historian David Nasaw observed, Carnegie "abandoned the moral economy of his Scottish forefathers for the political economy of his new employers."[8]

Unlike his father and grandfather, Carnegie prospered materially, drawing a salary and profiting from a growing investment portfolio. A stake in the Woodruff Sleeping Car Company alone earned him three times his railroad salary. Scott's patronage, moreover, boosted Carnegie up the company ladder. In 1859, when Scott became the PRR's vice president, Carnegie, just twenty-four years old, took over as the Western Division's superintendent.[9] Carnegie and his sixteen-year-old brother Tom, who was his personal assistant and telegraph operator, resided near the railyards with their mother. Will Carnegie had died by then, and Andy was the family's principal breadwinner. But downtown Pittsburgh upset the usually irrepressible Carnegie. "The smoke permeated and penetrated everything. If you placed your hand on the balustrade of the stair it came away black: if you washed face and hands, they were as dirty as ever in an hour. The soot gathered in the hair and irritated the skin, and for a time after our return from the mountain atmosphere of Altoona, life was more or less miserable."[10] They soon moved to Homewood (today's Point Breeze section), a leafy and affluent residential suburb. As superintendent, Carnegie traveled in the city's upper social circles. Like many manufacturers and industrialists, he was a strong supporter of the Republican Party, abolition, and Abraham Lincoln, for whom he cast his ballot in 1860.[11] Carnegie chafed as southern states seceded and waited eagerly for the South to provoke war. He did not wait long.

Carnegie was not the only one spoiling for a fight. Pittsburghers heeded Lincoln's request to pray and fast on January 4, 1861, and blocked the departure of the *Silver Wave*, which carried a load of weapons bound for southern waters, forcing the government to revoke the boat's orders. And they cheered the president-elect in February as he addressed a wildly enthusiastic crowd from the balcony of the Monongahela Hotel en route to Washington.

War fever swept across western Pennsylvania and volunteer companies arrived in Pittsburgh after the attack on Fort Sumter. They were fervent but poorly trained and ill-equipped. Some were long-standing militias; others recently formed. The Wide-Awakes, a young Republican club active during the campaign, reconstituted as a militia, while Birmingham glassblowers, Fort Pitt Foundry workers, and trainmen raised companies. African Americans formed the Hannibal Guards, German gymnastic societies became the Turner Rifles, and volunteer fire companies put down their hoses and picked up weapons. Some men, fearing the war would end quickly, bribed their way into companies. Overall, Allegheny County contributed twenty-four thousand Union soldiers, a staggering figure given that its 1860 population, including women, children, and the elderly, was only 179,000.[12]

Soon after Fort Sumter the War Department summoned Tom Scott to Washington to keep Union rail lines open. Carnegie accompanied him, ensuring that troops and armaments flowed smoothly. Assembling a corps of telegraph operators, he organized transportation for Union forces in the Capitol and northern Virginia, where the Confederates were mobilizing. After the Union army's debacle at Bull Run in late July, Carnegie helped evacuate the wounded. But sunstroke, poor health, and fear of typhoid, which was ravaging Union camps, convinced him to return to Pittsburgh in September 1861 and resume his position with the railroad.[13]

The Pennsylvania Railroad was critical to the Union effort, but Carnegie's own business interests vied for his time. Despite his rhetorical commitment to the Union, he was disinclined to join the military. In the summer of 1864, when the twenty-eight-year-old and unmarried Carnegie was drafted, he paid $850 for John Lindew, an Irish immigrant, to go in his place. Rather than fight, Carnegie focused on capitalizing on the industrial society he saw emerging in the wake of the war.[14] Pittsburgh, like Carnegie, escaped direct conflict. In June 1863, after Robert E. Lee led Confederate forces into south-west Pennsylvania, Pittsburgh feared an attack was imminent. Mills shut down, and workers built twelve miles of entrenchments and fortified twenty outposts on Mount Washington, Herron Hill, Stanton Heights, and other sites. But Confederate troops halted short of the city.[15]

THE IRON CITY

By the war's end Pittsburgh was the Iron City. Its iron girded the nation's military and continental expansion, forging rails for a transcontinental rail-road system and bridges spanning the Ohio, Mississippi, and Missouri Rivers. Iron in turn shaped Pittsburgh during the third quarter of the century. No one understood this better than the manufacturers and craftsmen who made it, men like B. F. Jones, Andrew Carnegie, Henry Oliver, and James Davis.

Mid-century had been a challenging time for iron makers. After years of profitably producing cast-iron products, iron plate for steam engines and boilers, and wrought iron for agricultural tools, they faced a market shifting to industrial machinery, rails and equipment, bridges, and large buildings. These new markets and the war's heightened demands presented attractive opportunities for firms able to adjust their operations accordingly. Pittsburgh firms succeeded so well in this new environment that by 1880 they produced one-eighth of the nation's iron and steel tonnage, and metalworkers comprised 62 percent of the city's industrial workforce.[16]

Benjamin Franklin Jones and James Laughlin epitomized the local economy's reorientation. Not only meeting the challenges of new markets, they built an integrated firm that presaged the direction other Pittsburgh iron and eventually steel companies would take. Smaller, narrowly focused, and less capitalized firms either succeeded within their niche or struggled to meet rapidly changing economic conditions. Jones & Laughlin would change and prosper for over a century.

Born in Washington County in 1824 to parents of Welsh and German ancestry, Jones began clerking for businessman Samuel Kier in Pittsburgh in 1842. Soon Jones joined Kier in operating boats on the Pennsylvania Main Line Canal. Recognizing that railroads were fast approaching Pittsburgh, they sold their canal business in 1850 and became iron merchants. They became acquainted with brothers Bernard and John Lauth, immigrant German craftsmen who operated puddling furnaces and a rolling mill on the South Side. When the Lauths needed capital to expand in 1853, they partnered with Jones and Kier, creating the American Iron Works. When they required additional investment, Jones brokered an infusion of considerable capital from banker James Laughlin. A Scotch-Irish member of the city's elite, the older Laughlin became a partner and principal financier of the rapidly growing firm.[17]

Their partnership combined technical knowledge, entrepreneurial vision, and capital, essential ingredients to flourish in the new iron markets critical to American industrialization. They needed to vertically integrate iron production, which a few iron mills east of the mountains and Johnstown's Cambria Iron Company had done. That meant building blast furnaces, securing access to raw materials, and processing greater quantities of pig iron and blooms than before the war. To make rails, ironmasters had to overcome inconsistencies in the pig iron, charcoal, and coke they acquired and mixed. Those raw materials came from disparate sources—central Pennsylvania, the Allegheny and Shenango Valleys north of the city, and Fayette County to the south—and in ever larger quantities.[18]

With the technically gifted Lauths overseeing operations and Laughlin supplying capital, Jones engineered the American Iron Works' vertical integration of smelting, puddling, rolling, and marketing. In 1860 the partnership blew in the two Eliza blast furnaces and built beehive ovens to furnish coke in Hazelwood, across the Monongahela from their South Side mill. A "forward" linkage preceded this "backward" integration, when Jones opened a warehouse in Chicago to service western markets and put his younger brother Tom in charge of sales.[19] Like the city in which the works was located, Jones had moved from the world of commerce to the vanguard of iron manufacturing.

The Civil War's tremendous appetite for iron goods magnified the challenges and opportunities of the 1850s. Pittsburgh firms prospered from unprecedented military demands for cannon, cannon balls, guns, shot, and shells, as well as ironclad vessels for western rivers. The Allegheny Arsenal in Lawrenceville supplied armaments, while the Fort Pitt Foundry in the Strip District made tons of shot and shells and three thousand cannon and mortars, including two unusually large, twenty-inch Columbiads. Singer, Nimick & Co. fabricated muzzle-loading field guns, while a Massachusetts firm fashioned four hundred thousand sabers out of Pittsburgh cast steel. Local rolling mills turned out iron plate for one hundred mortar boats and ironclad gunboats built in the city. Orders for rails, locomotives, cars, couplings, wheels, and axles added immensely to the frenzied demands on iron manufacturers.[20]

These wartime opportunities attracted Carnegie, whose career was evolving alongside the iron business. Foreseeing that iron bridges would replace wooden structures as the railroads deployed heavier trains and expanded westward, Carnegie organized the Keystone Bridge Company in the Strip District in 1862. His involvement in iron manufacturing, which defined much of his career, resulted from a dispute among boyhood friends. In 1859 Tom Miller and Henry Phipps had partnered with two skilled Prussian immigrant metalworkers, Anthony and Andrew Kloman, who produced high-quality railroad axles at their small Millvale forge. After Miller and Phipps underwrote the Klomans' expansion to fulfill railroad orders, the business grew and moved across the Allegheny River. Prosperity, however, created discord among the partners, who asked Carnegie to broker a settlement. That prompted Carnegie to join forces with them to form the Union Iron Mills, which sold beams and plates to Carnegie's nearby bridge works. More important, their collaboration merged the technical genius of Andrew Kloman, the managerial skills of Andrew Carnegie's brother Tom Carnegie and Henry Phipps, and Carnegie's capital resources—the same combination of attributes that powered Jones & Laughlin.[21]

The Union Iron Mills and other local firms positioned themselves to supply iron for America's postwar boom. As the nation industrialized, cities grew and the railroads surged, adding twenty-five thousand miles of new track by 1871 and another fifty thousand miles during the next decade. Much of that growth occurred west of the Allegheny Mountains. Pittsburgh's two dozen iron and steel mills before the war grew to thirty-eight in 1874. Eight produced high-value crucible steel; the rest were iron puddling and rolling mills. Doubling its number of puddling furnaces, the American Iron Works alone rolled fifty thousand tons of iron annually. Eleven more mills opened during the 1880s, including a few producing large quantities of steel from Bessemer and open-hearth furnaces.[22]

Pittsburgh's foundries, forges, and rolling mills ramped up production and were joined by the city's first blast furnace, built by Graf, Bennett & Company in 1859, and six more during the war. These seven furnaces produced forty-eight thousand tons of pig iron in 1870, which was not enough to satisfy the hunger of local mills. But with the addition of the huge Isabella Furnace in Etna, Carnegie's Lucy Furnaces in Lawrenceville, and other furnaces, local pig iron production rose sixfold by the end of the decade.[23]

Blast furnaces needed iron ore and coke, its essential fuel. Ore mines in the upper Great Lakes supplemented ore from Pennsylvania, while coke was found closer to home. The Connellsville coal seam, which ran from Latrobe southwest parallel to Chestnut Ridge to the Monongahela River, possessed special properties for iron making that made it superior to other bituminous coal seams. Connellsville coal was baked for forty-eight hours in brick beehive-shaped ovens, twelve feet in diameter and six feet high. After expelling waste gases through a hole at the top, the ovens yielded a strong, porous, silvery coke with few impurities to impart to pig iron during smelting. Easily carried to Pittsburgh by river and rail, it sustained blast furnaces and cut the cost of producing iron and steel. Investors from the Connellsville coke district, including Henry Clay Frick, began buying up coal lands and erecting beehive oven plants. An estimated 70 ovens in 1860 mushroomed to 3,600 in 1873. That number doubled by 1880, when more than two million tons of coke were shipped from the district. Young Frick, with the financial backing of Judge Thomas Mellon, and other entrepreneurs amassed lands and ovens throughout the 1870s depression. By 1882 Frick dominated with three hundred acres of coal land and over 1,000 ovens.[24]

Carnegie, charting his own course, resigned from the Pennsylvania Railroad in 1865. By then he understood the company's modernizing strategies and sensed industrialization's trajectory. Moreover, his stakes in several companies had enabled him to devote full attention to his investments and iron interests. Seizing opportunities that railroads afforded after the war, Carnegie traveled frequently, marketing his Keystone Bridge Company's products. Pittsburgh mills rolled and rerolled iron rails in great quantities and supplied railroads with other essential equipment. But Carnegie and other ironmasters realized that iron rails wore out quickly, enticing them to experiment with Englishman Henry Bessemer's process for cheaply producing large quantities of steel.[25]

By adding carbon to wrought iron to make steel, early producers made small batches of high-quality blister steel through a costly, labor intensive cementation process. In the 1850s Pittsburgh firms adopted the crucible process, which yielded a higher-quality steel more quickly and cheaply. But it was still a slow, skilled operation yielding small batches. While crucible firms such as Black Diamond and Hussey, Howe, and Wells flourished in making fine tools, shears, and knives, they could not roll competitively priced rails.[26]

Englishman Henry Bessemer discovered that blowing cold air through molten pig iron removed carbon and then stopping the process at the right moment produced steel. Enormous Bessemer furnaces began economically producing steel in large quantities. Benjamin Jones contracted with engineer Alexander Holley to construct a Bessemer steel mill, but the results were unsatisfactory. A few years later, Carnegie engaged Holley, who had designed eleven Bessemer mills in the United States, to build one at Braddock. The Edgar Thomson Works, which Holley considered his finest effort, opened in 1875 and changed the iron and steel industry and Pittsburgh forever.[27]

Although iron defined Pittsburgh between 1850 and 1880, other industries were also important. George Westinghouse, a twenty-two-year-old, Schenectady, New York, inventor, began his enormously prolific career in Pittsburgh when he contracted with an iron firm in 1868 to manufacture his car replacer, a device that quickly put derailed trains back on the tracks. A year later he patented his revolutionary air-brake system for safely stopping trains and started the Westinghouse Air Brake Company. The entrepreneur invented an array of devices for railroads and formed the Union Switch and Signal Company to manufacture electric control signals in 1881.[28] Other Pittsburgh companies made railroad wheels, axles, couplings, cars, and locomotives.

Meanwhile, the discovery of oil in northwest Pennsylvania in 1859 triggered a frenzied rush to exploit what lay beneath the ground. Iron manufacturer William Coleman invited Carnegie, his Homewood neighbor, to join him in drilling along Oil Creek. Their Columbia Oil Company soon reaped generous profits.[29] Although Carnegie never devoted himself to the industry, other local investors did. Drillers rafted oil down the Allegheny to small refineries that lined Lawrenceville's riverfront, while manufacturers and machinists made pipe and drilling equipment for the nascent industry. Pittsburgh's future in the industry looked bright until Cleveland hardware merchant John D. Rockefeller devised a strategy to ship crude oil via railroads and revolutionized the industry.

As promising as railroad equipment and oil refining were, glassmaking remained the city's second largest industry. In 1880 fifty firms employing six thousand workers produced 27 percent of the nation's glass, far more than any other center. Whether crafting tableware or window glass, skilled workers dominated the manufacturing process. Concentrated heavily on the South Side, glass firms attracted mold makers, machine shops, and material suppliers. These craftsmen and entrepreneurs spawned an innovative environment for designing, manufacturing, and marketing glass products. Across the river from the South Side, glassmakers displayed their products in waterfront warehouses. Expanding sales via illustrated trade catalogs and improving production with new technologies such as replacing coal with cleaner burning natural gas, they laid the foundation for dramatic changes in the glass industry toward the turn of the century.[30]

THE BIG CITY

As Pittsburgh became the epicenter of the nation's iron industry, manufacturing claimed its riverbanks. Carnegie opened his Cyclops Iron Company at Thirty-Third Street in the Strip and the Lucy Furnaces at Fifty-First Street in Lawrenceville, joining manufacturers lining the Allegheny's riverfront. Other factories colonized the north shore from Herr's Island (today called Washington's Landing) to Manchester along the Ohio River and from the South Side to Hazelwood along the Monongahela. No longer simply a walking city, Pittsburgh and its neighbors numbered 235,000 people in 1880.[31]

A few new, small industrial towns took shape beyond the original cluster of communities. Butcheries and tanneries performed their noxious tasks in

Millvale, small ironworks located in Etna and Sharpsburg, and the Pennsylvania Salt Manufacturing Company began operations in Natrona farther up the Allegheny. The National Tube Works in McKeesport and Carnegie's Bessemer steel mill in Braddock extended south the incipient industrial zone of the Monongahela Valley. Railroads, rivers, and capital connected these towns with Pittsburgh.

Both Pittsburgh and Allegheny City tried to annex contiguous communities to enhance tax revenues and their national profiles. Though the state legislature nixed consolidation attempts in 1854, Pittsburgh successfully annexed most of today's East End—nearly twenty-two square miles—after the Civil War and later added South Side communities. At the same time Allegheny City swallowed up Manchester and small areas to its east, including Troy Hill and Herr's Island.[32]

Industrial and residential development beyond the original urban core necessitated improving the means of movement and communication A few businesses maintained their own telegraph connections, while messenger boys like Andrew Carnegie and Henry Oliver delivered information from central telegraph offices. By the 1870s the telegraph allowed police and fire services to communicate with each other and seek help when confronting riots or large fires. But technology and cost limited the telegraph's reach.[33]

After mid-century bridges replaced the ferries crossing the three rivers and spanned the streams and valleys that made navigating the region's rugged topography so difficult. Years before he began designing the Brooklyn Bridge, John Augustus Roebling introduced his iron rope or wire cable suspension for the bridge carrying the Main Line Canal across the Allegheny. He then used that technology for the Monongahela Bridge at Smithfield Street in 1846, replacing a bridge destroyed by the great fire a year earlier, and in 1859 for the Sixth Street Bridge that connected the sibling cities.[34] As Carnegie had foreseen, iron was replacing wood in bridge building. Innovations in ground transportation also linked new areas with older core communities. Horse-drawn omnibuses carrying a dozen passengers first plied routes to Lawrenceville, Herron Hill, Oakland, and Allegheny City in the 1840s. Slow and expensive, omnibuses carried businessmen calling on clients and travelers disembarking at the wharves and railroad depots. More affluent Pittsburghers used them for social visits or commuting.[35]

In the 1850s the railroads enticed some wealthy Pittsburghers to build homes beyond the noise, dirt, and density of the city. The Pennsylvania Railroad offered commuting to East Liberty, Homewood, Wilkinsburg, and Edgewood, while the Pittsburgh, Fort Wayne, and Chicago Railway carried passengers to Bellevue and Sewickley. The Pittsburgh and Connellsville Railroad encouraged construction in Hazelwood, and a projected railroad on the river's south shore prompted speculators to start a suburban community in Homestead before industry moved there.[36]

Horsecars, introduced in 1859, had the greatest impact on shaping the city. One or two horses pulled cars carrying fifteen to twenty passengers along rails. Smoother and faster than omnibuses, horsecars rapidly gained popularity. The initial four lines connected downtown to Lawrenceville, the South Side, Oakland and East Liberty, and Allegheny City and Manchester. By 1880 nearly forty miles of track crossed the city and soon extended five miles from downtown. But the nickel fare and time to traverse Pittsburgh's hills limited commuting to people who were better off.[37]

These new means of communication and transportation transformed Pittsburgh's social geography. Prior to mid-century most people walked about the city, limiting development to about two miles from its compact core. Commuting by horsecar and railroad allowed middle- and upper-income people to leave older residential areas. Horsecars pushed middle-class residential development incrementally outward, while railroads allowed wealthier families to move more than five miles away. Population rose in the newly annexed districts, causing a long residential decline downtown. Offices, banks, firms such as the newly formed T. Mellon & Sons, and retail establishments replaced departing residents. Imposing, architecturally fashionable banks, churches, and public buildings graced downtown's landscape. New warehouses and commercial buildings, some with cast-iron facades, proliferated alongside humbler carts, drays, delivery wagons, and stables. Omnibuses and horsecars added to the congestion residents endured.[38]

Mill workers and unskilled day laborers, however, could not afford the cost and time to commute. They lived within walking distance of their jobs on the flats along the rivers of the South Side, the Strip, and Allegheny City. The introduction of inclines in the 1870s opened up hilltops such as Mt. Washington and Herron Hill to working-class and middle-income residents. Altogether, the distinctive character of individual districts in the coming decades—commercial downtown, industrial and working-class sections along the floodplains, middle-income residential neighborhoods, and distant wealthy enclaves—was emerging at mid-century.

Municipalities struggled to keep abreast of constituent demands for services. Residents wanted running water, waste disposal, street lighting, and graded and paved streets. Newly annexed areas anticipated the extension of services, but older wards resisted paying for them because their needs had already been addressed. Municipal councils initially provided services for the downtown district and then for middle-class and elite neighborhoods where property owners could afford assessments for improvements. In the 1870s the capacity to provide water was augmented with new pumps and reservoirs; but sewers, largely built to drain stormwater, were not adequately extended and most residents relied on privies. The city of Pittsburgh began improving fire and police services, initiating public schools, and erecting streetlighting, but only Allegheny City created a public park. It transformed the West Common into a designed space with a lake, fountains, and monuments. Pittsburgh residents had to be content with picnics, carriage drives, and strolling in the Allegheny Cemetery for comparable recreation.[39]

Critical as these public services were, public officials did not spread them evenly across municipalities. Many working-class districts lacked adequate running water, sewage disposal, gas lighting, and paved streets. Thick black smoke spread across the urban area, blanketing industrial neighborhoods and downtown. Visiting Englishman Anthony Trollope described Pittsburgh in 1861 as "without exception the blackest place which I ever saw. The three English towns which I named are pretty dirty, but all their combined soot and grease and dinginess do not equal that of Pittsburgh."[40] This choking air weighed more heavily on the Strip and the South Side than on newer East End neighborhoods.

Horses, essential for the movement of people and goods about the city and used as stationary power sources for ferries and some factories, aggravated environmental burdens. Thousands of them trod through the city, requiring stabling, feeding, and outfitting by saddlers, harness makers, and farriers. A central hay market, dozens of feed stores and stables, and a massive stock exchange in East Liberty supported the ubiquity of horses. Clattering loudly on paved streets, horses dropped roughly twenty-five pounds of manure and two gallons of urine apiece every day, attracting flies and grinding dirt that released airborne particles. Poorly maintained stables were health and fire hazards, while decomposing horse carcasses remained on the streets where they had collapsed until authorities or glue factory crews retrieved them. These conditions, like smoke, intensely affected downtown and industrial districts, with adjacent working-class neighborhoods suffering the most.[41]

THE CRAFTSMEN'S EMPIRE

Before the turn to mass production in the late nineteenth century, expertise in iron making, glassblowing, and other trades made craftsmen the princes of production. Their skills, which took years to attain and often remained a mystery to employers, laid the foundation for what historians call the craftsmen's empire. Unlike later generations of industrial workers, these men exerted extraordinary control over their work, and their presence was keenly felt in many neighborhoods and city politics. Their power, though, was vulnerable to economic cycles and the new technologies adopted between the Civil War and World War I.

By the time eighteen-year-old James Davis arrived in Pittsburgh in 1891, he was a master puddler. With "muscled arms as big as a bookkeeper's legs" and self-confidence based on knowledge of the intricacies of iron making, Davis sensed his own budding strength.[42] His power and that of workers like him derived from their workplace skills and willingness to stand together on and off the job. That power enabled them to virtually control production. Davis, who became the US secretary of labor in 1921, was deeply embedded in a culture stressing mutualism at home, work, and the community. The young puddler personified the blend of physical strength, intelligence, and activism that made Pittsburgh as much a craftsmen's empire after the Civil War as an ironmasters' fiefdom. A third-generation ironworker, Davis was fiercely committed to his family and proud of his craft and the identity he shared with other Welsh immigrants. His grandfather, a peripatetic artisan from Tredegar, Wales, who helped build blast furnaces in Russia and Maryland, advised his sons to seek their fortunes in America.

So did another Tredegar ironworker, Arthur Rooney. The Rooneys left Newry, Ireland, during the famine, heading first to Montreal. They sailed back across the Atlantic to Tredegar where Arthur worked at the ironworks. But as steel undercut ironworkers there, the Rooneys returned to North America, eventually settling on the South Side of Pittsburgh where Arthur and his son Dan worked at the Jones & Laughlin mill. Despite being blacklisted for labor activism after the Homestead Steel lockout, they stayed in Pittsburgh. Daniel's son Art became one of the best all-around athletes in Pittsburgh during the 1920s, forming a sandlot football team that became the Pittsburgh Steelers. Though Irish Catholics, the Rooneys shared many of the values that animated Davis and his Welsh comrades.[43]

James Davis's grandfather taught the "secrets of the trade" to his sons, grandsons, and nephews but never shared them outside the family. James Davis's father immigrated to Sharon, a Shenango River mill town sixty miles northwest of Pittsburgh, and saved enough money to send for his family. Traveling in steerage, they arrived in New York in 1881 and rode trains to Sharon. A Welsh compatriot allowed James's father to work his furnace for a few days to raise enough money to move to Pittsburgh, where he soon found work. But the city appalled James's mother. Contrasting Pittsburgh with her memories of sunlight and greenery in Tredegar, she found the city wanting. As Davis reflected, "The lords of steel in Pittsburgh were too new at the game to practise the customs of the nobility in beautifying their surroundings."[44] Before long the family was back in Sharon, living in a company-owned house with flower boxes and a garden.

The gregarious James hung around the train depot, shining shoes, carrying satchels, and delivering telegrams. Unlike Andrew Carnegie, whose dispatches concerned business, eight-year-old James frequently brought word of workplace accidents. A father's death often meant hunger for his survivors, because mill towns offered few occupations for women other than housewife, washerwoman, or seamstress. "Of the many death messages that I bore to the workers' homes in Sharon," Davis remembered, "few found a home that was able to last a day after the burial of the bread-winner."[45] A man's mates invariably took up a generous collection for the widow, who used it to pay for the funeral and travel to a relative's home. But as children were often distributed among kinsmen to ease the burden, the family split apart.

Even in good times the Davises lived with the specter of insecurity. The children realized that the family was "upheld by a single prop, our father's labor."[46] Davis concluded that the only safeguard against endemic insecurity was acquiring property, something few families could do. Others saw the answer not so much in upward mobility as in collective political and industrial action. Davis embodied both the individual and collective approach. The entire household worked to ensure the family's survival and nationality reinforced its obligations. Davis's home was always open to Welsh wayfarers. "Whether a blood relation or not, we regarded all Welshmen as belonging to our clan."[47]

Boys were bound for the mill, where each puddler had a helper and older puddlers had a "boy" to assist him. Helpers and boys allowed puddlers to conserve their strength. When he was twelve, James entered this proletarian fraternity as an older puddler's boy before becoming his father's helper. He considered mill life heroic, with manly craftsmen battling nature to make iron, which James considered civilization's cornerstone.[48] In this smoky, hot, and filthy world, half-naked men mastered elemental forces. As a helper's boy, James tended the furnace, leveling the fire but keeping it hot enough to melt pig iron. His father initiated James into the mysteries and craft of puddling just as his father had done for him. "None of us ever went to school and learned the chemistry of it from books," Davis scoffed. "We learned the trick by doing it, standing with our faces in the scorching heat while our hands puddled the metal in its glaring bath." At the unusually young age of sixteen, he became a master puddler.[49]

To puddle iron, Davis stared into the furnace through a working porthole. Stoking coal into a sea of flame, he placed a charge of pig iron weighing six hundred pounds inside. Smelted from ore, the pig iron contained traces of silicon, sulfur, and phosphorous which made it brittle and virtually unusable. By turning pig iron into a molten blob, puddlers boiled out these impurities. After melting pig iron in the hearth, Davis thickened the heat by stirring iron oxide into the batch. Firing the mixture until it melted, he let it cool until it was thick as hoe cake batter.[50] With his hands wrapped in thick rags, Davis stirred the batch with a twenty-five-pound iron bar called a rabble. The iron oxide produced slag, triggering a chemical reaction oxidizing the impurities. It also created a tableau in which flames of light broke through a lake of molten slag, a sight Davis compared to the ancients' vision of hell. While gaseous combinations of unwanted elements bubbled out, the slag overflowed and escaped the hearth through a hole into a buggy placed below.

At that point, "I have the job of my life on my hands," Davis wrote. "I must stir my boiling mess with all the strength in my body."[51] After kneading the batch with the rabble until it was uniformly mixed, he separated and shaped the sponge of pure iron with a long paddle and hook into three balls each weighing two hundred pounds. Davis was especially proud of his "batting eye" which helped him shape the balls to these specifications. Using long tongs, he then removed the iron balls and placed them on a buggy for delivery to machines that squeezed out more slag. From there the iron was rolled into blooms. A puddler directed a helper, a helper's assistant, and men who cleaned and refueled his furnace, while rollers supervised a dozen men and boys. The roller watched carefully as the muck rollers, hookers, catchers, and roughers squeezed and manipulated the iron through rolling machines before turning it over to the heater. The roller's pay depended on workers executing their labors correctly, and he was not hesitant to intervene.[52]

This amalgam of knowledge, strength, skill, and endurance made puddlers like Davis essential. Their traditional knowledge was their principal asset, giving them an unusual measure of autonomy on the job and power over their terms of employment.[53] The same applied to rollers, heaters, and other skilled craftsmen in the iron, steel, glass, and related industries. But it was no guarantee of steady work or a decent life. Craftsmen thus tried to translate this autonomy into work rules and union contracts.

Davis was a union man. "Love of comrades had always been a ruling passion with me," he later wrote. "I joined my union as soon as I had learned my trade," and became an officer in the Amalgamated Association of Iron, Steel and Tin Workers.[54] Irreplaceable skills and unions allowed these men to exert a measure of collective control over production after the Civil War. "Around their autonomous work," historian David Montgomery wrote, "craftsmen wove an ethical code to govern their own conduct."[55] Establishing and preserving dignity required a manly bearing toward the boss and each other. That meant sticking together and refusing to undermine fellow workers for personal gain. Setting a "stint"—a production quota not to be exceeded—became central to the code. Unrestricted output, while profitable in the short run, could lead to overproduction, falling wages, and unemployment. A stint preserved health, stabilized employment, and allowed for time to cultivate outside pursuits and citizenship. As unions formed, members swore not to exceed the stint they had imposed and sanctioned violators.

These work rules were incorporated into contracts, but ultimately depended on workers' vigilance and willingness to stand together.[56]

No earlier industrial workers, not the Allegheny City textile girls who rioted in 1848 nor the railroad workers who rebelled in 1877, had as much say over their working lives. No foreman watched over James Davis; no factory bell regimented his day. Nor did he work for hourly wages. Davis decided for himself how he would work, set his work schedule, and negotiated via his union to be paid based on what he produced.

By 1877 Pittsburgh was a hotbed of craft unionism. Soaring prices during the Civil War created tremendous demands for labor. As trade unionism revived, iron puddlers and boilers asserted their power.[57] An earlier union, the Iron City Forge of the United Sons of Vulcan, had crumbled in 1858 when manufacturers fired and blacklisted members. But if ironmasters had the upper hand in the 1850s, craftsmen regained momentum during the war and maintained it until the early 1890s.[58] Miles Humphreys revived the Sons of Vulcan in 1861 and organized a Grand Forge with affiliates in eight states. Most of its strength was in Pittsburgh, where it was headquartered, and Ohio. During the war skilled workers were in such demand that ironmasters acceded to most of their demands, with puddlers almost tripling their wages.[59]

When iron prices weakened after the war and ironmasters cut rates, the Vulcans walked off the job. The mills remained silent for eight months until ironmasters and puddlers found common ground with a sliding scale in 1867. The innovation of a sliding scale, which the Amalgamated Association of Iron, Steel and Tin Workers hailed as their most important contribution to labor relations, was first raised by ironmaster B. F. Jones. Though often their toughest foe, Jones respected workers and appreciated their commonality of interests enough to want to routinize it. Given that puddlers, rollers, and other craftsmen hired and supervised production teams and decided among themselves how the tonnage rate would be distributed, they could become partners with ironmasters, albeit quite junior ones.[60] The strike ended when Sons of Vulcan grand master Miles Humphreys devised a system by which puddlers' wages rose and fell with the price of a billet of iron, creating unprecedented mutual self-interest. Committees representing the Vulcans and manufacturers resolved their differences and set the scale. By the 1880s the sliding scale agreement was seventy-four pages long.[61]

The 1867 strike was a tremendous triumph, allowing puddlers to formally restrict output and legitimize their place at the bargaining table.[62] Although strikes and lockouts interrupted labor peace, puddlers largely held their ground and maintained an enviable standard of living.[63] In the aftermath of the 1873 financial panic, however, lockouts and related impasses grew more frequent, with mills closing for months at a time. Slackening demand slashed wages and ironworkers faced at least three lockouts during the long 1870s depression, sorely testing their collaboration with owners. In the midst of one shutdown, the Pittsburgh Bolt Company. brought forty-eight black puddlers to town to break the strike. Few African Americans had ever worked in the region's mines, mills, and factories, and several hundred screaming strikers descended on the mill. They intimidated the black puddlers, who decided not to go to work, and the lockout crumbled, allowing the union to maintain its pay scale. But owners would again use race to weaken labor solidarity during later walkouts.[64]

Despite ferocious conflicts, historian John Ingham argued that "mutual respect and accommodation" characterized labor relations into the 1880s.[65] Most mill owners in Pittsburgh complied with union requests to shut down to allow annual meetings, picnics, and for a month each summer to provide a respite from the heat.[66] Although antagonists, they reached a consensus on the sliding scale, collective bargaining, support for tariffs, and the ideology of republicanism (if not always the Republican Party). This alliance between bosses and craftsmen, however, was a shaky one, and their consensus ultimately fractured over class interests.[67]

Puddlers and boilers were not the only iron- and steelworkers seeking the benefits of unions. Heaters, rollers, roughers, and other craftsmen organized in the early 1870s. Though belonging to separate trade unions, they worked in close quarters and for the same companies. Merging their unions in 1876, they formed the Amalgamated Association of Iron, Steel and Tin Workers. Each year, new craftsmen joined—axle turners, wire drawers, picklers, and hammer men—until most skilled mill workers belonged. But unskilled laborers were not welcomed into the union, leaving most southern and eastern Europeans and African Americans, who began entering the industry later in the century, on the outside. "The craftsmen's definition of who could live up to their code of 'manly behavior,'" David Montgomery cautioned, "was usually cast in ethnic and racial terms."[68] Craftsmen in other industries, especially glass, had comparable success. According to Francis Couvares, they became "co-custodians of the trade." Lobbying alongside manufacturers for tariffs, they worked together to restrict output and establish industry-wide wages and prices. Despite periodic clashes and bouts of unemployment, their lifestyle made them labor aristocrats.[69]

Maintaining their relatively exalted status depended on their ability to negotiate favorable contracts. These agreements in turn were affected by the economy and technology. When railroad construction resumed its breakneck pace after the depression of the 1870s, iron and steel prices and thus wages rose. But when railroad expansion abruptly ceased in 1882, companies asked the union for a one-third cut in tonnage rates. The union struck but lost. By 1885 two-thirds of its membership and many lodges, especially in steel mills, were gone. When economic conditions revived later in the decade, so did the union's fortunes, but an even more intractable problem lay on the horizon—technological change.

The adoption of new technologies during the 1880s led to steel displacing iron, ending the craft workers' ascendancy. David Montgomery calculated that while 4 percent of the country's pig iron was made into Bessemer steel in 1872, it reached more than 50 percent by 1892. Steel also tended toward consolidated ownership.[70] Ultimately, the shift to mass-produced steel by bigger, more centralized concerns undercut craftsmen's autonomy. The epic labor battle at Homestead in 1892, which took place against this backdrop, was a turning point, ushering in the age of steel.

PLEBEIAN CULTURE

Workers' control, their moral code, and the network supporting it extended beyond the workplace. The "glow of brotherhood" James Davis experienced when iron puddlers shared their jobs with "brothers" out of work was felt in taverns, fraternal and sporting associations, and factory neighborhoods. Craftsmen read about themselves and their concerns in the *National Labor Tribune*, voted for candidates who vowed to represent their interests, and engaged in a broader, more inclusive movement to reform industrial life.[71] Francis Couvares described this epoch as revolving around a plebeian culture of working people and their "social equals," deeply and broadly rooted in the city's past.[72] Encompassing more than craftsmen and laborers, plebeian culture included shopkeepers, saloon owners, and professionals, whom workers patronized and knew as neighbors. The elites, for the most part, did not challenge plebeian Pittsburgh for cultural hegemony. Elite culture remained austere, relatively undeveloped, and insular, in stark contrast to the lively, vernacular, and often bawdy network of taverns, soirees, bands, melodramas, and sporting contests that defined plebeian culture.

This culture affirmed people's identity and worth as citizens and workers. Whether sitting in the audience of *The Lower Million*, a play about the 1877 insurrection and its aftermath set in a Pittsburgh iron mill, or competing in rowing races on the Allegheny, or dancing to bands made up of fellow plebes at soirees organized by their fire and militia companies, most Pittsburghers could celebrate themselves and their values. No sport exemplified plebeian culture more than rowing. Pittsburghers turned to the rivers for recreation, and by mid-century skilled craftsmen—especially ironworkers and glassblowers—put the city on the sporting map. Neighborhood and workplace rowing clubs such as the Juniata, the Diamond Alley Boat Club, and the Columbia built dozens of boathouses along the rivers. Some were two-story affairs; others sat atop barges. They made rowing the city's first mass spectator sport and produced its first national champions. Crowds of ten thousand or more lined riverbanks, stood on bridges, and bet heavily on races that drew rowers and spectators from other cities. James Hamill, a glassblower, and Eph Morris, a puddler's helper, won regattas across the United States and abroad. While craftsmen were well suited to rowing's physical demands, the sport attracted women and wealthier Pittsburghers too. But ever-greater river traffic and industrial use of the waterways eventually pushed rowing to the sidelines.[73]

Baseball, like rowing, was organized from the bottom up. The Civil War first exposed many Union soldiers to the sport, and they formed sandlot teams in neighborhoods and surrounding towns when they came home. The first attempt to establish a fully salaried professional baseball club in Pittsburgh, the Alleghenies of the International Association, folded in 1878 after a little more than two seasons. The club could not compete on the field or at the gate with stronger independent squads like the East Liberty Stars, the Olympics, and all-black Keystones. These teams, rooted in neighborhoods and workplaces, were part of a sporting life that encompassed boat clubs, volunteer fire companies, sandlot baseball, and traditional pastimes such as horse racing, boxing, and cockfighting. Membership in a fire company usually meant participating in a range of competitive endeavors. This sporting network was decidedly noncommercial and nonprofessional, and partially because of its strength, support for a professional club was slow to materialize.

Sometimes plebeian culture was infused with a class consciousness. At their summer reunions, the Amalgamated attracted up to twenty-five thousand people who danced and competed in games and contests interspersed with speeches and acts of labor solidarity. A glass presser and a laborer on the South Side formed the Mechanics Institute to build a library and hold lectures, while Andrew Burtt, a Knights of Labor activist and former glassblower, devoted himself to educating workers and their children. The *Labor Tribune* encouraged readers to form book-buying clubs and to read, discuss, and learn how to advance their interests as workers and citizens.[74] Their voices resonated in local politics. In addition to electing glass pressman William McCarthy as mayor of Pittsburgh, workers helped elect typographer Alexander Callow as Allegheny City's mayor and sent Vulcan Miles Humphreys to the state legislature three times.[75]

During the 1870s craft workers not only amalgamated their trades on an industrial basis and took part in a broader national movement; they drew strength from a city labor council, several labor newspapers, and a vibrant Knights of Labor assembly. The Knights, whose organizing spirit swept through mills, factories, mines, and workshops during the 1870s and 1880s, espoused the eight-hour workday and welcomed diverse workers. Over a hundred locals belonged to Pittsburgh's district assembly. The labor movement's militancy would soon be apparent to all.[76]

THE FINANCIAL PANIC AND ITS AFTERMATH

The 1877 insurrection came four years after Jay Cooke's banking empire collapsed. The sudden failure of the nation's leading banker, who had financed the Union during the Civil War and railroad expansion after, initiated a prolonged depression. "Apprehension and excitement spread everywhere," Thomas Mellon recalled, "and became more and more intensified every day by successive failures all over the country, until by the 1st of October we were in the midst of the most disastrous and extensive panic and collapse since that of 1819."[77]

While Mellon, who had opened the bank T. Mellon and Sons, was thrown off stride, he soon found ways to profit from the depression. Most Pittsburghers did not. For those accustomed to economic expansion, the depression exposed the fragility of an industrial economy and their sense of well-being. Skilled and unskilled, native-born and immigrant alike agonized as unemployment reached 25 percent nationally. By 1877 almost five million people had lost their jobs and hundreds of thousands tramped across the countryside seeking work or bread. Forty-seven thousand businesses failed, wholesale prices fell almost 30 percent, and industrial growth ceased.[78]

As one of the country's most industrialized centers, Pittsburgh was especially sensitive to the economy's trajectory. A tableau of cold desolation replaced the fires from hundreds of iron mills and glass plants that had lit up the evening skies during better times. Mills stood silent and empty. "From 1873 to 1879," Judge James Reed asserted, "you could not give away a rolling mill." Only in Braddock, where Andrew Carnegie's Edgar Thomson Works was rising on the banks of the Monongahela River, was there a sign of Pittsburgh's latent industrial strength.[79]

Wilson Howell Carpenter, a young steam pump manufacturer, worried that he would never be able to pay off his debts. In 1875 he lamented in his diary that "business prospects were 'Blue, Bluer, Bluest.'" When business sagged even deeper in 1876, the nation's centennial year, he wrote, "It does not seem possible that things can get worse. Some of our largest and most solid firms have gone under during the past winter." By then ten of Pittsburgh's largest iron firms had suspended operations, along with half of its oil companies and two-thirds of furniture and jewelry makers. Letting eight of his eleven workmen go, Carpenter cut hours and pay for the three he kept on. "Hope itself has almost died out," he wrote, "and the gloomiest prognostications are indulged."[80]

By 1877 Pittsburgh's workers had endured almost four years of increasing joblessness and falling wages. With even seasonal work hard to obtain, many joined the laboring poor. Former breadwinners wandered the city looking for work while skilled workers saw their status in the workplace and community jeopardized. The craftsmen's empire they had constructed in shops and factories, the voice they had raised in politics, and the cultural life they had created were at stake. They would not countenance these changes lightly, and the number of strikes, especially by miners, ironworkers, and other craftsmen, soared, peaking in 1877.[81]

Working people vented their discontent in the *National Labor Tribune*. "A Subscriber's Wife" from Leechburg wrote in April 1876 that the mill had been shuttered since October and notice served to vacate company houses. There was still blood left in the veins of the wives and children, she warned. "When that blood is heated, and heated until it boils over, then they will do what at other times they would be ashamed to even think of."[82] On New Year's Day 1876 the *Tribune* predicted growing resistance. "The workingmen are preparing to lift themselves out of this serfdom established by Capital." Sooner or later, it warned, the bottom would fall out of the economic system. The paper reminded readers that Charles Sumner once predicted that "unless the question of Capital and Labor was satisfactorily settled, it would one day drench the land in blood."[83] Working people would not surrender, the paper prophesied. "They will not submit to see their savings wrested from their grasp always. They will not starve in idleness by the millions in the midst of mountains heaped with plenty. . . . Look out for the slumbering tornado among the toiling millions. When all else fails them they will speak, and the whole land will tremble."[84]

The *National Labor Tribune* lambasted capital as a whole but held special scorn for the railroads. That rage was widely shared and cut across class lines. The Pennsylvania Railroad had helped make Pittsburgh the Iron City after connecting it to Philadelphia in 1852. The railroad industry's demands for iron, steel, and coal, and rail connections to other regions were indispensable. Yet by 1877 the Pennsylvania Railroad had become the focus for local frustrations with industrial society. Pittsburghers saw this railroad as an octopus strangling their city.

The railroad industry was corporate capitalism's vanguard. Unifying the vast national market, it ushered in an age of mechanization and mass production that propelled the country's rise as the world's leading economy. The most advanced and powerful corporate sector of the century, the railroad industry's need for capital, scale of operations, and internal complexities dwarfed other enterprises. Consequently, railroads exerted massive clout, winning whopping concessions and aid from all levels of government.

But their land grants, tax breaks, and loans provoked resentment by towns and citizens who saw their economic well-being held hostage to railroad interests.[85]

Pittsburghers hailed the Pennsylvania Railroad as a transportation breakthrough but wearied of the corporate behemoth in their midst. By the mid-1850s the region had subsidized rail connections through public subscription and assumed millions in bonded debt. But expectations of what the railroad would do crashed against unfavorable freight rates. Many accused the Pennsylvania Railroad of ruining the city's oil-refining business by keeping rates to Philadelphia artificially high; others resented paying interest on the railroad bonds that local governments had subscribed. Arguments over repudiating these payments were a constant in electoral races, with both parties opposing tax hikes to pay for them.[86]

Most Pittsburghers agreed that to some extent railroads charged discriminatory rates, wielded enormous political power despotically, and undermined not only workers' standard of living but the very essence of American republicanism. "Our wages go direct from our pockets into the pockets of the people who own the railroads," the *Tribune* howled, "and they build fine homes with them, and go to Europe, dress in silks and broadcloth, while we poor devils live on our corn meal and bacon." Many believed the legislatures, courts, and press were beholden to the industry. "The law-making powers are their servants instead of servants of the people," the *Tribune* argued. "This power is in violation of republican institutions."[87]

Pittsburgh and the region felt especially victimized. The Philadelphia-based company did its best to block the Baltimore and Ohio Railroad (B&O) and other lines from entering the city and competing for its traffic. Although rival railroads eventually began servicing Pittsburgh, local businessmen were embittered.[88] "Western Pennsylvania has suffered greatly," the *Tribune* pointed out. "The consequence is, our industries are under railroad control, [and] are healthy or sick, as freights allow."[89] The *Pittsburgh Post* was less temperate, calling the corporation "Railroad Vultures," scheming and speculating to amass princely fortunes.[90]

THE 1877 INSURRECTION

In the summer of 1877 anger at the railroads boiled over. Railroad workers, already working part-time, seethed over policies requiring them to put up at company hotels during layovers, buy at company stores, and rent company shacks. Many had died or were mutilated on the job, especially as trains began running doubleheaders. Instead of one locomotive pulling seventeen cars, two locomotives hauled thirty-four cars, cutting in half the number of brakemen, flagmen, and conductors, and leaving crews especially vulnerable to accidents. The Pennsylvania Railroad, however, required workers to waive claims for compensation due to accidents as a condition of employment.[91]

On July 11 the B&O board of directors declared a 10 percent dividend for stockholders while slashing wages 10 percent, the third pay cut since 1873. Furious firemen and brakemen retorted they would be forced to "steal or starve" to survive on that amount. On Tuesday, July 16, workers in Camden Junction, Maryland, and Martinsburg, West Virginia, refused to take their trains out. When the B&O requested troops to reopen traffic, workers defied the soldiers and the walkout spread. In Baltimore an angry crowd of workingmen and boys stoned the militia, leaving at least eleven protesters dead and forty wounded. There and elsewhere, other workers and their communities were solidly behind railroad employees.[92]

The upsurge spread to Pittsburgh after the Pennsylvania Railroad ordered that all trains east to Altoona would run as doubleheaders. Resistance to the company had been building for months. Weeks earlier engineers, brakemen, conductors, firemen, and yard workers had gathered in Allegheny City to form the Trainmen's Union. It vowed to restore lost wages, end doubleheaders, and address other grievances.[93]

Andy Carnegie's Allegheny City chum and former fellow telegraph messenger, Robert Pitcairn, was ill-prepared for the uprising. Pitcairn, who had replaced Carnegie as the railroad's Pittsburgh superintendent in 1865, should have realized that posting notice of the railroad's intention to run doubleheaders on July 16, only weeks after a 10 percent wage cut and the same day as the B&O walkouts, would spark outrage. When a crew refused to take a doubleheader out, the strike was on.

Striking coal miners from Wilkinsburg and unemployed men in the Strip joined rail workers in shutting down the Pittsburgh yards. Pitcairn's assistant implored Pittsburgh mayor William McCarthy to intervene, but the former glassworker was no friend of the corporation. He had let half of his police force go just days before due to budget shortfalls caused by the depression. Before long hundreds of freight cars, many carrying perishable commodities, jammed the yards. That evening the Trainmen's Union convened a meeting to call for ending doubleheaders, rescinding the pay cut, and rehiring all of the strikers. They linked their job action to the men on the B&O line and called for "all workingmen to make common cause" with railroad workers. "We're with you," a rolling mill worker shouted. "We're in the same boat."[94]

Pennsylvania Railroad officials responded by requesting the state mobilize its militia. The governor complied, but many local militiamen failed to report, and the loyalties of those who did were suspect. After surveying the scene that Friday from atop his horse, manufacturer Wilson Carpenter wrote in his journal, "The sympathy of the people and troops were [sic] entirely with the strikers. Many of the soldiers openly declared they would not fire on them and turned out with the greatest reluctance."[95] Related to protesters by blood, neighborhood, and work, local units were unlikely to suppress them.

That evening the First Division of the Pennsylvania militia was dispatched from Philadelphia. Like the protesters, these guardsmen were workers and Civil War veterans, but they did not come as brothers-in-arms. "These men will come here strangers to you, and they will come regarding you as we regarded the rebels during the rebellion," Dr. Edward Donnelly warned strikers. "I implore you, for God's sake, to stand back when they arrive."[96] While the Philadelphia militia was en route, the Pittsburgh militia units maintained their positions. Their arms stacked, they mixed easily with the crowd amid an almost festive atmosphere. But animus and competition between Philadelphia and Pittsburgh had deep roots, and crowds had pelted the troop trains in Harrisburg, Johnstown, and Altoona. The Philadelphia troops arrived early Saturday afternoon, just as shifts in the Strip ended, those workers swelling the ranks of the protesters. Local manufacturers begged railroad officials to do nothing that weekend. "I think I know the temper of our men pretty well," Black Diamond Steel Company owner James Park Jr. told Pennsylvania Railroad vice president Alexander Cassatt, "and you would be wise not to do anything until Monday" when many people would be back at work. His advice went unheeded.[97]

At five o'clock a phalanx of Philadelphia troops relieved Pittsburgh units at Twenty-Eighth Street, where a crowd of between five and seven thousand had congregated. Protesters taunted the troops as they began clearing the tracks. Several standing close to the troops, unable to move because of the crowd behind them, were stabbed by bayonets. Stones began flying, a few state militia rifles were seized, and firing commenced with shots coming from both sides. Within minutes, perhaps twenty in the crowd lay dead and a greater number were wounded.[98] "Women fainted," the *Labor Tribune*'s correspondent reported. "Children ran screaming through the streets, and strong men, with blanched cheeks, quailed and turning their eyes heavenward, seemed to invoke the intervention of a Supreme hand to stay the slaughter of the innocent."[99]

The bloodshed failed to reopen rail traffic. Instead, the *Tribune* wrote, it provoked "a condition of affairs bordering on anarchy."[100] More people converged on the Strip, including six hundred men who marched from the South Side, following a brass band and carrying their union colors. The crush of angry workers left the state militia with two options—engage in wholesale slaughter or retreat to the railroad's roundhouse. When state militia commanders chose the latter, some in the crowd took that as their cue to riot. Men, women, and children raided freight cars, and the streets filled with looters weighed down by hams, cheeses, and dry goods. "The moral relaxation was so supreme," Carpenter wrote, "that the most respectable people caught the contagion and scrupled not to scramble for the spoils. I myself felt mightily like 'hooking' a box of cigars, being only prevented by the difficulty of hiding it."[101]

An artillery piece was wheeled into place and loaded with chains, bolts, and coupling pins. State militia sharpshooters killed several men before they could use it but could not stop others from loading cars with petroleum and coal, setting them afire, and rolling them toward the roundhouse. The flames spread to cars loaded with oil, lumber, and coke, and soon the yards from the roundhouse to Thirty-Second Street were ablaze, consuming machine shops, office buildings, and houses. The glow of Pittsburgh burning could be seen twelve miles away. Large crowds stayed up through the night, sitting on hillsides overlooking the inferno.[102] Protesters targeted the Union Depot Hotel and the large grain elevator near it on Liberty Avenue. Though not railroad property, they were seen as symbols of monopoly. "Everything in these monopolies has got to burn," an American Iron Works machinist remarked. When firemen pleaded to be given the chance to put out the fire in the grain elevator, another man yelled: "It's owned by a damned monopoly—let it burn."[103]

"All night long the conflict raged, lit up by the grand conflagration," Carpenter wrote, while "the poor soldiers stifled with heat, raging with thirst and hunger, were penned up in a doomed building by a remorseless mob more cruel than the flames themselves."[104] The next day the troops left the roundhouse and fought their way out of town, taking casualties and returning fire. Crossing the Allegheny River, they marched upriver for eight miles before encamping.

Wilson Carpenter returned on Sunday to view the desolation. From the hill overlooking the roundhouse he gazed at more than a mile of smoking ruins. "Of over two thousand cars, nothing was left but the wheels, strung dismally along the twisted tracks. Over a hundred engines in the round houses were blasted and shrunken wrecks. The machine shops were shapeless masses."[105] Mayor McCarthy closed saloons, ordered crowds to disperse, and pleaded for citizens to stop the destruction. That afternoon a Committee of Public Safety formed that brought together labor stalwarts with manufacturers, religious figures, and community leaders and met with delegations of strikers and railroad officials.[106] But the Pennsylvania Railroad's reluctance to negotiate what it believed it would win with federal and state troops dashed hopes. The committee's efforts to mollify workers were marginally more successful. Crowds continued to assault railroad property but stopped short of rolling burning cars into the Duquesne Depot. "Had this not been hindered," Wilson Carpenter observed, "the whole city would have been in ashes."[107]

Pittsburghers restored order on their own. The fires burned out, and with little railroad property left to destroy, people dispersed. Many feared that armed bands were on their way to Pittsburgh, and on Monday several hundred miners boarded a boat in Elizabeth and steamed down the Monongahela to join their comrades. An impassioned Mayor McCarthy met them on the wharf and explained that the riot was over. Therefore, miners reasoned, they had little to do but return home. For several days, groups of strikers, merchants, and citizens patrolled the streets, ending the mayhem.

The strikes, however, spread elsewhere. Shutting down the National Tube Works in McKeesport, workers paraded through town, cajoling men to join them. After an open-air meeting, they marched behind a brass band to Carnegie's Edgar Thomson Works in Braddock and persuaded most of the new mill's workers to lay down their tools. Coal miners in Castle Shannon, Elizabeth, Brownsville, and elsewhere joined the strike movement.[108] So did two thousand men at the American Iron Works on the South Side, who demanded a 25 percent wage hike. But these disputes remained peaceful. When a compromise was reached at American Iron two months later, owner B. F. Jones wrote in his diary, "Great rejoicing among all that the mill will start up tomorrow morning. So the strike is ended and we are all glad of it for it was becoming very monotonous."[109]

Nor did riots rock Allegheny City. The Trainmen's Union preserved order and guarded the railyards from vandalism. But it did not allow the state militia uncontested entrance to their town. Arming themselves, workers put up fortifications near the Allegheny Depot and patrolled the streets. Neither rioters from across the river nor troops were welcome. Inspecting trains to ensure that no troops were aboard, they refused to let freight move for three days while the union's Robert Ammon ran the division, dispatching passenger traffic as if he were the district superintendent.[110] By the time Pennsylvania governor J. F. Hartranft arrived in town on Tuesday, order had already been restored.[111]

The insurrection reverberated across the nation. While no other city matched the magnitude of violence in Pittsburgh, many places witnessed death and destruction. President Hayes resolved to open the railroad to Pittsburgh, and a force of three thousand federal troops and a greater number of state militia boarded trains moving westward, reopening traffic along the way. Operations were soon restored.[112] Over one hundred men were subsequently arrested in Pittsburgh, most of them for looting, but charges were dismissed at preliminary hearings or punished with short workhouse sentences.[113] Pennsylvania Railroad's suit against Allegheny County for damages suffered during the riot was of greater consequence. After the 1848 textile riots, the county was held responsible for losses incurred by factories. That legal precedent convinced the county to settle with the railroad in 1880 for $1.4 million plus interest. The bond issued to pay for the claim was not retired until 1906.[114]

One Pittsburgh newspaper described those arrested as "vagabonds, tramps, mudlarks, thieves and cutthroats of the worst possible description."[115] However, many had roots in the city and a stake in the conflict. Most were railroad workers, with mill workers, laborers, glassblowers, and miners also well represented. Some were sporadically employed, illiterate laborers; others were better-off craftsmen. Most were men in their twenties and thirties and married with children. Virtually all had endured the depression and needed little prompting to take to the streets. Despite accounts accusing the Irish and Germans of perpetrating the riot, those arrested included native-born white people and immigrant Germans, Irish, and English in numbers close to the city's composition. Only three African Americans were arrested.[116]

As a general strike, the 1877 insurrection was a dismal failure. However, many Pittsburghers gained a sense of their power by engaging in collective action.[117] Within days of the bloody weekend, Karl Marx wrote Friedrich Engels that the conflict was "the first uprising against the oligarchy of capital which had developed since the Civil War."[118] While 1877 was a popular revolt against capital, it reflected considerable cross-class solidarity. Large elements of Pittsburgh capital were supportive of striking workers or remained neutral.

Though some claimed that communists, foreigners, and tramps had fomented the eruption, most Pittsburghers placed the blame squarely on the Pennsylvania Railroad. The company, they believed, had reduced wages to the point of starvation and, by calling for the state militia, bore the most responsibility. Even Joseph Weeks, associate editor for the *Iron Age*, and most local newspapers found the railroad at fault. The *Boston Globe* concluded that "The cowardice and imbecility of the railroad sharks" had at last "met its proper rebuke."[119]

The upsurge of 1877 arose from a deep depression and the insensitivity of a monopolistic corporation. Labor conflict was not new to Pittsburgh, but capital and labor had found ways to diminish or resolve differences before. Renewed economic growth after 1877 reduced tensions, but the conflagration anticipated the problems that would arise as mechanization and mass production, increasing numbers of unskilled immigrant workers, and growing corporate and financial power undermined the craftsmen's empire and profoundly transformed Pittsburgh. By World War I the region was hardly familiar to residents who had grown up during the nineteenth century.

FIVE

SECOND INDUSTRIAL REVOLUTION

1880 TO 1920

AFTER SETTLING INTO CLAYTON, HIS ITALIANATE-STYLE MANSION IN Point Breeze, Henry Clay Frick hosted weekly poker games in the breakfast room. "Papsie," as Helen Clay Frick called her industrialist father, loved to compete, whether at poker with his Pittsburgh peers or at bridge with his wife. A founding member of the Schenley Riding Club, he raced horse-drawn buggies a few blocks away at a small racetrack and on Brunot's Island in the Ohio River. He even relished competing with himself. "Papsie played solitaire a great, great deal," Helen recalled, "at odd times . . . even right after breakfast." Playing his cards deliberately, Frick rarely missed the right move.[1]

Frick embraced the ethos of competition that characterized late nineteenth-century industrial capitalism, something he shared with the other men at the table. Some of the players, like George Westinghouse and Thomas Carnegie, lived within shouting distance. Every now and then, Thomas's brother Andrew stopped by when in town. Others, like the Mellon brothers, Andrew and Richard, came by carriage from their East End estates, while iron and steel industry pioneers Henry Oliver and Benjamin F. Jones traveled the farthest, from across the river where they were neighbors on Ridge Avenue in Allegheny City, which was annexed by Pittsburgh in 1907.

Corporate lawyer Philander C. Knox, who served as the US attorney general and then secretary of state, was another regular. They talked politics and played draw poker, drinking whiskey from crystal decanters and enjoying cigars whose smell lingered the morning after. The plate glass windows, natural gas heat, electric lights, and aluminum leaf set within intricate plaster tracery on the walls of Frick's breakfast room surrounded them with products of their own innovative ventures. No matter how much they won or lost at the table, the stakes paled in comparison to the consequences of their conversations. Their small talk might determine Republican Party nominees, a company's survival, or philanthropic commitments.[2]

A student of the game, Frick owned first editions of John Blackridge's *The Complete Poker Player* and W. J. Florence's *The Gentlemen's Hand-book on Poker*. Blackridge's probabilistic analysis of draw poker appealed to Frick, who considered the odds, potential losses, and returns at the table much as he did in business. Blackridge wrote that gambling was simply trading in risk, no different than what bankers and insurance providers did. Florence, a Shakespearian actor, cautioned readers to never lose their temper. "Always keep cool. If you lose your head you will lose all your chips." On the other hand, he reflected, "a man who never bluffs in poker is not in sympathy with the game." These poker authorities reinforced Frick's business philosophy and that of his friends.[3]

By the late nineteenth century Frick, his tablemates, and their peers were among the most influential men in Pittsburgh, remaking the city in ways that reflected their growing clout. The industrialists gravitated to neighborhoods befitting their aspirations. As historians Edward Muller and John Bauman noted, "Beginning in the 1880s a sizeable segment of the city's wealthy began abandoning the din, pollution and ethnic mottle of the industrial city for bucolic suburban retreats in the East End and Sewickley areas." Their neighborhoods of stately mansions surrounded by sumptuously landscaped grounds became "a crucible where a new, more cosmopolitan upper-class culture was forming. Once caricatured as stern, self-abnegating Calvinists who shunned luxury as a sin, Pittsburgh elites increasingly immersed themselves in the cult of consumption, especially of a more beautiful, residential environment."[4]

When not competing in cards or business, they crossed paths at their churches and clubs. Most of them were Scottish or Scotch-Irish Presbyterians. Frick, Andrew Mellon, and Philander Knox were early members of the Pittsburgh and Oakmont golf clubs. During the week, while their husbands played cards and cut deals at the Duquesne Club downtown, the women often gathered on their own to play. In warm months the men joined their families to swim, boat, shoot, and fish at the South Fork Hunting and Fishing Club above Johnstown in the Allegheny Mountains. Andrew W. Mellon and Henry Clay Frick were especially close, traveling to Europe where Frick schooled his friend on art. Mellon introduced Frick to the woman he wed, while Frick did the same for Mellon. Their leisure time, business affairs, and proximity to each other's homes reinforced a sense of who they were as Pittsburgh's most powerful families.[5]

The power brokers at Frick's poker table, while celebrated for leading the region's remarkable industrialization, also left their mark on the nation. Like their counterparts in other cities, they created the workings of the modern corporation that propelled the United States to center stage in the global economy. Prior to the 1880s most manufacturers relied on skilled workers, specialized in a few product lines, and sold in limited geographical markets. But larger markets and new technologies expanded their horizons. Carnegie and a few others turned to mass production of steel. They held down costs by diminishing dependence on skilled craftsmen and employing less-skilled, often immigrant workers. In order to ensure steady supplies, they purchased companies that provided critical raw materials and fuels, exemplified by Carnegie's investment in Frick's coal mines and coke plants. They added new product lines and even sales departments instead of relying on middlemen to find markets. Assembling these components within one organization, what was often called vertical integration, fashioned the modern corporation.

The modern corporation, however, was not insulated from either local or national competitors. As aggressive in business as they were at poker, the industrialists faced perilous challenges in the marketplace, which they decried as "ruinous competition." They sometimes addressed competition by purchasing or merging with rival firms to reduce an industry's total production and raise prices. Carnegie opted for this strategy when he acquired rival mills at Homestead and Duquesne before selling his giant corporation in the 1901 merger that created U.S. Steel. Another option was innovation, developing cheaper manufacturing processes, new product lines, and even new companies. No one was more state of the art than George Westinghouse, who personally filed 362 patents and started sixty-two companies.[6]

Mass production, multiple plants, vertical integration, and mergers depended on access to unprecedented capital resources and new managerial arrangements.[7] When the intimate partnerships of merchants and manufacturers could no longer muster the necessary funds to underwrite this rapid industrialization, Andrew "A.W." Mellon and other bankers developed the financial means to meet the demand. Still, close relationships between Pittsburgh industrialists and financiers persisted. Oliver relied on local banks to finance his ambitious expansion and restructure his debt when he ran into capital difficulties. Frick began a financial relationship with the Mellons in the early 1870s that continued as he and A.W. Mellon bonded personally. Business dealings among the city's elite were not always so chummy. Westinghouse was willing to gamble with the Mellon brothers at Frick's table, but he turned to New York bankers, fearing that the Mellons would use their loans to interfere with his control of his firms.

With multiple plants in several locations, the industrialists also had to develop ways to coordinate ever-more complex operations. In addition to employing thousands of production workers, they centralized ever-larger administrative and professional staffs in downtown headquarters. Their eponymously named skyscrapers signified the industrialists' tremendous power, while the heights to which those buildings rose reflected their rivalries and animosities. Their modern corporations, ranging from the emblematic U.S. Steel Corporation to H. J. Heinz's food processing firm, branded Pittsburgh to the region and to the nation by the early twentieth century.[8]

Pittsburgh's regional economy, however, was more complex than just the giant iron and steel corporations associated with the Steel City. Older industries such as glass and railroad equipment expanded, while newer ones such as natural gas, electrical equipment, and aluminum became essential cogs in the corporate community. Many firms focused on specialized products for national and local market niches. Geared to meet changing customer demands, they limited production to batches rather than continuous mass runs.[9] Others, including highly skilled metalworking shops, Mesta Machine, and firebrick firms, serviced local industries. Together these modern corporations and smaller manufacturers created a dense web of relationships that stimulated innovation and entrepreneurship. Henry Oliver, George Westinghouse, Charles Martin Hall, and several of Carnegie's managers were among those who exemplified these dynamics as their discoveries changed America.

Historians call this convergence of new power sources (steam, petroleum, and electricity), new transportation and communication systems (railroads, telegraph, and telephone), mass production, scientific research, and modern management the Second Industrial Revolution. Pittsburgh was on its front lines. Its mines, mills, and workshops produced the iron, steel, fuel, glass, locomotive engines, and turbines that laid the transcontinental railroad, built the Brooklyn Bridge, erected Manhattan's skyscrapers, and armored the ships that expanded American naval power. The industrialists who sat around poker tables, lunched at their clubs, and raced their horse-drawn buggies orchestrated not just the city's remarkable industrial growth but that of the nation.

IRON CITY BEGINNINGS

Handsome and respected, forty-two-year-old Henry C. Oliver strode to the podium at the annual meeting of the American Institute of Mining Engineers in 1882 and announced the installation of an innovative Clapp-Griffiths furnace. The furnace, which would provide steel for the iron manufacturer's South Side works, signaled his intent to shift away from iron, a transformation other companies were considering. Clapp-Griffiths steel, he declared, would replace bar-iron for ironware, nail-plate, tank-steel, fish bars, and related products.[10] After installing the Clapp-Griffiths as well as a small Bessemer furnace, Oliver began to vertically integrate his iron- and steelworks from the mining of essential ingredients like iron ore and coal to marketing finished goods. By century's end Oliver, Andrew Carnegie, Henry Clay Frick, Benjamin Jones, and James Laughlin were in the vanguard that created the nation's steel industry.[11]

Oliver, like Carnegie, Frick, Heinz, and Westinghouse, epitomized industrializing Pittsburgh. At his death in 1904 an obituary observed that "the story of his career is bound up with the rise of Pittsburgh from a manufacturing town to a world-center of industry, for his business activities were an integral part of the process."[12] But when this Ulster-born immigrant embarked on his business life, he could not have imagined the vast fortune his entrepreneurial, visionary, and daring behavior would amass.

Both Oliver's and Carnegie's careers began and ended in strikingly similar ways. Oliver was the third son of a Dungannon saddler in County Tyrone, Ireland. Born in 1840, he immigrated with his family at age two and settled near the Pennsylvania Canal basin in Allegheny City on the flats called the First Bank. The neighborhood, which centered on General Robinson Street, later became the site for Exposition Park, Three Rivers Stadium, PNC Park, and Heinz Field. When the slightly older Andy Carnegie arrived six years later, he lived near the Olivers. Amid First Bank's clamor Henry and his five siblings played in a relatively secure neighborhood filled with Scots and Ulstermen, some of whom became lifelong acquaintances. Henry and his mates swam in the "pool" formed between an offshore sandbar and the riverbank. They also helped at home and gave what they earned to their parents, as most children then did. Henry helped his mother Margaret shop at the Allegheny Market, went to the First Ward Public School, and attended weekly church services.

The First Bank's floodplain offered a front row seat to the spectacle of Pittsburgh commerce and industry. When high water annually flooded the neighborhood, Margaret Oliver and her children moved to higher ground, while her husband and a son carted household goods upstairs. But once the waters receded, Henry witnessed canal boats stream into the Allegheny basin, scores of steamboats on the river, and dozens of flatboats tied up along the riverbank. He watched as the railroad arrived in Pittsburgh and listened to the shrill cry of steam whistles, clatter of hooves, and cacophony of shouting workers and boys. A transportation nexus, the First Bank moved to the beat of Pittsburgh's dynamic mid-century economy.

After finishing public school, Henry crossed the river for two years of private education. But like most of his friends, he also began working. During summers and holidays he helped at his father's saddlery on Wood Street downtown, where an extensive wagon trade provided ample business. Not inclined to working with his hands, the gregarious boy made deliveries and charmed customers, foreshadowing the sales and political skills that would serve him well. In 1853 thirteen-year-old Henry secured a position delivering messages for the Atlantic & Ohio Telegraph Company, where several companions also worked. Young Andy Carnegie toiled there as a telegraph operator, before leaving to work with Thomas Scott, superintendent of the Pennsylvania Railroad's Western Division. Like Carnegie, Henry familiarized himself with the business machinations of a bustling city by delivering telegrams.[13]

He used that knowledge to maneuver strategically among Pittsburgh's business community. After three years at the telegraph company, Oliver joined a freight forwarding firm, Clarke and Thaw, which operated canal boats and steamboats. He soon realized that railroads were eroding canal and river commerce, so in 1859 he became a shipping clerk for Graf, Bennett and Company, an innovative iron firm with puddling and rolling mills on the Monongahela River's south shore. It was a propitious moment to join the firm. Graf, Bennett blew in the city's first blast furnace that year.[14]

While still at Graf, Bennett and not yet twenty years old, Oliver partnered with two steamboat captains and his brother, David B. Oliver, to buy and refurbish a dormant puddling mill in Kittanning, forty miles northeast of the city along the Allegheny. Although his career was launched, he could not ignore the crisis tearing apart the nation. When Pennsylvania governor Andrew Gregg Curtin called for volunteers in April 1861 days after the Civil War began, Oliver joined the Twelfth Regiment and marched to York to patrol the state's border with Maryland. Private Oliver mustered out four months later and returned home to run his iron business. He married Edith Anne Cassidy and moved to Minersville, a pleasant community in the upper Hill District served by horsecars on Centre Avenue. In June 1863 Oliver helped build fortifications around the city should Robert E. Lee and his troops turn west to attack Pittsburgh during their march into Pennsylvania. Lee infamously chose Gettysburg instead, suffering a crippling defeat.[15]

With Pittsburgh spared, the volunteers resumed their normal business, allowing Oliver to establish another firm in 1863 with John Phillips and

William J. Lewis, an inventive bolt and nut manufacturer with a small plant in the Strip District. With the affable Oliver as salesman, the firm of Lewis, Oliver, and Phillips prospered and purchased a plant at Tenth and Muriel Streets on the South Side. Specializing in bar iron, plate, hardware, and wagon parts, its puddling furnaces and roll stands could handle forty thousand tons of iron annually by the end of the 1870s, making it one of the largest ironworks in the city.[16]

As the firm flourished, Oliver plunged into civic affairs. Already a Republican stalwart, he became a member of the Masons and joined the boards of the new Homeopathic Hospital, Dollar Savings Bank, and a horsecar railway firm. In 1871 voters elected Oliver to Pittsburgh's Common Council where he was promptly chosen as its president. He cowrote the Republican Party's protective tariff planks for American manufactures and narrowly lost a protracted battle to become a US senator from Pennsylvania (until 1913 all US senators were chosen by their state legislatures). In his early thirties Oliver joined other leading businessmen in forming the Duquesne Club, and a few years later moved his family to a mansion on Allegheny City's prestigious Ridge Avenue. But the immigrant boy's already impressive rise during the city's iron era was not even half completed. Nor was Pittsburgh's ascent as an industrial metropolis.[17]

CARNEGIE, FRICK, AND THE SHIFT TO STEEL

Reorganizing his firm as Oliver Brothers & Phillips in 1880, Oliver pivoted to steel. As other iron manufacturers were discovering, customers increasingly wanted steel products. Although local production of rolled iron goods grew throughout the 1880s, Carnegie Steel and Jones & Laughlin began dismantling their iron puddling furnaces. By 1901 only nineteen of the city's sixty-three iron and steel plants producing wrought iron by puddling remained. Meanwhile, with Carnegie's Edgar Thomson Works leading the way, the city's proportion of national steel output more than tripled to 30 percent.[18]

At Edgar Thomson, Carnegie demonstrated that steel could be mass-produced with remarkable efficiency. Carnegie had the railroad rail market in mind when he named the steelworks for Edgar Thomson, Pennsylvania Railroad's president from 1852 until his death in 1874. He had engaged Alexander Holley, America's leading designer of Bessemer plants, to build the mill. When it opened in 1875, Carnegie touted it as the most modern steel rail mill in the world. Holley incorporated the railroad into its layout to allow a continuous flow from ore and coal yards to blast furnaces to rolling stands and finally warehouses. Ironically, the depression of the 1870s allowed Carnegie to save considerably on construction costs.

He located Edgar Thomson ten miles southeast of Pittsburgh at Braddock Fields, where Turtle Creek meets the Monongahela River. General Braddock had suffered his ignominious defeat there more than a century earlier, and the Whiskey Rebels had massed on the spot in 1794. Two major railroads, the Pennsylvania and the Baltimore and Ohio, served the site, while barges arrived by river.[19] To these locational and design advantages, Carnegie applied managerial strategies he learned at the Pennsylvania Railroad and his iron mills. He also hired well. Carnegie persuaded Captain William Jones from Johnstown's Cambria Iron Works to become its superintendent and the stringent taskmaster William P. Shinn its general manager. Captain Jones streamlined production, while Shinn devised a detailed accounting method to assess and reduce unit costs.

Meanwhile the irrepressible Scottish owner with long-standing ties to the railroad industry was Edgar Thomson's chief salesman. Despite opening amid the depression, the mill enjoyed an initial order for two thousand rails from the Pennsylvania Railroad. Tightly coordinating and controlling all phases of production, Edgar Thomson delivered high volumes of steel and captured greater market share. The mill reflected Carnegie's famous aphorisms: "Watch the costs and the profits will take care of themselves,"[20] and "Cut the prices; scoop the market; run the mills full."[21] Carnegie's Bessemer works was, in historian John Ingham's words, "an enormous departure from the hovering, personal, idiosyncratic rule-of-thumb methods practiced by most Pittsburgh iron masters."[22] Under Carnegie's close supervision and his team's brilliant performance, costs per rail fell rapidly and profits rose dramatically. Less durable iron rails could not compete with Edgar Thomson's longer-lasting, cheaper steel rails. Edgar Thomson provided the steel for America's Centennial celebration in Philadelphia in 1876 and the Brooklyn Bridge two years later.

But the Edgar Thomson Works was not unchallenged. Several local ironmasters contested Carnegie's command of rail markets in 1881 by forming the Pittsburgh Bessemer Steel Company and opening a state-of-the-art works with Bessemer converters and rolling mills in Homestead, one mile downriver from Braddock. Two years later they encountered labor, management, and demand problems during a national recession, and their investors were too financially stressed to bail them out. Carnegie swooped in. He bought the works and started producing the structural beams and plates needed to construct rapidly growing cities.[23] Three years later his rivals tried again. The Allegheny Bessemer Steel Company built a Bessemer rail works at Duquesne, a mile upriver from Edgar Thomson. The owners instituted a novel continuous process by which ingots went directly from the soaking pits to the roll stands without the expense of reheating and additional handling. Cutting costs, these improvements would make the new company's rails cheaper than Edgar Thomson's. But when the works opened in 1889, labor problems buffeted the mill. More daunting, customers shunned its rails when Carnegie informed associates in the railroad industry that its products were flawed. This bald-faced lie diminished the firm's revenue at a time when its investors were financially overextended and anxious for relief. In his capacity as chairman of Carnegie Brothers and Company, Henry Clay Frick engineered the rival company's purchase. Suddenly, Allegheny Bessemer Steel's rails were no longer inferior, and Carnegie entered the 1890s commanding three large Bessemer steelworks just miles apart in the Monongahela Valley, more through uncanny opportunism than by grand design.[24]

The 1890s were no less momentous for Carnegie than the previous decade. With Frick at the helm, according to biographer Joseph Frazier Wall, Carnegie "changed his company from a highly successful business into an industrial empire."[25] Relentlessly cutting costs, Carnegie stressed innovation and control of each stage of steelmaking through vertical integration from the acquisition of raw materials to the marketing of finished products. He preached constantly about updating machinery and handling materials more efficiently. Contrary to iron industry tradition, the Scotsman pushed his managers to drive their machinery and men hard. Machines could be replaced with improved equipment and craftsmen supplanted by cheaper immigrant laborers. He greatly benefited from Henry Phipps's and Captain William Jones's innovations. Phipps, Carnegie's longtime associate and boyhood chum, devised ways to turn flue-cinder waste from blast furnaces and metal shavings from the rolling process into profitable by-products. Captain Jones, Edgar Thomson's remarkable general superintendent, installed cost-saving means of moving materials through the mill. His famous Jones mixer box homogenized liquid pig metal of varying compositions from several blast furnaces, eliminating the need to remelt pig iron in the Bessemer converter's cupola.[26] Not only did Carnegie encourage his men to innovate, he took side trips to mills in search of new methods during frequent European excursions. He was an early American adopter of open-hearth furnaces using the Thomas process to remove phosphorous from cheap and plentiful iron ores unsuited for Bessemer converters. These open-hearth furnaces had a significant cost advantage and produced better-quality steel.[27] Carnegie never wanted competitors to gain an advantage.

In the early 1890s Carnegie envisioned controlling the sources of each raw material needed to produce steel. He secured the limestone used in blast furnaces to draw out impurities from ore and, more important, ensured a steady supply of coke. In 1881 Carnegie famously proposed a partnership to Frick at a dinner in New York, which he and his mother hosted for the honeymooning coke baron and his wife, Adelaide Childs. By then Frick was a key figure in the Connellsville coke district.[28]

Frick had built his company through disciplined management and audacious investments during the 1870s depression. Born in 1849, he grew up on a small, struggling Westmoreland County farm near the West Overton homestead of his maternal grandfather, Abraham Overholt. This wealthy Mennonite operated flour mills, a cooperage, and rye whiskey distilleries in the rolling hills west of Chestnut Ridge. After enrolling at Otterbein College near Columbus, Ohio, Frick realized that he preferred the practical life of business. Withdrawing from school, he clerked in a relative's store near Mt. Pleasant and spent a year as a salesman in Pittsburgh before becoming chief bookkeeper for his grandfather's distillery in Broadford on the Youghiogheny River.[29]

Farms dominated the countryside, but coal outcroppings, which annoyed farmers like his father as they plowed, indicated the coalfields below the surface. A three-mile-wide coal seam ran southwest from Latrobe for fifty to sixty miles in front of Chestnut Ridge to the Monongahela River near the West Virginia border. Although some farmers harvested these outcroppings for fuel and sale, the real value lay in the seam's unmatched qualities for making coke. The area would become known as the Connellsville coke district.[30]

Although baking bituminous coal into a purer form of carbon called coke had been employed for decades in England, local entrepreneurs did not purchase coal lands and erect beehive coke ovens until blast furnaces began operating in Pittsburgh in the 1860s. Grasping coke's potential, Frick parleyed his initial investments in the fuel into a fortune. Like Carnegie, he was not averse to taking risks when most investors were retrenching. One of Frick's cousins and two other men had established the profitable Morgan mine and coke works in 1868. Three years later Frick raised funds from relatives to buy into the partnership, soon becoming its manager. Purchasing 123 acres near Broadford, he borrowed $10,000 from Pittsburgh's Judge Thomas Mellon to build fifty ovens. Obtaining another loan from the judge to construct fifty more ovens a few months later, the young firm erected a second coke plant. When the 1870s depression slashed demand for coke, investors scrambled to resolve their debt woes. But like Carnegie, who continued constructing the Edgar Thomson Works during the depression, Frick saw opportunity in economic distress. He bought out his partners, obtained additional loans from the Mellons, acquired more coal land, and leased and built coke plants. In 1877 Frick also secured funds from Edmund Ferguson, an investor who later frequented his poker games. By 1880 Frick had amassed three thousand acres of coal land and over 1,000 ovens in the coke district. He had bet correctly on expansion, for the appetite for iron and steel burgeoned following the 1870s depression. The number of coke ovens in the district climbed from approximately 550 to more than 4,200 during the decade, and Frick operated one-quarter of them. Making his first million dollars by the age of thirty, he moved to Pittsburgh. Grandfather Overholt would have beamed with pride.[31]

Frick's partnership with Carnegie was fruitful for both men, though often tempestuous. Frick supplied coke to Carnegie's blast furnaces; in turn Carnegie purchased 11.25 percent of Frick's coke company. With more working capital, Frick aggressively expanded his coke domain, while Carnegie rapidly increased his stake in the coke company. By 1883 Frick controlled roughly one-third of the region's coke production, and Carnegie had obtained majority ownership of the H. C. Frick Coke Company.[32] Carnegie forced Frick to settle with striking miners in 1887 to ensure a steady supply of coke for his mills. Angered by Carnegie's intervention, Frick resigned as head of the company, only to be coaxed back months later.

––––––––––

Although Carnegie had gained control of two of the three principal raw materials necessary to make steel, he did not control iron ore mines nor had he fully integrated his company. In 1886 he organized his iron and steel facilities into two companies—Carnegie Brothers and the Carnegie, Phipps Companies—with essentially the same ownership. When Carnegie's brother Thomas died that fall, Phipps temporarily replaced Thomas as the manager of Carnegie Brothers. In early 1887 Carnegie aligned Frick's interests more closely to his steel companies by selling the King of Coke 2 percent of Carnegie Brothers. Not wanting to lose his able manager, Carnegie appointed Frick chairman of Carnegie Brothers in 1889 and increased his stake to 11 percent.[33]

Frick completed the vertical integration of Carnegie's disparate iron and steel assets. Gaining the Scotsman's trust as profits surged, Frick bought the Duquesne mill and merged the two Carnegie companies into one, the Carnegie Steel Company. He further reduced costs by constructing the Union Railway to move materials among Carnegie plants on the Monongahela and Allegheny Rivers. After the 1892 Homestead Strike, Frick persuaded Carnegie to make a half-million-dollar loan to Henry Oliver's iron ore mining company in the Mesabi iron range of Minnesota and Wisconsin. Though Carnegie viewed Oliver as an unreliable speculator who made but also lost fortunes, Frick recognized the advantages of controlling iron ore resources.[34]

Several more moves completed Carnegie Steel integration, but Frick was gone by then. The mercurial Carnegie clashed with his implacable manager and removed Frick as chairman in 1894. By then the loan to Henry Oliver for half-interest in his Mesabi mining company gave Carnegie Steel a stake in iron ore, the one essential resource it lacked. But Carnegie still needed to secure a more reliable supply of ore and find a competitive means of transporting the raw material from the western end of Lake Superior to the Lake Erie port of Conneaut, Ohio. That meant bypassing the Pennsylvania Railroad, which controlled the rail connections that carried iron ore to Pittsburgh. Taking over a rundown railroad connecting Butler to Conneaut in 1896, the old railway man rebuilt it and extended the tracks to the town of Bessemer within Penn Hills Township to connect with the Union Railway. With the newly named Pittsburgh, Bessemer, and Lake Erie Railroad, Carnegie Steel finally controlled the movement of ore between the Great Lakes and its mills.[35]

John D. Rockefeller's entry into the Mesabi range, however, stoked fears that he might try to monopolize iron ore as he had dominated oil. When the 1893 depression exposed the fragile finances of Mountain Iron, an important iron mining operation, Rockefeller seized control of its mines and railroad to the Lake Superior port of Duluth. Oliver opened negotiations with Rockefeller and in 1896 the Oliver Iron Mining Company and Carnegie Steel agreed to lease Rockefeller's mines, produce six hundred thousand tons of ore at a fixed price, and ship that amount and an additional six hundred thousand tons of Oliver's ore on Rockefeller's railroad and ore boats. The agreement ensured Carnegie Steel the iron ore it needed at a competitive cost. A year later Carnegie Steel obtained a five-sixths interest in the Oliver Iron Mining Company. Carnegie Steel then bought and refurbished Conneaut Harbor and put its own fleet of ore boats on the Great Lakes. The company also created an in-house sales department with offices throughout North America. Carnegie Steel was now fully integrated, controlling every aspect of production, from extracting raw materials to producing, transporting, and selling its array of iron and steel output. At century's end Carnegie Steel outproduced the entire British industry and reaped the fabulous annual profit of forty million dollars.[36]

MORE THAN CARNEGIE STEEL

Carnegie Steel's dramatic growth does not capture the full story of Pittsburgh's rise as the center of the nation's iron and steel industry. Mushrooming demand for steel products induced traditional iron and crucible steel companies outside of Carnegie Steel's orbit to adapt to a new, competitive environment and changing technologies. While Carnegie took over the Bessemer Steel Company in Homestead and Allegheny Bessemer Steel in Duquesne in the 1880s, a few firms remained independent and integrated with varying degrees of success. Most avoided direct competition with Carnegie Steel's primary products, markets, and organizational strategies.[37]

But Henry Oliver took Carnegie on. Shifting to steel, he aggressively expanded his product line, while integrating backward to control steelmaking's first stages. In 1881 he constructed a wire mill on the South Side near his puddling and rolling mill, then purchased an Illinois barbed wire plant, and reopened it in Pittsburgh as part of the Oliver Wire Company. Oliver added a wire nail firm, and in a step toward integration, erected a wire rod rolling mill to supply his wire and nail plants. Oliver then added the capacity to make steel. At this juncture Oliver companies sprawled from Fourth to Fifteenth Streets on the South Side and specialized in iron and steel products from barbed wire and nails to hardware, but did not compete with the mass production of Carnegie's steelworks.[38]

Oliver was undaunted when the experiment with the Clapp-Griffith furnace failed and imperiled his finances. Working out credit extensions with Pittsburgh bankers, he continued to integrate his iron and steel business by acquiring companies and new product lines. Oliver established the Monongahela Tin Plate Company near his South Side mills and purchased the Hainsworth Steel Company's casting works in Lawrenceville. He also allied with the Schultz Bridge Company, a prominent bridge builder and structural steel fabricator. In 1891 he entered the emerging steel freight car business with Charles Schoen of Philadelphia. Bringing the inventor to Pittsburgh, they opened the Schoen Pressed Steel Car Company to build all-steel freight cars that would replace traditional wooden ones. It was later known as the Pressed Steel Car Company and the site of a violent labor conflict. Oliver also created a company to forge parts for steel cars. While the bridge and steel car companies were customers of Oliver's iron- and steelworks, these acquisitions and plants had not yet fulfilled his vision of a fully integrated iron and steel company.[39]

Oliver still needed to guarantee supplies of basic materials for his steelmaking facilities. After leasing a blast furnace in New Castle and the Edith blast furnace along the Allegheny River in 1891, he purchased coal properties, accumulating more than one thousand acres near Uniontown, and building three coke plants to ensure a fuel supply. He and his partners also established the Monongahela Natural Gas Company to provide their plants with this new source of energy. In 1892 Oliver made his initial foray into the booming Mesabi iron range. Iron ore was the new "gold," and the Oliver Iron Mining Company began producing prodigious amounts of it. But an economic slump forced Oliver to ask Carnegie Steel to invest in his Mesabi iron mining operations.[40]

Oliver's far-flung assets stretched from southwestern Pennsylvania coalfields to northern Minnesota iron mines. Like Carnegie, his complex holdings required an efficient transportation system to carry raw and finished materials. Accordingly Oliver created a better local railroad network. In 1875 he and several others, including Benjamin F. Jones, formed the Pittsburgh and Lake Erie Railroad (P&LE) to challenge Pennsylvania Railroad's access to the Midwest. The P&LE ran from a terminal at the southern end of the Smithfield Street Bridge (currently Station Square) to Youngstown, Ohio, where it connected with William Vanderbilt's New York Central Railroad. Oliver and his partners sold their interest to Vanderbilt in the early 1880s. They then built the Pittsburgh, McKeesport, and Youghiogheny Railroad from Connellsville along the Youghiogheny River to McKeesport and down the Monongahela to serve his South Side plants. The P&LE absorbed this new line and over the years hauled enormous amounts of coal, coke, limestone, and iron ore via its connections to Lake Erie ports. Oliver also added a fleet of ships, the Pittsburgh Steamship Company, to carry ore across the lakes to Fairport, Ohio.[41]

Having achieved railroad access for his South Side plants, Oliver turned to improving transportation connections for manufacturers along the Allegheny River. He joined other investors in engineering a route from Allegheny City to New Castle, where his new Pittsburgh and Western Railroad line connected to the Midwest. The partners then built the Junction Railroad to connect the Pittsburgh and Western in Allegheny City north to the Baltimore and Ohio Railroad along the Monongahela River by tunneling under Oakland and skirting Schenley Park. The Pennsylvania Railroad, which had exercised its rate-setting power to the dismay of local manufacturers, finally faced a viable east–west competitor.[42]

By 1893 Oliver sat atop a robust, integrated complex of iron and steel companies with control over basic raw materials and access to vital transportation. But the severe depression of 1893 was not kind to Oliver and many other Pittsburgh businessmen. It weakened demand for steel goods, reduced orders for iron ore, coal, and coke, and threw Oliver's finances into disarray. With Oliver Iron and Steel Company in receivership, he partnered with prominent businessman William Penn Snyder and reorganized his holdings to weather the financial storm. Oliver's rapid development of an iron and steel empire, which then faced repeated financial difficulties, confirmed Carnegie's assessment. Though Carnegie and others admired Oliver's enterprise and farsighted understanding of industrial trends, they worried about his expansive, speculative, and at times reckless ventures.[43] Still, Oliver's rise to prominence in iron and steel mirrored Pittsburgh's rise as a great industrial city at the center of a dynamic region of coal mining, coke plants, railroading, and iron and steel mills.

Just upstream from Oliver's South Side mills, another even larger and older integrated iron and steel company dwarfed both sides of the Monongahela River. Unlike Carnegie and Oliver, whose impressive companies succumbed to the turn-of-the-century merger movement, Jones & Laughlin Steel Corporation (J&L) remained independent until the LTV Corporation purchased it in 1968. Benjamin F. Jones and James Laughlin, who established their ironworks on the South Side before the Civil War, later erected blast furnaces and coke ovens across the river in Hazelwood. Under the direction of Jones, its senior partner, J&L became the city's largest iron producer by the 1880s, with seventy-five puddling furnaces, twenty rolling mill stands, and three to four thousand employees. Moreover, Jones had integrated J&L with coal mines, coke works, and a national sales force. Like Oliver, he embraced the shift to steel and blew in two Bessemer converters in 1886. Adding to its Bessemer capacity, J&L erected open-hearth furnaces and began dismantling its iron puddling capacity. Producing steel rails, beams, sheets, and structural shapes of all kinds, it competed directly with the Carnegie Steel Company.[44]

Though Oliver, Jones, Carnegie, and a few others scaled up their companies into massive, integrated corporations, most Pittsburgh iron- and steel masters chose a different strategy. They specialized on finished, less standardized products not well suited for mass production. These companies sought market niches that required small product batches, precision work, individualized service, and the flexibility to meet fluctuating customer demands. Compared to J&L or Oliver Steel, these firms were relatively small, disinclined to integrate production, and cautious about overexpanding. They were neither exciting nor spectacular. A few long-standing firms, the Sable Rolling Mill, Vesuvius Iron, and A. M. Byers Pipe Works, successfully remained committed to their iron product lines and never made steel, surviving into the turbulent post–World War I era. Byers, for example, produced iron pipe for the booming oil, gas, and irrigation industries. Others that stuck to iron, however, succumbed during the 1893 depression, the acquisitive appetite of large firms, or the pitfalls of familial ownership.[45] By century's end Pittsburgh's enormous mass production works and its many specialized firms produced one third of the nation's iron and steel.[46] But the final years of the century disrupted the Steel City's leading industry.

MERGERS COME TO PITTSBURGH

By the 1890s depression the movement consolidating iron and steel firms into giant trusts and holding companies enveloped Oliver, posing challenges but offering opportunities. U.S. Steel's formation in 1901 absorbed twenty-six southwestern Pennsylvania companies, most significantly the hugely productive Carnegie Steel Company. That shifted ownership of 40 percent of the city's iron and steel production to the new firm, headquartered in New York. Suddenly Pittsburgh's brash, risk-taking entrepreneurs, including a few from Frick's poker soirees, no longer towered over the nation's iron and steel industry. Even so, the city's total tonnage continued to increase, as many older companies survived the merger movement and new ones were soon organized.[47]

Midwestern speculators John W. Gates and James H. Moore, as well as Wall Street impresario J. P. Morgan, consolidated several rival companies in specific sectors of the industry. Oliver, forced to sell assets during the depression, began unwinding his iron and steel empire when he sold his wire firms to Gates's American Steel Wire Company; the Monongahela Tin Plate Company to the new American Tin Plate Company trust; and parts of Oliver & Snyder Steel to the National Steel Company. He also exited the iron ore business, selling his remaining interest in the Oliver Iron Mining Company. At that point Oliver retained only his original Oliver Iron and Steel firm and what was left of Oliver & Snyder Steel. Decades of tireless expansion were over. "The result of nearly forty years of active connection with iron and steel manufacture," the *Pittsburgh Dispatch* observed, was "merged in the great consolidations . . . [and] recognized as among the most important in the country." Oliver, still quite wealthy, dabbled in mining and steel ventures and turned his attention to real estate in downtown Pittsburgh.[48]

Oliver was not the only Pittsburgh steel magnate in eclipse. Between 1895 and 1904 over one hundred consolidations of five or more manufacturing firms occurred across the nation. Many were capital-intensive companies holding excessive debt accrued during their rapid growth and faced high fixed costs because of their extensive operations. During the 1893 depression they often experienced debilitating financial pressure. Confronting declining demand, producers often consolidated with their rivals to diminish competition and stabilize prices. Several Pittsburgh steel and glass firms were subsumed by new trusts such as the American Window Glass Company, American Tin Plate Company, and National Steel Company.[49]

Even Carnegie finally agreed to sell his beloved company. While Oliver cashed in by selling his assets, Carnegie prepared to battle speculators John Gates, James Moore, and, more ominously, J. P. Morgan. Characteristically, Carnegie exuded confidence in overcoming a challenge from Federal Steel, the Morgan syndicate's new combination. "I think Federal the greatest concern the world ever saw for manufacturing stock certificates," he blustered, "but they will fail sadly in steel."[50] Carnegie Steel was the most efficient and profitable producer of semifinished billets, bars, and structural shapes purchased by wire, nail, hoop, tin plate, and tube manufacturers. But Federal Steel, linked to new trusts that would buy its steel instead of Carnegie's, had an edge. Determined not to lose these markets, Carnegie loudly threatened to enter the finishing end of the industry to compete with them. His longstanding associates, particularly Phipps, Frick, and George Lauder, were not so confident. Besides, after decades of brutal competition, they were tired and ready to cash out. Like Oliver, they wanted to extract the wealth of their labors before old age prevented them from enjoying it. A failed attempt by Frick and Phipps to engineer a sale of Carnegie Steel to James Moore, whom Carnegie detested, steeled the Scotsman's resolve to continue the battle. But not for long.

Morgan and the steel trusts considered Carnegie and his powerful company a menace to their success. With Carnegie associate Charles Schwab acting as an intermediary, Morgan offered to purchase Carnegie Steel. No longer willing to battle it out, Carnegie stipulated his price and conditions, which Morgan readily accepted. Despite his instinct to fight, Carnegie was sixty-five and his wife Louise was pressuring him to retire. Moreover, it would have taken years to build the finishing capacity necessary to compete with Morgan, and Carnegie was committed to his philanthropic goals. Quickly and surprisingly, Pittsburgh's signature iron and steel company became the foundation of the new U.S. Steel Corporation in 1901. It was the world's first billion-dollar corporation. Reaping nearly $300 million from the sale, Carnegie now had the daunting task of constructively giving away as much as he could (see Chapter 8).[51]

The formation of U.S. Steel rearranged the landscape of Pittsburgh's iron and steel industry, absorbing steelworks from around the country, including twenty firms in the region. Three former Oliver plants sold earlier to the trusts or directly to U.S. Steel were now part of Morgan's behemoth, which accounted for nearly two-thirds of US iron and steel production. But U.S. Steel did not eliminate many firms that sought to remain independent. Financier Andrew W. Mellon consolidated thirteen crucible steelworks into the Crucible Steel Company. Most of these long-standing partnerships operated as nearly autonomous subsidiaries for several years after consolidation. Twenty-three firms founded before the merger movement remained independent of both U.S. Steel and Crucible, and fourteen new works were established between 1895 and 1901.[52]

After the merger wave ended, a few new, large steel mills began operating in the region. A.W. Mellon and Frick joined William Donner in establishing Union Steel to challenge U.S. Steel at the new town of Donora. Crucible Steel, which Oliver advised, built a plant at Clairton, and the newly formed Pittsburgh Steel Company constructed a large works at Monessen. These three new plants were located on the Monongahela River upstream (south) from Carnegie's complex of mills. U.S. Steel purchased the mills at Donora and Clairton, and Crucible tried again with a mill at Midland on the Ohio River in 1914. Out of space to expand in Pittsburgh, Jones & Laughlin built an enormous new works and company town at Aliquippa on the Ohio twenty-six miles north of the city in 1909. Financial panic in 1903 and an especially damaging economic downturn in 1907, as well as the sale of several companies, reduced the forty independent companies in 1901 to thirty-one in 1920. Though still the epicenter of American iron and steel production, the dynamic era of forming new steelworks in the region was coming to an end.[53]

LINKED TO IRON AND STEEL

Several industries linked to iron and steel, some of which achieved national importance, fleshed out a robust industrial complex. Both small independent iron and steel mills and large integrated works depended on specialized, subcontracting, and service companies. Metalworking and metal-serving businesses and dozens of foundries and machine shops fashioned, serviced, and repaired parts for mill machinery. Model and pattern-makers worked in concert with these mills, while larger machine tool firms such as Mackintosh-Hemphill and Mesta Machine made heavy equipment for mills and mines. Iron and steel construction and fabricating companies such as American Bridge and McClintic-Marshall Construction used local semifinished products. Initially specializing in industrial machinery, Dravo Corporation diversified into general industrial contracting, concrete construction, and waterway improvements. Engineering firms were in constant demand, river and railroad companies transported goods, and horse-drawn haulers distributed materials around the city. Jobbers or wholesalers sold finished products for companies without sales departments, and scrap dealers assembled metals to feed open-hearth furnaces. Larger iron and steel firms such as Carnegie, Oliver, and J&L had their own machine shops, patternmakers, chemists, and engineers, but even they subcontracted for services. Together these iron and steel companies and hundreds of subcontracting, servicing, and finishing firms formed a vigorous production system.[54]

With mining coal and turning it into coke indispensable to the iron and steel economy, coal mines and coke plants seemed ubiquitous, and towns like Greensburg, Connellsville, and Uniontown began providing essential services to the industry. By some accounts the region's 240 mines produced thirteen million tons of bituminous coal in 1884; thirty years later they produced fifty-seven million tons.[55] Mine entrances, outbuildings, tipples, refuse piles, and adjacent company houses and stores in infamous patch towns occupied ravines outside the city.[56] Coke plants were first concentrated around Connellsville, but increased demand and the exhaustion of older mines spread mining toward the Monongahela River into the "Klondike" area and after 1910 west of the river into Greene and Washington Counties.

At times more than eighty thousand miners extracted coal, and thirty to forty thousand beehive ovens baked it into coke, releasing waste gases into the air. The title of Muriel Sheppard's book describing the industry, *Cloud by Day*, depicted its pervasive gaseous presence in southwestern Pennsylvania.[57] By then European engineers were developing ovens that captured the gases freed during coking and distilled them into tars, ammonia, benzene, naphtha, and toluene. These by-products fostered a nascent chemical industry. But local companies, with huge and profitable investments in beehive ovens, were reluctant to incur the costs of adopting this new technology, and besides, German companies already met US demand for the chemicals. U.S. Steel and other big coke producers, however, concluded that new ovens could capture waste gases and pipe it to nearby mills as fuel. In 1910 the Mellons invested in the Illinois German Koppers Company, which built by-product ovens, and moved it to Pittsburgh, where it became a stalwart of the corporate community. Koppers built hundreds of ovens for U.S. Steel at Clairton in 1917, J&L at Hazelwood and Aliquippa, and Crucible Steel at Midland. Resistance to investing in by-product ovens waned when World War I disrupted chemical importations. As by-product technology spread to steel mills nationally, the Connellsville coke district slipped into protracted decline.[58]

Local railroad equipment manufacturers thrived on their links to the coal, iron, and steel industries. The region's rail network included the Pennsylvania Railroad, the Baltimore and Ohio (B&O), and the P&LE; numerous feeder and short line railroads; and small switching lines used within plants. By 1902 this dense rail network supported thirteen repair shops, including the B&O shops in Glenwood, the P&LE's in McKees Rocks, and the enormous Conway and Pitcairn switching yards.[59] In addition to rails, local companies made railroad equipment, including wheels, axles, couplers, frogs (which allowed trains to switch tracks), and springs. Locomotive (four at one point) and railroad car manufacturers employed thousands. So did dozens of parts suppliers surrounding the Pittsburgh Locomotive Works in Allegheny City and the H.K. Porter Company, which manufactured powerful, narrow gauge locomotives for logging, mining, and switching in Lawrenceville.

George Westinghouse, who opened an air brake plant in 1870 in the Strip District, moved operations to Allegheny City and then in 1889 to the Turtle Creek valley, where he constructed Wilmerding, a model workers' town. Westinghouse also focused on railroad signals and switches. After purchasing the Interlocking Switch and Signal Company of Harrisburg and investing in a Massachusetts company, he consolidated them as the Union Switch and Signal Company, initially in the Strip District and then in an enormous Swissvale plant.[60]

Glass, iron, and steel industry furnaces, beehive ovens, steam engines, and other high heat equipment needed fire or refractory brick to withstand the heat. Tapping clay deposits in northern Pennsylvania in 1865, the Star

Fire Brick Company launched the local refractory brick industry in the Strip. New investors kept it afloat during the 1870s downturn. After changing its name to the Harbison-Walker Company, it increased mining operations in northern counties, enlarged its Pittsburgh works, and constructed a brick plant at Hays near Homestead. In 1902 several refractory brick companies merged into a large trust named Harbison-Walker Refractories Company. Supplying the region's industries, Harbison-Walker, like some of its customers, became a national concern with a modern corporate structure.[61]

MORE THAN IRON AND STEEL

Iron and steel were not the only industries driving Pittsburgh's astonishing growth. Glassmaking had deep roots in Pittsburgh, while several remarkable innovators like George Westinghouse and Charles Martin Hall, who developed a process for smelting aluminum, flourished in Pittsburgh's entrepreneurial, risk-taking environment. They launched firms that shared characteristics with iron and steel corporations in their reliance on mass production, innovation, vertical integration, and multifaceted financial organization. By 1920 the Pittsburgh region encompassed a sprawling industrial complex with a population of more than one and a half million, making it the nation's sixth largest metropolitan area.[62]

Glass manufacturing centered on the South Side was well established by the mid-1800s. Though other plants operated along the Monongahela River in Washington and Fayette Counties, a critical mass of skilled workers, patternmakers, and financiers gave the city a competitive advantage. However, labor tensions in the 1880s and the need to build larger factories with access to natural gas deposits spurred some firms to abandon the South Side. James Chambers and H. Sellers McKee erected plants in Jeannette and Arnold in Westmoreland County. Captain John Ford and John Pitcairn built their new Pittsburgh Plate Glass Company (PPG) in Creighton and Ford City northeast of Pittsburgh on the Allegheny River, adding research facilities at Creighton and establishing plants around the United States and in Belgium. Like steel firms, glass companies consolidated on a massive level. Chambers formed the American Window Glass Company in 1899 with forty firms, marshalling 40 percent of all national window glass capacity. The Independent Glass Company combined thirty-six firms. These arrangements were not long-lasting, and southwestern Pennsylvania still had nearly fifty glass manufacturers in 1919.[63]

The discovery of oil in northwestern Pennsylvania in 1859 spawned another Pittsburgh industry. Although drilling and refining crude oil eventually moved to Texas and Oklahoma and then overseas, the Pennsylvania boom left a substantial local legacy. In the 1860s drillers rafted oil down the Allegheny to five dozen small refineries lining the city's riverbanks. But then Clevelander John D. Rockefeller began using railroads and pipelines to monopolize the industry, marginalizing Pittsburgh refiners. By 1884 only nineteen refineries remained, producing mostly lubricants, solvents, and kerosene. However, the boom had stimulated the manufacture of rivercraft, wooden and iron barrels, tanks, hoops, tubes and pipes, drilling equipment, chemicals, and oil-burning lamps, as well as a local Petroleum Exchange for trading in the commodity and shares of related companies. Pittsburghers like Jacob Jay Vandergrift, who participated in the drilling rush, and those like Carnegie, who invested in it, accumulated wealth and knowledge about the industry they would exploit in other regions.[64]

Though Rockefeller's Standard Oil Company squeezed out independent producers and refiners, new discoveries in the region and West Virginia finally attracted the Mellons' attention. William Larimer Mellon partnered with local businessmen and wildcatters James Guffey and John Gayley, opening the McDonald field in northern Allegheny and southern Beaver Counties. His uncles, financiers A.W. and R. B. Mellon, supported his venture, which included short feeder pipelines from the wells to a refinery in Coraopolis. In order to circumvent Rockefeller's effort to break their well-financed upstart, the Mellons funded a pipeline across Pennsylvania to Chester on the Delaware River near Philadelphia, where they refined their crude and exported petroleum products. Combining their oil assets into the Crescent Oil Company, the Mellons integrated production, transportation, refining, and marketing. But weak demand during the depression of mid-1890s and Rockefeller's price manipulations led the Mellons to sell Crescent Oil to Rockefeller's Standard Oil in 1895 and exit the industry.[65]

They returned a few years later when Gayley and Guffey asked them to back their Texas oil explorations. The wildcatters' discovery of the massive Spindletop field near Beaumont and the construction of transportation facilities and a refinery in Port Arthur persuaded the Mellons to increase their investment. When Guffey proved to be a poor manager, they took over the Texas operations, opened a rich field in Oklahoma, and reorganized as the Gulf Oil Corporation with their nephew William Larimer Mellon leading the venture. Immensely profitable by World War I, Gulf Oil became one of America's largest corporations.[66]

Natural gas often came along with oil drilling of western Pennsylvania wells. Because distributing gas was dangerous and limited its commercialization, drillers either burned it off or sold it locally for fuel. The discovery of gas in Murrysville, east of Pittsburgh, in the mid-1870s stimulated regional exploration. Gas was piped to iron mills and glassworks, but leaks, inadequately regulated pressure, and hand-controlled shut-off valves delayed widespread adoption by city residents. After entering the natural gas business in 1883, George Westinghouse drilled a well on his Homewood property (now Westinghouse Park). It blew in under high pressure, startling neighbors but inspiring the inventor to address distribution and safety issues and form the Philadelphia Company to supply gas to homes and businesses. Westinghouse ultimately registered thirty-eight patents, resolving distribution and safety problems. The profitable company operated four dozen wells and three hundred miles of pipelines in the city and Monongahela Valley.

Other firms, particularly Joseph Pew's Peoples Natural Gas and the Chartiers Valley Gas Company, rivalled the Philadelphia Company. Their success distributing natural gas temporarily eroded residential and industrial use of coal, and Pittsburghers delighted in the clearing skies. Unfortunately, regional gas supplies became less reliable after 1890. As many users switched back to coal, Pittsburgh soon regained its smoky reputation. Nonetheless, natural gas did not disappear from the region; wells continued to be drilled, firms distributed the fuel, and companies manufactured gas meters, pipes, and valves.[67]

In addition to railroad equipment and natural gas businesses, Westinghouse developed other major industries in the region. In 1880 he and his brother Herman established the Westinghouse Machine Company to make high-speed steam engines powering dynamos that produced electricity. Experimenting with electricity for railroad signals at his laboratory, the inventor entered the infant field of electricity and took on Thomas Edison. Westinghouse tinkered with electricity to light his factories and established a company to light downtown businesses. Organizing the Westinghouse Electric Company in 1886, he produced generators, transformers, meters, motors, and power plants. These forays convinced Westinghouse that alternating electrical current, unlike Edison's direct current, could be successfully transmitted over long distances. With Westinghouse championing his approach and J. P. Morgan backing Edison, the two inventors engaged in a bitter, protracted battle for primacy in the field.

Two large projects decided the Edison–Westinghouse struggle. One contract was to harness the power of Niagara Falls to generate electricity and transmit it as far as New York City. The other was to light the 1893 Chicago World's Fair. The latter endeavor, Westinghouse believed, would demonstrate alternating current and his company's capabilities, and secure the Niagara Falls contract. After opening a glassworks in Allegheny City that produced more than 250,000 incandescent lights to illuminate the World's Fair, he won the opportunity to generate electricity from the falls. With municipal and business demand for electrical power escalating, Westinghouse Electric soon outgrew its downtown facility and relocated to the Turtle Creek valley. A foundry that cast parts for machines and turbines completed a complex of Westinghouse companies from Trafford to Wilmerding and

East Pittsburgh. Known as the Electric Valley, more than thirty thousand people lived there early in the twentieth century.[68]

Much like George Westinghouse twenty years earlier, a young chemist, Charles Martin Hall, came to Pittsburgh in 1888 in search of partners and capital to commercialize his electrolytic process for smelting aluminum. Alfred E. Hunt, cooperator of the Pittsburgh Testing Laboratory, saw the process's potential and organized the Pittsburgh Reduction Company. Hall and his even younger collaborator, Arthur Vining Davis, labored in a small Strip District factory to make the process commercially feasible. Their success led the company to build a smelter in Niagara Falls in 1895 to tap cheap hydroelectric power and build a larger factory in New Kensington. The Mellon brothers supplied the considerable capital that expansion required.

Hall and Davis realized that making aluminum a viable substitute for other metals required lower cost and enhanced markets for aluminum products. That meant integration and innovation. Reaching backward, they acquired bauxite mines in Georgia, Alabama, Arkansas, and eventually South America. Ore, shipped to their reduction facility in East St. Louis on the firm's own rail lines and riverboats, was refined into alumina ingots and sent to smelters at Niagara Falls and Massena, New York. At the same time Hall and Davis experimented at New Kensington with methods to manufacture ingots into sheets, rods, wire, tubes, and castings and to fabricate aluminum electrical wires, cables, cook- and kitchenware, machinery parts, and even automobile parts. The entrepreneurs also bought out competitors, tapped international markets, and sought tariff protections and control of patents. By World War I they had transformed the Pittsburgh Reduction Company, its company historian David Smith wrote, "from a small producer of a proprietary product for limited markets into a center of industry of the national economy." The renamed Aluminum Company of America (Alcoa) was vertically integrated and connected to Pittsburgh's capital resources: the Mellons and their Union Trust Bank, which held substantial stakes in it. By 1920 Alcoa was another Pittsburgh modern corporation with approximately fourteen thousand employees in eleven locations around the United States and abroad.[69]

While Westinghouse and Hall were developing new industries, Henry J. Heinz experimented in bottling and canning food products. Raised in Sharpsburg across the Allegheny River from Pittsburgh, young Heinz peddled surplus vegetables from his family's garden, bottled horseradish, and eventually bought into his father's brickworks. In 1869 he focused on preparing food condiments. He and his partners built up the business, barely surviving the financial difficulties of the 1870s. Incessantly promoting his products, Heinz dreamed up the widely recognized "57 Varieties" slogan, erected a large electric promotional sign in New York City, and constructed the nine-hundred-foot-long Heinz Pier in Atlantic City. Opening a London plant and establishing sales agencies worldwide, the company had more than two hundred products by the turn of the century, leading the nation in bottling pickles, vinegar, and ketchup. Purchasing agricultural products from around the world and farming sixteen thousand acres of its own land, Heinz operated eight buildings on the North Side, nine branch plants, and its London site, while a fleet of railroad cars moved materials from field to factory to grocers. As he made the Heinz Company into an integrated corporation, Henry J. Heinz built Greenlawn, his estate in Point Breeze near where Westinghouse, Frick, and Thomas Carnegie resided, but he did not join his neighbors for poker.[70]

Though the sobriquet "Steel City" aptly characterized Pittsburgh, the region's industrial economy was far more complex than simply smoke-belching iron and steel mills. Southwestern Pennsylvania also thrived because of coal and coke, steel construction and bridge building, industrial machinery, and railroad, oil, and gas equipment industries. Glass manufacturing continued to grow, while entrepreneurs such as Westinghouse and Heinz developed new companies that joined the nation's roster of corporate powers. In the nearly half-century before 1920 Pittsburgh displayed an innovative, calculated risk-taking propensity, just as Frick and his poker mates did, unmatched in its earlier years and for decades to come.[71]

FINANCING THE MODERN CORPORATION

Carnegie, Frick, Oliver, Westinghouse, Heinz, and other industrialists required enormous infusions of capital to expand and operate their corporations. Heinz, Carnegie, and a few others relied principally on retained earnings to grow their firms. But self-financing and traditional partnerships were generally incapable of amassing sufficient capital for the multiple acquisitions that built modern corporations. Oliver and Westinghouse turned to capital markets in Pittsburgh and New York, respectively, where investment bankers such as J. P. Morgan could marshal enormous resources. Private investment banks, trust banks, and stock exchanges became financial intermediaries, creating markets for funded corporate debt. In Pittsburgh, A.W. Mellon spearheaded these deals through the private investment banks he led: T. Mellon and Sons and the Union Trust Company.[72]

Andrew W. Mellon, Andy to family and friends when he was younger, had grown up in the family business. Born in 1855 the fourth son of Judge Thomas Mellon lived in a privileged, though somber, home surrounded by pleasant grounds on North Negley Avenue in East Liberty. Under the judge's stern rule, home life was austere, without frivolity. He preached traditional Scotch-Irish Presbyterian values of hard work, thrift, and moral rectitude. His wife Sarah Jane Negley presided over the household and saw to their children's attendance at the East Liberty Presbyterian Church, while the judge groomed his sons for their careers. He stressed acquiring wealth and provided them with a pragmatic education and a leg up in business. In 1867 the judge established a partnership for his two older sons, Thomas Alexander and James Ross, to develop land in East Liberty and sell building supplies and coal. To finance the enterprise, he established a new East End bank. At age nine, when Andrew began commuting with his father to school downtown, they forged a close, trusting relationship.[73] On retiring from the court in 1869, the judge opened a private bank, T. Mellon & Sons, which dealt primarily in real estate, mortgages, and coal. Financial success came quickly, and he built a four-story building on 116 Smithfield Street to house the growing bank. When not at school, sixteen-year-old Andrew (later known as A.W.) joined his father at the bank and three years later began working there full-time. In 1882 failing eyesight caused the judge to withdraw from active management, and he chose Andrew to head the bank. Younger brothers Richard Beatty (Dick or R.B.) and George Negley tended to Mellon investments in real estate and ranching in North Dakota. After George died at a young age, R.B. closed their North Dakota operations and returned to Pittsburgh to join A.W. as a partner in T. Mellon & Sons.[74]

At the helm of a profitable investment bank, they worked closely to fashion the financial means that underwrote much of Pittsburgh's astonishing industrial growth. In so doing, they built Pittsburgh's leading financial institution. In the 1880s A.W. began transforming the Mellon banking interests, buying two banks and an insurance company, as well as establishing a new bank and two trust companies. He also expanded T. Mellon & Sons' portfolio with investments in natural gas, the Pittsburgh Plate Glass Company, and local utilities. Though the Mellon banking activities remained relatively small, the establishment of the Union Trust Company in 1889 and the brothers' involvement in the nascent Pittsburgh Reduction Company (Alcoa) foreshadowed their emerging financial empire.[75]

Pittsburgh financial institutions grew exponentially as they organized investment syndicates to underwrite bonds and stocks during the national merger frenzy between 1895 and 1904. As the value of its bank loans quadrupled and that of the securities it held quintupled, the Union Trust Company facilitated dozens of consolidations. To enhance profits, A.W. Mellon mingled his banking interests with industrial firms, closely overseeing a company's performance, forming interlocking boards of directors, and sometimes gaining majority control. By 1906 the Union Trust Company commanded scores of industrial and financial corporations, and A.W. was on the board of forty-one companies. Some of these locally based companies became cornerstones of the Mellon empire. The brothers intervened in companies in which they had large investments, including Alcoa, Gulf Oil, and Koppers. When a company underperformed, the brothers replaced the inventor-founder with one of their own men.[76]

When Carnegie and Frick's tempestuous relationship ruptured, A.W. moved into steel, which he had avoided until the turn of the century. Mellon and his longtime friend Frick profited by investing in Union Steel in Donora. The frequent investment partners brought in Henry Oliver and financed Standard Steel Car in Lenora near Butler to produce steel railroad cars. The Mellons funded Standard Steel Car's suppliers of wheels, bolts, and rivets and added six new plants in the United States and two more in France and Brazil. They backed two engineers, Howard McClintic and Charles Marshall, in a structural steel fabricating business located in Braddock and Rankin. The company played a role in high-profile construction projects around the world, including the Panama Canal, the Golden Gate Bridge, and the University of Pittsburgh's Cathedral of Learning. Beside joining Frick in the formation of the New York Shipbuilding Company of Camden, New Jersey, A.W. consolidated thirteen specialty steel companies into the Crucible Steel Company.[77]

While establishing a presence in steel, Mellon attempted to consolidate the region's fragmented coal industry by assembling the numerous small coal companies that depended on rail connections into the Pittsburgh Coal Company. The new entity included eighty thousand acres of coal land, five thousand railcars, and a railcar shop in Montour. Mellon also organized coal companies that depended on river transportation into the Monongahela River Consolidated Coal and Coke Company, which encompassed barges, coal tipples, barge-building facilities, coal ports, and riverboat companies. When the combination struggled, the two holding companies were consolidated as the Pittsburgh Coal Company with sixty-four mines and five thousand coal patch houses in 1917.[78]

But the notoriously individualistic coal industry never met Mellon's profit expectations. Other corporate investments, however, wildly exceeded expectations. The Mellons acquired majority or minority positions in scores of major corporations. Andrew Mellon, his biographer David Cannadine wrote, "had established himself by the mid-1900s decade as the single most significant individual in the economic life and progress of western Pennsylvania." Overall, their investments and speculative ventures in industry, streetcar lines, real estate, and banking, had elevated the Mellons to the top echelons of American wealth.[79]

SKYSCRAPERS AND THE CORPORATE ECONOMY

When news broke of Henry Oliver's death on the morning of February 8, 1904, newspapers extolled his contributions to Pittsburgh's industrial growth. They noted that Oliver, along with Frick and Phipps, had become a major investor in downtown real estate. In addition to scattered properties, he owned most of the block bounded by Smithfield Street, Sixth Avenue, Wood Street, and Virgin Alley (soon to be widened and renamed Oliver Avenue). The *Pittsburgh Dispatch* observed that since the sale of his industrial companies, Oliver had invested in real estate "for the improvement of the city." But he had also anticipated real estate's rewards.[80] Frick's poker mates on Thursday evenings viewed downtown real estate in a similar manner, almost as if they were playing Monopoly, as Oliver, Westinghouse, Carnegie, and Frick erected eponymously named downtown skyscrapers.

Soaring industrial growth had generated demand for offices to accommodate clerical, management, and professional personnel staffing corporations, financial institutions, and business service firms. Prior to the mid-1880s most administrative offices of manufacturing companies were attached to their production facilities or housed in walk-up buildings of five stories or less. The original buildings of T. Mellon & Sons, for example, were typical low-rise structures on Smithfield Street. The grander of the two, a four-story, cast-iron and masonry building, opened in 1871. By 1917 Pittsburgh's transit commissioner calculated that eighty-seven thousand people worked downtown.[81]

Elevators and steel frame construction made building skyscrapers possible. The industrialists and financiers occupied several floors and rented the remaining space. Not only good investments, skyscrapers proclaimed their owners' wealth and prominence. As railroads diminished the city's river trade, businesses gravitated to the center of downtown, away from the Monongahela wharf. Banks, insurance companies, brokerages, and the Pittsburgh Stock Exchange clustered around Fourth Avenue. During the first phase of erecting skyscrapers, oil, steel, and banking entrepreneur Jacob J. Vandergrift built an eight-story tower on Fourth Avenue, while iron and steel men David and William Park constructed the fifteen-story Park Building on Smithfield Street. Andrew Carnegie put up a fourteen-story tower on Fifth Avenue, famously leaving its steel frame exposed for a year to advertise the suitability of steel for skyscrapers. The Park and Carnegie buildings, which rose in the mid-1890s, were the city's earliest steel frame towers. Not to be left out, Westinghouse built a nine-story building, eventually expanding to twelve stories, on Penn Avenue near his Garrison Alley factory.[82]

With the city's financial and industrial companies flourishing as the economy rebounded after the 1893 depression, skyscrapers proliferated. By 1908 three dozen new ones, many over twenty stories, dramatically altered downtown's skyline. One-third of them were built by banks and financial service firms clustered in the Fourth Avenue financial district. Others were scattered from river to river. Henry Phipps's two towers facing the Sixth Avenue bridge across from Allegheny City were among the most notable.

So were H. C. Frick's buildings. He engaged architect Daniel Burnham, in demand after overseeing the hugely successful 1893 Chicago World's Fair, to erect the Frick and the Allegheny buildings. They towered over Carnegie's building, leading many to believe they were a deliberate snub of Carnegie, his former antagonistic partner. Grand railroad terminals complemented the city's close relationship with railroads. The B&O opened its station at Smithfield and the Monongahela wharf, Burnham designed the impressive Pennsylvania (Penn) Station at Grant Street and Liberty, P&LE placed its majestic terminal next to the Smithfield Street Bridge on the South Side, and the Wabash Terminal was located near the Point.[83]

Investing in skyscrapers declined after a severe flood and the financial panic in 1907. Before he died in 1904, Oliver considered building an office tower on Smithfield Street. After his death his executors hired architect Burnham and erected the handsome, twenty-five-story Oliver Building, another major contribution to the skyline. Frick also added the William Penn Hotel and the ornate Union Arcade (the Union Trust Building), both on Grant Street, before America's entry into World War I. The city, after years of debate, then lowered the hill (called the Hump) on Grant Street by sixteen feet, making the street even more attractive for investment. After the war the city constructed the City-County Building, which complemented architect H. H. Richardson's masterpiece, the Allegheny County Courthouse (1888). They were joined by other governmental buildings and corporate towers along Grant Street. Nevertheless, with stagnating industrial growth, downtown investment in office buildings lagged until the Pittsburgh Renaissance redevelopment began in the 1950s.[84] Half a century of investment downtown after the Civil War left a legacy of architectural distinction, landmarks to the region's industrial titans, and evidence of Pittsburgh's national significance.

INDUSTRIAL GROWTH SLOWS

Pittsburgh's industrial and corporate growth slowed in late October 1907 when financial panic erupted. The insolvency of several New York banks and brokerages spread to other financial centers, including Pittsburgh. The impending failure of the severely indebted local Whitney and Stephenson brokerage, linked to New York banks and widely connected within Pittsburgh's financial network, jeopardized several Pittsburgh banks. Simultaneously, three Westinghouse companies faced bankruptcy when an attempt to raise capital was undersubscribed. Share prices on the Pittsburgh Stock Exchange, especially those of the Westinghouse Electric and Manufacturing Company, plunged and the exchange suspended all trading for three months. Liquidity dried up and local bankers feared not being able to meet their obligations.

As business across the region rapidly declined, many predicted a prolonged depression.

Led by J. P. Morgan, America's wealthiest capitalists poured money into the national financial system to prevent the panic becoming a depression. The US Treasury supplied currency to many banks, while A.W. Mellon's financial maneuvering, some of which angered local bankers, tempered the damage to Pittsburgh's financial community from Whitney and Stephenson's bankruptcy. Even so, Fort Pitt National Bank, Hostetter-Connellsville Coal and Coke Company, and the large National Glass holding company collapsed. Meanwhile the receiverships of Westinghouse Electric, Westinghouse Machine, and Westinghouse's financial arm, the Security Investment Company, jeopardized the city's financial stability. In search of capital to fund expansion in the early 1890s, George Westinghouse had snubbed a deal with A.W. Mellon because it would have given the banker considerable influence over his affairs. Instead, he had turned to New York financiers. But the 1907 crisis allowed the Mellons to gain a foothold in Westinghouse's companies anyway. Despite its financial difficulties, Westinghouse Electric continued to attract worldwide orders for generators, transformers, and power plants. Reorganizing its finances prevented collapse, which would have had devastating consequences for the region, and the Westinghouse companies regained their solvency. But George Westinghouse lost control of his own creations, and the Mellons finally got a stake in them.

Though the local response and national intervention spared Pittsburgh a near fatal blow to its economy, the panic plunged the region into steep industrial decline. Demand for locally produced goods deteriorated and production of railroad locomotives and cars stalled. During 1908 regional steel output declined by one-third, coal and coke shipments by 50 percent, and manufacturing employment by one-third. Companies slashed dividends or ceased production altogether. As unemployment climbed, breadlines appeared. Although the Pittsburgh Stock Exchange reopened in late January 1908, it had been pushed to the margins of the nation's capital markets.[85]

A prolonged depression did not set in, but the ensuing recovery was slow. Most economic indicators returned to pre-panic levels by 1914, and World War I matériel orders completed the recovery. A few new steel and coke plants were constructed after the panic. Jones & Laughlin blew in its first blast furnaces at Aliquippa in 1909.[86] Two years later Crucible Steel opened an integrated mill at Midland down the Ohio River from Aliquippa, and U.S. Steel built its enormous by-product coke plant at Clairton in the waning years of the decade. Several key corporations, including Westinghouse Air Brake, Westinghouse Electric, Alcoa, Gulf Oil, and Heinz, rebounded.

However, the prosperity of the war years masked serious problems troubling the regional economy. Pittsburgh was too specialized in its emblematic iron and steel, coal and coke, and railroad industries. These industries stagnated or grew slowly during the 1920s and suffered during the Great Depression, never regaining their vigor of the pre–1907 panic years. Some companies faced strong competition from Chicago and elsewhere, while coal struggled. But several profitable non-steel firms such as Alcoa expanded nationally and abroad. However, Carnegie, Oliver, Westinghouse, Frick, and their fellow poker players no longer sat atop the city's industries. Some had retired, others had died, and a had few just played their cards poorly. The Pittsburgh region, which they and their fellow business leaders had labored to build, remained an industrial powerhouse for several decades, but it was unable to recover the buoyancy of the three decades following the 1870s depression and railroad strike. After 1920 Pittsburgh began a long, relative—much later absolute—decline in its national industrial and population stature.[87]

SIX

COMING TO PITTSBURGH

IN THE FALL OF 1881 TWENTY-ONE-YEAR-OLD GEORGE KRACHA LEFT A
highland village in the Austro-Hungarian province of Abavuska. His pregnant wife, a widowed mother, and an unmarried sister remained behind in a
one-room hut with a dirt floor, while Kracha traveled to Bremen, a port in
northwest Germany. There he boarded a ship for the voyage across the
North Atlantic, traveling in steerage, the cheapest, most basic accommodation. Thomas Bell, who created Kracha in *Out of This Furnace*, his multigen-
erational novel of immigrants in the Monongahela Valley, wrote that Kracha may have hoped that "he was likewise leaving behind the endless
poverty and oppression which were the birthrights of Slovak peasants in
Franz Joseph's regime." After spending eight years on a railroad gang in rural
Pennsylvania, Kracha headed to Homestead to work in a steel mill. He never
set foot outside the Monongahela Valley again. Although he escaped injury
on the job, Kracha neither climbed the mill's job ladder nor took pride in his
labor. Instead, he suffered the contempt that immigrants from the Austro-
Hungarian empire incurred. His grandson Dobie, however, joined the vanguard of steelworkers who organized a union during the Great Depression
and gave working people a measure of control over their lives.[1]

A few years after Kracha came to Pittsburgh, Agostino Carlino left his family in San Pietro Avellino, a town in Abruzzi, Italy, and traveled to Colorado.[2] Working alongside his brother in the mines, he saved enough to return to Italy and marry. But Carlino could not find satisfactory work in Italy and recrossed the Atlantic, this time to New York City. His third sojourn to America brought the stonemason to Pittsburgh. There Carlino stayed, making Bloomfield his home until his death in 1946. He and his wife Palmira bequeathed an enduring legacy to their children and grandchildren. Agostino's grandson became the Democratic Party ward chair in 1976 in the heavily Italian-American community. His great-grandson August R. Carlino blocked for future Hall of Famer Dan Marino at Central Catholic High School, attended the University of Pittsburgh, and after watching the steel industry collapse, led efforts to reclaim the city's steel heritage.[3]

A quarter of a century after Kracha and Carlino came to Pittsburgh, William Edlow Tinker joined them in the Steel City. Born on a plantation called Tinker's Farm before slavery's demise, William left sharecropping and the Alabama countryside for Birmingham when he was a young man. After several years of success as a barber and a realtor in the "Pittsburgh of the South," William lost his business and his home. He, like hundreds of thousands of African Americans, joined the great northern migration. Along with his oldest son Leon, William boarded a train for Pittsburgh, seeking work and the chance to leave Jim Crow behind. A year later the family reunited in the city's Hill District, where William stayed for the next half-century. Like most African Americans in Pittsburgh, he struggled to find secure work and equal rights. But at least the discrimination they encountered was less pernicious than what it had been in the South. They persevered and made a mark on the city. William and Mamie Tinker's young son Harold left his impression on the ballfield, where black Pittsburgh spearheaded a sporting renaissance in the 1930s. Harold captained the Pittsburgh Crawfords as they emerged on the Hill before becoming one of the most renowned ball clubs in baseball.

By the time Kracha, Carlino, and Tinker made Pittsburgh their home, James Davis was long gone. Steel chased the Welsh iron puddler away, welcoming new cohorts of European and African American laborers in his stead. The transition from iron to steel, largely complete by 1900, meant that skilled craftsmen like Davis were no longer so crucial to metal making. The craftsmen's empire they created in the region's mills and workshops had faded away. But for every native-born white or English-speaking craftsman made redundant by sweeping technological change, several new immigrants and black migrants found work in Pittsburgh and its industrializing river valleys.

The "old working classes" that Davis personified did not disappear quietly. Yet their decline in the workplace and at the ballot box established the parameters for those who came after them. These newcomers, the so-called new immigrants from southern, central, and eastern Europe, as well as those from the American South, poured into the region from the 1880s through World War I. Entering workplaces in the grasp of a self-confident and powerful industrial and financial elite, they were little more than disposable labor commodities. Working mind-numbing shifts, they frequently met death or dismemberment on the job and endured the scorn of native-born white people.

Pittsburgh attracted so many of these sojourners after 1880 that its population almost doubled to 451,000 by 1900. It grew by about a third again over the next two decades, to 588,343. Including the mill towns proliferating along the rivers, the region surged to roughly 1.3 million people in 1920, making it the nation's sixth largest metropolitan area.[4] As Pittsburgh and the region grew, their ethnic and racial makeup changed. Between 1880 and 1920 over half of the city's population was either foreign-born or had at least one foreign parent. Native-born white people whose parents had also been born in the United States were not in the majority until after 1930. Moreover, immigrants from England, Scotland, Wales, Germany, and Ireland, who made up over 90 percent of the foreign-born and almost one-fourth of the city's population in 1880, saw their proportion of the population shrink. By 1920 they comprised fewer than 35 percent of the foreign-born and only 7 percent of the overall population.[5]

These demographic transitions remade the city. In 1880 few "new immigrants" could be found in or near Pittsburgh, while African Americans, numbering over four thousand, constituted just 2.6 percent of the city. But their numbers in the city and nearby mill towns swelled, especially after 1900 as the Polish contingent in Pittsburgh increased by over a third and the population of Italians more than doubled. Though these foreign-born contingents began shrinking before World War I, Pittsburgh's black population continued to climb, reaching 37,725, or 6.4 percent of the city and 4.5 percent of the county, by 1920.[6] If their combined economic and cultural impact had been scant in 1880, it was strikingly evident by the twentieth century.

Many, perhaps a third of all immigrants, went back to Europe. Never intending to stay, they had only wanted to save enough to return to their homelands and live better than before. Those who stayed created their own neighborhoods. And when conditions, especially at work, became unbearable, they resisted the powerful corporate forces for whom they labored. These new immigrants could be found throughout the region. Slavs created multinational enclaves in Braddock, Duquesne, Homestead, and other mill towns, where in 1910 they and their children made up over 40 percent of the population. Poles settled on the South Side, in the Strip District, Lawrenceville, and on Polish (or Herron) Hill; Italians gravitated to the lower Hill, Bloomfield, East Liberty, Manchester, and McKees Rocks; and a majority of African Americans made the Hill their home, with sizable outposts in Manchester, Beltzhoover, and Homewood. Their legacies are still evident.[7]

These newcomers remade Pittsburgh's working classes but remained distant from the old working class and its once strong ethic of labor republicanism. Not only did they have little dialogue with the native-born or the Irish, Germans, and "Johnny Bulls,"[8] who had once comprised Pittsburgh's working-class vanguard; the new immigrants saw their predecessors more as part of management than fellow proletarians. Though their struggles were similar to those of the old immigrants, and they used comparable strategies for coping with life, they did so with fewer applicable craft skills, facing cultural and linguistic obstacles, against ever-stronger corporate opponents.

Several decades before either James Davis or Kracha arrived in Pittsburgh, Karl Marx argued that people made history, but not, he cautioned, under conditions they could choose for themselves. Instead, they lived and acted within their historical circumstances, "given and transmitted from the past," in which "the tradition of all dead generations weighs like a nightmare on the brains of the living."[9] Unlike James Davis's generation of skilled workers, the new immigrants that Kracha personified encountered a hard-charging, increasingly industrialized, corporate capitalism. They did not gain their voice at work, in the city's cultural and social life, or in politics until well after World War I. It took African Americans longer, and even then, their power remained constrained by racial disparities. Nevertheless, people like Kracha, Carlino, and Tinker, like earlier migrants, left as much of an imprint on Pittsburgh as its industrial and financial kingpins.

THE NEW IMMIGRANTS

As the global economy enveloped Europe's rural backwaters in the late 1800s, its relatively static peasant world began eroding. Economic power shifted west to cities where industrial capitalism had matured, leaving much of central, eastern, and southern Europe behind. Many peasants and rural workers had little choice but to leave their villages and find work elsewhere. The emancipation of the serfs had weakened the bonds holding people to the land. Owning small, fragmented pieces of land or nothing at all, they were unable to wring a living from the poor soil. Nor could the millions of "dwarf holders" with tiny plots of land or landless peasants find suitable local alternatives.[10]

Many looked for work elsewhere in Europe or headed to the Americas.

According to historian Ewa Morawska, at least one-third of the adults from the tremendous agrarian expanses of central and eastern Europe had lived and worked away from their birthplaces by the early twentieth century. Nine million people alone left Polish territories, another six million migrated either seasonally or permanently from Hungary before World War I, and in one intense wave of departures between 1906 and 1911, almost three million people left Austria.[11] By the twentieth century millions of peasant families had become habituated to seasonal migrations.[12]

There were two currents to this wave of unprecedented proletarian globetrotting. Part of it was a rural-to-rural movement as peasants hired themselves out as farm laborers in Germany, the Hungarian lowlands, and the Americas. The other current carried people to cities and factories. Men found jobs in Galician textile factories, Silesian mines, and as unskilled laborers in Warsaw, Budapest, and Lodz.[13] Groups of young women traveled to work on farms or in light industry, where they rolled cigars and operated looms, before returning home. Children often joined them, working for wages by the age of thirteen.[14]

Immigrants gravitated to the global economy's more dynamic centers. Some worked elsewhere in Europe. Others, because a route developed from their village or region to a particular city in the Americas, went directly overseas. Western Pennsylvania attracted disproportionate numbers of these émigrés to work in the complex of mills and mines that Pittsburgh's power brokers controlled.[15] In 1907 eastern Europeans held over 80 percent of the 14,359 common laborer jobs at Carnegie Steel's mills in Allegheny County.[16] For some immigrants the sojourn was temporary. For Kracha, who never returned home, going to America was a one-way voyage.[17]

By the turn of the century the peasant who had never ventured from his or her native village was the exception. Some eleven to twelve million people left eastern and central European seaports to cross the Atlantic between 1870 and the outbreak of World War I.[18] Far from being pulled kicking and screaming into the twentieth century, many sought new experiences and options. Exposed to wage labor, shift work, machinery, and managerial expectations before embarking for the United States, they were already partially enmeshed in cash economies. Rather than seeing themselves as passive objects of forces beyond their control, many willingly chased their own destinies. Their world was ever more secular, geared toward obtaining the tangible material rewards that capitalism offered. Countless émigrés never realized their dreams of greater security, status, and affluence in Pittsburgh and its satellite mill and mining towns. But coming to Pittsburgh at least offered the chance to create a new life abroad for themselves and their children or return home men of means.[19]

COMING TO AMERICA

Thomas Bell, born in Braddock in 1903, was the son of Mary and Michael Belejcak, who left the Slovak province of Sarisa in Austria-Hungary in 1890. Though he wrote *Out of This Furnace* as a work of fiction in 1941, Bell noted that he had "been as true to the events, the people and the place as lay within [his] power."[20] He based his characters on composites of family and neighbors. Few have so poignantly captured life in Pittsburgh's mill towns or captured their reality so clearly. George Kracha, who represented the first wave of immigrants, was full of foibles. Splurging on liquor to impress a young woman during the Atlantic crossing, he had less than a dollar left when he set foot on the docks in New York City. Thus he had to walk and hitch rides to White Haven, a town in Pennsylvania's anthracite coal region, where his sister Francka lived. Her husband, Andrej, worked on a railroad section gang made up of eastern Europeans. Kracha joined the gang, making ten cents an hour. When work was steady, he made as much as $25 in a month. But work was rarely steady.[21]

A few months after arriving in White Haven, Kracha learned that his wife, Elena, had given birth to a son. The following month's mail brought word of his son's death from a fever. Within a year Kracha saved enough to pay off the $20 he had borrowed from his brother-in-law for his passage over and to send for his wife. Elena by then had developed a disfiguring goiter, and though she bore three daughters, her relationship with Kracha was mutually unsatisfying. Kracha found some solace in his friendship with Joe Dubik, a Greek Catholic Slovak from Sarisa, with whom he shared a bed and many a bottle after arriving in White Haven.[22]

After a few years Dubik left for Pittsburgh's mills where a man, especially one from eastern Europe, could find more hours of work than on the railroads. He began working at the Edgar Thomson Works in Braddock. Kracha's sister and brother-in-law followed Dubik to the Monongahela River Valley, settling in Homestead instead of Braddock after Dubik warned them that Edgar Thomson's superintendent Captain Bill Jones had locked the workers out to force a wage cut and return of the twelve-hour day. After closing the mill for five months, the company won. Homestead's skilled steelworkers, however, retained their union and better working conditions until 1892. Unskilled laborers there, although not covered by their contract, fared better than in nonunion shops.[23]

Kracha, Elena, and their daughters joined friends and relations in the Monongahela Valley in 1889. Francka met the family at the Homestead train station and led them across the tracks into a murky, shabby, and crowded immigrant ghetto close to the mill known as the Ward. The air was so acrid that the newcomers began coughing and asked if it was always this smoky. Francka responded that "it was no worse than usual." During the strike, she added, there had been no smoke. "But no money, either."[24]

Kracha and Elena confronted the two questions newcomers faced: where to live and how to find work. Familial and ethnic connections were crucial in each case, just as they had been for the Carnegies in 1848 and for James Davis's family in 1881. Kracha and Elena stayed with Franka in her family's tiny apartment in a crowded tenement built around a courtyard with a communal privy until they were able to rent their own rooms, furnishing them with secondhand items. In the meantime Franka's husband spoke to his "pusher" about Kracha. Meeting the Irish assistant foreman at a saloon, Kracha bought him a shot of imported whiskey, while Andrej gave him a cigar and three dollars. With that transaction, Kracha joined the Irishman's work gang.[25]

Like many immigrants coming to Pittsburgh, Kracha had few marketable skills other than his ability to push and pull, shovel and lift. Once employed, these immigrants did not readily abandon their jobs despite the hardships they stomached at work. Prizing steady work, they helped compatriots get hired alongside them, creating beachheads in certain departments and mills. The densest concentrations were in steel- and metalworking, which employed about half of all the central and eastern European men working in Pittsburgh by 1900. They slotted in at the bottom of an industrial hierarchy largely defined by nationality and race. Native-born white, English-speaking immigrants, and their sons filled the ranks of skilled labor and supervisory positions. Eastern and central Europeans and African Americans took what was left. Mixing nationalities and races discouraged workers from banding together. Captain Bill Jones, who directed the construction of the Edgar Thomson Works for Andrew Carnegie and served as its supervisor, wrote in 1875 that "my experience has shown that Germans and Irish, Swedes and what I denominate 'Buckwheats' (young American country boys), judiciously mixed, make the most effective and tractable force you can find." Adding Slavs, Poles, and other nationalities made workers even easier to control.[26]

On his first day off, Kracha visited Dubik in nearby Braddock. His friend had lost weight, and Kracha thought he looked tired even as he slept. Dubik spoke of saving enough to leave the mills and buy land to farm. "Not for me," Kracha responded. "I got my fill of farming in the old country." Dubik retorted, "You will get your fill of the mills, too." Dubik showed Kracha the town's Carnegie Library, which he had never entered. "When do I have the time for such things?" Dubik lamented. "Since they cut wages and put us on twelve hours I've even stopped going to church. I was going to learn English, take out my first papers, try to educate myself a little." But Dubik was unable to fulfill his plans, hoping instead that his children would receive the benefits of his new homeland. "After all," he pointed out, "my children will be Americans, real Americans."[27]

Kracha and his family moved to Braddock, where he bribed his way onto a mill's work gang, and Dorta, Dubik's wife, found them two rooms built on a cinder dump. Depending on his shift, Kracha set out for work at 5:30 in the morning or 5:30 in the afternoon. His work gang tended a Bessemer blast furnace. Unlike James Davis, for whom iron making was the source of splendid self-esteem, Kracha simply followed orders. His work, difficult and dangerous, instilled little sense of worth.[28] Accident rates were markedly higher for men whose rudimentary English and lack of industrial experience rendered them more vulnerable than native-born skilled workers. The physician at Carnegie's Duquesne Works testified that, despite a company safety campaign, he routinely treated sixty to seventy men a day for injuries. In a single year 127 eastern Europeans died in Allegheny County steel mills. Crystal Eastman, who in 1910 wrote *Work, Accidents and the Law* for the Pittsburgh Survey, charged that Pittsburgh and its environs were responsible for "45 one-legged men; 100 hopeless cripples; . . . 45 men with a twisted useless arm; 30 men with an empty sleeve; 20 men with but one hand; . . . 70 one-eyed men—500 such wrecks in all" on an annual basis. She tallied 526 workplace fatalities in one year, almost half in steel mills.[29] Dubik, burnt badly in an accident, was one of the latter. His death was the catalyst to Kracha leaving the mill.

Twelve-hour shifts, seven days a week, contributed to the toll. A man worked days one week, nights the next. To get every other Sunday off, he put in a twenty-four-hour-shift on the Sunday of the week he worked days. Arriving home in the morning after that daylong shift, he returned to work that evening for the night turn. On those shifts, Bell wrote, "it was fatally easy to be careless." Kracha felt alive only when he worked days. "Night-turn weeks were periods of mental fog; he went back and forth to the mill in half a daze, which lasted until the end of his turn. . . . Only whiskey could pierce the shell of his weariness, warm him, and make him think well of himself and his world again."[30] Most mill workers, Bell wrote, endured their lot, believing it would someday change for the better. "But it never did. When human flesh and blood could stand no more it got up at five in the morning as usual and put on its work clothes and went into the mill; and when the whistle blew it came home."[31]

Dubik had been right that Kracha would have his fill of the mill. Steelmaking ebbed and flowed seasonally and in response to business conditions. Though Kracha accumulated money when work was steady, layoffs or underemployment routinely eroded his savings. In 1903, 1907–1908, and again in 1921–1922, severe economic downturns forced industry-wide layoffs. In those periods more foreign-born left than arrived.[32] But somewhere between Abavuska and Braddock, Kracha began internalizing a capitalist mentality. "The way to get rich in America," Kracha told Dorta, "is to go into business." Saving enough to buy a butcher shop in the fall of 1895, Kracha owned two horses and wagons, employed a man and two boys, and had a thousand dollars hidden in a steel box in his bedroom a year later.[33]

Kracha's prosperity was temporary. His downfall began with the return of Zuska, the woman on whom he had squandered his money during the Atlantic crossing. Zuska and her husband had settled on Pittsburgh's South Side. After her husband died from silicosis contracted while working at J&L's Second Avenue steelworks, Zuska moved to Braddock to stay with her sister. She walked into Kracha's shop one day, and they soon began an affair. Kracha's wife, Elena, frail and looking much older than her thirty-something years, rarely ventured from her home except to go to St. Michael's Church. She died not long after. The costs of Elena's funeral and keeping Zuska's household, in addition to losing customers upset over his behavior, rendered Kracha's finances precarious.[34] He married Zuska soon after Elena's death and promptly went on a two-month-long drunk. Sentenced to ten days in jail for beating Zuska, Kracha emerged from confinement in 1898 to find that his wife, his home, his business, and his property were gone. Two of his daughters found refuge with his sister Francka while the third, Mary, began working as a domestic for a well-to-do family.[35]

HOME AND COMMUNITY

By the time Kracha lost everything he had attained during twenty years in the United States, Mihal "Mike" Dobrejcak, another character in Bell's novel, had worked in Braddock for nine years. After his father died when he was fourteen, Mike, the eldest son, wrote Joe Dubik, who was from his village, to ask for assistance in finding work and a place to stay. Dubik helped Mike land a job as a water boy at Edgar Thomson and invited him to board with his family. Mike became a blast furnace laborer and then the furnace keeper's helper. He was in every respect, the "good man" that *dobrejcak* signified.[36]

Unlike many compatriots, Mike attended English classes and became literate in the language. Though paid the same fourteen cents an hour that most laborers made, he possessed a slightly better status as the furnace keeper's helper. Ethnic and racial patterns of hiring and job assignment were institutionalized in industry. In 1925 the Central Tube Company in McKeesport went so far as to chart the jobs and working conditions for which they thought each nationality was suited. Native-born white people were ranked as capable of almost any position, while Hungarians and Slovaks fared best among the thirty-four immigrant groups on the chart. They were viewed as good hires for most types of labor, whether wielding picks and shovels, working under hot and dry or cold and wet conditions, or on the day or night shift. Italians were considered less reliable, unable to work as boilermakers or engineers' helpers, while African Americans were of little value for anything but cleaning and demolition work. Jews were a lost cause as laborers, rated as helpless in almost every capacity.[37]

Unskilled immigrant laborers in an industry which bottomed out every few years were especially vulnerable to layoffs. After a decade in the mill Mike lamented his inability to save. Unlike Kracha, who sought his fortune in business, Mike wanted a good job that would allow him to raise a family with a degree of security. He wanted that even more when Kracha's daughter, Mary, paid a Sunday visit to Dorta on an afternoon when Mike was off work. Mary had been living with the family of a small manufacturer for whom she worked since Kracha's household fell apart. Now a woman, Mary dazzled Mike. "You don't look the same," he told her. "You look more like an American now."[38]

Mary worked and lived in a home with a telephone, bathroom, steam heat, and an icebox. Mike had never stepped foot inside such a house. One Sunday afternoon when the owners went to Kennywood, Mary took Mike through the home, where he gaped at furniture, beds, silverware, and other household things that "were desirable and beautiful in themselves and not merely as articles of use." Mary "proudly" showed the home, "almost as though it were her own," She looked like she belonged in such a setting. Attractive and Americanized, Mary understood the contrast in conditions that awaited her should she decide to marry Mike. He blurted out in Slovak, "This is the way a man should live." They dreamed of how they would accomplish such social mobility.[39]

After a brief courtship, they wed, and Mary gave birth to John Joseph "Dobie" Dobrejcak and three other children. But Mike's expectation of a better job was never realized. "There was a time when I thought I'd surely get a good job sometime," Mike reflected after twenty years in the mill. "I worked hard. I did what I was told and more. And I've seen them hire Irish, Johnny Bulls, Scotties, just off the boat . . . and in a year they're giving me orders. . . . But I'm a Hunky; and they don't give good jobs to Hunkies. God damn their souls to hell."[40]

Though Mike resisted taking in boarders because he felt the work would make a drudge out of Mary, perpetual financial distress forced him to relent. The physical toll of laundering clothes soiled in the mill and keeping a home clean not far from belching smokestacks without running water was taxing. Mary rose by 4:30 each morning to pack a half-dozen boarders' double-decker lunch buckets with hot drinks in the bottom and thick meat sandwiches in the upper compartment, along with pickles, pastry, and fruit.[41] Boardinghouses were home for better or worse to a majority of single immigrants and those separated from their own families. Each house usually accommodated men of the same nationality with Serbian, Slovak, Croatian, and Hungarian boardinghouses side by side in multiethnic mill-worker ghettoes.[42]

While boarders frequently had personal or familial connections to their hosts, the relationship was a calculated business transaction. For a man on his own, boarding was a viable strategy. An immigrant's pay was insufficient to support a family, but a man who boarded could take care of most needs and still save a third of his wages. The boarder relinquished privacy, sharing a room and often a bed with other men. The host family lost its privacy too, and Mike feared that he would end up feeling like a boarder in his own home. But boarders contributed thirty dollars a month to his household, enough to allow the family to pay down debts and begin to save.[43] For an unattached immigrant man, boarding was an expedient way to live until he returned to Europe or married. Sitting on plank benches and dining with his hosts and fellow boarders came as close to a family setting as he would likely find. Neighborhood taverns, where men often stopped for a drink both to and from work, offered additional chances for socializing within a mostly male domain. Braddock, Duquesne, and McKeesport together had 164 saloons.[44]

Boarding drained women but mill towns offered them few alternatives to earn money. Young girls worked as domestics and older women laundered other families' clothes, but work in the mills and workshops that powered the regional economy was off limits to females. More women worked for wages across the river in Pittsburgh, rolling cigars and in the garment trades, but domestic service was the biggest employer of female labor well into the twentieth century.

Women were more visible in churches and fraternal associations, which bolstered kinship and boardinghouse bonds. Organized throughout the Monongahela Valley by the 1890s, fraternal societies brought together immigrants from similar European backgrounds in groups of fifty to four hundred members. Most formed out of necessity. The dangers millworkers confronted compelled them to pool some of their limited earnings in mutual aid societies, to which they turned in case of sickness, accident, or death. The National Slavonic Society paid $1,000 after the death of a member and five dollars a week when a member was sick. Dues were sixty cents a month.[45]

The associations, which numbered in the hundreds in the Monongahela Valley alone, shaped social life, sponsoring dances at Christmas and before and after Lent. Offering a treasured cultural counterpoint to the drudgery of mill town life, fraternal groups also reinforced national identities. They distributed newspapers published in the immigrants' native languages and helped to organize their spiritual lives. Fraternal associations were often cat-

157

alysts to the creation of new parishes for nationality groups. In Braddock the Slovak steelworkers, who formed the Sick-Benefit Society of Saint Michael the Archangel, petitioned for the creation of St. Michael's Church in 1890. Purchasing the building that had housed the First Christian Church since the Civil War, the Society required its members to join the church. St. Michael's symbolized a larger transition in the valley's demography. As older, English-speaking residents moved out, the new immigrants took over their churches and residences. After a church was in place, the fraternal association raised funds to create a parochial school, usually staffed by European priests and nuns. The church–fraternal association relationship also spawned gymnastic societies modeled on the Sokol movement from the Czech region of the Austro-Hungarian Empire as well as basketball and baseball teams.[46]

While strengthening local ties, the churches stitched together a more inclusive identity. St. Michael's, the first Slovak church in the Pittsburgh diocese, drew members from over a dozen Monongahela Valley and Turtle Creek towns. Though churches, the ethnic press, and fraternal associations reinforced ethnic identities, they also helped immigrants cope and, to an extent, become more "American." St. Michael's priest, Alderbert Kazincy, held English classes to prepare Slovaks for citizenship examinations. The Slovak League of America in Duquesne and the Kosciusko Political Club in Homestead similarly promoted citizenship along with welfare and cultural endeavors.[47]

WHEN THE RIVER RAN RED

Kracha and Mike labored in a setting that would have been increasingly alien to James Davis and the skilled men of earlier decades. The introduction of Bessemer converters and open-hearth furnaces had radically altered the workplace. These new processes demanded a greater number of unskilled hands but had less need for the craftsmen who once controlled production. Comparable technological changes remade glass factories with a similar downside for craftsmen. Losing its purchase in the workplace, the labor movement subsequently exerted less clout in politics and the neighborhoods. Labor's energy and will flagged throughout the region, as it did nationally. Homestead, the only unionized steel mill left in the region by 1889, was labor's last redoubt. In 1892 Homestead's workers lost their war too.

During the days when craftsmen could hire and direct their own helpers and bargain over output and wages from a position of strength, laborers worked on teams led by skilled workers. They shared a mutual self-interest over working conditions and pay. Usually of similar ethnic backgrounds and often related to each other, the unskilled hoped to one day fill skilled positions. But steel's radical transformation of the workplace altered the composition of the workforce and eroded the common ground between the skilled and unskilled. They no longer worked together in teams or came from the same heritage. "Workers in the same plant," David Brody concluded, "skilled and unskilled men shared little more than a common employer."[48]

Though working for the same company, they lived, prayed, and played apart from each other. The skilled worker's vision of his household included a stay-at-home wife and children enrolled in school without strangers in their midst. Taking in boarders signified that a man was not making it on his own labor and by the turn of the century, few semiskilled or skilled workers took in lodgers. Nor did their children work outside the home as frequently as did those of the new immigrants. By the 1880s the children of better-off workers stayed in school longer to enhance their prospects. Deferring work to gain more education, historian S. J. Kleinberg argued, was a luxury few unskilled families could afford.[49] The differences in living conditions and their consequences were graphic. Native-born white people were twice as likely to have running water and much more likely to have a toilet in their homes. Twice as many Slavic children died before the age of two as their English-speaking contemporaries, nor did they stay in school or live as long. Divisions over religion and nationality undermined solidarity at work and in the community, just as they had when Irish and German immigrants flooded the city before the Civil War.[50]

According to historian Paul Krause, Homestead's working classes in the 1880s bucked the xenophobic tide overtaking much of the nation. He described the mill town as "the last bastion of labor republicanism in Greater Pittsburgh," where workers were able to overcome their differences to defend their rights. But if Homestead's labor movement welcomed unskilled immigrants, its counterparts elsewhere reflected nativist sentiments and retreated to a more conservative stance.[51] Consequently, solidarity that cut across nationality lines was hardly in evidence. America's embrace of the oppressed of the earth, the *National Labor Tribune* wrote in 1882, "certainly never contemplated the introduction of so miserly low carrion as these Huns, the worst probably of the civilized world's people. . . . The republic cannot afford to have such ignorant animals within its borders." In language and logic earlier employed to characterize Irish and German immigrants as carriers of disease, disorder, and crime, editor Thomas Armstrong warned that this new wave of immigrants would have dire consequences. "No words that can be formulated can exaggerate the utter brutality of the Huns now in Pennsylvania. Their uncleanliness of person is only equaled by their beastliness as to morals and depravity of appetite."[52] The *Tribune* called for strict limits on immigration in 1882 and continued to see the immigrants as a threat a quarter of a century later. "The Poles, Slavs, Huns and Italians," it wrote, "come over without any ambition to live as Americans live and . . . accept work at any wages at all, thereby lowering the tone of American labor as a whole."[53]

But in Homestead, according to Krause, the new immigrants had found common ground with labor republicanism rooted in notions of communal solidarity and the desire for security. In the old country decisions were often made collectively by families or villages. The eastern and central Europeans who began arriving in the early 1880s also pursued *ist' za chlebom*. This Slovak saying conveyed the desire for bread and a livelihood. To Krause, these goals were similar to what skilled workers sought and made it in their self-interest to shore up support among the unskilled. In return, the immigrants' pay and working conditions were linked to those of the skilled.[54] Cutting against the grain of the Amalgamated Association's national leadership, some Homestead lodges even admitted unskilled workers. Slavic workers also mingled with skilled workers at a few bars and billiard parlors, but for the most part the new immigrants were isolated from the English-speaking men in the mill.[55]

Up to a thousand eastern Europeans worked at the Homestead Steel Works in 1892. Some had taken part in the 1882 strike and again in the 1889 lockout, during which their solidarity with the craftsmen was indispensable to labor's victory. But Andrew Carnegie, who purchased the Homestead Works in 1883, and Henry Clay Frick, the antiunion president of Carnegie Steel, bridled at the union's power. They vowed to crush the union, revamp production, and replace skilled workers with machines and un-skilled laborers. After turning the mill into an armed camp, the company locked the men out on June 30, 1892. If workers did not return on management's terms, Carnegie and Frick would bring in men who would.

When Carnegie and Frick forced a showdown, eastern and central Europeans were loyal partners of the skilled men. Though most did not belong to the union, they knew their working conditions would deteriorate if the union was ousted. When the mill's seven hundred unionized skilled men stayed off the job, over four times that number—virtually the entire workforce—joined them in an act of solidarity. During the lockout many immigrant workers joined the Knights of Labor, a progressive labor federation which collaborated with the Amalgamated Association. But Carnegie and Frick were undeterred. On July 6, 1892, barges packed with three hundred armed Pinkerton guards came up the Monongahela River to escort strikebreakers into the steelworks to resume production. When armed workers met them at the landing, the river ran red as almost a dozen Pinkertons and workers died.[56] The strikebreakers were routed. Peter Fares, a Slovak who worked as a helper in the open-hearth department, was among those shot dead during the July 6 battle. So were another Slovak, two skilled

Welsh steelworkers, two English mill hands, a German teamster, and a native-born American.[57] Though the workers won the battle of Homestead, Carnegie called on Pennsylvania governor Robert Pattison to intervene. Beholden to Carnegie, Pattison rushed in thousands of state militia to occupy Homestead and safeguard strikebreakers into the mill. Pittsburghers reviled the militia, spitting "Cossack" and other epithets at them, but the mill reopened and the union was crushed. The steel company would prevail on the shop floor until the revival of industrial unionism in the 1930s.[58]

Labor's loss in the Homestead clash was the handwriting on the wall. Though workers' resistance did not entirely disappear, it went underground.[59] Subsequent campaigns to rebuild a steelworkers union were defeated. People often told Margaret Byington, a contributor to the Pittsburgh Survey, that "if you want to talk in Homestead, you must talk to yourself."[60] In 1909 U.S. Steel announced that it would henceforth run as an open shop, free of unions. It also tried to Americanize immigrants and sons of immigrants, introducing piecemeal reforms. But these efforts did not eliminate worker discontent. If anything, the more these men felt themselves to be Americans, the more they resisted the company. That resistance flared during a decade-long labor upsurge that culminated in the steel strike of 1919.

BECOMING AMERICANS

By the early twentieth century sizable numbers of the foreign-born and their offspring had coalesced into communities throughout the region. Even while many cycled back and forth from Europe and remained physically detached from English-speaking sections of town, their communities were digging in. Most immigrants endured wretched work only as long as they thought it temporary, and eventually significant numbers did better their standing. The longer a man stayed, the greater the likelihood he would send for his wife or marry an immigrant woman or daughter of an immigrant and become invested in his new surroundings.[61] Once they had children and baptized and educated them in the United States, there was little chance they would return to Europe. As they began viewing their residence in Pittsburgh and its environs as permanent, they confronted what it meant to become Americans. But Americanization did not occur in a vacuum, nor did it mean shucking identities brought from Europe along with their few belongings.[62]

Often ignored by English-speaking Americans, the immigrants remained of great interest to the corporations for whom they comprised the bulk of the unskilled workforce. Steel companies, especially U.S. Steel, sought to control virtually every aspect of their lives. Since defeating the Amalgamated Association in 1892, the steel companies had gained increasing sway over the political and social affairs of the Monongahela Valley. U.S. Steel plant managers and superintendents directed local banks, held elective offices, and were prominent in churches, extending their influence well beyond the factory gates.[63]

As part of a multipronged strategy before World War I, U.S. Steel and other companies sought to Americanize foreign-born employees. Their actions were in response to unfavorable attention generated by the Pittsburgh Survey, but also a practical personnel calculation. The Russell Sage Foundation, a Progressive Era think tank, dispatched researchers to Pittsburgh in 1907. Their findings laid bare industrialization's devastating impact in the workplace and home. One of its researchers, Margaret Byington, spent the year talking with women in Homestead. She visited fetid tenement courtyards, where one in three Slavic children died before reaching two years of age, and saw the toll of millwork—crushed feet, lacerated hands, amputated limbs, and fatherless families. Her Pittsburgh Survey volume, *Homestead: The Households of a Milltown*, described how drinking water fouled by raw sewage spread disease and ravished children and their parents.[64] The Pittsburgh Survey painted a dystopian picture of working-class life in the city and its environs and prompted a minimalist corporate response. In 1908 U.S. Steel created a Bureau of Safety, Relief, Sanitation, and Welfare to focus on workplace safety, arrange English lessons, organize playground activities, and hold classes in cooking, sewing, and sanitation for wives and daughters. This Americanization from the top down dovetailed with pragmatic attempts to improve plant safety and working conditions, offering just enough to keep workers reasonably compliant and absolutely nonunion.[65] And if that did not snuff out union sentiments, companies turned to blacklists, informants, and security forces to enforce discipline.

Workplace reforms, especially profit-sharing and pension plans, targeted skilled native-born white workers, but did not entirely ignore new immigrant or black workers. Water fountains, day care nurseries for children of men killed at work, and instruction in English so that workers could better understand safety signs and orders did not require shortening twelve-hour shifts or significantly raising wages. The safety campaign, which led to a 43 percent decline in serious accidents nationally in four years, also cut costs.[66]

Other reforms focused on the world outside the plant and were designed to win community goodwill. U.S. Steel's community-based welfare activities included playgrounds, gardens, baseball leagues, English classes, and a nursing corps that made home visits. Homestead superintendent L. C. Gardner lauded his plant's efforts, arguing that it was good business to make the life of its workforce "as pleasant as possible." A recreation program, he explained, would ensure "workers coming to work refreshed and alert and in a happy frame of mind." Gardner even suggested that recreation instilled a sense of organization and ideology. "It trains leaders to work with the company and does so in non-controversial subjects, so that these leaders are likely to be anchors to windward when outside leaders attempt to gather a following." He proposed twenty-eight activities, including team sports, playgrounds, and festivals, that firms should consider. At the Schwab Manual Training School a few blocks from the Homestead mill, boys learned how to work with metal and wood, while girls practiced the domestic sciences in a technical school donated by the works' former general superintendent.[67]

While steel corporations advanced an agenda to win immigrants' allegiance and better control them at work and the ballot box, diverse voices inside ethnic communities also sought to persuade their compatriots to become citizens. Receptivity to becoming American reflected the degree to which immigrants felt the United States had become their permanent home. The gaps between American ideals and realities could be disconcerting, and many who remained never reconciled with their new country. Nor did Americanization hold only one meaning. Kracha viewed becoming an American in terms of upward mobility; his son-in-law, Mike, perceived it in terms of political rights and citizenship.[68]

Unlike Kracha, Mike never adjusted to the contempt he felt from native-born white people and "older" immigrants. Kracha, Bell wrote, could shrug off being called a Hunky, for "he had come to America to find work and save money, not to make friends with the Irish." But Kracha's resignation to inequality, Bell argued, was not acceptable to the next generation.[69] Mary too had been hurt by the insults of native-born classmates who belittled her and other immigrant girls because they did not wear undergarments. "I hated Braddock," Mary later confessed. "I didn't know anybody and the American girls were always making fun of us."[70]

Mike, though born abroad, identified more with the second generation and was barely able to contain his resentments. "You're a smart Hunky and I don't like smart Hunkies," a gang boss told him. With no union at his back, Mike was vulnerable. His closest friend warned him not to voice his thoughts too openly. "I can remember when people weren't afraid," Mike responded. "Now fear is everywhere, spreading suspicion and bitterness, draining every man's heart of courage and making honesty a sin against his family's bread." Close to despair, he asked, "Why must only poverty and meanness be our portion?"[71] Another time Mike cried out. "We can't even open our mouths. Even a dog is allowed to howl when he's kicked, but we? We have to carry it inside ourselves until it tastes so bitter we want to vomit. But blessed God, a man can hold only so much and one of these days they'll learn it. Someday ..."[72]

Mike applied for citizenship papers as soon as he could and exercised his franchise as a citizen. By World War I he wasn't the only immigrant seeking to be heard. Kracha, however, never became a citizen and wanted only to be left alone. "I've been in America long enough to learn that it's run just like any other country," he lectured Mike. While royalty ruled in Europe, "over here it's your millionaires and your trusts. . . . Your vote means nothing. The company man always wins." As novelist Bell wryly noted, the only uncertainty about an election in Braddock was the weather.[73]

Kracha reflected how deeply some immigrants had internalized notions of feudal privilege and inequality and how easily these attitudes were transferred to their new surroundings. Central European peasants were accustomed to a condescending paternalism laced with open contempt, but these "simple, religious, unwarlike people," as Bell described them, changed in America. Deference and detachment from politics were part of their cultural baggage, but many wanted to claim democratic rights and improve their quality of life and the quantity of their goods.[74]

In the 1916 presidential election Mike secretly cast his ballot for Socialist Party candidate Eugene Debs and lived in trepidation that his act of defiance would be discovered and cost him his job. Debs polled 15 percent of Allegheny County's vote in 1912 and 25 percent in sixteen western Pennsylvania steel towns. Socialist candidates did even better in local elections, electing councilmen or mayors in Turtle Creek, McKeesport, Pitcairn, and New Castle. But neither Socialists nor Democrats won in Braddock, Homestead, or Duquesne, mill towns closer to Pittsburgh. "I met more socialists in Homestead and Munhall than elsewhere," John Fitch wrote in his volume for the Pittsburgh Survey. But most men told him that "to be known as a socialist . . . would be to court discharge."[75] There the steelworks remained nonunion, a legacy of the workers' defeat in 1892 and subsequent defeats in 1895, 1899, and 1901. Mike did not live long enough to witness the laborers' redemption. His son Dobie would.[76]

LABOR'S UPSURGE

Neither Joe Dubik nor Mike Dobrejcak made it "out of this furnace" alive. Like thousands of workers, their lives were sacrificed on big steel's shop floor. Other men had their fill of twelve-hour shifts, nagging respiratory ailments, and ethnic slights and returned to their homelands, grateful not to have perished in a blast furnace explosion, from asphyxiation by furnace gas, or by falling into a molten pit. But those who stayed fashioned lives in Pittsburgh. An array of institutions—public schools, settlement houses, factories, and government agencies—tried to persuade immigrants and their children to exchange their ethnic identities and radical proclivities for values and behaviors inspiring patriotism and company loyalty. The onset of World War I and around-the-clock production accelerated those efforts. So did immigration laws in the 1920s which sharply limited the number of immigrants from southern, eastern, and central Europe.

But "Americanism," historian James Barrett pointed out, "was, in fact, a contested ideal." Industrial and urban reality looked different from the new immigrants' vantage point on the shop floor and in mill town apartments than it did from managerial offices or Pittsburgh's East End. Immigrants, Barrett observed, were not simply lumps of clay easily molded by paternalistic forces. They were committed to "Americanization from the bottom up," ever more serious about claiming their rights as citizens. For many that meant greater control over their working lives and engagement in civil society. Like Mike Dobrejcak's fictional son Dobie, they became Americans by dint of their own experiences, by defining notions of democracy and equality on their own terms, and by fighting for their rights.[77]

That was not what their employers had anticipated when they promoted a corporate version of Americanism. Ironically, by stressing the critical role of steel in the war effort, these corporations unintentionally boosted their workers' sense of self-worth. The foreign-born responded enthusiastically to wartime rhetoric that placed them on the metaphorical front lines. Buying war bonds and marching in loyalty day parades alongside German-American, Irish-American, and native-born workers, they sent their sons off to war. Most of all, they worked hard in the mills, where blast furnace laborers averaged eighty-two hours a week. U.S. Steel gave flagpoles to parochial schools, underwrote patriotic displays, and raised money for the war effort. During the Fourth Liberty Loan campaign, Homestead Works superintendent A. A. Corey urged each worker to buy twenty-five days' pay worth of bonds. It was more than a suggestion, and Corey claimed that 100 percent of "his men" had participated, allowing the steelworks to raise over two million dollars, an average of $176 per employee. Even though coerced, these sacrifices made immigrants feel that they belonged and were worthy of citizenship and rights.[78]

Pittsburgh's elites reaped what they had sown. They had looked down on the new immigrants ever since they arrived, viewing them as a source of disease and social chaos. But immigrants were a necessary and seemingly inexhaustible source of cheap labor, and corporations successfully thwarted their desire for higher wages and excluded them from civic and political life. But their fear of the immigrants was a self-fulfilling prophecy, and Americanization became a double-edged sword. Given wartime demands for labor, manufacturing concerns treated immigrant workers and their sons better during the conflict, promoting some to skilled positions. Accorded greater respect and new opportunities, they expected that their lot at work would continue to improve. But after the war these expectations were shattered as returning veterans bumped many new immigrants back to common labor status. The economy's sharp postwar recession meant they were no longer in demand. Valued for their patriotism during the war, they were "Hunkies" again when it was over. Frustrated and angry, steelworkers revolted in a massive strike for union recognition in 1919.[79] The steel strike, in which a quarter of a million men across the nation walked off the job, was the culmination of a decade-long national labor upsurge that began in 1909. In 1919 one in five workers across the country went on strike. As in 1877 and 1892 Pittsburgh was ground zero for labor's insurgency.

American workers rode a roller coaster after the Civil War, buffeted by a boom-and-bust economy marked by deep depressions. Even in the best of times workers were frequently overwhelmed by corporate forces able to call on state power to settle strikes on management's behalf. The 1909–1919 labor upsurge occurred against a backdrop of corporate consolidation and a changing workplace. By the twentieth century corporations were ever bigger, more powerful, and more complex. With multiple plants across the country and supply chains and markets crossing national boundaries, modern corporations had diversified product lines and increased market share. They embraced the gospel of scientific management as the means to increase efficiency, production, and profitability. But industrial efficiency squeezed take-home pay and encouraged managers to relentlessly drive their workers. In steel, labor plummeted from 22 to 16 percent of production costs between 1890 and 1910. For workers, this reorganizing production meant speedups, frequent layoffs, and a loss of control over the process of work itself. They wanted more than that and responded with direct, often militant, action.[80]

By the early twentieth century the intense labor activism of the 1890s, which erupted in Homestead in 1892, had largely dissipated. Craft unions became more conservative, representing skilled white males and protecting their place in the workplace hierarchy. Unskilled workers, especially if they were immigrant, black, or female, were without a collective voice. But when the economy revived following the swift downturn of 1907–1908, so did working-class agitation. These struggles defied both managerial authority and the more conservative strategies of the American Federation of Labor (AFL). Two currents of protest emerged, one of the unskilled and semi-skilled over wages and working conditions, the other of skilled workers seeking greater control over production. They struggled, however, to unite their own ranks, and rarely submerged ethnic and skill differences long enough to win their demands. These divisions over skill and nationality led to defeats at the Pressed Steel Car Company in McKees Rocks in 1909, the

Westinghouse complex of factories in Turtle Creek and East Pittsburgh be-tween 1914 and 1916, and the 1919 strike in steel.

Corporate leaders might have shrugged off the Pittsburgh Survey's mul-tifaceted critique of life in the region, which lambasted their callous disre-gard of labor and the environment, but they could not ignore the ferocious conflicts that reinforced the national image of Pittsburgh as a hotbed of la-bor militancy. Although this generation of working people would not reach labor's promised land, their children would renew their struggle in the 1930s.[81]

The Pressed Steel labor impasse, though deadlier than the 1892 shoot-out in Homestead, left much less of a mark in accounts of these times. Pressed Steel's leaders could not match Carnegie's panache or Frick's unfeel-ing demeanor, and its principal working-class protagonists were foreign-born. About five miles down the Ohio River from the Point, McKees Rocks was one of several industrial suburbs along Pittsburgh's rivers. Over two-thirds of its residents were foreign-born or their children, the majority from eastern Europe. Most worked for the Pressed Steel Car Company, the na-tion's second-largest manufacturer of railroad cars. They lived in the "Bot-toms" by the river or in Presston, a company town commonly derided as "Hunky Town," where residents were required to shop at a company store. About three-quarters of Pressed Steel's 4,700 employees were unskilled or semiskilled immigrants; the remainder were native-born or English-speaking immigrants holding skilled positions. In all, sixteen different na-tionalities worked there.[82]

Relations between the company's foreign-born and English-speaking workers had never been good; interactions between workers and manage-ment were worse. The company's first owners had earned a reputation, even among their peers, as callous autocrats. Their factory was commonly re-ferred to as "The Slaughterhouse" or "The Last Chance." A former coroner claimed that on average, somebody died on the job once a day. A. F. Toner, a priest at St. Mary's Roman Catholic Church, told the *Pittsburgh Leader* that "men are persecuted, robbed, and slaughtered, and their wives are abused in a manner worse than death—all to obtain or retain positions that barely keep starvation from the door."[83] New management sought to repair labor relations by tying an incentive pay system to a revamped assembly line that allowed some unskilled immigrants to earn almost as much skilled workers. But after virtually shutting down for eighteen months during the 1907–1908 recession, management terminated the incentive pay scheme when production resumed in early 1909.[84]

Foreign-born workers were dismayed when they received their pay in late July, convinced that the company had shorted them. When manage-ment refused to listen to their grievances, all except for the skilled native-born workers put down their tools and vowed to shut down the plant. Strikers marched through McKees Rocks, taking positions on the bridge connecting the town with Pittsburgh's North Side. In the morning they stopped nearly all American-born workers, most of whom lived on the North Side, from crossing the Ohio River to go to work. Skilled workers had shown little inclination to strike, but after realizing that the foreign-born were adamant about the shutdown and management just as stubborn in its refusal to negotiate, they formed a common front with the strikers. Their unity was short-lived. Skilled workers, eager to return to work as soon as possible, were willing to compromise on demands of concern to the unskilled. Unsurprisingly, the foreign-born were not. Meeting on their own, they twice rejected proposed settlements and contacted the Industrial Workers of the World (IWW) for help. Founded just a few years before, the IWW espoused a revolutionary industrial unionism that appealed to the great majority of workers who had been ignored by the craft unions. By then unity with skilled workers had splintered.

The company announced that it would no longer negotiate and hired Pearl Bergoff, an infamous strikebreaker, to restore production. Bergoff's private force of thugs, supported by five hundred state constables and deputy sheriffs, clashed with strikers when they escorted strikebreakers down the river from Pittsburgh. Skirmishes climaxed on "Bloody Sunday," August 22, when gun battles left as many as twenty-six people dead and scores injured. Martial law was declared the next day, and state troopers went door-to-door, seizing weapons from the foreign-born. Meanwhile, leaders representing skilled workers resumed secret discussions with the company and reached an agreement that restored their prestrike status quo and made a few concessions. This induced most men to return to work. While many foreign-born workers protested at the plant gates, nearly two thousand other workers, some armed and many of whom were also foreign-born, easily broke through the picket lines. The strike was over but not foreign-born laborers' discontent.

The inability of unskilled and skilled workers to forge a viable alliance reflected labor's fundamental dilemma. The struggles of one group were not necessarily embraced by the other. Most skilled workers, if inclined to seek union affiliation, turned to the AFL. Immigrant workers looked more favorably on the IWW. The Wobblies, as the IWW was called, maintained a strong presence in Pittsburgh after the McKees Rocks strike, organizing meat packers, miners, and mill workers. Strikes flared, but none of the magnitude of the Pressed Steel walkout. In the Hill District the center of the stogie industry, 1,200 women and men enrolled in the IWW Tobacco

Workers Local No. 101 demanded union recognition. Stogie manufacturers locked them out in 1912, but the mostly Jewish workers held out for eighteen weeks and won a union shop. That same year two thousand central and eastern Europeans, led by the local socialist journalist Fred Merrick, struck National Tube in McKeesport.[85] Enduring unity was hard to forge, but activists like Merrick tried anyway.

The Westinghouse strikes in 1914 and 1916 were the high-water mark for workers sticking together despite skill and ethnic differences. In 1914 fourteen thousand men and women walked off their jobs at the Westinghouse Electric and Manufacturing Company in Turtle Creek. Their independent union demanded recognition, a grievance process, rehiring workers fired for trying to organize the union, a fair system to determine layoffs, and an end to all piece, premium, and bonus pay systems. Once again workers sought out the IWW, trusting its radical leadership more than the AFL. While skilled, native-born men led the campaign, they saw the necessity of involving their foreign-born workmates. Each nationality chose its own delegates to speak and translate for them at meetings; ballots were printed in Slavic, Hungarian, and Croatian as well as in English and German. In Turtle Creek barbers cut strikers' hair for free one day a week, and bakers brought coffee and doughnuts to the picket line each morning. But impressive unity and community backing were not enough to defeat the giant Westinghouse Corporation, and the strike petered out.[86]

Two years later, on Good Friday, April 21, 1916, some forty thousand strikers shut down Westinghouse's massive complex in nearby East Pittsburgh. As in 1914 they showed little interest in AFL unions and acted on their own. This time immigrant and less-skilled workers were even more involved in the strike and its leadership. Their central demand was an eight-hour workday, which they saw as a way to avoid overwork and live fuller lives. For ten days growing numbers of men and women engaged in meetings, parades, mass picketing, and plant invasions. Amid sporadic violence and arrests, strikers shut down other Westinghouse companies, including the Union Switch and Signal in Swissvale, the Pittsburgh Meter Company, and the Westinghouse Machine Company. On May 1 several thousand people paraded through the Monongahela Valley into Braddock and Rankin. After disrupting passenger trains, they broke down the iron gates at the Edgar Thomson Works, overwhelmed eighty Coal and Iron Police, and exhorted workers inside to put down their tools.[87]

Strikers returned in greater numbers the next day. When a crowd converged on Edgar Thomson at noon, police with riot sticks backed up by armed guards confronted them. Rocks were thrown and shots fired as several thousand special deputies, railroad, and Coal and Iron Police rebuffed repeated attempts to enter the mill. The violence at Edgar Thomson was a turning point in the strike. After several people were killed and others wounded, the governor ordered National Guard units to patrol Braddock and East Pittsburgh. Despite their militancy and the unity forged among different national groups and between skilled and unskilled workers, they could not withstand state power. With troops guarding factories and mills, most workers soon returned to their jobs. A grand jury indicted Fred Merrick, radical activists, and a cross section of workers, and Pittsburgh's workers again suffered defeat.

THE 1919 STEEL STRIKE

Three years elapsed before labor's next great outburst. In 1919 steelworkers in Pittsburgh joined those in nine other states and struck for union recognition. The walkout had ramifications well beyond the steel industry. Union membership in mass-production industries had doubled during and after the war. But steel, the bastion of the open shop, stood in the way of further organizing. "If unionism entrenched itself here," labor historian David Brody reasoned, "the entire mass-production sector could be swept into the labor fold."[88]

World War I tested the industry's sway over its workforce. "The Gods," radical activist William Z. Foster later wrote, "were indeed fighting on the side of Labor. [It] was an opportunity to organize the industry such as might never again occur." As the mills ran full blast, the war in Europe constricted the flow of cheap, unskilled labor from overseas. The supply of labor diminished further when the United States entered the war, radically altering labor relations and prompting the federal government to intervene to ensure uninterrupted production.[89] Though steel corporations resisted bargaining with unions, they had to accept government directives protecting the right to organize. With the National War Labor Board and a tight labor market bolstering workers' confidence, many compared their struggles to bring democracy to the workplace to the effort to end autocracy in Europe.[90]

The impetus for organizing steelworkers began in Chicago, a hotbed of union militancy during the war. The Chicago Federation of Labor pressed the AFL to lead the fight. The national labor body created the National Committee for Organizing Iron and Steel Workers to conduct a drive in the summer of 1918 led by John Fitzpatrick and William Z. Foster, two veterans of the Chicago movement. The National Committee was a coalition of twenty-five national unions, which meant that the steelworkers it organized would be divided into two dozen unions depending on the work they did. An industrial union would instead have enrolled all steelworkers regardless of their level of skill or craft. The National Committee's approach placed unskilled laborers in the Amalgamated Association of Iron, Steel, and Tin Workers or the Mine, Mill and Smelter Workers (MMSW), which focused on blast furnace workers. Skilled workers wound up in their respective craft unions, which had never evinced much interest in unskilled workers. The behind-the-scenes compromises and the implications of avoiding an industrial union approach were hidden to most steelworkers but severely compromised the National Committee's effectiveness. Underfinanced and understaffed, it was made up of individual unions far more concerned with their own organization's fortunes than those of the larger campaign.[91]

The National Committee presented twelve demands, including collective bargaining, an eight-hour day, one day off each week, an end to twenty-four-hour-long shifts, and wages that guaranteed an "American" standard of living. A strike vote overwhelmingly endorsed a walkout for September 22, 1919. In its leaflet announcing the strike, printed in seven different languages, the National Committee argued that "if we stand together like men, our demands will soon be granted and a golden era of prosperity will open for us in the steel industry. . . . The welfare of our wives and children is at stake. Now is the time to insist upon our rights as human beings."[92]

Foster, concerned that it would be hard going in the Pittsburgh district, which had been inhospitable to labor since the Homestead defeat in 1892, moved the National Committee's headquarters to Pittsburgh on October 1, 1918. The steel industry countered by announcing that an eight-hour day would be instituted the same day the strike headquarters opened. The end of the war on November 17, 1918, had an even greater impact. As production slowed, workers worried about layoffs. Meanwhile the influenza epidemic curtailed meetings, and winter was not far away.[93]

Nor was exercising the right to free speech and assembly a given in company towns such as Aliquippa, Weirton, and Midland, where authorities routinely denied permits to meet. In a display of solidarity on April 1, thousands of miners converged on Monessen, a mill town forty miles up the Monongahela River from Pittsburgh, defying the local burgess's refusal to allow a rally. Intimidated by the miners, the burgess backed down, and the crowd listened to legendary organizer Mother Jones and Philip Murray, president of United Mine Workers District Five. In nearby Donora a miners' boycott of merchants also forced the mayor to permit meetings, and organizers established a union presence there too.[94]

In McKeesport, Homestead, and Duquesne, organizers were less successful, as local officials frequently arrested Mother Jones, Foster, and other activists. When Rabbi Stephen Wise sought permission to speak in Duquesne, the mayor retorted that "Jesus Christ himself could not speak in Duquesne for the A.F. of L.!" The union gradually won limited rights to assemble in Monongahela Valley towns but could not stop companies from discharging thousands of men for union sympathies.[95]

The strike came at the end of a summer of turmoil, during which race riots, labor unrest, and the aftershocks of the Russian Revolution fueled pervasive anxieties across the nation. A near-record 22 percent of workers took part in strikes nationally in 1919, culminating in a Red Scare that targeted immigrant activists and deported thousands. In steel, half of the workforce joined the walkout.[96] The steel corporations fueled the growing sense of unease by labeling the strike as a radical movement of foreign-born workers. They were not entirely off the mark; the foreign-born constituted a majority of strikers. But steel companies inflated the strike's subversive character, and the press in Pittsburgh obliged with alarmist headlines and stories about a radical reign of terror. The Interchurch World Movement's investigation of the strike found most of these stories groundless. If anything, the foreign-born workers' struggle was their way of becoming Americans, of gaining democracy. Foster described steelworkers' meetings as "schools in practical Americanization."[97]

"Pittsburgh," Foster wrote, "was the storm center." The steel companies there had fortified the mills, "surrounding them with stockades topped off with heavily charged electric wires, and bristling with machine guns." From the start the strike was much stronger elsewhere. In the Pittsburgh district the Donora and Monessen mills shut down, but other mills, including U.S. Steel's Duquesne Works and J&L's plants in Aliquippa and the city, were hardly affected. By October production was off by a third nationally, but down only an eighth in the Pittsburgh region, where steelworkers feared company retaliation. According to David Brody, "the terror" had begun the day before the strike commenced. As three thousand workers from the Clairton Works gathered in a field to discuss the strike, mounted state police charged into them. A union meeting in nearby Glassport was also dispersed by force. The county sheriff deputized five thousand men, chosen and paid for by the steel companies, who routinely arrested organizers and held them without charges.[98]

Flush with wartime profits, steel corporations were prepared to withstand a stoppage. Now that the government had ended its wartime role in labor relations, no outside force could make them enter negotiations. The companies took out full-page advertisements urging employees to report to work, and newspapers generally exaggerated the number of men returning and the degree to which production had resumed. With a few notable exceptions, clergy espoused the company line from the pulpit. One dissenter, Father Adelbert Kazincy of St. Michael's Church in Braddock, opened his church to strikers. When the companies threatened retaliation, he said he would put a sign on the steeple proclaiming: "This church destroyed by the Steel Trust." Homestead, the only Monongahela Valley town to allow meetings, permitted the union to hold just one mass meeting a week. Coal and

Iron Police sat on the podium, permitting only English to be spoken and cutting off speakers who aroused their displeasure.[99]

The steel companies relied on sympathetic officials and an army of deputies and security guards. The Pennsylvania State Constabulary, derided as Cossacks in mill towns, trampled workers in the streets and even attacked a striker's funeral procession in Braddock. On several occasions they rode their horses onto workers' porches and into kitchens and front parlors. Father Kazincy wrote that his congregation had been "attacked on the very steps of the Temple of God, by the Constables, and dispersed by the iron-hoofed Huns."[100]

Company tactics worked. Though production in the Pittsburgh district was off noticeably at first, it returned to normal within two months. Foster claimed that about ninety-two thousand men were on strike in Pittsburgh on September 29, but only a third remained out on December 10. Given the centrality of Pittsburgh to the industry, the steelworkers could not win without shutting down the district. Ethnic divisions, however, made that almost impossible.[101] Most eastern and central Europeans were ready to strike, especially in the Monongahela Valley. Slovaks, the most populous nationality in Pittsburgh's mills, provided the largest group of strikers. "Throughout the steel strike," Mary Heaton Vorse wrote, "there was no group of people who stuck so firmly as did the Slovaks down in the Braddock slums. . . . This strike, to them, had meant an opportunity; it had meant a road of escape; it had meant, besides, a court of appeal at last for grievances."[102]

English-speaking steelworkers, on the other hand, were lukewarm, even hostile to the strike. Many native-born and old immigrants saw the conflict as a "Hunky strike," from which they could lose more than gain. A few years earlier John Fitch had interviewed a Scotch-Irishman who had worked his way from laborer to furnace boss. His remarks reflected how much the solidarity evident in 1892 had evaporated. The skilled worker lamented that few of his former kinsman still worked in the mills. He saw them about town, riding in carriages and wearing white shirts, while "here I am with these Hunkies. They don't seem like men to me hardly. They can't talk United States. . . . And I'm here with them all the time, twelve hours a day and every day and I'm all alone—not a mother's son of 'em that I can talk to."[103]

Racial prejudice, Foster contended, was also a factor. African American steelworkers did not embrace the strike. The companies, he stressed, did their best to heighten racial divisions by recruiting thousands of them as strikebreakers.[104] According to Foster, only a score of the thousands of African Americans working in Pittsburgh mills joined the walkout. Acknowledging the trade unions' history of discrimination, he warned that company tactics "would make our industrial disputes take on more and more the character of race wars."[105]

By December most strike leaders understood that the companies were too strong to defeat. The campaign, poorly financed and with too few organizers, was unable to gain support from other unions that might have helped turn the tide. The railroad brotherhoods, for example, could have stopped trains supplying the mills with coal and iron ore or carrying their products to the marketplace. Foster acknowledged that the campaign made a critical error in not waging its battle while the war was still on and government more likely to intervene on the workers' side.[106]

On January 8, 1920, the National Committee called off the strike. Unionism was all but extinguished in the steel industry for the remainder of the decade. Though skilled craftsmen, operatives, and unskilled laborers had their grievances, they could not make the vast industrial enterprises dominating Pittsburgh's landscape address them. Their hard-won triumphs over labor secured, corporations were unwilling to surrender the upper hand. Rather than depend only on the stick, the steel industry offered workers a carrot, the "American Plan," to keep the peace and ensure that workers did not make common cause.

Mike Dobrejcak missed the great steel strike of 1919. He died in 1914 in a mill accident that burned his body and crushed his skull.[107] Widowed at thirty, with four children aged two to eleven, a little over $1,000 in savings, and only domestic skills to fall back on, Mary struggled to keep her family together. She picked up work sewing, washing, or cleaning homes and offices whenever it was available. Her children scavenged for wood and coal, sold newspapers, and collected bottles, rags, and scrap for the junkman. Mary left Braddock and returned to Homestead where she persuaded Kracha to board with the family. Johnny, the oldest child, whom most people called Dobie, worked after school and in the summer at a glass factory that employed children. The glassworks served, Bell wrote, as a "preparatory school for future employees of the steel mills and the Westinghouse." Missing the first month of school that fall, Dobie found himself behind the other students and never caught up. In high school "he found himself more than ever a Hunky."[108] Dropping out, he forged working papers that made him out to be old enough to get a job as an apprentice armature winder. Mary's health, meanwhile, weakened. Diagnosed with "consumption," the term then used for tuberculosis, she was sent to a state sanitarium, while Johnny moved in with his aunt. Like Thomas Bell's mother, Mary died in the sanitarium. Following his father's footsteps, Dobie labored in the steelworks.

But there he would fulfill his father's vision of a better future for workers in the Monongahela Valley. Just as Kracha, Mike, and their generation of new immigrants sacrificed to build a foundation for Dobie and his generation, other newcomers less dependent on the steel industry scrambled to leave for their children a solid footing for life in Pittsburgh and southwestern Pennsylvania.

SEVEN

ITALIANS AND AFRICAN AMERICANS IN PITTSBURGH

IN 1885 AGOSTINO CARLINO LEFT SAN PIETRO AVELLINO, A TOWN IN THE mountains of Abruzzi, Italy, and made his way across the sea to a mining town in the Rockies. The seventeen-year-old son of a granite cutter had been away from home before to fight for Italy in a dispute with Turkey at the edge of the Ottoman Empire. When the fighting subsided, he and his comrades walked for four months to return to Italy. Once home, Agostino surveyed his prospects and left for America.[1] Agostino was not the first Carlino to leave San Pietro. His older brother Luigi was already digging in a Colorado mine.[2] Agostino labored alongside Luigi for a year before saving enough to return home and marry Palmira Frazzini, a young woman from his village. He was soon on the go again, and like other Italians, his destination was the United States. Many migrated several times, some seasonally, returning to Italy each year after the harvest or when hiring sagged. They were called "the birds of passage."

After unification in 1871, Italy experienced a series of traumas which convinced many to emigrate. Though the north was industrializing, the southern countryside, where population was growing, was in disarray. Prices for agricultural commodities were falling due to competition from abroad, while cutbacks in mining and craft production compounded the cri-

176

sis. As rural residents were reduced to day labor or tenancy at the mercy of speculators and absentee landlords, many from Abruzzi, Calabria, Sicily, and Campania, in the southern region of Italy known as the Mezzogiorno, ventured abroad for employment.[3]

The same factors that persuaded many to emigrate had already forced them to find new ways of coping before they left home. Neither a peasantry nor an industrial proletariat, these southern Italians blended work on the land with work for hire. Some switched to wage labor; others mixed wage or craft work with cultivating small parcels of land. They fished, made shoes and clothes, labored in sulfur mines and quarries, and acquired construction skills. If they still could not adequately support themselves or wanted more than those skills could procure, emigration was an option.[4]

Like eastern and central Europeans, most Italian immigrants first worked elsewhere in Europe. Many from Abruzzi headed to France to work on railroads or in mines and factories. But by the 1890s a majority of emigrants ventured farther afield, making the Western Hemisphere, especially the United States, their preferred destination. Overall, about seventeen million Italians left their homeland between 1876 and 1926, with most traveling to the United States, Argentina, Brazil, or Canada.[5]

Agostino settled in Pittsburgh on his third sojourn to America and never left.[6] He joined other Italians who built robust communities in the city, in Agostino's case Bloomfield. On a foundation of common labor, craft skills, and entrepreneurial drive, they erected a scaffold of social and religious institutions. Each was anchored to their families. The first Italians to come struggled, and not all stayed, but those who did helped successive generations gain relatively secure jobs, acquire homes, establish local businesses, and sustain a network of fraternal clubs and churches. Capitalizing on trades learned in Italy, they created about sixty carpentry, cement, and marble-cutting businesses in Pittsburgh by 1928. Some of these became powerful construction companies. But along the way Pittsburgh's Italian community confronted recessions and anti-immigrant backlash.

The Italians who ended up in Pittsburgh were, as historians John Bodnar, Roger Simon, and Michael Weber stressed, "more than simply impoverished, tradition-bound peasants."[7] Many were relatively skilled and resourceful, experienced in a variety of endeavors. As historian Virginia Yans-McLaughlin noted, most "joined the ranks of an impoverished working class" in the United States but not with the intention of staying poor.[8]

Like Agostino Carlino, Alabama-born William Tinker came to Pittsburgh to improve his prospects. Arriving in 1916 as part of the Great Migration of African Americans from the Deep South, Tinker and fellow migrants found work but did not fare as well as earlier black wayfarers to the city who came from Virginia, Maryland, and the upper South. They occupied lower rungs on the economic ladder. Even for those with some education, work was insecure and opportunities for advancement limited. Like the Italians, they established shops and fraternal organizations. But inferior job prospects made it more difficult to acquire homes and build political power, and caused many to leave. These disadvantages limited their capacity to establish the strong communities so important for the health and welfare of families during at a time when industrial capitalism emphasized individual responsibility. Tinker's children gained professional training, but apart from the youngest son Harold, they found opportunity in other cities. Though African Americans faced many of the same issues as their European counterparts, race indisputably shaped their lives in Pittsburgh.

BUILDING A FOUNDATION

After marrying Palmira, Agostino Carlino left her behind in San Pietro and rejoined his brother, Luigi, who by then was working in a New York City granite shop. The brothers had already learned how to cut stone by helping their father carve monuments, statues, and tombstones from marble and granite in San Pietro. After a brief stay Agostino returned to Italy to bring his wife back with him. When an immigration problem delayed Palmira, who was pregnant, Agostino left for Pittsburgh without her. Setting out from Naples aboard the *Archimendia*, he arrived in New York City on May 2, 1892, and made his way to Pittsburgh. Palmira came later, losing the baby during the voyage.

They reunited in Pittsburgh. A robust economic rebound and a downtown building boom following the 1890s depression meant that work was readily available for stonemasons.[9] The local Italian community grew from only 1,889 in 1890 to 14,120 in 1910. About half of them were from southern Italy.[10] Their first neighborhood was a four-block area downtown clustered around Virgin Alley (later Oliver Avenue) and bordered by Sixth, Smithfield, Fifth, and Grant. But the growth of the central business district pushed most of Little Italy's residents and later arrivals to one of three neighborhoods: the lower Hill, East Liberty and Larimer, and Bloomfield. Smaller enclaves developed around the city and region.[11]

Like Kracha and other turn-of-the-century immigrants, Agostino and his fellow Italians relied on kin and village connections to find work and lodging. Many came with skills that gave them options beyond factory work and unskilled labor. Most, especially southern Italians, were illiterate. In 1910 a majority of the southern and a fifth of northern Italians arriving in the United States could not read or write in any language. Virtually all of the men who stayed in Pittsburgh for more than a few years, however, learned to converse in English.[12]

Work dominated Agostino's daily existence. Many Italian men, especially those from Abruzzi, came with experience in construction trades and had worked with stone, granite, and marble. They gathered early each morning on street corners or at social clubs that acted as hiring halls. Trucks took those chosen for the day to a work site and returned them to Bloomfield in the evening. Work was often seasonal and underemployment a problem. Many searched for jobs that allowed them to work outside, free from direct supervision. In 1900 over 70 percent of all Italian men in Pittsburgh worked as unskilled laborers, a smaller percentage than their Russian, German, or Austrian counterparts, but still twice the citywide average. Fewer than 2 percent did white-collar work. Many employers saw Italians as docile and submissive, willing to work long hours for the lowest of wages "without a murmur." But some workplaces remained off limits to Italians because of their nationality.[13]

Almost a quarter of Italian men held skilled jobs, a figure higher than the city average or that of Russian, Austrian, German, and African American men. Those craft positions became a foundation for economic advancement, as skilled workers could become their own bosses: men with construction skills could often acquire enough capital to become subcontractors.[14] If successful, they could attempt to scale up the jobs they tackled. Nor did grocers, shoemakers, tailors, and fruit vendors need much capital to open shops. A 1920s study identified almost a hundred of these Italian-owned establishments in East Liberty alone. Some of these tradesmen and small shopkeepers invested in property and facilitated their descendants' mobility. Though the first generation often discounted investment in education, over nine hundred Italians and Italian Americans were attending the University of Pittsburgh (also called Pitt) by the 1920s.[15] Overall, Italian immigrants displayed a more entrepreneurial inclination than many other newcomers to the region in the late nineteenth century.

Large families and extended kinship groups created a self-help network through which men found jobs. Consequently they clustered in particular workplaces and trades, especially masonry, cement-finishing, bricklaying, and construction. Recent arrivals from the village of Ateleta were hired by the pipeline department of Equitable Gas. Their passport to the job came from the Ateleta Beneficial Association in Bloomfield. Others worked for the railroad on section gangs and in coal mines outside the city. Once employed, newcomers benefited from working alongside compatriots in what some described as a "sheltered apprenticeship" during the crucial period of adjustment to American life.[16]

Agostino's *paesans* from San Pietro told him he could find work at Campbell-Horigan Memorials, a shop on Penn Avenue in Bloomfield which made gravestones. He worked there on and off for decades, as did several of his sons and grandsons. Like his father, Agostino was a stonemason. He worked with slabs of granite cut from quarries, squaring, grinding, polishing, and buffing the stone until it was ready for use. Though safer than the steel mills, stonework meant laboring amid a cloud of stone particles and dust in poorly ventilated shops with nothing more than a handkerchief over one's face for protection. "I remember the first time walking in a shop when I was a kid," recalled Agostino's grandson Augustine Carlino, the third generation of the family to work at Campbell-Horigan. "Whew! I just wanted to get the hell out of there." Three of his uncles died from silicosis.[17]

In 1912 Agostino had been cutting and polishing stone for Campbell-Horigan for more than a decade when work began on lowering the "hump" on Grant Street downtown to ease the flow of traffic. Agostino helped to reface the courthouse's foundation facade, which had been exposed by the excavation. One day in the yard a cable snapped on a crane lifting a slab of granite intended for the courthouse. The slab rolled onto Agostino's leg, pinning him beneath it. To stop the bleeding before he died, Agostino's leg was amputated on the spot.[18]

He was off work for a year before returning with a wooden leg strapped to his stump. Though Agostino went back to the doctors periodically to have what was left of his leg honed clean, he continued working. The $1,200 compensation Agostino received allowed him to pay off the mortgage on their home and survive the year without pay. He would work for Campbell-Horigan until the mid-1930s. "If his leg hadn't come off," Agostino's grandson reasoned, "I don't know if he would have stayed in Pittsburgh." One study of the Italian migration concluded that about forty-four thousand of the seventy-three thousand who came to Allegheny County between 1870 and 1920 went back home. Like most immigrant groups, Italian migrants were sensitive to economic and political conditions. More left than arrived during the severe economic downturn in 1908 and during other recessions.[19]

BUILDING A COMMUNITY

Agostino, however, stayed, becoming ever more rooted in his workplace and neighborhood. Like most Pittsburghers, a majority of whom lived less than two miles from their workplace before World War I, the Carlinos resided within walking distance of Campbell-Horigan. "My grandfather lived down in the Hollow, Little Italy, where all the Italians lived," Augustine Carlino explained.[20] Little Italy fit compactly between Liberty Avenue and the ravine separating Bloomfield from Oakland. Bloomfield had been sparsely populated farmland dotted with small gardens and dairies until a German immigrant, Joseph Conrad Winebiddle, began developing residential properties there in the 1870s. Germans and German Americans, many of whom worked nearby in Lawrenceville's mills, predominated until the early twentieth century. Native-born white people, Germans, and some

Irish lived north of Liberty Avenue, the neighborhood's main shopping thoroughfare and a barrier Italian families did not cross for decades. Several black families lived at the margins of the Italian community, where the land plunged down to the railroad tracks.[21]

The Italian community sprawled over several blocks of Lorigan, Juniper, and Pearl Streets in tightly packed houses fronting narrow streets in the shadow of the Bloomfield Bridge. Some called it Skunk Hollow to disparage those living there. In the Pittsburgh Survey Florence Lattimore described the crowded district as a squalid, demoralizing pocket of civic neglect. Ella Myers, a graduate student conducting home visits for the Tuberculosis League in 1919, noted that trash was rarely picked up in the neighborhood and heaps of rubbish disfigured the hillside. Residents said the only way to ensure even sporadic collection was to tip the garbagemen. Myers also reported a high incidence of tuberculosis, pneumonia, and other respiratory infections. These problems were hardly unique to Bloomfield; Myers would have found trash and disease in many neighborhoods.[22] But Italians encountered uncommon scorn. In 1905 a *Pittsburgh Leader* story depicted "throngs of greasy, unkempt Italians standing around in front of crazy little grocery stores, jabbering or smoking, while slovenly women with filthy youngsters sit on steps or parade up and down in the street strewn with old vegetables, filthy water, and rubbish of all kinds."[23]

Residents saw their neighborhood not as Skunk Hollow but as Little Italy with a church, fraternal societies, a branch of the Bank of Italy, and a score of mom-and-pop stores, bakeries, and butcher shops. Chickens and goats, the latter to make mozzarella, grazed in backyards alongside statues of the Madonna. Italian was spoken on the street and at home. Even Florence Lattimore noted the presence of "bright-faced, thrifty Italians" amid what she described as squalor. Though some outsiders considered the neighborhood a shantytown, its residents helped each other improve their properties. "Everything you create," Agostino told his children and grandchildren, "consider it your monument and be proud of it. You plant a garden, plant a good one. You make a bridge, make a good one."[24] Within a few decades, descendants of families like the Carlinos comprised much of the area; they still predominate in the twenty-first century. Life revolved around work, home, and neighborhood, as it did in other immigrant neighborhoods. Italians parleyed their investments in these three essential areas of life into substantial legacies they bequeathed to children and grandchildren.

Homeownership was the most common means by which immigrants acquired capital in early twentieth-century Pittsburgh. Owning a home meant freedom from the whims of a landlord, better social standing, and a sense of greater security. A home also meant that a family could provide shelter to grown children and relatives or take in boarders to help pay for the house.

As the mortgage dwindled, a family's equity in its home increased. But purchasing a house required sacrifices to hold on to the dwelling, especially when work was not steady. In 1900 when a quarter of occupants owned their own homes in Pittsburgh, less than a tenth of all Italian households did so. But by the 1930s, when two-fifths of all Pittsburgh households owned their own homes, half of all Italian households did. Poles also owned homes at a rate above the city average, underscoring how much value recent immigrants placed on homeownership. Italian and Polish families in neighborhoods like Bloomfield and Polish Hill sometimes built a second dwelling in their backyards for one of their children or as a rental property. As historians Bodnar, Simon, and Weber concluded: "A house was tangible proof that the long struggle to get to Pittsburgh, acquire a job, and render mutual assistance had not been in vain."[25]

The Carlinos owned a home on Pearl Street in the midst of a community which welcomed them. Their home, a two-story wooden frame house with an attic, shared a common wall with an adjoining structure. A living room, dining room, and kitchen took up the first floor, with three bedrooms on the second, and two small rooms in the attic. They had indoor plumbing and put a bathtub in their basement. Illuminated first by gas, then by electricity, the house had running water that had to be heated up on a coal stove.[26] The lot was about twenty-five feet wide and eighty feet deep. On one side of this deep backyard, Agostino planted grapevines to make wine. On the other he built a bocce court. The rectangular court was framed by railroad ties and drained by gutters and grates. Inside the ties Agostino pounded, rolled, and tamped down red dog, a coal by-product, until it formed a smooth surface on which bocce balls were rolled. He replenished the red dog from a coal mine in Harmarville each year. The goal of the game was to roll heavy wooden bocce balls closer to the *palin*, a smaller ball, than those of the other team. Playing bocce, a sport they had created for themselves, reinforced elements of a common culture that crossed the Atlantic. In backyards and on local sandlots, recreation was not purchased for consumption but largely self-organized.

Agostino and Palmira raised a large family on Pearl Street, though two children did not survive infancy. In later years they kept two rooms available for sons who married. The son and his family could stay there for a few years while saving for their own place. When relatives or friends came over from Italy, they also stayed with the family until finding their own lodgings. The couple lived there until their deaths. Palmira died in late December 1946, Agostino a few months later.

Joseph Carlino stayed with his parents until he was twenty-five years old. Leaving school after the eighth grade, he worked for a year as a messenger for Fisher Scientific downtown until his father brought him to work at Campbell-Horigan Memorials. There he became a stonemason, learning how to create crosses, rosettes, and fine detail work on tombstones with diamond blades that cut to a sixteenth of an inch. Joseph worked on the granite columns adorning Allegheny Cemetery and the granite base for the statue of Honus Wagner, one of baseball's nonpareils. The statue, originally placed outside Forbes Field, was later moved across the Allegheny to Three Rivers Stadium and then PNC Park.[27]

Joseph chipped in some of his earnings when he was single. After he wed he paid his father ten dollars a month for board and saved what he could from the rest of his pay. His wife, Anna Capretta, who had grown up across the street, helped her mother-in-law with the laundry and cleaning. They moved two years later when Anna was pregnant with their second child, renting three rooms from a stonecutter down the street. The money they saved while living with Joseph's parents eventually helped them purchase a home close by on Millgate Street, near one of his sisters. They never moved again.

Agostino and Palmira's children in turn helped their parents. During the Great Depression the children contributed five dollars every other week to support their parents, and the youngest son remained at home to help around the house. "There was always enough food to put on the table," Augustine recalled. The strain of hard times was not that apparent, but neither would there ever be a windfall. "My grandfather would have a meeting with his sons every so often and tell them 'I have nothing to leave you, just the house.'"

COMMUNITY INSTITUTIONS

In Bloomfield, like other Italian neighborhoods, immigrants built their own world of religious, educational, social, and business organizations. Part of the impetus was that they were uncomfortable patronizing businesses where they felt they were treated badly. Resentment over poor reception at stores lingered for decades, prompting them to create alternatives that met their specific needs. They also promoted a sense of belonging and identity, mediated immigrants' transition to their new city, and helped their offspring become Americans without renouncing their heritage. The first Italians in Pittsburgh celebrated mass in the basement of St. Paul's Church downtown before building Help of All Christians in East Liberty in 1897. A parochial school came a decade later. Other churches and affiliated schools began serving Italians in the early twentieth century, including Calvary Church on Lorigan Street in Bloomfield in 1905. Before Calvary opened, Bloomfield's Italians had met in a blacksmith shop because they felt unwelcome at St.

Joseph's, a German parish formed in 1872. Calvary Church opened a school which many Italian children attended through eighth grade before either leaving school for good or entering a public high school. The church later moved across Liberty Avenue to Edmonds Street and was renamed Immaculate Conception; its cornerstone was laid in 1925.[28]

Locally published, foreign language newspapers catered to Pittsburgh's immigrant communities. Agostino Carlino could choose from three local Italian-language newspapers, *La Trinacria*, *Vita*, and the *Unione*, which began serving the community in 1890 with a weekly run of 2,300 copies. The Italian-language press not only focused on news of interest to Italians but defended them against nativist prejudice. The newspapers also served as guides to employment, housing, and schools, matters of great practical assistance.[29]

Like newspapers, fraternal clubs helped immigrants and their children retain a sense of nationality while adjusting to Pittsburgh. Originally organized to provide insurance for sickness and death, clubs also vouched for members applying for loans or mortgages. Some affiliated with the Order of the Sons of Italy, the Independent Sons of Italy, and the Sons of Columbus. But provincial and town identities were strong, and membership often reflected which province or town a person was from.[30]

In Bloomfield, the Ateleta, Castel di Sangro, Rocca Cinque Miglia, Pesco Costanza, and Italian Independent clubs represented villages in Abruzzi and could be found within a few blocks of each other in houses renovated by club members. Agostino helped to organize the Bloomfield Italian Citizens Club and became its president. Sundays revolved around mass and then socializing at the clubs. Joseph Carlino's family also belonged to the Castel di Sangro club because his wife, Anna Capretta, was the daughter of two Castel di Sangro villagers.[31] At their peak each of Bloomfield's clubs had memberships of several hundred individuals with dues of five to ten dollars a year. Men often congregated at the clubs in the evenings for bocce, to play cards, inquire about work, or just hang out with friends. On Sundays the clubs were jammed with entire families, even men and women of Irish and German descent who came because alcohol could be served there despite the state's Sabbatarian legislation restricting its sale. Though women belonged to the societies and cooked for parties and saint's days, they attended less frequently. They formed their own affiliated societies and had their own bocce league, but the clubs remained a mostly male domain, except for dances and celebrations. The fetes, held until the mid-1950s, included yearly festivals honoring the Assumption of the Blessed Mother and the feast of San Rocco, the patron saint of Rocco Cinque Miglia. During the latter celebration, club members carried a statue of San Rocco through the streets of Little Italy as people pinned currency to it and threw money onto a flag.[32]

Meetings were originally held in Italian, but in later years blended Italian and English. The first generation's children, who attended schools where instruction was in English, helped their parents learn a second language. "The older members were very proud that they could get up and speak in 'the English,'" Augustine Carlino recalled.[33] The clubs also celebrated members who gained citizenship. One leader claimed that 80 percent of those who remained in Pittsburgh for five years became naturalized and cast five thousand votes in a city election prior to World War I. Agostino declared his intent to become a US citizen in 1914, for which he renounced "all allegiance and fidelity" to any foreign power and affirmed he was neither an anarchist nor a polygamist.[34] By 1919, 70 percent of Italians had naturalized and another 10 percent had taken out their first citizenship papers. According to the Pittsburgh Survey, they sought citizenship in greater numbers than eastern and central Europeans. Agostino and his paesans did so to vote for the Democratic Party. In fifteen wards, the Pittsburgh Survey noted, the combined Italian and Polish vote held the balance of power before the war.[35]

Most immigrants patronized the Bloomfield branch of the Bank of Italy, whose manager acted as banker, realtor, and conduit for remitting money to families in Italy. Many, including the Carlinos, sent money back. "They were proud of it," their grandson recalled. The remittances helped to maintain ties between families separated by thousands of miles. The bank held funds saved to bring family members over or to purchase a home, for which it also provided the mortgage. During the Great Depression Joseph Carlino lost his savings at one bank but not the Bank of Italy. "It was just about the only bank to stay open," his son Augustine remembered.

Though clubs reinforced village attachments, Bloomfield's Italians embraced a wider identity. Migration had heightened the sense of their own "Italianness." Scorned by native-born Americans for their origins, Pittsburgh's Italians became more aware of their common cultural, linguistic, and political identities in the United States. Though Agostino and Palmira were both from San Pietro, their children did not necessarily find spouses from the same village. Joseph married a girl from Castel de Sangro, a town across the river from San Pietro, whose parents met on the boat coming from Italy. Four other children married either a man or a woman from Abruzzi; the remaining three wed Poles or Germans.

The mother was the center of the family. As an Italian proverb put it, "If the father should die, the family would suffer; if the mother should die, the family ceases to exist."[36] The city's heavy manufacturing base, large families, and the tendency of children to contribute to family income meant that few

Italian women—5 percent according to one sample—worked outside the home. Those who did work likely did so as domestics, laundresses, and seamstresses, usually before marriage. In the early twentieth century, especially during World War I, opportunities for women increased in manufacturing, but most employed outside the home continued to do domestic work or work in the needle trades and sales.[37] Boarding was also a common source of income in the Hollow. Though the Capretta and Carlino families were too big to take in boarders, the women did laundry for doctors at West Penn Hospital, and several daughters worked at laundries or in cigar factories on the Hill until they wed.[38]

The family, enmeshed in an extended network of kinship and village relationships, absorbed the shocks and disruptions of immigration and provided practical and psychological sustenance to its members. This network meant that most Italians were never completely on their own. Though not all relationships fostered a sense of mutualism and community, they contributed to neighborhood cohesion. At times, as with other nationalities, these relationships sacrificed children's education to the desire to own property and stifled cultural and social freedoms, especially for women. Social control could become intense in neighborhoods where it seemed as if almost everybody was connected to everybody else.[39]

By the 1920s Bloomfield had not only grown but become increasingly segregated by race and ethnicity. Italians and Italian Americans, who outnumbered residents of German descent, comprised about 70 percent of the neighborhood in 1930. A majority of them were American-born. Restrictive immigration laws passed in 1921 and 1924 curtailed the number of eastern, central, and southern Europeans who could enter the country. Even though the foreign-born population in Pittsburgh as a whole began to shrink, their neighborhoods grew due to the next generation of American-born offspring and their propensity to remain in their ethnic communities. While immigrants were not cut off from contact with their countries of origin, and some continued to arrive in the city, their ethnic neighborhoods were no longer just immigrant communities. They were part of Pittsburgh.[40]

REMAKING BLACK PITTSBURGH, 1870–1920

When William Edlow Tinker and his eldest son Leon disembarked at Union Station and walked up Centre Avenue in the summer of 1916, the Hill District was jumping. Pittsburgh's economy had rallied with the onset of war in Europe. Trolleys, trucks, and teams of horses jostled with pedestrians and pushcarts on the Hill. Southern dialects mingled with a half-dozen European and Mediterranean languages in the city's most chaotic, densely populated, and cosmopolitan neighborhood. African Americans, though not yet a majority, were poised to make the Hill what the Jamaican-born, Harlem Renaissance poet Claude McKay called the crossroads of the world.

The migration of African Americans northward, what became known as the Great Migration, was now a full-fledged exodus. With war in Europe boosting production, native-born workers entering the armed services, and the flow of immigrants cut off, the region's mills and mines hired record numbers of African Americans. Newcomers like the Tinkers arrived daily on trains from the South, and many headed to the Hill, where Martin Delany and other African Americans had congregated in a neighborhood called Little Hayti before the Civil War. During the Great Migration more African Americans settled there than elsewhere in the city.

African Americans had been making their way northward long before the war. Between 1890 and 1910, some 300,000 black people departed the South, leaving behind a deteriorating social climate and historically low cotton prices. An even greater number followed between 1910 and 1920.[41] In Pittsburgh the number of African Americans leaped from 20,355 in 1900 to 37,725 in 1920 and more than 50,000 in 1930. Their share of the population climbed to 8.2 percent, a harbinger of continuing demographic change. Several thousand more lived in Allegheny County outside the city limits, especially in mill towns along the rivers, where their numbers almost doubled.[42] But a surging population did not secure African Americans a proportional, much less equitable, share of power in the city. They lacked a strong voice in politics, were absent from the most vital sectors of the economy, and lived in neighborhoods with the highest rates of disease and death. Despite these obstacles, African Americans nurtured an entrepreneurial element that created the most influential black newspaper in the country, the *Pittsburgh Courier*, and two of the greatest ever baseball clubs, the Homestead Grays and Pittsburgh Crawfords. The Hill became a mecca for jazz and was the neighborhood that the preeminent playwright and native son August Wilson used as the backdrop for his cycle of ten plays depicting the African American experience in the twentieth century.

The Great Migration did not create black Pittsburgh but did dramatically remake it. After the Fugitive Slave Law forced hundreds of African Americans to abandon Pittsburgh in 1851, the black community languished. It recouped some of its population during and after the Civil War, but they numbered fewer than eight thousand in 1890, before more than doubling that decade. William Tinker, like George Kracha and Agostino Carlino, came to Pittsburgh searching for better-paying work. But black migrants crossing the Mason-Dixon Line also hoped that reaching Pittsburgh would become the path to greater freedom and equality. They came in two waves. The first, during the 1890s, hailed from the upper South. The second, during

World War I, included the Tinkers and African Americans with roots in Alabama, Georgia, and the Black Belt's rural hinterlands.

THE FIRST WAVE

By the late nineteenth century many gains won during Reconstruction had been reversed. Jim Crow, sharecropping, and the rise of the Ku Klux Klan imposed a new form of bondage, especially in the rural South, where almost two-thirds of the nation's African Americans still lived in 1910. Sharecropping and tenant farming offered a bleak future, especially after the boll weevil began its devastating assault on cotton fields. Farmers fell into debt, which their children inherited. Black children received a separate and terribly unequal education, spending more time in fields than classrooms. Like their parents, they encountered segregation wherever they turned. By the 1890s white supremacists had regained power in most southern states and driven all but a few African Americans from the voting rolls. Lynchings took place on average one hundred times a year and were celebrated by many white people as "festivals of violence." Nor was anyone brought to justice. "Crossing over Jordan," as the *Chicago Defender* called the migration north, meant not only the chance to gain better work and escape white supremacist terror, but to educate children, vote, and experience a greater taste of personal freedom.[43]

In the first wave most southern émigrés to Pittsburgh came from Virginia, Maryland, the District of Columbia, North Carolina, and Tennessee. They doubled the city's black population between 1890 and 1900 to more than twenty thousand.[44] Overwhelmingly working class in income and occupation and often from southern towns and cities, they settled in half a dozen Pittsburgh neighborhoods and nearby mill towns.[45] A majority had been born in Virginia, especially in the more economically diverse Shenandoah Valley or Richmond, the South's industrial metropolis. By heading north, they gambled that they could forge better lives. They were a self-selecting group, inclined to embark on an adventure whose outcome was uncertain. According to historian Laurence Glasco, many were ambitious, not averse to risk, and generally better off socially and economically than those in the rural South. "Advocates of the self-made man," he argued, "they had great confidence in their abilities and in their own entrepreneurial future."[46]

More than a few, most notably Cumberland Posey Sr., Robert L. Vann, and Mary Cardwell Dawson, fulfilled their ambitions. Posey built a commercial empire, Vann made the *Pittsburgh Courier* a voice for African Americans in Pittsburgh and beyond, and Dawson created the Negro National Opera Company, the first black opera company in the country. Building a critical mass of black-controlled businesses and social and cultural institutions, the first wave brought with them a degree of high culture—of classical music, literary societies, and orchestras—that permeated working-class as well as middle-class and elite black homes.

But African Americans were marginalized in the city's industrial economy until the war. Few worked in its burgeoning network of mills, factories, and offices. Instead, they labored in many of the same occupations African Americans had held before the Civil War. More than a hundred ran their own businesses, operating barbershops, pool halls, print shops, and pharmacies, or contracted for construction, hauling, and catering work. A far greater number labored as porters, waiters, domestics, and coachmen. Except for a small cluster who gained a foothold in the iron and steel industry, most worked in unskilled positions.[47]

Pittsburgh was the nation's leading steel center, but African Americans were underrepresented, comprising roughly 3 percent of steel's workforce. A surprising share of those, however, held relatively skilled positions. Some had entered the industry when hired to break strikes and remained afterward. In Lawrenceville, about a third of the 110 black men at the Clark mill worked as puddlers, heaters, rollers, roughers, finishers, or millwrights. Another cluster of skilled black men emerged at the Homestead Steel Works. This cohort had more in common with James Davis and other skilled workers than with Kracha and Mike Dobrejcak, at least at work. They took enormous satisfaction in their workplace competence, modeled respectability, and sought uplift for themselves and their children. They even supervised white workers.[48]

By World War I this early wave of migrants was known as the "OPs," the Old Pittsburghers. They lived on Sugar Top on the Hill, Hilltop in Homestead, and in a few enclaves in otherwise white neighborhoods. Those arriving later, especially during and after the war, were from the deeper South. More accustomed to farm than factory and not well educated, they had fewer employable skills and were poorer and darker skinned. They lived apart, prayed apart, and worked apart from the OPs. In Homestead, Hilltoppers attended Clark Memorial Baptist Church and participated in its clubs, auxiliaries, educational programs, and foreign mission. Migrants in the Ward were more likely to turn to Second Baptist church, which moved among storefronts and provided fellowship but little status. Some OPs feared that newcomers with country ways would jeopardize their hard-won standing in the city. As migrants swamped neighborhoods already lacking adequate housing and social services, black Pittsburgh was at odds with itself, divided between Pittsburgh-born and newer migrants, which undercut collective efforts in politics and the community. Black Pittsburgh did not come to terms with itself and emerge with a renewed identity as a community and part of an emerging national black consciousness until later in the century.[49]

Black Pittsburgh, Laurence Glasco observed, was shaped not only by racial discrimination and intra-racial tensions, but by bad timing and topography. The primary problem was that most black migrants to Pittsburgh arrived as the region's economy was cresting. Its steel companies never regained their prewar energy after World War I. Unlike their European counterparts, African Americans had not yet established themselves in the region's steel- and manufacturing works when those industries plateaued. Arriving too late to establish a secure grip on employment, few black workers benefited from promotion. Last hired in steel, they were the first pushed out. Nor did they attain skilled positions or enough seniority to resist frequent layoffs. Many never established the occupational and residential security attained by European immigrants. That had repercussions not only for them, but for their children and grandchildren. Men were unable to get jobs for their cousins, sons, and nephews in the mills like Slavic steelworkers did, or like the Carlinos, who brought kin into the stone trades. Few acquired homes that they could pass on to children.[50]

Additionally, rather than forming one contiguous ghetto, African Americans settled into a handful of neighborhoods and mill towns, undercutting their economic and political clout. The area's rivers and hillsides cut the city into scores of neighborhoods whose borders were defined by physical boundaries. The Hill did not become a majority black community until the 1930s, nor did the city's topography allow it to become a concentrated political and economic force like New York City's Harlem or Chicago's South Side. This geography made it difficult for a strong black middle and professional class to thrive or a viable black political movement to coalesce.

OLD PITTSBURGHERS

Most who came during the Great Migration, like the Tinkers, were from rural, agrarian backgrounds in the Deep South. But William Tinker had spent time in Birmingham after leaving Tinkers Farm, Alabama. His mother was of Chippewa and African American heritage, and he could have passed for an OP. Light-skinned and literate, William Tinker had known success in business and was familiar with city life. He and his wife, Mamie Willhite Tinker, the daughter of a preacher and a high school graduate, were on the fringes of the city's more established black elements.[51]

If William had entered the mines or worked on the river, he might have labored for Captain Cumberland Willis Posey. The son of a Maryland slave, Posey worked as a deck sweeper aboard a ferry on the Ohio and Little Kanawha Rivers (West Virginia) before becoming the first African American to earn a chief engineer's license (thus his sobriquet, "the Captain"). Posey moved to Homestead in 1892 where he supervised the construction of vessels working Pittsburgh's rivers. By the turn of century he had diversified his interests. His Diamond Coke and Coal Company, the largest black-owned business in the region, employed a thousand workers and contracted with Andrew Carnegie. A self-made man, Posey acquired substantial real estate in Homestead and was the director of a bank. He was also the president of the Loendi Club, the Warren Methodist Episcopal Church, and the *Pittsburgh Courier*, which noted his death at the age of sixty-seven in 1925 as the passing of a "pioneer of industry." Posey, Laurence Glasco wrote, epitomized a cohort of black entrepreneurs, of whom he was the most successful.[52]

The Poseys lived in an integrated neighborhood called Hilltop, several blocks up the slope overlooking the Homestead Steel Works along the Monongahela River. White and black professionals, shopkeepers, and skilled workers owned homes in this pleasant neighborhood. In contrast, black migrants who came during the war crowded into the Ward, where they lived within shouting distance of saloons, brothels, gambling houses, and each other. The hulking steelworks belched iron filings and sulfur fumes into the air and provided an inescapable soundtrack of whistles, clangs, trains, and occasional explosions to daily life. Unlike the single-family homes on Hilltop, company-built bunkhouses and overcrowded tenements filled the Ward. Posey's neighbors included the Goodes and the Veneys. William Goode reached the highest position a black man could fill at the Homestead Steel Works: first helper on a blast furnace. Though he had been illiterate when he left Virginia for Pittsburgh, his wife Mary had taught school in Staunton in the Shenandoah Valley and taught him to read and write. Years later, their children graduated from Howard University and the University of Pittsburgh. One son would own a pharmacy on the Hill, another was a broadcast pioneer, and a daughter, the charismatic Mary Dee, won acclaim as the country's first female black radio host. The Veney brothers were from another Shenandoah Valley town. Jerry and John Veney, engineers on the Homestead plant's railroad, formed a black sandlot baseball team in 1900 and guided the club during its formative years. Captain Posey's son, Cumberland Willis Posey Jr., turned that ball club into a sporting legend—the Homestead Grays. William Tinker may not have had much contact with Captain Posey, but it was the ambition of his youngest son, Harold, to assemble a ball club that could beat the Grays. With help from Satchel Paige, other sons of the Great Migration, and numbers baron Gus Greenlee, Harold achieved that goal during the 1920s.

William Tinker read Robert L. Vann's weekly paper, the *Pittsburgh Courier*. Vann, the son a black woman who cooked for a white farmer in rural

North Carolina, was born in 1879. He came to Pittsburgh in 1903 to attend the University of Pittsburgh on an Avery Scholarship, a legacy of local abolitionist and philanthropist Charles Avery. While at Pitt, Vann lodged with a black family in Allegheny City. Light-skinned, ambitious, and one of the few African Americans in college, Vann was welcomed by Old Pittsburgh. He went to services at the Brown Chapel of the American Methodist Evangelical Church and attended literary gatherings at the Loendi Club. The Loendi, founded in 1897 and named for a river in Africa, was *the* club for the city's growing black business and professional class. Vann also crossed into previously all-white arenas, joining Pitt's debate squad, and becoming the first black editor in chief of *The Courant*, its literary journal. That Vann graduated college was an exceptional achievement; fewer than a dozen African Americans had earned degrees from the University of Pittsburgh during the preceding two decades. After graduating, he entered the university's law school in 1906, its only black student.[53]

During Vann's first year in law school, he boarded the Pennsylvania and Lake Erie Railroad most afternoons after class and served dinner on its evening run to Connellsville. Overnighting in the small industrial town on the Youghiogheny River, Vann worked the breakfast shift on his way back to Pittsburgh. After earning a law degree, Vann became the city's fifth black attorney, opening an office in 1910. A decade later there were still only eight black lawyers in the city. Many African Americans hesitated to employ a black attorney, believing that they stood a better chance in court with white representation. Reflecting on Vann and other black lawyers' difficulty in securing black clients, correspondent Mal Goode remarked, "As we so often said, they believed the 'white man's ice was colder.'"[54]

In 1910 a group of influential black men, including Captain Posey, approached Vann to incorporate the *Pittsburgh Courier*. Begun in 1907 by Edwin Harleston, a guard with a journalistic bent at the H.J. Heinz plant on the North Side, the paper was a two-page, nickel-a-copy weekly. With Posey and other backers the *Courier* expanded distribution and the scope of its coverage. It was a corrective to the mainstream press, which paid little attention to the black community other than melodramatic crime stories. Vann, the paper's counsel, contributed to editorial copy and, when Harleston quit after a dispute with the board, became its editor. Though paid little, Vann's legal efforts and public speaking received front-page attention. He proclaimed that the *Courier* would continue the fight "to abolish every vestige of Jim Crowism in Pittsburgh."[55]

Crusading for social change, the *Courier* filled a leadership void that the fragmented and often conservative fraternal, social, religious, and political groups did not address. According to his biographer Andrew Buni, Vann was hardly a radical activist, but his paper critiqued problems and proposed solutions. There was no dearth of issues. The *Courier* focused on substandard housing, workplace discrimination, public health problems, and a lack of political power. Black mortality rates had soared during the migration, climbing by almost a third between 1910 and 1917, while white mortality rates, already substantially lower, declined slightly. Despite this gap only one hospital in the city accepted black patients.[56] By the late 1920s the *Courier* was regarded by some as the nation's finest black weekly newspaper. With a circulation approaching fifty-five thousand, both a city and national edition, and distribution by Pullman porters throughout the South and Midwest, the *Courier* and Vann gained a local and a national voice.

Posey and Vann were among the most illustrious members of black Pittsburgh, which by the turn of the century had crafted its own set of institutions. African Americans started fraternal lodges; built a network of charitable institutions for the aged, orphaned, and destitute; and organized an array of cultural bodies. The last included scores of clubs and literary societies, and three concert and symphony orchestras. Many were the work of migrants from the Shenandoah Valley and Richmond, who brought their affinity for high culture with them to Pittsburgh.

The black community, however, changed profoundly during the migration. Its internal social distinctions, already well drawn, became even clearer. By then Vann had moved from an enclave of Old Pittsburghers in Allegheny City to Homewood, where he was the nucleus of a newer black, middle-class section. Other pockets of relatively affluent and secure African Americans resided in the upper Hill, Beltzhoover, and East Liberty.[57] On the lower Hill a larger, more transient, and less secure black community took shape. That's where the Tinkers made their home, among southern African Americans pouring into the city in record numbers. Between 1915 and 1917 the region's black workforce tripled. Some migrants stayed only a few weeks, others traveled back and forth between Pittsburgh and the South, but a sizable proportion stayed and made Pittsburgh their home.[58]

WILLIAM TINKER

After securing lodging on the Hill, William and Leon Tinker found work downtown at Joseph Horne's department store. Leon, fifteen years old, shined shoes, while his father was a porter, cleaning furniture, dusting, and sweeping. A few years later a fellow parishioner at Central Baptist Church told William of a job cutting hair at Mason's Barbershop on Wylie Avenue. That was more to his liking. Barbering in an arena of black male conviviality, William worked there until moving to Red Moore's Barbershop downtown, a job he kept as long as he stayed in Pittsburgh.[59]

A barber in Birmingham, William also had partnered in a real estate business and an undertaking establishment. Hard-working and sober, he owned a bungalow with indoor plumbing and hardwood floors. "It was one of the finest homes among colored people there," his youngest son Harold recalled. The family had a buggy and a horse. "When you rode around in a horse and buggy in those days," Harold explained, "you were a well-to-do man." But William lost his share of the businesses. Harold believed his father's partners swindled him. "We lost our home and had to move out. That's why Dad came here and made a place for us in Pittsburgh." After a year, William sent for his wife, Mamie Willhite Tinker, daughter Katherine, and two remaining sons, Carl and Harold.

While relatives and acquaintances had preceded the Tinkers to the city, easing their transition, Pittsburgh was a different world. Though most downtown hotels, restaurants, and theaters were segregated, and African Americans absent from city leadership, the Tinkers interacted with white people more than in Birmingham. "Everything there was segregated," recalled Harold, "but my mother and dad didn't dwell on that stuff." The children had attended all-black schools and lived in an all-black neighborhood whose men worked in Birmingham's mills and nearby mines. When Harold saw minor league baseball's Birmingham Barons play, he sat in the "colored bleachers." His local nickelodeon was for black people only. "We stayed mostly in black neighborhoods," Harold explained, "and when you ventured through a white neighborhood you'd know you were going to have some trouble. They'd throw rocks at you and if they came in our neighborhood, we'd throw rocks at them." But in Pittsburgh Harold lived in integrated neighborhoods and went to school with white children. Getting accustomed to white folks took time, he laughed. "It was strange for a while."

William found a three-room apartment for his family in Duquesne Heights, south of the Monongahela River. Harold, twelve, was lonely at first, missing the daily pickup games on the street near his home in Birmingham. From the South Side bluffs he could see semipro teams playing baseball across the river at Exposition Park on the North Side, where the Pittsburgh Pirates had played before decamping for Forbes Field in Oakland in 1909. Harold adjusted to Pittsburgh, especially after the Tinkers moved to Mahon Street on the Hill, where his brother Carl tended a vegetable garden and kept chickens in the backyard. It was a short walk to Schenley High School, which Harold attended until late in the eleventh grade. Most of his friends were children of the Great Migration, and some, like Neal Harris, his best friend and sandlot teammate, were also from Alabama. The five Harris brothers, from Calhoun, Alabama, excelled on the baseball diamond. Bill Harris cofounded the Pittsburgh Crawfords with Teenie Harris (no relation), who gained acclaim as a photographic chronicler of black Pittsburgh. Neal joined Harold on the Crawfords, while Vic Harris won fame playing for, then managing, the Homestead Grays. Harold's closest friends were black, but he was no longer in a black-only setting. "We were all mixed together," Harold recalled. They played pickup ball together and were often in each other's homes. "When we got in trouble," he laughed, "we got a *whuppin'* from our black mama and our white mama."

THE SECOND WAVE

The Hill became black Pittsburgh's focal point. At the turn of the century it was a multiethnic, multiracial neighborhood overlooking downtown, the Strip, Bloomfield, Oakland, and the South Side. During the 1890s most native-born, white professionals, who numbered in the hundreds, left the Hill. They were replaced by Italians, Russian Jews, Syrians, Hungarians, and African Americans, who joined the Germans and Irish who had remained.[60] About two-fifths of the city's black population lived on the Hill during World War I, but they did not constitute a majority there. Over a third of black households had white neighbors, and most African Americans lived on streets mixed by class as well as race. The upper Hill from Herron Avenue toward Bloomfield and Oakland was more affluent, especially the Schenley Heights area known as Sugar Top. Far more black families owned houses there than on the lower Hill, which extended from Herron Avenue to the central business district. But overall only 4 percent of African Americans on the Hill owned a home in the 1920s.[61]

Those who came during the Great Migration gravitated to the lower Hill or mill towns along the rivers, forming pockets of people from the same southern towns. These recent arrivals were less secure economically and less familiar with urban life than families that had been in the city for a generation or more. They crowded into ramshackle dwellings, squatted in abandoned boxcars, and lived in boardinghouses where they shared beds in dark, dank rooms. Soon the most densely populated part of Pittsburgh, the Hill suffered from an exploding crime rate and a high incidence of tuberculosis, venereal disease, whooping cough, and influenza.[62]

Many of the new migrants, like William Tinker, had been born on a plantation or grown up in a sharecropper's or tenant farmer's shack. They left home in an ever-widening series of seasonal migrations for cash labor. At sawmills and logging camps, on railroad gangs and the docks, or in southern coal mines and steel mills, they heard of the possibilities that northern cities offered. Some, like Tinker, traveled directly to Pittsburgh. Others came more circuitously, moving from city to city, leaving whenever prospects seemed better elsewhere. Unattached men between the ages of fifteen and fifty-five predominated, but hundreds of single women and families came north too.[63]

Most already knew something of Pittsburgh, and many had friends or family members there. Some traveled in groups, planning their journey with great deliberation. During wartime labor shortages, others were re-cruited by labor agents working for the Pennsylvania Railroad, Standard Steel Car, Carnegie Steel, and other industrial concerns. Agents often gave men tickets for the train ride, paid for out of future wages. The trains deliv-ered them directly to the mill, where they were immediately put to work.[64]

Those who came after 1915 were less likely than earlier migrants to ben-efit from a gradual introduction to urban life via short stays in southern cities. Although they spoke English, these men and women were almost as bewildered as European immigrants by what they encountered in factories and on city streets. Difficulty in adjusting contributed to astounding turn-over rates at work, especially for young black males. In 1923 the A. M. Byers Steel Company had to hire 1,408 black workers to keep an average of 228 men on the job daily.[65]

The migration heightened residential segregation. On the Hill the in-crease in the number of African Americans between 1910 and 1920 almost doubled the decline in the foreign-born population, many of whom left for East End neighborhoods. Black enclaves also emerged in Lawrenceville, Ha-zelwood, and the North Side. In Braddock black migrants clustered in Port Perry; in Duquesne, they lived in Castle Garden; in Homestead, they settled in the Ward. Another two thousand black workers lived in segregated mill town quarters provided by their employers.[66]

WORK AND RACE

These enclaves reflected a growing black industrial presence. Overall, the number of black steelworkers soared to seven thousand in 1918, 13 percent of the region's steel workforce. By 1923 almost seventeen thousand, over a fifth of western Pennsylvania's steelworkers, were black. This industrial pro-letariat was much bigger than the prewar cohort of skilled black steelwork-ers, but not nearly as well positioned. As thousands of black people entered mills where few had worked before, virtually all of them were assigned to labor on blast furnaces and other unskilled work.[67]

Although black migrants shared common ground with eastern and southern European immigrants, they differed in critical respects. Few black people in Pittsburgh prior to the Great Migration were employed in indus-tries that hired additional workers during and after the war. Laboring in smaller shops more vulnerable to layoffs, they were less able to help family and friends get hired. Foreign-born immigrants, however, had already es-tablished beachheads in particular departments at many larger plants. Slavs fit industry's stereotypes of what made for a desirable worker, while man-agement often viewed black men as less suited for industrial labor.[68]

Though not entirely segregated at work, African Americans were rou-tinely assigned to what became known as "black jobs." They found themselves clustered in the lowest-paying, dirtiest, and most dangerous jobs with little chance of promotion. They attained no position higher than first helper on a blast furnace and were generally excluded from skilled trades. During the summer heat supervisors assigned them to coking operations or to tearing down and rebuilding furnaces. In the winter, when working next to a furnace was more tolerable, they were sent outside to work.[69]

Though aggrieved by this treatment, black workers had nowhere to turn for help. Resentment lingered over the decades-old use of black workers to break strikes at a few Pittsburgh mills, and most African Americans did unskilled work at a time when the AFL ignored unskilled workers. Many AFL craft unions refused to admit black members, while others organized trades with few or no black workers. Black workers did join unions where possible, especially the local Hod (brick) Carriers Union and the Hoisting Engineers Union—but they were exceptions.[70]

Consequently, when the steel industry convulsed during the 1919 strike, most black workers stayed on the job. The Amalgamated Association had made only half-hearted efforts to win them over, a mistake for which it paid heavily. During the strike companies brought in additional southern black workers, who often ate and slept in the mills protected by armed guards. Along with black workers who did not strike and native-born workers who looked at the walkout as a "Hunky" affair, these new recruits were vital to the companies' ultimate victory.[71]

African American women found conditions in the labor market even more daunting. The regional economy's heavy manufacturing preponderance marginalized women of all races. Outside the home, most were employed as domestics, seamstresses, or laundresses. While half of all unmarried white women worked as domestics at the turn of the century, 90 percent of all unmarried black women did so. Few joined the growing number of white women entering factories during World War I. Nevertheless, black women were more likely to work for wages outside the home, especially after marriage. Despite obstacles to employment, women headed almost a fifth of all black households in 1900, a higher percentage than in the white community.[72]

WORK AND COMMUNITY

In contrast to European immigrants, African Americans had a harder time building stable communities and aiding their children. They were not as successful as eastern Europeans in establishing a solid employment base in manufacturing, especially in steel. Nor could they parley craft and entrepreneurial skills into a network of small businesses and skilled jobs as readily as Pittsburgh's Italians. One consequence was that black households owned homes at one-third the city average in 1900. Years later African

Americans still owned homes below the city's average. As a result, fewer black children inherited homes, most families' greatest source of wealth. Nor did homeownership anchor families to neighborhoods as much as it did for European immigrant groups.[73]

Unable to gain secure employment and own a home, many African Americans saw little reason to stay in Pittsburgh. Like foreign-born new-comers, black migrants were sensitive to the regional economy's gyrations. Studies tracking those who arrived during the Great Migration show that fewer than half remained a decade after their arrival. By one estimate two-thirds of all African Americans in Pittsburgh in 1910 were gone within a decade.[74] By the 1920s the children of foreign-born immigrants—a second generation—outnumbered their parents in Pittsburgh. But higher turnover in the black community meant that most African Americans were still relatively new to the city.[75]

William and Mamie Tinker remained in Pittsburgh until 1941, when they moved to Los Angeles to live with their son, Carl. William died there at the age of 102; Mamie passed away two weeks short of her 102nd birthday. Their daughter, Katherine, married and moved to Buffalo. Leon, who worked as a bellhop at the Monongahela House downtown after leaving Horne's department store, wound up in Buffalo too. Only Harold remained in Pittsburgh.

Despite obstacles in the workplace, some African Americans in Pittsburgh held high expectations for the future. They perceived that leaving the South for Pittsburgh was the means to make a better life. They saw education, especially for their children, as critical to attaining this end. Black youth were more likely to attend high school than their European counterparts. Two-fifths of black high school students questioned in 1928 wanted to pursue teaching, dentistry, pharmacy, law, or another profession. Carl Tinker did just that, becoming a pharmacist after completing his studies at the University of Pittsburgh. But many black college graduates could not enter their chosen profession in Pittsburgh. City schools did not hire African American teachers in significant numbers until after World War II, and many black graduates left town. Carl, who paid for tuition at Pitt by working as a porter at the Pittsburgh Athletic Association, worked for a black pharmacist on the Hill after graduation. He later moved to Los Angeles and opened a drugstore of his own.[76]

CORPORATE WELFARE

Given their growing numbers in the mills and their pro-company stance during the 1919 Steel Strike, African Americans were welcomed by management as an important part of the region's workforce. In contrast, the participation of eastern and central Europeans in the labor upsurge of these years, compounded by the 1921 and 1924 immigration quota acts, made companies more skeptical of foreign-born workers as a source of labor. For many native-born white people, European immigrants constituted a threatening, potentially subversive element.[77] But industrialists believed that black workers needed to improve their work habits and reliability. Turnover and absenteeism were especially alarming. Many migrants, historian Peter Gottlieb pointed out, had little intention of staying with a job for long.[78] Their youthfulness and the disagreeable nature of the work contributed to a footloose attitude. It was also far easier to return to the South than it was for European immigrants to cross the Atlantic again, and it was often necessary to help with their families' harvest or other troubles. To ensure their labor supply, some local companies took steps to help black workers adjust to urban life and industrial work.

These measures fit into the larger "American Plan" of the period, in which companies stuck to an open (nonunion) shop stance while initiating sweeping welfare measures. The plan offered English classes, clean restrooms, company newspapers, and athletic programs. Efforts targeting black workers were like campaigns to Americanize and acculturate European immigrants. Of special interest to management was how workers spent their leisure time. Black workers, they felt, were too easily seduced by pool halls, saloons, crap games, and the sporting life.[79]

The companies offered alternatives, employing a score of black welfare workers to implement segregated programs. Earl Johnson (who won bronze and silver medals in distance running at the 1924 Paris Olympics) at the Edgar Thomson Steel Works, William "Pimp" Young (who became Pennsylvania's secretary of labor) at Lockhart Iron and Steel, Charles "Greasy" Betts at the Homestead Steel Works, Cyrus T. Green at Westinghouse, and Charles Deevers and J. D. Barr at the Pennsylvania Railways Company mediated the concerns of local industry and the needs of black workers. They sought to reduce turnover and absenteeism, improve morale and company loyalty, and make men harder-working, more dependable employees. They also helped workers, especially those fresh off the farm, adjust to urban ways and industrial discipline. Pimp Young sponsored dances for the workers at Lockhart Iron and Steel, encouraged them to open bank accounts, and persuaded the company to refurbish the depressing bunkhouses where many slept. Earl Johnson sponsored a black baseball team at Edgar Thomson, for which Harold Tinker played. Grover Nelson ran the Homestead Steel Works' community center for black workers. Built in 1918, the center held classes in English, arithmetic, and civics, housed newly arrived workers in a third-floor dormitory, and welcomed workers and their dependents to its reading, card, and billiard rooms. Several of these college-educated welfare workers played for the Loendis and Monticellos, basketball teams that

Cum Posey Jr. played for and ran. The teams were black America's unofficial champions for several seasons.[80]

Welfare workers cooperated with churches, settlement agencies, the Centre Avenue YMCA, and the Urban League to advance a common agenda. Stressing thrift, sobriety, and diligence, the church and social agencies sought to better workers' lives. The companies, which contributed to churches and the Urban League, benefited from more efficient and loyal employees. As Dennis Dickerson pointed out, these programs were not intended to eliminate racial discrimination or raise wages but did make social and living conditions more tolerable.[81]

Local companies were not the only institutions helping black workers adjust. The Centre Avenue YMCA, the Soho, Bryant, and Morgan Community Centers, and scores of churches offered an array of programs. The Pittsburgh Council of Social Services Among Negroes, which formed in 1915, affiliated with the National Urban League and worked closely with Carnegie Steel, Jones & Laughlin, and other plants. Its Traveler's Aid Program met migrants at Union Station, helped them find housing and jobs, and sponsored recreation for youth. When Harold Tinker needed a job, his father took him to the Urban League, which provided him with a letter of introduction at Pathé Films. Harold held the job of shipping clerk for over a half a century.[82]

Much of the impetus for corporate welfare work, however, dissipated with the Great Depression. With unemployment soaring, turnover and absenteeism were no longer problems for the companies, and they felt less concern about workers' attitudes. The Urban League, churches, settlement houses, and other community groups were left on their own, while the problems they confronted worsened. Public agencies struggled to find their role in the provision of social services, while the network of private voluntary welfare organizations was overwhelmed. Communities and families remained the bulwark for those in need. Nevertheless, black Pittsburgh would come into its own during the 1930s and 1940s. A minority of African Americans, especially those from families with longer residence in the city, moved up the job ladder in the first quarter of the century. Some attained white-collar or professional positions and refused to accept menial labor. But workplace gains were difficult to sustain for those who came later. Upward mobility was offset by a substantial number whose standing at work dropped over time. Still, despite the serious obstacles African Americans encountered, the community taking shape on the Hill and across black Pittsburgh in the 1930s and 1940s would make its mark on music, politics, and sport.[83]

Fig. 18. "Industrial Wreckage in the Pennsylvania Steel District." Death and injury struck almost daily in local mills and mines, devastating the lives of the men and their families. Photo by Lewis W. Hine. Courtesy of the George Eastman Museum.

Fig. 19. "Man Playing the Accordion." Immigrant steelworkers often spent a little
    time after work to relax with their families by playing music from the old
    country as a means to keep some connection with their roots. Photo by
    Lewis W. Hine. Courtesy of the George Eastman Museum.

Fig. 20. "Steelworker Washing Up at the Bosh." Though steelworkers cleaned up as well as they could before leaving work, their wives or the women they boarded with washed their clothes, often without running water. Photo by Lewis W. Hine. Courtesy of the George Eastman Museum.

Fig. 21. Making steel required both skill and brawn. Photo by Lewis W. Hine. Courtesy of the George Eastman Museum.

Fig. 22. Agostino and Palmira Carlino were immigrants whose focus on work, family, and community over several decades in Bloomfield built a foundation for subsequent generations to have fruitful lives. Courtesy of the Carlino Family; all rights reserved.

Fig. 23. William Edlow and Mamie Willhite Tinker, photographed by Teenie Harris at their fiftieth wedding anniversary, came from Birmingham to Pittsburgh during the Great Migration. Their son Harold captained the Pittsburgh Crawfords. Courtesy of Marion, Natalie, Eric, Kirk and Kent Davis; all rights reserved.

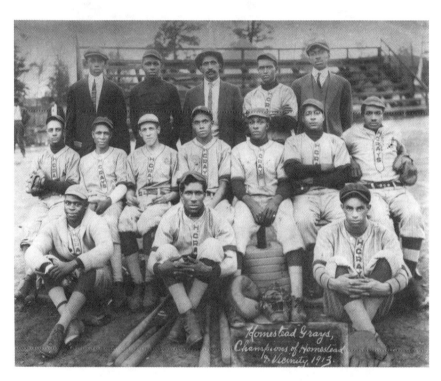

Fig. 24. The Homestead Grays, which began as a sandlot ball club of skilled workers, became black baseball's premier franchise. Its owner, Cumberland Posey Jr. (middle row, third from left) is the only person in both baseball's and basketball's hall of fame. Courtesy of Carnegie Library of Pittsburgh.

BASIN ALLEY
In the Italian quarter on the Hill, Pittsburgh

Fig. 25. These children lived on Basin Alley in the Italian quarter of the Hill, one of
the most cosmopolitan and multinational neighborhoods in Pittsburgh.
Photo by Lewis W. Hine. Courtesy of Carnegie Library of Pittsburgh.

PLAY IN SKUNK HOLLOW
The Ball Team

Fig. 26. The Skunk Hollow baseball team. Though some disparaged the Italian
    section of Bloomfield as Skunk Hollow, the Italian and African American
    children who lived there created their own sporting life, while their parents
    worked to build a neighborhood. Photo by Lewis W. Hine. Courtesy of
    Carnegie Library of Pittsburgh.

Fig. 27. "Two Boys Going to a Glassworks." The fifteen-year-old boy on the left, who could not speak English, and his friend are heading to work the night shift at a local glassworks. Photo by Lewis W. Hine. Courtesy of the National Child Labor Committee collection, Library of Congress.

Fig. 28. Women, many of whom were Jewish immigrants from Europe, worked in the needle trades and rolled small, inexpensive stogies in Hill District workshops. Photo by Lewis W. Hine. Courtesy of the George Eastman Museum.

Fig. 29. No athlete better captured Pittsburgh and much of the nation's sporting imagination than its native son Honus Wagner, one of the Baseball Hall of Fame's five inaugural inductees. Photo by Charles Condon. Courtesy of the National Baseball Library and Hall of Fame.

Fig. 30. After becoming the Pittsburgh Pirates' owner in 1900, Barney Dreyfuss inaugurated the World Series, built Forbes Field, and led the club to its first championships. Courtesy of the Pittsburgh Pirates.

Fig. 31. The Rooneys lived on two floors atop Dan Rooney's Café and Bar close by the Allegheny River on the North Side, near where the Steelers, founded by Daniel and Margaret Murray Rooney's son Art in 1933, now play. Courtesy of Kathy Rooney.

Fig. 32. Westinghouse Electric Corporation employed many women in its operations, including those who wound coils and armatures for electric motors
in what was referred to as the winding room shown in this photograph.
During massive strikes in 1914 and 1916, they joined their male coworkers
to fight for better working conditions. Courtesy of the Heinz History Center,
Library and Archives.

Fig. 33. "Smoke Means Prosperity." Most Pittsburghers saw mills and factories belching smoke and particulates as the source of profits and jobs, accepting the trade-off of polluted, unhealthy air then and for much of the twentieth century. Photo by Lewis W. Hine. Courtesy of the George Eastman Museum.

EIGHT

"LARGELY INEFFECTUAL"

DURING THE EARLY TWENTIETH CENTURY PITTSBURGH'S ETHNIC BALANCE flipped. Immigrants from eastern, southern, and central Europe and migrants from the American Black Belt began outnumbering earlier waves of émigrés and their offspring from the British Isles, Ireland, and Germany. By then many descendants of Irish and German immigrants had experienced considerable socioeconomic mobility, securing better jobs and establishing communities with vigorous retail, religious, and social organizations. As James Barrett and David Roediger pointed out, Irish Catholics could be found everywhere in a city like Pittsburgh. To the new European immigrants and black migrants remaking the city, they were inescapable. "Whether they wanted to save their souls, get a drink, find a job, or just take a walk around the corner, the newcomers had to deal with the entrenched Irish."[1]

Though Irish and German immigration to Pittsburgh had slackened and their numbers were dwindling as a proportion of the city, they and their offspring had achieved greater economic and political power. Irish ward heelers and politicians helped resolve neighborhood problems and controlled patronage at city hall. They were gatekeepers to the Catholic Church, labor unions, hiring halls, both the Republican and Democratic Parties, and the city's sporting life. More than any other nationality, the Irish could open doors for the new immigrants and black migrants or slam them shut. Even Pittsburgh's best-known athletes were of Irish or German descent. While sometimes an obstacle to other nationalities' progress, the Irish became a model for mobility and an ally for those seeking a measure of power.[2]

Despite the socioeconomic mobility that many Irish and German immigrants and their children achieved by World War I, a far greater proportion of Pittsburgh workers and their families lived precariously. Industrial capitalism provided substantial opportunities, even security or wealth, for those fortunate enough to be able to take advantage of them. But layoffs frequently impoverished families and left them with few options. The Pittsburgh Survey, an independent appraisal of Pittsburgh in the early twentieth century, painted a dismal picture of the city and its industrial surroundings. It detailed squalid housing and neighborhoods, abysmal public health, dangerous working conditions, a degraded environment, and local governments largely incapable or unwilling to address these problems. There were those, however, who sought to change conditions for the better. In Pittsburgh and around the country, churches, voluntary organizations, and political challengers loosely affiliated in what became known as the Progressive movement advanced a broad reform agenda. Workers often resisted on the job, although they struggled to maintain the gains they won. Wealthy Pittsburgh philanthropists bolstered the city's educational, health, and cultural institutions. But these reform activities, labor organizing, and philanthropic efforts were unable to resolve the most serious problems accompanying industrial capitalism.

THE IRISH

Pittsburgh's Irish came from different parts of the island. The Lawrence and Conwell families were from Belfast, the Murrays and Coynes from Galway and County Mayo, while the Rooneys hailed from Newry. Arriving during and after the late 1840s famine, they settled at the Point, in the Strip, and along both shores of the Allegheny and Monongahela Rivers. They crowded into neighborhoods close to the mills and railroad tracks and congregated in nearby mining and mill towns. At the lowest rungs of the economy's hierarchy, the Irish worked as unskilled laborers, teamsters, and stonecutters. As their numbers grew, some opened saloons and small shops, and began to pursue patronage and union positions.

Though most Irish Catholic immigrants to Pittsburgh came from rural areas and arrived with little wealth, they tapped their social capital and culture and found a place in politics and the Church. Targeted by nativists at mid-century and blamed for spreading disease, crime, and depravity, the Irish retained a sense of grievance and kept a chip on their shoulder even as they climbed the socioeconomic ladder. Over time both the Irish and

Germans sunk deep roots in Pittsburgh and showed the new immigrants who started arriving later in the century that overcoming discrimination and amassing power were possible. Their version of Americanization appealed to newcomers because the Irish had also once been at the bottom of society.

Perhaps no family better personified the Irish ascent in Pittsburgh than the Rooneys, whose roots were in iron mills and coal mines. Arthur J. Rooney, whose football team captured the city's sporting soul, was the third generation of the family to live in Pittsburgh. His paternal ancestors were forged in the iron furnaces of Ireland, Montreal, Wales, Youngstown, and Pittsburgh's South Side. His mother's people, the Murrays, wielded picks and shovels in Irish coal mines before settling along the Youghiogheny River, where they again descended into the mines. They were often on the move, chasing work as industrialization revamped the global economy. No one traveled more frequently than Arthur J. Rooney's grandfather, also named Arthur. He was born in Canada and worked at the Ebbw Vale Iron and Steel Works in Tredegar, Wales, as an apprentice to his father James before returning to North America. After a stint in Youngstown, Ohio, he came to Pittsburgh in the 1870s. Arthur worked at the Jones & Laughlin Steel Company on the South Side and, according to his grandchildren, was blacklisted after the steelworkers' union was crushed in Homestead in 1892. "You better believe I grew up as a union guy," his grandson Art attested. "I used to listen to all the stories about my grandfather fighting the Pinkertons." His grandfather, who never again worked in the mills, opened a saloon on East Carson Street on the South Side. His son Daniel, who also left the mills after the Homestead lockout, married Maggie Murray from Coultersville, a mining patch along the Youghiogheny River. They ran a boardinghouse and saloon in the small town, where their first son, Art, was born in 1901. Moving to the North Side in 1913, they lived atop Dan Rooney's Café and Bar on General Robinson Street, close to Exposition Park. That rough-and-tumble part of the North Side was known as the Ward.[3]

Maggie Murray Rooney gave birth to nine children, each baptized in the Catholic Church. Her six sons were baptized a second time on North Side sandlots. Their children became gatekeepers in local politics, the Church, and most of all sport. Art, the patriarch of the Pittsburgh Steelers, might have been the city's best all-around athlete after World War I, but he left a greater mark by making Pittsburgh sandlots and fight clubs a hothouse for generations of athletes and the Steelers a National Football League titan. His teams welcomed youth from other nationalities, just as long as they were tough enough to play. Art's brother Dan, with whom he played on the sandlots and in the minor leagues, turned down a contract with the New York Yankees to enter the seminary. James, who starred in football for the

University of Pittsburgh, became a state legislator and, like his father, dabbled in bootlegging. Vincent and Duke played for their brother's football clubs and boxed; Tommie, the youngest, died when the Marines hit the beaches on Guam in 1944. Their sisters were also involved with Pittsburgh's sporting life. Margaret married Jack McGinley, whose father Barney was Art Rooney's partner in both boxing and the Steelers, while Marie wed Johnny Laughlin, a restaurateur whose Shamrock Inn became a gathering spot for the sporting set. Laughlin organized Shamrock Specials, train coaches filled with fans, food, alcohol, and a band for Steelers games on the road.[4]

The Rooneys were also drawn into local politics, where Irish influence was evident. "Coming from the Ward," Art Rooney said, "you knew politics from the day you were able to speak." And every Irishman, he added, was a politician. His nephew Jamie Rooney, who made a career in politics, observed that "for Irish Catholics coming to Allegheny County, politics was the venue to advance." Dan Rooney's Café and Bar was a hangout for both the political and sporting set. "My grandfather owned a bar," Jamie Rooney said. "That's as much social politics as you can get." As Rooney's biographers wrote, "An Irish barkeep heard stories, witnessed deal-making, and often brokered peace and power."[5] James J. Coyne and David Lawrence were regulars at Dan Rooney's saloon as they rose through their parties' ranks in the early 1900s.

Christopher L. Magee and William Flinn sculpted Pittsburgh's late nineteenth-century political landscape. Though neither had ever held the city's mayoral reins, they ran the Republican Party and fashioned a powerful machine that controlled spending and patronage during the 1880s and 1890s. The city's explosive growth allowed the Magee-Flinn ring to reward those loyal to them with contracts, jobs, and services. Small businessmen deferred to them, as did builders and developers willing to engage in quid pro quo dealings. Those receiving city or county jobs and contracts provided their votes and monetary contributions in return.[6] Pittsburgh-born Magee, from a better-off family, graduated from the University of Pittsburgh and used his family's political connections to jump-start his career. He was city treasurer in the 1870s and later a state senator. In addition to wielding political influence, Magee owned streetcar companies, the *Pittsburgh Times* newspaper, and substantial real estate about the city. He sat on the boards of nonprofit institutions and was a benefactor of the Pittsburgh Zoo. His estate at Forbes and Halket streets later became a maternity hospital, the Magee-Women's Hospital.

Flinn, born in Manchester, England, to an Irish father and English mother, emigrated with his family as an infant, dropped out of school when he was nine, and worked his way up the ranks of the Republican Party. Although raised as a Catholic, he joined a Presbyterian church in Pittsburgh. Winning election to the state legislature, he chaired the Pittsburgh Republican Party for two decades. His Booth & Flinn Ltd. construction company was ubiquitous, and the city and county awarded it a disproportionate number of projects. Booth & Flinn built tunnels, roads, and bridges, and the men who worked on those projects voted accordingly. Lincoln Steffens's famous muckraking book, *The Shame of the Cities*, devoted a chapter to Pittsburgh's deeply ingrained corruption. "Magee wanted power," Steffens wrote, "Flinn wealth. . . . Magee spent his wealth for more power, and Flinn spent his power for more wealth. . . . Magee attracted followers, Flinn employed them. He was useful to Magee, Magee was indispensable to him. . . . Molasses and vinegar, diplomacy and force, mind and will, they were well mated."[7] Flinn owned a country manor in Fox Chapel Borough where he raised cattle; it later became the Audubon Society's Beechwood Farms Nature Reserve. His daughter Mary had a nearby estate, now Allegheny County's Hartwood Acres Park.

After Magee's death in 1901, political power shifted at the grass roots. By the early 1900s James Coyne and David Lawrence were building their own organizations, Coyne in the Republican Party, Lawrence for the relatively powerless Democrats. Both men brought Irish Catholics into their parties' infrastructure at the ward level. Coyne was born in 1882 in the Galway countryside and labored in England before joining fourteen siblings in Pittsburgh. He worked as a teamster and in construction before finding his calling in ward politics and winning election to the state legislature. He became a kingpin in county politics and secured the votes of working people and immigrants for the Republican Party, which was led by Scotch-Irish elites and the Mellons. He and his North Side lieutenants, including Art Rooney, the Hill District's Gus Greenlee, and the Strip District's Pat O'Malley, often met at Dan Rooney's saloon or Greenlee's Crawford Grill. Coyne and Lawrence were fixtures in Pittsburgh's sporting life, which mixed politics, the rackets, and night life. They also became Art Rooney's lifelong political mentors.[8]

David Lawrence's grandparents, the Lawrences and the Conwells, came from Belfast and settled at the Point, a chaotic jumble of modest homes, workshops, and gambling dens. Most of the people living there were from Galway on Ireland's west coast and spoke more Gaelic than English. Lawrence's grandfathers worked as stonemasons and stonecutters; his mother bottled whiskey, some of which she sold to Dan Rooney for his saloon across the Allegheny River. David Lawrence's father toiled as a hauler and warehouseman and gravitated to the Democratic Party. His brothers championed the labor movement and sports. One, who played professional base-ball before working as a carpenter, would use his political connections to become the county's superintendent of maintenance; the other was elected president of the plumbers' union local.[9] David played sandlot ball and man-aged semipro ball clubs and a few boxers. "I was always his batboy, ballboy, and waterboy," Art Rooney recalled, "whenever Lawrence's teams played on the North Side." Plunging into Democratic Party politics, Lawrence took his cues from William Brennen, who began working at the American Iron Works (Jones & Laughlin's predecessor) when he was eleven. Brennen be-came a machinist and then a lawyer, serving as counsel to the Homestead steelworkers after the 1892 strike and becoming the Democrats' local leader. He schooled Lawrence, his protégé, who became the Democratic Party county chairman in 1920.[10]

Coyne and Lawrence might have represented different parties, but they worked together and found common ground. Coyne's political bonds were based on personal connections and dependability more than ideology. His pragmatic alliance with the Mellons acknowledged the reality of their power in the region. But, Art Rooney's son Tim sniffed, "we never thought of the Mellons as Irish." They were Northern Ireland Presbyterians, not Catholic. Still, Coyne and later Lawrence collaborated with them to take care of their constituencies.[11] Coyne and Lawrence were just as likely to join forces with each other in the wards. Coyne lived in Oakland but owned a farm north of the city. Lawrence had an adjoining property and often met Coyne and Rooney at Coyne's farmhouse, where party politics mattered less than na-tionality, religion, and class. That approach molded Rooney's work as the Republican ward chairman on the North Side in the 1920s. When Lawrence became the city's mayor in the 1940s, he opened the door to new immi-grants, integrating their descendants into his organization.

The Irish were even more in charge of Pittsburgh's Catholic Church than the city's political parties. While parish priests, like St. Michael's Adalbert Kazinczy in Braddock, were often of a different nationality than the Irish, all but one of the diocese's first ten bishops from its inception in 1843 until 1883 were either Irish-born or of Irish parentage.[12] Michael O'Connor, the first of them, brought seminarians from Maynooth College and Sisters of Mercy from Dublin to build the diocese. They opened schools, an orphan-age, the *Pittsburgh Catholic* newspaper, and added Benedictine monks to serve German-speaking immigrants. When the new immigrants from cen-tral, southern, and eastern Europe reached critical mass, the bishop sought priests who spoke their languages, but the Irish retained control of the dio-cese. The Irish influence in the spiritual lives of the new immigrants and black Catholics was inescapable. In the Catholic Church, as in politics, the Irish were the gatekeepers.

THE GERMANS

The Germans and their descendants were not as visible as the Irish in Pittsburgh, nor were they as homogenous. They came from different regions of Germany, which had yet to cohere into a nation, and made up 10 to 15 percent of the city and county population in 1870. Their ranks included Lutherans, Catholics, and Jews, and were divided by class, occupation, and politics. Before the Civil War their circumstances at work were similar to the Irish. Women worked as domestic servants and laundresses, while men held unskilled manual jobs. Many skilled and professionally trained Germans came to Pittsburgh, too, and they experienced substantial occupational and economic mobility after the Civil War. Many could be found in small shops, working as tailors, butchers, shoemakers, bakers, and brewers; some established large, successful mercantile and manufacturing concerns. They lived in working-class wards in Lawrenceville and the Strip and south across the lower Hill to Uptown, but notably clustered in the eastern area of Allegheny City, commonly called Deutschtown. By 1870 the Germans had built a vibrant community life there. In addition to local retail shops and churches, they organized fraternal and reading societies, musical clubs, gymnasiums, and labor unions.[13]

Henry John "H.J." Heinz was among the most successful progeny of this early immigration, personifying the entrepreneurial skills and familial inclinations to develop small businesses that both German Protestants and Jews parleyed into larger, more successful enterprises. Heinz's Lutheran parents came during the 1840s and settled in Birmingham (which became the South Side), H.J.'s birthplace. The family moved to Sharpsburg, a town across the Allegheny River from Morningside. H.J. worked as a towpath boy, leading canal boats down the Pennsylvania Main Line Canal, and at his father's brickyards before he began peddling surplus produce that the family grew in its garden. Before long he was making and selling horseradish, using clear vinegar and glass bottles to demonstrate his product's purity. After starting Heinz, Noble, and Company with a partner in 1869, he made horseradish, mustard, pickles, fruit preserves, and the product with which Heinz would be forever linked, ketchup. The company successfully marketed its products beyond the city until the depression of 1873 bankrupted it. Although distraught and embarrassed over his failure, Heinz soon rebounded and diversified his business as he built what became a global manufacturing power. The H.J. Heinz Company employed hundreds of young immigrant women, not all of whom were German, at its manufacturing complex on the North Side. The company was in the vanguard of corporate welfare in Pittsburgh, offering its workers access to swimming pools, gymnasiums, lectures, concerts, and most of all, medical care.[14] That philanthropic approach continued in the 1900s, culminating in the creation of the Heinz Endowments through his son Howard Heinz's bequeath at his death in 1941.

Another successful entrepreneur of German descent, Henry Buhl Jr. made his fortune in Allegheny City a few blocks from Heinz's manufacturing and administrative headquarters. Only twenty-one years old, Buhl left Zelienople in Butler County to join Russell H. Boggs, a slightly older friend of Scotch-Irish descent, in 1869. They opened a small dry goods shop on Federal Street, Allegheny City's main shopping venue. Moving across the street, the partners transformed their venture into a full-service department store, named Boggs and Buhl. They catered to the carriage trade, the wealthy folks living along nearby Ridge Avenue area and other well-to-do streets, delivering purchases by attractive horse-and-wagon rigs. Boggs saw the growing market north of Allegheny City and orchestrated the construction of an interurban electric trolley line in 1908, commonly known as the Harmony Short Line, through Butler County to New Castle. Regular railroad service through the Ohio Valley made it possible for shoppers to come to the North Side from Sewickley and suburban towns along the river. Boggs and Buhl's reputation for excellence survived for several years after Buhl's death in 1927, but the combined impact of the Great Depression, World War II, the rise of automobiles, and suburban shopping led to the store's demise in 1958. Two years later the building was demolished during the Allegheny Center urban renewal project. Unlike Heinz, Buhl had no heirs to carry on a family philanthropic tradition, but he established the Buhl Foundation in a bequest, which continues that legacy today.[15]

GERMAN JEWS

Meanwhile, Pittsburgh's Jewish population exploded during the 1880s, rising from two thousand in 1880 to fifty-three thousand at the end of World War I, as new immigrants from eastern and central Europe joined the local German Jewish community. Rather than enter the mines and mills, German Jews more often ventured into manufacturing and retailing clothing, liquor, and other merchandise such as dry goods, shoes, and jewelry. William Frank arrived in Philadelphia from Bavaria in 1840, peddled goods around Lancaster County, and ran general stores in Ohio before opening a dry goods store in Pittsburgh. He joined the other clothing manufacturers that clustered around Liberty Avenue downtown and employed hundreds of garment workers and machine operators, many who were Jewish. A far smaller number of Jews worked in Pittsburgh's industrial corporations, notably Westinghouse and National Tube Company in McKeesport. One of William Frank's sons, Isaac, became an engineer and later organized the successful United Engineering and Foundry Company that made equipment for rolling mills.[16]

The German Jews left a more visible mark on Pittsburgh by creating department stores. In addition to Jacob Gusky's and Max Rosenbaum's stores, three German brothers, Morris, Jacob, and Isaac Kaufmann, began their retail venture with a small store on the South Side in 1871. They moved across the river to downtown and eventually to Fifth and Smithfield, where Kaufmann's Department Store became a landmark for the next century. It was the best known and consequential of these commercial efforts by Jewish immigrants. Morris's son, Edgar J. Kaufmann, became one of the city's leading businessmen and philanthropists in the first half of the twentieth century.[17]

The Rauhs, another family that built its fortunes in retail, left a comparable philanthropic legacy. Bavarian immigrants Solomon Rauh and Rosalia Lippman arrived in Pittsburgh about 1870 where Solomon worked with his brother-in-law at a downtown dry goods store. Their sons began wholesaling men's clothing and opened Rauh Brothers and Company downtown. Few families became more involved in philanthropic efforts. Rosalia was president of the Hebrew Ladies Aid Society and on the boards of the Women's Auxiliary of the Gusky Orphanage, the Montefiore Hospital Ladies' Aid Society, and the Jewish Home for the Aged. Her son Enoch continued his parent's philanthropic initiatives and served on the city council, where he helped pass an eight-hour workday ordinance and anti–child labor laws. His wife, Bertha Floersheim, performed as a singer and actress while serving on the boards of thirty organizations and presiding over Pittsburgh's chapter of the National Council of Jewish Women, which among other projects bridged the gap between established German Jews and the eastern European newcomers. She helped spread "penny lunches" for students at city schools and worked to initiate juvenile courts, public baths, and access to pasteurized milk and clean water in poorer neighborhoods. Their descendants continued the family's commitment to culture, the arts, and social welfare.[18]

Eastern European Jews, like Russian immigrants Jacob Frank and Isaac Seder, joined their German counterparts in the manufacturing and merchandising niche. Frank and Seder, who began wholesaling women's wear, opened a seven-story department building downtown in 1918 that expanded to branches in Detroit, Philadelphia, and Cleveland. Other Jewish wholesalers, like Trau & Loevner, clustered on Fifth Avenue in the Uptown section adjoining downtown. Gus Trau and Philip Loevner, immigrants from what was the Austro-Hungarian empire in the 1890s, began peddling long underwear as they rode the train from town to town along the Allegheny River.[19] Not all Jews became merchants or businessmen; eastern European Jews worked in the needle trades and rolled small, inexpensive stogies in Hill District workshops and at their homes in tenements.

GERMAN SPORTS FIGURES

Besides H. J. Heinz and Henry Buhl, the two best-known Germans in Pittsburgh and beyond had little to do with manufacturing or merchandising. For Barney Dreyfuss and Honus Wagner the baseball diamond was their field of play. The duo not only established Pittsburgh as a major league city, they broadened the sport's stature as the national pastime. While the first effort to establish professional baseball in Pittsburgh floundered, the next attempt succeeded. In 1882 a local syndicate received a charter franchise in the American Association, the forerunner of the American League. When an opening developed in the National League in 1887, the local American Association club, known as the Alleghenies, jumped leagues. The National League was but ten years old at the time and hardly in the monopolistic position vis-à-vis baseball that it and the American League would attain in the twentieth century. With its onerous reserve clause and stingy salary scales, the league alienated a majority of its players, who revolted and, with the backing of their union, the Brotherhood of Professional Baseball Players, formed a rival league, the Players' League.

The upstarts went head-to-head with the National League, placing teams in Pittsburgh and other cities. Almost the entire Pittsburgh club went over to the Players' League, and their fans were not far behind. Pittsburgh's National League's franchise fielded a mediocre lineup and its 23–113 record, the worst won–lost percentage compiled in more than a century of club baseball, earned the team a last-place finish. But the Brotherhood-backed league disbanded after the 1890 season, and the National League soon regained the upper hand. Most Brotherhood players returned to their former teams. The Pittsburgh team quickly signed up its former players and also retained the services of Louis Bierbauer of the recently dismantled Philadelphia Athletics of the American Association. The American Association claimed first rights to Bierbauer, but they had inadvertently left him off a list of players claimed from the defunct Philadelphia franchise, giving Pittsburgh the opening to sign him.

The American Association appealed the matter but an arbitration board ruled in Pittsburgh's favor. The Association responded by abrogating their agreements with the National League and denouncing Pittsburgh for its "act of piracy." Pittsburgh, rather pleased with its newly won notoriety, kept not only Bierbauer but the name as well. But the new moniker did little to help the club on the field or at the gate. The club reorganized in 1891 but escaped the second division only once before the end of the century. Unable to turn a profit, its owners sold the club to Barney Dreyfuss in 1900.[20]

Leaving Freiburg, Germany, in 1882, seventeen-year-old Dreyfuss embraced baseball as a rite of Americanization. A year after arriving in the

United States, he organized a semipro ball club in Paducah, Kentucky, where he kept the books for his cousins' distillery. When the company moved to Louisville, so did Dreyfuss. But he left its employ to devote himself to baseball and acquired control of Louisville's franchise in the American Association. Louisville joined the twelve-team National League, but the league contracted in 1899 and eliminated four franchises. As compensation for losing his National League franchise in Louisville, Dreyfuss was offered part ownership of the Pittsburgh Pirates. Before signing the deal, he traded several of his best Louisville players, including Honus Wagner, to the Pirates.

The club had been major league baseball's laughingstock in the 1890s but responded to the infusion of talent and their new owner's acumen by reeling off three consecutive National League championships and becoming a success at the gate. In 1903 the Pirates met the Boston Americans in the first World Series, losing five games to three in a best-of-nine contest played in Boston's Huntington Avenue Grounds and Allegheny City's Exposition Park. The franchise modeled stability. Before Dreyfuss the team had gone through seven presidents and eleven managers in thirteen seasons; from 1900 through 1946 either Dreyfuss or his daughter Eleanor and her husband, William Benswanger, ran the club.

Soon after acquiring the Pirates, Dreyfuss sought better home grounds than flood-prone Exposition Park on the rough-and-tumble North Side where Andrew Carnegie and Henry Oliver grew up. Espying Pittsburgh's eastward expansion, he bought land in Oakland, where the University of Pittsburgh's Posvar Hall sits today. Six months later Forbes Field opened on June 30, 1909. Named after General John Forbes, who took Fort Duquesne for the British in 1758, it was the most impressive of the dozen classic concrete and steel ballparks built between 1909 and 1915.

No athlete better captured Pittsburgh and much of the nation's sporting imagination than Dreyfuss's German compatriot, Honus Wagner. The Pirates' iconic bowlegged shortstop, who scooped balls out of the dirt at Forbes Field and led the league in batting eight times, was one of the Baseball Hall of Fame's five inaugural inductees. Born in 1874 to immigrants in Carnegie, a coal mining town a few miles west of Pittsburgh, Wagner lived there until his death in 1955. He dropped out of school and followed his father and brothers into the coal mines when he was twelve years old. Baseball, however, became Wagner's ticket out of the mines and the other blue-collar jobs he held. He played professionally for several teams before joining the National League's and Dreyfuss's Louisville Colonels. Once Barney Dreyfuss brought Wagner back to Pittsburgh in 1900, he never left and led the squad to its first World Series title. Wagner, who said that he let his bat do his talking, personified Pittsburgh's working-class ways. When he retired after twenty-one seasons, Wagner held virtually every batting record in the National League. Bloomfield's Joseph Carlino helped build the base for the statue of Wagner that stood outside Forbes Field before its relocation to Three Rivers Stadium and finally PNC Park. Wagner's unpretentious ways bolstered his popularity. He was approachable and understood working-class life because that was what he knew. His father and eight siblings never had it easy and his mother died from typhus, for which Pittsburgh led the nation in fatalities.[21]

By the end of World War I southwestern Pennsylvania's diverse German population was experiencing economic mobility and stability in the business community and in their neighborhoods. Though many had risen to the growing middle class, the majority remained part of the city's working classes. America's entry into World War I led German Americans to mute their ethnic origins, in some cases abandoning them altogether. Names, food preferences, community cultural institutions, and businesses still revealed their Germanic origins, but in other ways, such as language, German Pittsburghers assimilated rapidly into the city's mainstream.

PITTSBURGH PROGRESSIVES AND REFORM

The surge of strikes after 1900 failed to appreciably improve wages and working conditions for the region's industrial workers, especially unskilled immigrants. Corporate benefit efforts such as U.S. Steel's American Plan did no more than modestly improve conditions or extend much beyond skilled workers. These workers, many of whom were the sons and grandsons of British, Irish, and German immigrants, began achieving lifestyles virtually indistinguishable from those fashioned by white-collar employees in the middle classes. But they were the exceptions. Most Pittsburgh industrial workers, especially those with roots in eastern, central, and southern Europe or the American South, did not attain comparable working and living conditions. The Pittsburgh Survey, the Russell Sage Foundation's extensive study of the city beginning in 1907, reported extreme poverty, wretched housing, a degraded physical environment, and municipal corruption.[22] The survey writers lamented the stark and pernicious contrast between the region's powerful, efficient industrial sector and its weak, fragmented civic institutions. Pittsburgh, they stressed, exemplified industrial capitalism's labor, social, and municipal problems. The survey was part of a national Progressive reform movement that aimed to mitigate them. In Pittsburgh and beyond Progressivism brought together reformers and institutions whose goals and strategies achieved mixed results. While unable to address many of the most severe problems facing the nation, a wave of Progressive Era reform surged again during the 1930s New Deal and the 1960s Great Society and left more lasting impressions.[23]

In the 1880s and 1990s powerful reform energies built up in response to the ills of industrial America. After 1900 they mushroomed into a reform movement known as Progressivism, as well as a radical movement that went well beyond reform and embraced socialist, anarchist, even communist ideologies. Pittsburgh's labor upsurge reflected these radical currents, while the city's Progressive movement was more of a middle- and upper-class effort. In some cities corrupt political rings that ran city halls were overthrown, an army of social workers invaded the slums, and new federal and state regulatory agencies began operating. City playgrounds were built, food made purer, and schools improved. The Federal Reserve System reformed the country's financial system, tariffs were lowered, conservation efforts were initiated on a federal level, and more democratic means of conducting politics were introduced. The last gave voters the chance to initiate referendums on issues, recall candidates, and directly elect senators. In 1920 women won the right to vote in federal elections.

The roots of this Progressive movement can be found in the revolt against Social Darwinism, the social philosophy that presupposed society evolved via competition and a fight for survival in which allegedly superior races came out on top. Herbert Spencer, the British polymath scholar who coined the term, preached that nothing could or should be done about social problems. Instead, society should rely on natural evolution. Social Darwinists argued that people must stand alone, relying on their own capacities. Those who did not make it, they reasoned, were neither fit nor deserved to succeed. Society, despite the grief those unfortunates suffered, would be better off in the long run if they succumbed. This was social survival of the fittest, and for many it meant that government should do little but maintain order, prevent crime, and protect property. Shunning reform as soft-headed sentimentalism that only delayed the inevitable, Social Darwinists rejected trying to soften or prevent the losers' plight.

But to the generation coming out of universities with training in medicine, social work, teaching, and government service, doing nothing was unacceptable. Additionally, many liberal Protestant clergy and laity, in what was termed the Social Gospel, felt that the kingdom of God should be brought to earth through the application of biblical principles that ameliorated social problems.[24] Both types of reformers refused to accept that the savage dynamics of the social jungle were the only option. Spencer, they argued, did not take into consideration the human mind. Society must not be left without goals but should be planned and perfected to whatever degree possible. Putting these sentiments into action, they created settlement houses and social agencies, became muckraking journalists who exposed corruption and suggested solutions, and advocated for specific reforms in government and how cities should build infrastructure.

Andrew Carnegie, who believed that Social Darwinism justified his ferociously competitive bent, was enamored with Spencer and called himself Spencer's "Disciple" in his autobiography. They met for the first time aboard the *Servia* en route from Liverpool to New York in 1882. During the nine-day voyage Carnegie endeavored to spend as much time with Spencer as possible, persuading the chief steward to assign them to the same table for dining. He charmed Spencer and persuaded him to visit Pittsburgh during his US visit. A few weeks later Carnegie welcomed Spencer at the Pittsburgh train station, believing, historian John White wrote, that his "Edgar Thomson Steel Works represented, in embryo, the industrial order predicted by Spencer in its purest form." Spencer, however, was appalled by Pittsburgh's pollution and told Carnegie that "six months residence here would justify suicide." That did not deter the irrepressible Carnegie from continuing to venerate Spencer. He often said that "before Spencer, all for me had been darkness, after him, all had become light—and right." But Social Darwinism did not stop Carnegie from contributing to Progressive reforms.[25]

Pittsburgh reformers, like Progressives elsewhere, constituted a movement more than a cohesive organization. Loosely aligned, they adopted an environmental approach to society's problems, believing that people would respond positively to a restructured city designed to elicit better social behavior. They agreed that Pittsburgh urgently needed to tackle its many problems. While some reformers focused on issues affecting economic and city-building success, others addressed social and health conditions. Despite these differences, they shared common concerns, including a defiled environment and public corruption. They believed that cleaner, healthier, and more orderly physical and social environments would "uplift" the city and its residents' prospects.[26]

The Pittsburgh Chamber of Commerce was part of that Progressive current of reform. It viewed rationalizing and modernizing urban space and infrastructure as necessary to create an efficient, orderly city. Sprawling development, fragmented services, and divided political authority were both inefficient and encouraged corruption. The chamber promoted the creation of a political entity known as Greater Pittsburgh, essentially all of Allegheny County. It reasoned that the new urban entity would rank among the largest nationally, rationalize infrastructure development, and centralize decision making. The county had scores of separate municipalities with their own police, fire, and administrative staffs, redundancies that reformers found ineffective and expensive. Short of creating a Greater Pittsburgh, the chamber supported annexing municipalities contiguous with the city, including the infamous absorption of Allegheny City that began in 1906. Pittsburgh pushed an act through the state legislature providing for a referendum to consolidate the two cities, in which a simple majority of voters would decide the issue. Although the citizens of Allegheny City voted two to one against it, the far larger Pittsburgh electorate easily carried the day. Efforts to find the state's legislation and the referendum unconstitutional failed in state courts and the US Supreme Court, and Allegheny City formally became part of Pittsburgh in December 1907. In response to Allegheny City's annexation and the chamber's appetite for consolidation, suburban municipalities formed a league to ward off further takeovers.[27] Fragmentation of municipal government in Allegheny County persisted. Though Pittsburgh annexed a few more adjacent boroughs over the next fifteen years, an attempt in 1929 to consolidate county municipalities, including the city, into a federated government narrowly failed. In the view of many fragmentation remained a problem for the city and county into the twenty-first century.[28]

Reformers also pressed for increasing executive power in city government by changing the city charter. The Magee-Flinn political machine secured the state legislature's approval to reform Pittsburgh's charter and create executive departments, though the city's machine-controlled councils still appointed the units' heads. Charter reform in 1901 gave the mayor power over city departments, further centralizing executive power. Ten years later Progressives achieved a major victory against machine political power, or so they thought. The 1911 charter reduced the city's two ward-elected councils to one body of nine, at-large representatives. The charter diminished the power of ward bosses and parochial interests in council business, centralizing decision making at the expense of community power. But political machines adapted to the new governmental structure and remained powerful until 1970. The 1911 charter also established the City Planning Commission to bring order to development. However, the commission had only an advisory capacity, except for approval of private subdivision plans. Although augmenting executive power, the planning provision was a weak step and was soon gutted by political opponents. The 1911 charter also established a Municipal Arts Commission with power to veto city art initiatives such as purchasing sculptures and paintings and approving building designs and other city construction projects. Though a minor presence in city planning, the Arts Commission kept the idea of planning alive while the Planning Commission itself languished before 1920.

Despite the consolidation of Allegheny City with Pittsburgh, the dozens of autonomous municipal governments within Allegheny County under-

scored the Chamber of Commerce's argument that a mishmash of small jurisdictions with their own police, fire, sewage, and other services was unnec-
essarily expensive and delivered subpar results. Consolidating many of
these services into networks of greater geographical scope, the chamber reasoned, would diminish the costs of coping with the region's complex topography and suburban development. Private businesses and the public sector,
sometimes in combination, networked Pittsburgh with "pipes, wires, streets,
tracks, and other technological systems."[29] As the population increased in
outlying wards and towns, the city and county opened new streets and built
bridges. Paving and lighting followed, but in an uneven pattern that favored
middle- and upper-class areas. To boost transportation, the city awarded
private companies franchises to operate horsecars on 56 miles of track. In
the 1890s the companies switched to electric streetcars, expanded the track
network to 470 miles, and carried 168 million passengers in 1902 alone. By
then the companies led by Christopher Magee had consolidated into a more
interconnected system. Nearly a dozen incline railroads climbed steep hillsides for workers and freight haulers, while commuter railroads, interurban
tracks, and streetcar lines connected outlying communities. Similarly, private companies powered industries with natural gas and electricity. Other
companies facilitated regional communications via telegraph and then the
telephone.

Distressing diseases, most notoriously typhoid, engendered considerable
debate over improving water and sewer services. Pittsburgh had the highest
death rate from typhoid in the country at the turn of the century with low-
income immigrants especially vulnerable. The city's spatial growth required
the extension of the water system, but water was drawn from polluted rivers
and remained untreated until completion of the slow sand filtration works
in O'Hara Township in 1907, after which the typhoid death rate fell precipitously. Political disagreements had delayed that decision for a decade, accounting for many unnecessary deaths. Similarly, contention over whether
to erect separate sanitary waste and stormwater sewers or combined ones in
larger pipes was finally resolved in favor of a combined system. The city
subsequently built more than four hundred miles of combined sewers.
However, the costs borne by residents and businesses to connect to the sewers slowed the system's efficacy and consequently reduced its health benefits. As historian Joel Tarr later observed: "The legacy of the decision to com-
bine stormwater and sanitary sewerage in one pipe is the pollution of the
rivers during heavy rain events and the high costs of undoing the combined
sewers system."[30]

New expansive infrastructure networks necessitated a centralized approach to planning and construction, unlike the piecemeal efforts of the
nineteenth century. With reformers leading the way, city departments and

bureaus increasingly tackled infrastructure projects. The Department of Public Works and the Bureau of Lighting were among the government bodies that hired professional staff and consultants to plan and implement projects. But politicians representing private and local interests often impeded centralized, professional decisions. Approval for projects by the mayor, city council, or departments became entangled in politics, causing long delays or even rejection. Consequently, the provision of infrastructure, though improved by centralization and professionalism, remained uneven. Working-class neighborhoods lacked sufficient political power and were disadvantaged in the distribution of services dependent on property assessments. Families often could not afford to pay the assessments, and landlords were unwilling to bear the expense necessary to improve conditions.[31]

The Civic Club of Allegheny County (CCAC) found common ground with the Chamber of Commerce through a shared belief that moral environmentalism was a path to civic betterment. Founded in 1895 by socially active, elite members of two women's groups, the Women's Health Protective Association and the Twentieth Century Club in Oakland, the CCAC argued that a physically degraded environment and overcrowded neighborhoods contributed to social, health, and labor problems. Both the chamber and the CCAC felt that large city parks offered "breathing spots" in otherwise poorly ventilated and overcrowded cities. In addition to this health benefit, they contended that parks provided moral uplift through the connection with nature missing in the industrial city. Embracing this ideology, Pittsburgh Public Works director Edward Bigelow oversaw the establishment of Schenley, Highland, and Riverview Parks. However, working-class families did not have the time or money to enjoy them regularly. Small neighborhood parklets, playground advocates believed, offered more convenient outdoor recreation. Sometimes supervised by trained aides, they encouraged children to learn cooperative, disciplined behavior through play.[32]

The parks were an enduring legacy and over time became well used by the city's working classes. In 1889 Mary Schenley gifted the city three hundred acres of her Schenley Farms estate. One of her grandfathers, William Croghan Sr., had been a Revolutionary War officer, as had the other, James O'Hara, whose fingerprints were all over Pittsburgh's emergence during and after the war. In 1842 the not-quite-fifteen-year-old Mary eloped with a British officer, forty-two-year-old Captain Edward Wyndham Schenley, whom she had met while attending the Brighton School in Staten Island, New York. Her elopement scandalized her family and much of Pittsburgh, but the marriage lasted. After several years in the Dutch colony of Suriname, where her husband was a judge on an antislavery tribunal which

Great Britain had forced the Dutch to accept in an 1818 treaty, the couple headed to England. Mary Schenley came back to Pittsburgh briefly when she turned twenty-one to claim her estate before returning to England. In 1889 Edward Bigelow visited her to request that she make the city a beneficiary of her extensive Pittsburgh holdings, which James O'Hara had assembled. The city turned this land into its first park.[33]

The next year Andrew Carnegie, one of the three trustees for her gift, began work on the library, music hall, and museum complex that bears his name. In 1905 his largesse led to the creation of the Carnegie Technical Institute. The University of Pittsburgh moved to Oakland in 1907 and a year later, apparently at Carnegie's suggestion, Barney Dreyfuss purchased seven acres of Schenley's properties to build Forbes Field, a new home for his Pittsburgh Pirates. The Pirates had been playing in Exposition Park in a section of Allegheny City called the Ward, which had acquired a notorious reputation. Some folks referred to Allegheny City as Little Canada because, they said, the law of the United States stopped at the north shore of the Allegheny River. "The better class of citizens," Dreyfuss reflected, "especially when accompanied by their womenfolk, were loath to go there." Moreover, the Allegheny River flooded the ballpark each spring and winds had twice destroyed its roof. Dreyfuss wanted a better venue for his club.[34]

Oakland offered a glimpse of Pittsburgh's future. "The more I looked over the property," Dreyfuss said, "the better I liked it. I had a strong hunch, which amounted to a conviction, that Pittsburgh would grow eastward." Anticipating that Oakland would attract a more genteel clientele and encouraged by his friend Franklin A. Nicola, Dreyfuss spent two million dollars to acquire the land and to design and construct the park. With a buff-colored terra cotta facade, green-painted steelwork, and red tile roof, Forbes Field was the biggest and most impressive of the concrete and steel ballparks then being built in the country when it opened in 1909.[35] Forbes Field furthered the vision of builder Nicola, who, having bought land north of Forbes Avenue, worked to attract major institutions to enhance his Schenley Farms residential development. The Schenley Hotel (now the University of Pittsburgh's William Pitt Union), Pittsburgh Athletic Association, Allegheny County's Soldiers' and Sailors' Memorial Hall, Masonic Temple, and Syria Mosque were all built between 1898 and 1915, and complemented Carnegie's Music Hall and Luna Park (an amusement park), as Oakland developed into the city's cultural, educational, and entertainment center.[36]

The overwhelming need for health and social services presented a difficult challenge for Progressives. During much of the nineteenth century the informal, mutual assistance of family, neighbors, and religious institutions

was the primary source of charity for those in need. There were no significant local governmental programs, much less a state or federal agency, they
could turn to for assistance. The experiences of the Carlino family and their
immigrant neighbors in Bloomfield underscored the role of mutual assistance and its persistence during the early twentieth century. Ethnic fraternal
organizations offered essential, but minimal, sick and funeral benefits.
Workers and unions held collections and raffles for those in need, and locally elected aldermen enforced community standards over injustices arising from abusive husbands, child neglect, and other conflicts. But explosive
population growth after the Civil War necessitated more formal and professional means of ameliorating social problems, an approach in tune with the
rise of scientific, systematic thinking during the industrial era.[37]

Women found opportunities for professional development and employment in the growth of schools, orphanages, old age homes, hospitals, and
immigrant charitable institutions. Many trained to become teachers, nurses,
social workers, and care-giving aides; some managed and directed schools
and agencies. Men were not excluded from progressive work and some powerful figures gave financial support. Henry Clay Frick donated the building
for the Kingsley House, while H. J. Heinz created the Sarah Heinz House as
a center for children in the vicinity of his factory on the North Side. The
world of charity also opened spaces for female participation in civic betterment, where their "natural maternalism" was presumed to give them special
insights and authority. Begun in 1869, the Pennsylvania Female College,
renamed in 1890 the Pittsburgh College for Women and later Chatham
University, prepared young women for expanded roles in society.[38]

Progressive efforts across several issues drew some wealthier women to
enter the public arena. Kate McKnight, Lucy Dorsey Iams, and Elizabeth
Dohrman Thaw, for example, were central to the formation and extensive
activities of the pivotally important Civic Club of Allegheny County and
other reform organizations. The president of the CCAC at her death in 1907,
Kate McKnight traced her elite social connections through her father, a US
congressman, and the O'Hara and Denny families of early Pittsburgh. Elizabeth Thaw was at thirty-one the widow of William Thaw Jr., making her
heir to a railroad and coal fortune. She was the Civic Club's treasurer for
forty-three years and organized arts and music programs for public school
children along with public health initiatives. Thaw was active in women's
suffrage campaigns and a founding member of the local chapter of both
the League of Women's Voters and the Birth Control League of Allegheny
County. Lucy Iams took a complementary path to Thaw. She married a lawyer, Franklin P. Iams, and learned the ins and outs of law by working with
her husband. Chairing the CCAC's Legislative Committee, Iams became well
known in the halls of state government for her effective lobbying for reform

legislation, notably for the passage of the 1903 tenement housing law. Acknowledging the breadth of her political work, historian Roy Lubove wrote that "she acted as an informal coordinator of reform legislation for Western Pennsylvania."[39] In a parallel social universe in Pittsburgh, wealthy Jewish women such as Rosalie Rauh and her daughter-in-law Bertha Floersheim worked across a broad area of Jewish charitable organizations for orphans and the elderly, ladies aid societies, and with the Montefiore Hospital.

This trio mobilized CCAC members to support endeavors to counter the many woes degrading city life. They coordinated their reform efforts with other organizations, including the Chamber of Commerce, to pursue through legislation improvements to sewers, water treatment, and smoke control. But, in concert with the prevailing thinking of private, voluntary reform groups, they balked at constraining the city's primary industries through actual enforcement, especially with respect to smoke abatement. Instead, the CCAC emphasized long-standing issues concerning indigent women and children, public health, and the deplorable conditions in tenements. It promoted a national trend of transforming local charity into more efficient, citywide welfare systems. In Allegheny County that took the form of the Associated Charities in 1907, the forerunner of the United Way, to coordinate the many charitable organizations competing for funding and even clients. The umbrella organization, Lubove argued, advocated the progressive "techniques of investigation, coordination, and personal service to lead the poor back to the ranks of the self-sustaining."[40]

The CCAC and other volunteer organizations eschewed public welfare, fearing that it would be corrupted and wind up supporting imposters and the unworthy. Instead, they lobbied state and city government for legislation setting minimum housing standards, implementing smoke abatement, and achieving other targeted reforms. Though public regulations were modest and weakly enforced, the public sector was not entirely absent. The city built critical infrastructure such as sewers, water treatment plants, and parks, and in 1901 established the Juvenile Court, which removed children from adult judiciary venues and became a place to adjudicate family issues.[41]

A sense of middle- and upper-class paternalism infused efforts by Progressives in Pittsburgh. Filling the gap between mutual assistance and public welfare, the CCAC and other groups emphasized individual character as both the cause of poverty and the basis for resolving social problems. Frequently rooted in Protestant teachings, charitable groups decried the moral failings of the poor, their ignorance, laziness, or fondness for alcohol. They advocated shaping behavior to meet middle-class community standards. Facilities like the Crawford Bath House on the Hill and the Oliver Bathhouse on the South Side that were open to the public lessened the health risks associated with inadequate hygiene in severely underserviced and over-crowded tenements.

No institution reflected this perspective more than the settlement houses that were located in low-income and immigrant neighborhoods. The Kingsley House and Irene Kaufmann Center in the Hill District epitomized the settlement house movement in Pittsburgh. Funded privately, settlement houses offered citizenship preparation, English language lessons, and cooking and sewing classes. Child care and recreation clubs aided overburdened mothers, while female "visitors" went to homes in surrounding neighborhoods stressing the imperative of cleanliness and proper behavior.

The philanthropy of wealthy men and women valued the importance of uplifting the individual while maintaining the sanctity of the free market, private property, and limited government. Andrew Carnegie codified his view of philanthropy in two essays published in 1900 as the *Gospel of Wealth*. Embracing a philosophy of the survival of the fittest in human affairs, Carnegie held that the wealthy had the responsibility to "prevent ignorance and disease" and create resources so that less-advantaged people, that is the worthy poor, could work on their own behalf. To that end he and others like him funded libraries, schools, churches, universities, hospitals, parks, museums, and concert halls. Carnegie built libraries in Allegheny City, the City of Pittsburgh, the Borough of Carnegie, and the steel towns of Braddock, Homestead, and Duquesne, as well as about 2,500 more in the United States and the English-speaking world. Because the Washington, DC, library was the first public building in the capital to desegregate, some southern towns refused Carnegie's money, fearing the specter of integration. Other towns rebuffed his offer because they considered Carnegie an enemy of working people.[42] In Pittsburgh he established the Carnegie Museum of Natural History, Music Hall, and Art Gallery in Oakland in the 1890s. Across the ravine from his cultural complex, he founded the Carnegie Institute of Technology, initially a set of secondary schools to train skilled craftsmen and reorganized in 1912 into a school of higher education with the Margaret Morrison Carnegie College for Women. Other Carnegie initiatives did not specifically target southwestern Pennsylvania but have benefited the region since their inception. In 1905 he launched the Carnegie Foundation for the Advancement of Teaching to "provide retiring pensions for the teachers of Universities, Colleges and Technical Schools," which in time evolved into the enormously significant Teachers Insurance and Annuity Association of America (TIAA). He created the Carnegie Corporation of New York in 1911 "to promote the advancement and diffusion of knowledge among the people of the United States." It was, in the words of biographer Joseph Wall, "the super-trust in the history of philanthropy" at the time.[43]

Carnegie did not stand alone in using his fortune to benefit southwestern Pennsylvania. It's unclear to what extent his philanthropic philosophy, exhortations for the wealthy to give back to society, and benevolent actions inspired other regional elites to follow suit, but Pittsburgh and the region benefited from such philanthropy. Bequeathing 80 percent of his fortune upon his death in 1919 to nonprofit institutions of public service, H. C. Frick donated to seven regional hospitals and Pittsburgh's public schools. He also gave the city 151 acres with an endowment to create and maintain Frick Park. Frick supported three eastern universities and prior to his death established his art collection in a museum in his house on Fifth Avenue across from Central Park in New York. In addition to giving the land for Schenley Park, Mary Schenley donated property to create the Western Pennsylvania Hospital and the Western Pennsylvania Institute for the Blind and made gifts to other local causes.[44] Other wealthy Pittsburghers of the period or their descendants created foundations that have endowed the region with resources for cultural, social, economic, and environmental initiatives long after the deaths of those who amassed the wealth. Sons of Andrew W. Mellon, Richard B. Mellon, Henry Buhl Jr., and H. J. Heinz, as well as the daughter of H. C. Frick, among others, established important foundations that have served the region well.[45]

The immediate charitable deeds and long-term endowments of philanthropic beneficence by Pittsburgh's richest people are incalculable, but critics correctly observed that their fortunes were in part amassed from wages too low to support a decent standard of living and the strenuous, dangerous labor of thousands of workers, who, along with their families, could have benefited from more generous working conditions. The combination of local mutual assistance, charitable institutions' programs, large philanthropic gifts, and regulatory legislation unquestionably contributed to the region's civic betterment. Many lives were made less onerous and disagreeable, and opportunities for personal advancement, however limited, became more accessible. In the end, however, the scale of social privation and environmental degradation, along with the unwillingness by civic leaders to impinge on business prerogatives and enlist significant public sector engagement, rendered the mostly voluntary, though spirited, charitable efforts, as Roy Lubove argued, "largely ineffectual."[46]

AFTERMATH

BY THE END OF WORLD WAR I PITTSBURGH RANKED AMONG NORTH
America's largest and most vibrant metropolitan areas. But even as the region's economic power peaked, dark clouds were gathering. Those who had
made Pittsburgh their home and the waves of newcomers arriving after
World War I confronted a troubling agenda that earlier generations had not
adequately addressed. If their intent was to remain, they had little choice but
to navigate the turmoil of the twentieth century on the foundation laid by
those who came before them.

The region epitomized both the dynamism of industrial capitalism and
the downside of a laissez-faire worldview embracing private markets, indi-
vidualism, and limited government. An innovative, economic powerhouse,
southwestern Pennsylvania produced goods ranging from glass and steel to
air brakes and pickles. Its demographic makeup was just as varied, with a
majority of the population being the foreign-born and their children. Pittsburgh's footprint spread more than thirty miles from the downtown core
through urban neighborhoods, nearby mill towns, farms, and forests. While
Pittsburgh's skyscrapers, department stores, and cultural institutions were
the hallmarks of early twentieth-century modernity, the factories and adjacent communities along the rivers reinforced the region's unpretentious,

gritty, ambiance. Thick streams of railroad and streetcar tracks, river barges, pipelines, and telephone wires held together the sprawling industrial complex of more than a million people.

But the region's remarkable upward economic trajectory had stalled. The rate of industrial growth was slowing and competitors, especially Chicago, were better placed to service the country's westward growth. Those with capital often sought higher returns in other industries and cities rather than reinvest locally. And in a little more than a decade, the Roaring Twenties gave way to the Great Depression. As the downturn deepened, the region paid a steep price for its perilous overspecialization in industries no longer among the nation's most rapidly growing sectors.[1]

Pittsburgh's power brokers accepted periodic downturns and economic inequality as the natural conditions of society. Supremely self-confident, they considered their web of factories, mines, mills, and corporations strong enough to survive the vicissitudes of the twentieth century. The immigrants from Europe and migrants from the American South who came to work for them were less sanguine about their prospects. While sometimes emerging from conflicts with management with hard-won gains, they more often succumbed to a powerful and cohesive elite who shared business, political, and social connections. They had yet to gain substantial leverage in the workplace or political power commensurate with their numbers.

Though the region had grown dramatically in the nearly 150 years since Pittsburgh took shape at the headwaters of the Ohio River, its twentieth-century future was uncertain. Inequality and rampant industrial development had spawned extreme poverty, a degraded environment, unhealthy living conditions, and impotent, often corrupt local governments. Nor had many of the working people who contributed to the region's wealth been rewarded with secure or adequate livelihoods. The elites leavened their embrace of laissez-faire capitalism with charitable and religious humanitarianism, but those efforts were insufficient. Progressive reformers and some religious leaders struggled valiantly to mitigate disconcerting social issues, but the prevailing worldview limited their ability to resolve them. Civic elites countenanced reforms and supported charitable interventions that nibbled at the edges of the region's problems, but they were unwilling to relinquish control. When pivotal decisions were made, private and public leaders prioritized industrial needs over labor and social concerns.[2]

The contradictions and problems of rapacious capitalism could not be ignored indefinitely. Both elites and working people shaped Pittsburgh, forming the bones and sinews of its industrial infrastructure and contributing to its hard-driving, hard-working ethos. Their successes and failures defined not only their lives but the prospects of their progeny. The fight for Pittsburgh was far from over.

Even from the vantage of the twenty-first century, the legacies of the people who built and fought for Pittsburgh remain tangible. Some are impossible to ignore. Their names—Carnegie, Mellon, Schenley, Heinz, Oliver, and Westinghouse—are affixed to buildings, parks, corporations, and schools. And though far fewer people remember those who labored in their factories or built those parks, there would have been no Pittsburgh without them. Many who participated in the making of the city decamped, but the hardscrabble farmers and working people who stayed, fortified by waves of immigrants from Europe and African Americans from the South, created the Steel City that shouted Pittsburgh's story to the world during the twentieth century. They and their descendants infused that city with a code stressing hard work, family, persistence, and the willingness to fight—for the city, for themselves, and often with each other.

Unable to forestall European colonization or find a modus vivendi with the settlers, Catahecassa Blackhoof and most indigenous people moved on. Those who replaced them were intent on owning and utilizing the land. Some wanted no more than to provide their families with a way to subsist and a measure of autonomy. Others razed forests to produce commodities for the marketplace or dug below the soil to extract coal. Few, however, ever appreciated how well the Native Americans they had displaced had performed as stewards of the land. If they had, perhaps they would not have scarred a pristine wilderness, fouled the air they breathed, and tainted the water they drank.

James Smith learned to value the indigenous way of life. As a captive and then a tribal member, he saw how they survived and waged war. Those insights made him a leader among backwoods Pennsylvanians after his release. Smith used those lessons to protect settlers from Native American attack and then to drive British forces from the colonies during the Revolution. But after he headed to Kentucky and explored western territories. Smith served in Kentucky's general assembly, then became a missionary proselytizing among indigenous people.

A century after Smith's death, Neil Swanson rescued him from historical oblivion. In a 1937 biography, *The First Rebel*, Swanson contended that the insurgency Smith led against British authority in 1765 was the first act of rebellion in the American War of Independence.[3] RKO Radio Pictures seized on the notion and released *Allegheny Uprising* two years later. Predictably, Hollywood's version ignored the years Smith spent living with the Caughnawaga, who adopted and treated him as their equal. Instead RKO made Smith part of America's heroic narrative. John Wayne portrayed Smith in the movie as a fearless, taciturn patriot ready to tangle with avaricious traders and arrogant British officers. The local militiamen riding to the rescue under his command were fiercely racist and full of braggadocio. They dismissed Native Americans as "dirty murdering heathen" and "bloodthirsty barbarians." The only African American in the movie was Governor John Penn's servant. Clair Trevor, the only woman with a speaking part, had been besotted with Smith before he was abducted while cutting a road for Braddock's campaign. A horse-riding sharpshooter with a dash of incipient feminism, she thought he was dead. Given a second chance, Trevor galloped after Wayne when he headed into the West at the movie's end.[4]

Wayne played Pittsburgh characters twice more. In *Pittsburgh* he starred alongside Marlene Dietrich and Randolph Scott as a coal miner seeking his fortune in the steel industry. His character, Charles "Pittsburgh" Markham, who many found redolent of the late nineteenth century's robber barons, was willing to betray his friends and values to gain the power he craved. This time Randolph Scott got the girl. A decade later Wayne played an Irish-born, Pittsburgh-bred, ex-prizefighter and steelworker forged in "steel and pig iron furnaces so hot a man forgets his fear of hell." *The Quiet Man*, which won two Academy Awards, was set in the village of Cong in County Mayo, the home of many Irish immigrants to Pittsburgh. Wayne's character, Sean Thornton, was a quintessential Pittsburgh male, tough and resolute, qualities Pittsburghers still revere.[5]

Mike Fink, unlike James Smith and most of the individuals profiled in this volume, was a native Pittsburgher, born in a cabin outside Fort Pitt's palisade. But he eventually left the fledgling town and died somewhere in the West. The circumstances of his death and the location of his grave remain unknown. Long after his demise, Fink also made it to Hollywood, appearing in the 1956 Walt Disney production, *Davy Crockett and the River Pirates* and several Disney television shows. Visitors to Walt Disney's Magic Kingdom and Disneyland floated along in Mike Fink Keelboats until one capsized in 1997 and dumped a boatload of guests into the water.[6] Fink often crossed paths with James O'Hara, the County Mayo–born Irish adventurer who left his mark on Pittsburgh as a Revolutionary War hero and entrepreneur. He died in his home on Water Street near the Point in 1819 after amassing one of the city's first fortunes. Heeding George Washington's counsel, O'Hara had acquired extensive real estate holdings, including the land that became Schenley Park, where a stone marker remembers Catahecassa Blackhoof.

O'Hara's contemporary, the Scottish-born Hugh Henry Brackenridge, made unparalleled contributions to the educational, cultural, and political infrastructure of the city. His greatest accomplishment was persuading the Whiskey Rebels not to burn it down in 1794. Brackenridge left in 1799 when appointed to the Pennsylvania supreme court and died in Carlisle, Pennsylvania, in 1816. His handiwork, including the formation of Allegheny County, the Pittsburgh Academy which later became the University of Pittsburgh, and the forerunner of the *Pittsburgh Post-Gazette*, are part of the region's bedrock. But William Miller, the farmer whose summons to appear in Philadelphia sparked the Whiskey Rebellion that Brackenridge diverted from sacking Pittsburgh, left for Kentucky. So did many of those who resented the excise on distilled spirits and what they saw as the heavy hand of a distant government. Though they departed, antigovernment attitudes remained strong, especially outside of the city.

It's likely that Miranda Hollander also left. Hollander, who took an axe to a textile factory door as she rallied her coworkers to fight for shorter hours in 1848, stood trial and was convicted on charges resulting from those protests. The textile girls shook up Pittsburgh in their fight for shorter hours, but Hollander disappeared from the historical record after standing trial. Later generations reprised her unabashed labor militancy. Hollander's contemporary Martin Delany found a vibrant black community when he arrived in 1831, but he did not stay for long. He left for Canada after the passage of the Fugitive Slave Act in 1850, one of many African Americans who fled the onerous legislation that extended the reach of slave masters into the North. Called the father of black nationalism, Delany made the same decision as many African Americans in Pittsburgh—to go elsewhere. Enduring severe conditions at work and squalor in dilapidated neighborhoods, African Americans were more likely to depart than European immigrants to Pittsburgh. Constant turnover made it harder for the black community to build social and economic strength.

James Davis, the peripatetic Welsh puddler whose memoir, *The Iron Puddler*, depicted his journey from Tredegar, Wales, to Pittsburgh, became the US secretary of labor in 1921 and then a US senator in 1930. He retained his class sympathies, backing the right to strike and helping to sway U.S. Steel to end the twelve-hour workday, but he also supported the eugenics movement, an unscientific, racist effort to "improve" the human race by eliminating those people the eugenicists considered less desirable. Unwilling to open the gate to allow the new immigrants to enter the country, Davis opposed continued migration from southern, eastern, and central Europe and learned to coexist with the likes of Andrew Carnegie and H. C. Frick. Both of these industrial titans left Pittsburgh after making their fortunes there. But their legacies include the Carnegie Libraries, the Carnegie Museum, Carnegie-Mellon University, Frick Art and Historical Center, and Frick Park. George Westinghouse, one of the most prolific inventors ever, did not abandon Solitude, his Point Breeze mansion. While he lost control over the constellation of companies he created and died on the eve of World War I, those companies endured long after him. Westinghouse High School, the Westinghouse Bridge, and Westinghouse Park still bear his name.

Members of the Mellon and Heinz families also stayed, and though not all of their corporate concerns remained in their descendants' control, they continue to hold an iconic status. The Mellon financial network grew ever larger, and Heinz became a global brand. Thomas Mellon's son Andrew was appointed secretary of the treasury and served alongside James Davis in presidential cabinets during the 1920s. It was often said that he was the only secretary under whom three different presidents served. His brother's son, Richard King Mellon, recognized the dangers that Pittsburgh's overspecialized industrial sector and severely polluted environment posed to the region's future. He collaborated with David Lawrence to launch the Pittsburgh Renaissance in 1946. Other children of Pittsburgh's wealthy industrialists and bankers, often imbued with a sense of security and class superiority, also shaped the city's future. Though some heirs to the city's elite withdrew into leisurely lives, others channeled a portion of their families' assets into foundations and philanthropy. Lucy Iams, Elizabeth Thaw, and other women founded and remained committed to the Civic Club of Allegheny County, a pivotal reform organization. During her forty-three years with the Civic Club, Thaw worked to strengthen the arts in public schools and achieve women's suffrage. Their philanthropic efforts and the work of the Heinz, Pittsburgh, Mellon, Buhl, and other foundations became instrumental in shaping the city during the twentieth century. These foundations continue to address problems that the industries that built their endowments had caused.

The Irish who came to Pittsburgh eventually fared well, despite a sometimes violent reception by American-born nativists like Joe Barker and de facto restrictions on where they could work and live. Immigrant Germans faced a less daunting reception than the Irish. Though often successful, Jewish immigrants from central and eastern Europe experienced insidious and persistent antisemitism. David Lawrence, Richard King Mellon's partner in the transformational Pittsburgh Renaissance, became the city's powerful mayor and then Pennsylvania's governor. He tackled some of the city's long-term problems, but could not resolve Western Pennsylvania's fragmentation into a multitude of small political entities. Consequently, the region still struggles to address issues which call for regional strategies. But Lawrence and other descendants of immigrants fashioned a more progressive counterpoint to the laissez faire elite.

Art Rooney, Lawrence's batboy when his teams played on the North Side, became a gatekeeper on the sandlots and in ward politics for other nationalities and races. The Hope-Harveys, his sandlot ball club of Irish

Catholic boys on the North Side, would become the Pittsburgh Steelers. Rooney collaborated with African American sportsmen like Cum Posey Jr. and Gus Greenlee and guided the NFL to the pinnacle of professional sport in the United States. And as Pittsburgh's identity as the Steel City crumbled during the collapse of steel and other manufacturing, the city acquired a new persona in the 1970s and 1980s as the City of Champions.

Slovaks and the other new immigrants whom Thomas Bell portrayed in *Out of This Furnace* comprised more than a quarter of the region's population by World War I. Bell's fictional character Dobie Dobrejcak was American-born but that birthright did not ensure social equality or a voice in the workplace. Due to the death of his parents, Dobie had little familial support. But he acted on his father's lament regarding the dangers, low pay, and ethnic prejudices of millwork. Rallying coworkers during the 1930s to stand together and join the CIO, Dobie and the steelworkers union succeeded where previous campaigns to organize the industry had failed. Overcoming divisions of race and nationality as well as between skilled and unskilled labor, they helped make the region a labor stronghold, propelling tens of thousands of families into the middle class.

Agostino and Palmyra Carlino, like so many other immigrants, enabled their children to establish rewarding lives in working-class and ethnic communities, in their case Bloomfield's Italian neighborhood. They helped their sons find employment in the stonecutting trades and shared their house with married children until they could save enough to afford their own homes. The Carlinos did not amass financial capital like the Mellon or Heinz families, but they did build social capital. The second, American generation married, moved to homes nearby, and aided their parents during the Great Depression years. They joined the social clubs and mutual aid societies the first generation had formed. Though the Carlino name does not grace the city's bridges, they helped to build some of them. Agostino and Palmyra's grandson August J. Carlino (Augie) became the first Italian ward chairman in the city. His son August R. Carlino (also Augie or, informally, Augie Junior) became the executive director of the Rivers of Steel National Heritage Area, which is based in Homestead in the Bost Building, the headquarters for steelworkers during the 1892 lockout in which Carnegie and Frick crushed unionism in the region. Rivers of Steel, which joined the region's roster of notable cultural arts institutions, operates in several southwestern Pennsylvania counties. It helps them preserve historically significant buildings that both tell the region's industrial and labor story and bolster economic development. Along with operating the *Explorer*, a laboratory boat for school-age students and river tours, Rivers of Steel preserved the century-old Carrie Blast Furnaces, which hosts a stream of events, exhibitions, and tours.

Most of Mamie and William Tinker's children moved away, but their youngest son stayed and left an indelible mark on the city's sporting life. Though Harold Tinker's prospects at work were forever limited by his race, those who played with or against him on city sandlots and basketball courts respected his athletic daring. The sort of player who made those around him better by his presence, Harold captained the renowned Pittsburgh Crawfords and recruited the son of another migrant to the team as it became a competitor to the Homestead Grays. While Harold admired Cum Posey Jr. and the Homestead Grays, he longed to defeat, not to join, them. Josh Gibson, a teenager and another child of the Great Migration whom Harold persuaded to join the Crawfords, became one of the greatest ballplayers of all time. The two Negro League teams Gibson played for, the Pittsburgh Crawfords and the Homestead Grays, made the city the crossroads of black baseball in the 1930s and 1940s. Pittsburgh became to sport what Harlem was to the arts, the center of a renaissance.

In work to come, historians will pick up their stories and that of the region, but understanding the trajectory of twentieth century Pittsburgh requires an appreciation of who and what came before. That legacy enabled Pittsburghers to fashion lives of their own and a city resilient enough to overcome economic trauma. But it was also a problematic legacy, in which many people were denied their due. Some left town; others fought to make a city more to their liking. Those struggles and triumphs continue as new generations author Pittsburgh's story.

ACKNOWLEDGMENTS

PETER ORESICK, THEN THE ACTING DIRECTOR OF THE UNIVERSITY OF
Pittsburgh Press, was the catalyst to this book. Over lunch many years ago,
he said that somebody ought to write a history of the city. That planted the
idea with one of us; the other already was considering doing just that. At a
chance encounter by the mailboxes in the Department of History at the
University of Pittsburgh one morning, we decided to collaborate. Neither of
us anticipated that completing this volume would take so long, but our understanding of the city and our friendship deepened during this extended
collaboration. We talked about Pittsburgh at coffee shops before class, at
ballgames, and while hiking in the Grand Canyon. Those years, during
which we taught about Pittsburgh and worked on other projects focusing on
the city, brought us into contact with a stunning constellation of scholars,
community activists, and Pittsburghers who enriched our efforts. This history of Pittsburgh's initial 170 years is both a synthesis and an overview
that would have been impossible to write without them. Though we've each
done research on the city, we also relied heavily on the rich foundation of
Pittsburgh history built block by block over the years by the dedicated archivists, librarians, and curators of local history at institutions and museums;
by colleagues and graduate students both in and beyond Pittsburgh; and by

independent scholars. To the degree that we have succeeded, it's because we climbed atop their shoulders.

Pittsburgh has long punched above its weight in both popular imagination and scholarly circles. It initially attracted historians as the geographic flashpoint in the global struggle for control of North America during the eighteenth century, then as an important early western city dubbed the Gateway to the West, and finally as the Steel City, the center of the nation's iron and steel industry. In the twentieth century its resilience and ability to reinvent itself after a devastating stretch of deindustrialization led to its acclaim as the City of Champions and America's Most Livable City. A range of scholars have concentrated on the business practices and lives of its wealthy and iconic industrialists and bankers. Labor and social historians, meanwhile, investigated the city's centrality to the emergence of a national labor movement and explored the cataclysmic workplace conflicts that punctuated the city's history. Others were fascinated by the waves of immigrants from the United Kingdom, then Ireland and Germany, and later southern, central, and eastern Europe, who not only labored in the mills and mines but shaped its culture of persistence and image as a city that worked hard and played harder. Despite the discrimination they encountered, Pittsburgh's African American population worked alongside and lived nearby many of these immigrants. They brought the city a special respect for its music, arts, and sports. Still other historians focused on the many roles that women played in the region, despite an emphasis on heavy manufacturing and mining that denied them opportunities in the workplace. We relied on these scholars' work along the way.

Protean Pittsburgh, as native son David McCullough once called it, has long fired the imagination of writers, artists, and scholars. It also attracted the attention of two men who made Pittsburgh a laboratory for the study of social and labor history. Sam Hays came to Pittsburgh in 1960 and built the Department of History at the University of Pittsburgh. Many of the men and women he brought to the city were our mentors, teachers, and colleagues. In 1962 Hays recruited David Montgomery to Pitt. Montgomery's history of radical activism might have dissuaded many departments to hire him, but Hays was undeterred. He and Montgomery were in the vanguard of the new social and labor history that refocused how historians explored the past. They encouraged students and colleagues to delve into questions and follow approaches few were then considering and emphasized a history-from-below approach that gave voice to those whose lives had long been ignored—including domestic servants, sharecroppers, shop floor workers, and immigrants. Their brilliance and energy attracted scores of graduate students to the department who concentrated on Pittsburgh and whose work we drew on countless times. The participants in their seminars in social and labor history at the University of Pittsburgh and those offered at Carnegie Mellon University penned scores of papers on Pittsburgh's history which became master's theses, doctoral dissertations, and books. Hays would edit a collection of essays on Pittsburgh, *City at the Point: Essays on the Social History of Pittsburgh* (1989), that remains the jumping-off point for understanding Pittsburgh's history.

Both of us came to Pitt because of the department that Sam Hays, David Montgomery, and their colleagues built. Exceptionally collegial, that department attracted faculty and students without whom this book would not have been written. The department's grad students were a remarkably talented cohort. One of us began at Pitt as a grad student in the department; the other, born in Pittsburgh, came back as a professor. The grad students taught the novice how to survive and become a historian; they and the faculty made the professor better at his craft. Jim Barrett, Nora Faires, Peter Gottlieb, Mark McColloch, Ron Schatz, Vic Walsh, Bernie Hagerty, Scott Smith, Laird Bergad, and Peter Rachleff shaped us as well as this book.

We learned from our colleagues by reading and critiquing each other's writing, over brown bag lunches in the department lounge, in exploring the city and beyond together, and by watching them teach. Starting mornings with coffee and the likes of Van Beck Hall, Sy Drescher, Hugh Kearney, and Liann Tsoukas was a workshop in how to engage in the craft of history and how to teach. Other colleagues, especially Dick Smethurst, Janelle Greenberg, Bill Chase, Bob Doherty, and Reid Andrews, added to the camaraderie that made the department a special place. Dave Bear, Mark Cohen, and Marcus Rediker read early drafts of the manuscript and suggested how to make it better on countless excursions. Colleagues in the city's historical community were also central to our understanding of the city. Foremost among them were the late Michael P. Weber and the late Morton Coleman, as well as Joe Trotter and Joel Tarr from Carnegie Mellon University. Pitt historians Laurence Glasco, Maurine Greenwald, and Dick Oestreicher have devoted years to explaining the city's history, and the more we read and re-read their appraisal of the past, the more we appreciated and benefited from their labor. Barbara Burstin deserves special recognition for her years of work on the city's Jewish community. The foundation of the department has been its staff, especially its unsung heroes: Grace Tomcho, Patty Landon, and Kathy Gibson. Other scholars, many of whom neither resided or taught in the city, honed our sense of its history, including John F. Bauman, Tracy Neumann, and Allen Dieterich-Ward. They contributed to our understanding through their writings, lectures, and conversations.

A number of institutions in Pittsburgh and the region contain documentary and photographic archives, old newspapers and records, artwork, and maps of various kinds. Over the long gestation of this book, some very fine archivists and librarians have come and gone. While there were too many to list, and we would unintentionally fail to include some of them if we tried, special thanks go to David Grinnell and Miriam Meislik of the Archives Services Center at the University of Pittsburgh, Gilbert Pietrzak of Carnegie Library of Pittsburgh, Anne Madarasz and Matt Strauss of the Senator John Heinz History Center, Dawn Brean and Julie Ludwig of the Frick Art and Historical Center, the late Walter Kidney and the late Al Tannler at the Pittsburgh History and Landmarks Foundation, Ron Baraff of the Rivers of Steel National Heritage Area, and Barbara Jones, art curator of the Westmoreland Museum of American Art. The City of Pittsburgh has gradually made its records more and more available, often online. In a similar manner, many institutions have scanned and put photographs online so that researchers do not have the expense of travel. Foremost for us were the Library of Congress and the George Eastman Museum in Rochester, New York, which provided several important images.

The Howard Heinz Endowment of Pittsburgh provided critical financial support that underwrote a prolonged period of research and writing. We are especially grateful to Janet Sarbaugh, a pillar of the foundation community whose endeavors have built the city's social capital. We also appreciate those who generously and graciously allowed us to interview them. Augie J. Carlino sat down with us several times to discuss his ancestors in Pittsburgh and served us unbelievable lunches while we talked. Then his son, Augie R. Carlino, uncovered a photograph of his great grandparents, the ancestral immigrants of the Carlino family. Similarly, the Tinker family shared its recollections of the Great Migration and the African American experience in Pittsburgh and unearthed a photo of the first Tinkers to come to Pittsburgh. We hope to explore more about both families' histories in the future. Joli Schroeder, who married into the extended Henry Oliver family, shared her recollections and the documentary materials in her possession. Finally, we appreciated the advice and encouragement of the director and staff of the University of Pittsburgh Press, especially the hands-on work of Acquisitions Editor Josh Shanholtzer, Managing Editor Amy Sherman, and Design and Production Manager Joel W. Coggins. We benefited a great deal from the meticulous work of copyeditor Judy Loeven.

Our greatest debt is to Maggie Jones Patterson and Kate Zander Muller, who withstood our ups and downs during this long-materializing project and the frenzied intensity of getting it over the finishing line. They seem to intuit when to offer suggestions and when to steer clear. It is a gift they have, and one we are grateful for in many ways.

NOTES

INTRODUCTION

1. George Kracha and Mike Dobrejcak are the fictional names of two principal characters in Thomas Bell's 1941 novel *Out of This Furnace.* Born Adalbert Thomas Belejcak in Braddock in 1903, Bell created a novel of immigrant life and work in the mills and towns of the Monongahela Valley, which is widely accepted as an accurate depiction. Thomas Bell, *Out of This Furnace* (Boston: Little, Brown, 1941; repr., Pittsburgh: University of Pittsburgh Press, 1977). The Carlinos and Tinkers, however, were not fictional characters and some of their descendants still live in Pittsburgh.

2. Pittsburgh-bred, renowned historian David McCullough stresses that people, both famous and ordinary, are the story of Pittsburgh. McCullough, "The Case for Pittsburgh," Distinguished Lecture in the Humanities, September 13, 1990, Pennsylvania Humanities Council, University of Pittsburgh, Pittsburgh.

3. Mike Dobrejcak was also a fictional character in Thomas Bell's *Out of This Furnace.*

4. While calling a mill worker or coal miner from eastern or central Europe a *hunky* was originally perceived as a scornful term, in later years some of these workers' descendants and others in Pittsburgh embraced the term as a marker of their

hardworking, tough identity. Some of them published a magazine titled the *Mill Hunk Herald* in the 1970s and 1980s.

5. Barbara S. Burstin, *Steel City Jews: A History of Pittsburgh and Its Jewish Community, 1840–1915* (Pittsburgh: Closson Press, 2000), 79–81.

6. John N. Ingham, *Making Iron and Steel: Independent Mills in Pittsburgh, 1820–1920* (Columbus: Ohio State University Press, 1991), 157–90.

7. John Cumbler, *A Social History of Economic Decline* (New Brunswick, NJ: Rutgers University Press, 1989), 3. Cumbler calls this era "civic capitalism" and argues that shifts to national forces (i.e., national capitalism) weakened local control during much of the twentieth century.

8. David Montgomery, *Workers' Control in America: Studies in the History of Work, Technology, and Labor Struggles* (Cambridge: Cambridge University Press, 1980).

9. Samuel P. Hays, "The Development of Pittsburgh as a Social Order," *Western Pennsylvania Historical Magazine* 57 (1974): 432–48.

10. Joel A. Tarr, "Infrastructure and City-Building in the Nineteenth and Twentieth Centuries," in Samuel P. Hays, ed., *City at the Point: Essays on the Social History of Pittsburgh* (Pittsburgh: University of Pittsburgh Press, 1989), 213–64.

11. Roy Lubove, *Twentieth Century Pittsburgh: Government, Business and Environmental Change* (New York: John Wiley & Sons, 1969), chaps. 2 and 3.

12. Cumbler, *Social History of Economic Decline*, 5.

13. During the 1975 NFL playoffs, the inimitable Pittsburgh Steeler announcer Myron Cope came up with the idea of a yellow and black towel—the Terrible Towel—for fans to twirl at games. It became one of the most iconic symbols of Pittsburgh and can be seen wherever the Steelers play.

ONE: ON THE FRONTIER

1. Col. James Smith, *An Account of the Remarkable Occurrences in the Life and Travels of Col. James Smith during His Captivity with the Indians* (Lexington, KY: John Bradford, 1799), 5.

2. Daniel P. Barr, *A Colony Sprung from Hell: Pittsburgh and the Struggle for Authority on the Western Pennsylvania Frontier, 1744–1794* (Kent, OH: Kent State University Press, 2014), 18–19; and Patrick Spero, *Frontier Rebels: The Fight for Independence in the American West, 1765–1776* (New York: W. W. Norton, 2018) offer a comprehensive account of the frontier's role in these struggles.

3. Martha Ann Atkins, "Colonel James Smith's Death Verified," Kentucky Ancestors with the Kentucky Historical Society, July 25, 2014, http://kentuckyancestors .org/colonel-james-smiths-death-verified/.

4. Smith, *Account of the Remarkable Occurrences*, 9.

5. Smith, *Account of the Remarkable Occurrences*, 10.

6. Daniel K. Richter, *Native Americans' Pennsylvania*, Pennsylvania History

Studies Series, no. 28 (University Park: Pennsylvania Historical Association, 2005), 7–8.

7. Francis Jennings, *Ambiguous Iroquois Empire* (New York: W. W. Norton, 1984), 243.

8. Jennings, *Ambiguous Iroquois Empire*, 223, 328–45.

9. Richter, *Native Americans' Pennsylvania*, 59.

10. Daniel K. Richter, *Facing East from Indian Country: A Native History of Early America* (Cambridge, MA: Harvard University Press, 2001), 41.

11. Richter, *Facing East from Indian Country*, 53–68.

12. Jennings, *Ambiguous Iroquois Empire*, 39–41, 111–14, quoted in Richard White, *Middle Ground: Indians, Empires, and Republics in Great Lakes Region, 1630–1815* (Cambridge: Cambridge University Press, 2012), 256.

13. It had not always been that way. The Meadowcroft rock shelter in southwestern Pennsylvania in today's Avella is the oldest-known inhabited, prehistoric site in the region, dating back sixteen thousand to nineteen thousand years. The people known as the Monongahelas later lived in stockade villages along hilltops above streams draining into the Monongahela, Youghiogheny, and Ohio Rivers. Their numbers grew as they became more sedentary and added maize and beans to their fishing and hunting.

14. Jennings, *Ambiguous Iroquois Empire*, 4–7.

15. Solon J. Buck and Elizabeth Hawthorn Buck, *The Planting of Civilization in Western Pennsylvania* (1939; repr. Pittsburgh: University of Pittsburgh Press, 1967), 56.

16. The French had traded with Native Americans, but it was a costly relationship to maintain. They were more interested in how trade tied Native Americans to France, paying political and military dividends.

17. They did manage to build Fort Le Boeuf, a stockade with artillery pieces on French Creek, and to fortify a trading post at Venango on the Allegheny River.

18. The Ohio Company argued that the royal concession would counter French influence, encourage trade with the Native Americans, boost sales of English goods, and promote settlement by the Crown's subjects. It might even help develop a route that would connect the Potomac River with the Mississippi.

19. John Harpster, ed., *Crossroads: Descriptions of Western Pennsylvania, 1720–1829* (Pittsburgh: University of Pittsburgh Press, 1938), 19–20.

20. Buck and Buck, *Planting of Civilization in Western Pennsylvania*, 60.

21. A few weeks later, Tanacharison told Conrad Weiser, Pennsylvania's representative to the Native Americans that while Washington was a good-natured man, he lacked experience and would not listen to them. Had he taken their advice, "he would certainly have beat the French off; that the French had acted as great Cowards, and the English as Fools in that engagement." C. Hale Sipe, *The Indian Wars of Pennsylvania* (Harrisburg, PA: Telegraph Press, 1929), 174.

22. C. Hale Sipe, *The Indian Wars of Pennsylvania* (Harrisburg, PA: Telegraph Press, 1929), 174.

23. White, *Middle Ground*, 234.

24. Smith, *Account of the Remarkable Occurrences*, 11.

25. Smith, *Account of the Remarkable Occurrences*, 11.

26. Pennsylvania Colony Council Minutes, 6:589, quoted in Jennings, *Ambiguous Iroquois Empire*, 152.

27. Benjamin Franklin, quoted in Thomas Harrison Montgomery, *History of the University of Pennsylvania* (Philadelphia: G. W. Jacobs, 1900), 225; Jennings, *Ambiguous Iroquois Empire*, 152.

28. Smith, *Account of the Remarkable Occurrences*, 15.

29. Smith, *Account of the Remarkable Occurrences*, 16–17.

30. William Cronon, *Changes in the Land: Indians, Colonists, and the Ecology of New England* (New York: Hill and Wang, 1983), 25.

31. Thomas Morton, quoted in Cronon, *Changes in the Land*, 33.

32. Indigenous populations along the North Atlantic coast and in the Ohio River Valley were relatively small. It is not known how much their numbers were kept down by the diseases, especially smallpox, which Europeans had inadvertently introduced. Estimates range from five to seven million North American indigenous people in 1650, falling to barely a million by the twentieth century.

33. Cronon, *Changes in the Land*, 37.

34. Smith, *Account of the Remarkable Occurrences*, 31, 46.

35. Smith, *Account of the Remarkable Occurrences*, 94.

36. Buck and Buck, *Planting of Civilization in Western Pennsylvania*, 87–88.

37. Smith, *Account of the Remarkable Occurrences*, 104.

38. White, *Middle Ground*, 253.

39. White, *Middle Ground*, 256.

40. White, *Middle Ground*, 275.

41. Quoted in White, *Middle Ground*, 278. For thunderclap, Simon Ecuyer to Henry Bouquet, March 11, 1763, 10:69; for despair, George Croghan to Bouquet, March 19, 1763, 10:80, both in Papers of Colonel Henry Bouquet, Pennsylvania Historical Commission, Department of Public Instruction, Harrisburg.

42. Jennings, *Ambiguous Iroquois Empire*, 298–99. General Amherst had written another officer earlier that month, urging such tactics to wreak havoc among Native Americans. Ecuyer's logic was similar as he sent the Delaware to their death.

43. Smith, *Account of the Remarkable Occurrences*, 107.

44. Buck and Buck, *Planting of Civilization in Western Pennsylvania*, 141–42.

45. Richter, *Facing East from Indian Country*, 208.

46. James Merrell, *Into the American Woods* (New York: W. W. Norton, 1999), 37.

47. Buck and Buck, *Planting of Civilization in Western Pennsylvania*, 113–14. Fort Pitt remained in service until 1792, when it was dismantled.

48. Buck and Buck, *Planting of Civilization in Western Pennsylvania*, 144–46.

49. Barr, *Colony Sprung from Hell*, 256–57; Buck and Buck, *Planting of Civilization in Western Pennsylvania*, 144, 168.

50. Buck and Buck, *Planting of Civilization in Western Pennsylvania*, 111, 156–58.

51. Leland Baldwin, *Pittsburgh: The Story of a City, 1750–1865* (Pittsburgh: University of Pittsburgh Press, 1937), 87.

52. Neil Harmon Swanson, *The First Rebel, Being a Lost Chapter of Our History* (New York: Farrar & Rinehart, 1937), https://archive.org/details/firstrebelbeing 00swangoog/page/n10/mode/2up.

53. Smith, *Account of the Remarkable Occurrences*, 109.

54. Smith, *Account of the Remarkable Occurrences*, 124.

55. Russell J. Ferguson, *Early Western Pennsylvania Politics* (Pittsburgh: University of Pittsburgh Press, 1938), 28–30.

56. Henry Adams, quoted in Buck and Buck, *Planting of Civilization in Western Pennsylvania*, 129.

57. Prior to the last ice age's glaciers, the rivers had been wider and drained north to Lake Erie, not south via the Ohio and Mississippi.

TWO: **FRONTIER CITY**

1. Hugh Henry Brackenridge, *Incidents of the Insurrection*, ed. Daniel Marder (1795; repr., New Haven, CT: College and University Press, 1972), 93, 95.

2. Brackenridge, *Incidents of the Insurrection*, 101–5.

3. *Niles' Register*, May 28, 1814, quoted in Richard C. Wade, *The Urban Frontier: The Rise of Western Cities 1790–1830* (Cambridge, MA: Harvard University Press, 1967), 46, 105–6.

4. Dorothy Fennell, "From Rebelliousness to Insurrection: A Social History of the Whiskey Rebellion, 1765–1802" (PhD diss., University of Pittsburgh, 1981), intro.

5. Jennifer Ford, "Migration on the Passage: Western Settlement, 1763–1840," in Edward K. Muller, ed., *Biking through History on the Great Allegheny Passage* (Pittsburgh: University of Pittsburgh Press, 2009), 120–22.

6. Solon J. Buck and Elizabeth Hawthorn Buck, *The Planting of Civilization in Western Pennsylvania* (Pittsburgh: University of Pittsburgh Press, 1939), 329–30.

7. Buck and Buck, *Planting of Civilization*, 275, 330.

8. Ford, *Biking through History*, 135–37.

9. Buck and Buck, *Planting of Civilization*, 275, 330.

10. Thomas P. Slaughter, *The Whiskey Rebellion: Frontier Epilogue to the American Revolution* (New York: Oxford University Press, 1986), 65, 122–25.

11. R. Eugene Harper, *The Transformation of Western Pennsylvania, 1770–1800* (Pittsburgh: University of Pittsburgh Press, 1991), 20–21, 29, 34–43.

12. Buck and Buck, *Planting of Civilization*, 136, 431.

13. Buck and Buck, *Planting of Civilization*, 144.

14. Slaughter, *Whiskey Rebellion*, 40–43, 94; Buck and Buck, *Planting of Civilization*, 459.

15. Slaughter, *Whiskey Rebellion*, 57.

16. Slaughter, *Whiskey Rebellion*, 87–89, 93–97.

17. The tax, about seven cents a gallon, amounted to a quarter of liquor's selling price in the West, double what it was in the East where liquor was more expensive.

18. Buck and Buck, *Planting of Civilization*, 465–67.

19. Fennell, "From Rebelliousness to Insurrection," 238–39.

20. Slaughter, *Whiskey Rebellion*, 151; Brackenridge, *Incidents of the Insurrection*, xi; Fennell, "From Rebelliousness to Insurrection," 251–52.

21. James Thomas Flexner, *George Washington*, 4 vols. (Boston: Little, Brown, 1965–1972), 1:302; and John C. Fitzpatrick, ed., *The Writings of George Washington*, 39 vols. (Washington, DC: George Washington Bicentennial Commission, US Government Printing Office, 1931–1944), 27:112, cited in Slaughter, *Whiskey Rebellion*, 75–89.

22. Slaughter, *Whiskey Rebellion*, 78.

23. Brackenridge, *Incidents of the Insurrection*, 157–58.

24. William Miller, quoted in Brackenridge, *Incidents of the Insurrection*, 157; Slaughter, *Whiskey Rebellion*, 177–78.

25. Slaughter, *Whiskey Rebellion*, 180–81.

26. Harper, *Transformation of Western Pennsylvania*, 54, 279–80.

27. *Pittsburgh Gazette*, April 26, 1794 (quote); and *Gazette of the United States* (Philadelphia, May 5, 1794), cited in Leland Baldwin, *Whiskey Rebels: The Story of a Frontier Uprising* (Pittsburgh: University of Pittsburgh Press, 1939), 98.

28. Brackenridge, *Incidents of the Insurrection*, 91–94.

29. Virginia K. Bartlett, *Keeping House: Women's Lives in Western Pennsylvania* (Pittsburgh: Western Pennsylvania Historical Society and University of Pittsburgh Press, 1994), 45–46.

30. Slaughter, *Whiskey Rebellion*, 70.

31. John Pope, *A Tour through the Southern and Western Territories of the United States* (New York: Charles L. Woodward, 1888), 25.

32. Slaughter, *Whiskey Rebellion*, 187 (quote); Brackenridge, *Incidents of the Insurrection*, 119, 131.

33. Brackenridge, *Incidents of the Insurrection*, 97.

34. Brackenridge, *Incidents of the Insurrection*, 98.

35. Brackenridge, *Incidents of the Insurrection*, 8–10.

36. Buck and Buck, *Planting of Civilization*, 232, 376, 394, 460–62.

37. Buck and Buck, *Planting of Civilization*, 462; Baldwin, *Whiskey Rebels*, 38–42; Brackenridge, *Incidents of the Insurrection*, 9.

38. Brackenridge, *Incidents of the Insurrection*, 104.

39. Brackenridge, *Incidents of the Insurrection*, 115–16.

40. Slaughter, *Whiskey Rebellion*, 194–98.

41. Slaughter, *Whiskey Rebellion*, 188–89, 194–98; Brackenridge, *Incidents of the Insurrection*, 5.

42. Slaughter, *Whiskey Rebellion*, 197–203.

43. Slaughter, *Whiskey Rebellion*, 216–18; Baldwin, *Whiskey Rebels*, 244–45.

44. Fennell, "From Rebelliousness to Insurrection," 90–91.

45. Slaughter, *Whiskey Rebellion*, 224.

46. Baldwin, *Whiskey Rebels*, 264.

47. James P. McClory, "Ends of the American Earth: Pittsburgh and the Upper Ohio Valley to 1795" (PhD diss., University of Michigan, 1983), 77–78; Buck and Buck, *Planting of Civilization*, 110.

48. Wade, *Urban Frontier*, 66–67.

49. O'Hara's father, like his father before him, had soldiered in Dillon's Irish Brigade, a unit of Irish expatriates in the service of France.

50. Susan J. Illis and Carolyn S. Schumacher, eds., *General James O'Hara: Captain of Early Industry in Western Pennsylvania* (Pittsburgh: Historical Society of Western Pennsylvania, 1993), 3–4; Eulalia Catherine Schramm, "General James O'Hara: Pittsburgh's First Captain of Industry" (master's thesis, University of Pittsburgh, 1931), 2–3.

51. Schramm, "General James O'Hara," 10–18.

52. McClory, "Ends of the American Earth," 488–89.

53. Schramm, "General James O'Hara," 29–31.

54. Anthony Wayne to Timothy Pickering, September 19, 1795, quoted in Schramm, "General James O'Hara," 49–50.

55. Schramm, "General James O'Hara," 38–54.

56. Illis and Schumacher, *General James O'Hara*, 8–10; Ella Chafant, *A Goodly Heritage* (Pittsburgh: University of Pittsburgh Press, 1955), 199; Schramm, "General James O'Hara," 103–4. His descendants built some of the city's classic nineteenth-century homes on these lots. A granddaughter, Mary Schenley, gave a large portion of the Mt. Airy tract to the city, which made it into Schenley Park.

57. Wade, *Urban Frontier*, 44.

58. Buck and Buck, *Planting of Civilization*, 227; Catherine Elizabeth Reiser, *Pittsburgh's Commercial Development, 1800–1850* (Harrisburg: Pennsylvania Historical and Museum Commission, 1951), 6.

59. Reiser, *Pittsburgh's Commercial Development*, 2, 45–46, 56–60, 137; Buck and Buck, *Planting of Civilization*, 244–52, 300.

60. James Hall, *Letters from the West, 1828* (Gainesville, FL: Scholars' Facsimiles & Reprints, 1967), 36–37; Reiser, *Pittsburgh's Commercial Development*, 76–77, 125.

61. Hall, *Letters from the West*, 36–37; Reiser, *Pittsburgh's Commercial Development*, 76–77, 125.

62. Zadok Cramer, *Cramer's Almanack* (Pittsburgh, 1814), 63, quoted in Wade, *Urban Frontier*, 48.

63. Walter Blair and Franklin J. Meine, eds., *Half Horse Half Alligator: The Growth of the Mike Fink Legend* (Chicago: University of Chicago Press, 1956), 10.

64. Blair and Meine, *Half Horse Half Alligator,* 47–52.

65. Emerson Bennett, "Mike Fink: A Legend of the Ohio," 1848, in Blair and Meine, *Half Horse Half Alligator,* 170–71.

66. Irwin Shapiro, *Davy Crockett and Mike Fink* (New York: Simon and Schuster, 1955). This book was published in connection with the Disney television series.

67. John S. Robb, "Trimming 'A Darky's Heel,'" 1847, 87–92; T. B. Thorpe, "The Disgraced Scalp-Lock," 1842, 67–86, both in Blair and Meine, *Half Horse Half Alligator.*

68. Zadok Cramer, *Pittsburgh Magazine Almanack 1817,* 43–44, quoted in Reiser, *Pittsburgh's Commercial Development,* 3; Buck and Buck, *Planting of Civilization,* 250–51.

69. Reiser, *Pittsburgh's Commercial Development,* 16–17.

70. Chafant, *Goodly Heritage,* 156, 172; Zadok Cramer, *Pittsburgh Magazine Almanack 1817,* 43–44, quoted in Reiser, *Pittsburgh's Commercial Development,* 3. For a counterargument to those who believe that by 1815 Pittsburgh was destined to be a great manufacturing city, see Edward K. Muller, "Was Pittsburgh's Economic Destiny Set in 1815?" *Indiana Magazine of History* 105 (2009): 203–18.

71. Schramm, "General James O'Hara," 64–67.

72. Anne Madarasz, *Glass: Shattering Notions* (Pittsburgh: Historical Society of Western Pennsylvania, 1998), 18–30. Construction began in 1797, the same year Albert Gallatin and his partners began building a glass manufactory at New Geneva on the Monongahela forty-five miles south of Pittsburgh.

73. Schramm, "General James O'Hara," 67–76; Buck and Buck, *Planting of Civilization,* 307–11; Reiser, *Pittsburgh's Commercial Development,* 26–27; Madarasz, *Glass,* 30–34.

74. Schramm, "General James O'Hara," 78–80.

75. Hall, *Letters from the West,* 36–37.

76. Schramm, "General James O'Hara," 80–82.

77. Buck and Buck, *Planting of Civilization,* 303–6; Wade, *Urban Frontier,* 46.

78. Reiser, *Pittsburgh's Commercial Development,* 20. In 1815 manufacturers employed 1,960 workers who produced goods valued at $2,617,833.

79. Wade, *Urban Frontier,* 161–62; Reiser, *Pittsburgh's Commercial Development,* 16–20.

80. Reiser, *Pittsburgh's Commercial Development,* 132–33.

81. James E. Vance Jr., *The Continuing: Urban Morphology in Western Civilization* (Baltimore: Johns Hopkins University Press, 1990), 263–68; Virginia Price, "Introduction to Planning in Early American Cities," *Journal of Planning History* 18, no. 3 (2019): 169–71.

82. Joel Tarr, "Infrastructure and City-Building in the Nineteenth and Twentieth

Centuries," in Samuel P. Hays, ed., *City at the Point: Essays on the Social History of Pittsburgh* (Pittsburgh: University of Pittsburgh Press, 1991), 219.

83. *Pittsburgh Directory*, 1826, quoted in Wade, *Urban Frontier*, 203–4.

84. Samuel Jones, quoted in Wade, *Urban Frontier*, 42–43.

85. Arthur Lee, 1784, quoted in Buck and Buck, *Planting of* Civilization, 147; S. Jones, *Pittsburgh in the Year Eighteen Hundred and Twenty-Six* (Pittsburgh: Johnston & Stockton, 1826), 42, quoted in Wade, *Urban Frontier*, 203–4.

86. Charles Cist, "The Last of the Girtys," *Western Literary Journal and Monthly Review* 1 (February 1845): 234; Wade, *Urban Frontier*, 120–21 (quote).

87. Chafant, *Goodly Heritage*, 98–99.

88. Reiser, *Pittsburgh's Commercial Development*, 20–22; Wade, *Urban Frontier*, 161–70.

89. George Dangerfield, *The Era of Good Feelings*, (New York: Harcourt Brace, 1952), 177, quoted in Wade, *Urban Frontier*, 162–63.

90. *Statesman*, August 28, 1819, and July 17, 1819; quoted in Wade, *Urban Frontier*, 167–68.

THREE: FRACTURES IN THE COMMERCIAL CITY

1. Monte A. Calvert, "The Allegheny City Cotton Mill Riot of 1848," *Western Pennsylvania Historical Magazine* 46, no. 2 (1963): 98–133.

2. "Local Affairs, Factory Riots," *Pittsburgh Daily Gazette*, August 2, 1848; *Pittsburgh Morning Post*, August 3, 1848, quoted in Calvert, "The Allegheny City Cotton Mill Riot," 115.

3. Eric Foner and John Garraty, eds., *The Readers Companion to American History* (Boston: Houghton Mifflin, 1991), 274.

4. John T. Cumbler, *A Social History of Economic Decline: Business, Politics, and Work in Trenton* (New Brunswick, NJ: Rutgers University Press, 1989), 3.

5. John N. Ingham, "Steel City Aristocrats," in Samuel P. Hays, ed., *City at the Point: Essays on the Social History of Pittsburgh* (Pittsburgh: University of Pittsburgh Press, 1989), 267; see also John N. Ingham, *Making Iron and Steel: Independent Mills in Pittsburgh, 1820–1920* (Columbus: Ohio State University Press, 1991).

6. Richard C. Wade, *The Urban Frontier: Pioneer Life in Early Pittsburgh, Cincinnati, Lexington, Louisville, and St. Louis* (Chicago: University of Chicago Press, 1959), 177–78; Edward K. Muller, "Was Pittsburgh's Economic Destiny Set in 1815?" *Indiana Magazine of History* 105, no. 3 (2009): 203–18.

7. Pittsburgh manufacturers and merchants also called for greater tariffs on European imports, a protectionist position that regional politicians maintained long thereafter.

8. A second turnpike followed a northern route from Harrisburg to Pittsburgh via Huntingdon.

9. Catherine Elizabeth Reiser, *Pittsburgh's Commercial Development, 1800–1850* (Harrisburg: Pennsylvania Historical and Museum Commission, 1951), 67–68. Annual low-water events on the Ohio River from the city to Wheeling also disadvantaged Pittsburgh merchants. Civic leaders urged the federal government to remove sand bars, boulders, snags, and other hazards, but efforts at dredging, blasting, and pulling yielded only marginal results.

10. Reiser, *Pittsburgh's Commercial Development*, 173–90.

11. Wade, *Urban Frontier*, 195.

12. Samuel Jones, *Pittsburgh in the Year of Eighteen Hundred and Twenty-Six* (Pittsburgh: Johnston & Stockton, 1826); Louis C. Hunter, "Financial Problems of the Early Pittsburgh Iron Manufacturers," *Journal of Economic and Business History* 2 (1930): 520–44.

13. Charles Dickens, *American Notes for General Circulation* (Paris: A and W Galignari, 1842); Hunter, *Financial Problems of the Early Pittsburgh Iron Manufacturers*; Richard Oestreicher, "Working-Class Formation, Development, and Consciousness in Pittsburgh 1790–1960," in Hays, *City at the Point*, 116–17; Ingham, *Making Iron and Steel*, 26–33. In Kenneth Warren, *The American Steel Industry, 1850–1970: A Geographical Interpretation* (1973; repr., Pittsburgh: University of Pittsburgh Press, 1988), 11, he observed that before 1850 the American iron industry was small, technically backward, and growing slowly because of British competition, high labor costs, lack of mineral fuel, and poor transportation.

14. Anne Madarasz, *Glass: Shattering Notions* (Pittsburgh: Historical Society of Western Pennsylvania, 1998), 45.

15. Oestreicher, "Working-Class Formation," 115–18; James C. Holmberg, "The Industrializing Community: Pittsburgh, 1850–1880" (PhD diss., University of Pittsburgh, 1981). Holmberg's data were based on 1850 US Census reports.

16. J. Ernest Wright, quoted in Stefan Lorant, *Pittsburgh: The Story of An American City* (Garden City, NY: Doubleday, 1964), 168.

17. Lorant, *Pittsburgh*, 117.

18. Oestreicher, "Working-Class Formation," 155.

19. Oestreicher, "Working-Class Formation," 117.

20. Letters to the editor, *Pittsburgh Post*, January 23, 26, 1850.

21. *Factory Riots in Allegheny: Judge Patton's Charge to the Jury* (Pittsburgh, 1849), 2. This pamphlet was published by the manufacturers.

22. Lawrence S. Thurman, "The Cotton Industry in Pittsburgh, 1800–1861" (MA thesis, University of Pittsburgh, 1947), 1–2; John N. Boucher, ed., *A Century and a Half of Pittsburgh and Her People*, 4 vols. (Pittsburgh: Lewis Publishing, 1908), 1:506–7.

23. Leland Baldwin, *Pittsburgh: The Story of a City* (Pittsburgh: University of Pittsburgh, 1938), 226, quoted in Calvert, "Allegheny City Cotton Mill Riot," 101.

24. Thurman, "The Cotton Industry in Pittsburgh," 45; *Pittsburgh Gazette*, August 1, 1848, cited in Calvert, "Allegheny City Cotton Mill Riot," 100–101.

25. Michael Fitzgibbon Holt, *Forging a Majority: The Formation of the Republican Party in Pittsburgh, 1848–1860* (New Haven, CT: Yale University Press, 1969), 30.

26. *Pennsylvania Senate Journal,* 1837–1838, 2:348, quoted in William A. Sullivan, *The Industrial Worker in Pennsylvania, 1800–1840* (Harrisburg: Pennsylvania Historical and Museum Commission, 1955), 32; Lorant, *Pittsburgh,* 102.

27. Editorial, *Gazette,* August 14, 1832.

28. *Gazette,* June 28, 1833.

29. Joseph Frazier Wall, *Andrew Carnegie* (Pittsburgh: University of Pittsburgh Press, 1989), 87.

30. James Lynn Barnard, *Factory Legislation in Pennsylvania: Its History and Administration* (Philadelphia: University of Pennsylvania, 1907), 11–14.

31. *Pennsylvania Senate Journal,* 1837–1838, 2:346, quoted in Sullivan, *Industrial Worker in Pennsylvania,* 38.

32. *Allegheny Democrat and Working Men's Advocate,* December 9, 1836, quoted in Sullivan, *Industrial Worker in Pennsylvania,* 38.

33. Barnard, *Factory Legislation in Pennsylvania,* 10–11.

34. Sullivan, *Industrial Worker in Pennsylvania,* 46, 317–18.

35. Sullivan, *Industrial Worker in Pennsylvania,* 46, 317–18; Barnard, *Factory Legislation in Pennsylvania,* 12.

36. Barnard, *Factory Legislation in Pennsylvania,* 14.

37. Barnard, *Factory Legislation in Pennsylvania,* 15.

38. *Post,* January 1, 1849.

39. Barnard, *Factory Legislation in Pennsylvania,* 22.

40. *Factory Riots in Allegheny City,* 1–2.

41. *Factory Riots in Allegheny City,* 2–4; *Gazette,* January 17, 1849.

42. *Gazette,* January 17, 1849.

43. *Post,* August 3, 1848, quoted in Calvert, "Allegheny City Cotton Mill Riot," 108–13.

44. Henry Mann, ed., *Our Police* (Pittsburgh, 1889), 81–82. Mann did not identify the paper that published this report.

45. *Gazette,* August 3, 1848.

46. *Gazette,* August 14, 1848.

47. *Gazette,* August 17, 1848.

48. *Post,* January 13, 1848.

49. *Post,* August 2, 1848.

50. "The Five Hour System: Something New in Factory Operations," *Post,* August 9, 1848; Calvert, "Allegheny Cotton Mill Riots," 116–17.

51. Calvert, "Allegheny Cotton Mill Riots," 116–20. At the Starr Factory, owned by Swiss-German immigrant Nicholas Voeghtly, a sizable number of the employees, mostly German immigrants, reported to work. Voeghtly, who had bought large chunks of Allegheny's eastern wards, established the first German church there, and sold lots to many other Germans in the 1840s. The heavily German neighborhood

became known as Deutschtown. Voeghtly had previously broken ranks with the other owners on a number of matters. He refused to contribute to their fund to prosecute the rioters and declared after the factory riot trial that "when we can't pay our girls a living share of our profits, we'll stop the mill." *Post*, Jan. 23, 1849; Nora Faires, "Ethnicity in Evolution: The German Community in Pittsburgh and Allegheny City, Pennsylvania, 1845–1885" (PhD diss., University of Pittsburgh, 1981), 205–8.

52. *Post*, January 17, 1849; *Factory Riots in Allegheny City*, 3.

53. *Post*, December 6, 1848, quoted in Calvert, "Allegheny City Cotton Mill Riot," 124.

54. *Post*, January 23, 1849.

55. Benjamin Parke, *Recollections of Seventy Years and Historical Gleanings of Allegheny, Pennsylvania* (Boston, 1886), 79, cited in Calvert, "Allegheny City Cotton Mill Riot," 121.

56. *Factory Riots in Allegheny City*, 11–12.

57. Calvert, "Allegheny City Cotton Mill Riot," 129.

58. Thurman, "Cotton Industry in Pittsburgh," 53.

59. W. D. Howard, "God's Goodness, and Our Ingratitude" (Pittsburgh, 1849), 6–8, 15, quoted in Calvert, "Allegheny City Cotton Mill Riot," 131.

60. Holt, *Forging a Majority*, 87–89.

61. Wall, *Andrew Carnegie*, 52–53, 62.

62. Wall, *Andrew Carnegie*, 73, 79.

63. Wall, *Andrew Carnegie*, 8–12, 32.

64. Wall, *Andrew Carnegie*, 13, 54.

65. Wall, *Andrew Carnegie*, 58–59.

66. Wall, *Andrew Carnegie*, 50–53, 65–66. Will Carnegie supported the movement to secure a charter to democratize Great Britain. He believed that political rights, in turn, would bring greater economic security.

67. Wall, *Andrew Carnegie*, 20–29.

68. Wall, *Andrew Carnegie*, 67n12.

69. Wall, *Andrew Carnegie*, 72–74.

70. Wall, *Andrew Carnegie*, 81n2.

71. Wall, *Andrew Carnegie*, 81–87.

72. Wall, *Andrew Carnegie*, 97.

73. Wall, *Andrew Carnegie*, 102n38.

74. Thomas Mellon, *Thomas Mellon and His Times* (Pittsburgh: University of Pittsburgh Press, 1994), 15–16. The Mellons did not come directly from Scotland. They initially left Scotland for Ulster in northern Ireland around 1660 and stayed until the early 1800s.

75. Solon J. Buck and Elizabeth Hawthorn Buck, *The Planting of Civilization in Western Pennsylvania* (Pittsburgh: University of Pittsburgh Press, 1939), 120–21, 153.

76. Mellon, *Thomas Mellon and His Times*, 15.

77. Mellon, *Thomas Mellon and His Times*, 21–23.

78. Mellon, *Thomas Mellon and His Times*, 23–26.

79. Buck and Buck, *Planting of Civilization*, 119–21.

80. Mellon, *Thomas Mellon and His Times*, 45–51.

81. Mellon, *Thomas Mellon and His Times*, 64–65.

82. Mellon, *Thomas Mellon and His Times*, 75–88.

83. Mellon, *Thomas Mellon and His Times*, 90–97.

84. Ingham, "Steel City Aristocrats," 268–69.

85. William W. McKinney, ed., *The Presbyterian Valley* (Pittsburgh: Davis & Warde, 1958), cited in Faires, "Ethnicity in Evolution," 165.

86. Holt, *Forging a Majority*, 30–34; Ingham, "Steel City Aristocrats," 267–69.

87. Joseph F. Rishel, *Founding Families of Pittsburgh: The Evolution of a Regional Elite, 1760–1910* (Pittsburgh: University of Pittsburgh Press, 1990); Holt, *Forging a Majority*, 269–71; Ingham, "Steel City Aristocrats," 266–67; Ingham, *Making Iron and Steel*, 18–19. In addition to his economic and political success, Thomas Mellon joined the upper class through his marriage to Sarah Jane Negley of the affluent and prominent Pittsburgh Negley family.

88. Victor A. Walsh "Across 'The Big Wather': Irish Community Life in Pittsburgh and Allegheny City, 1850–1885" (PhD diss., University of Pittsburgh, 1983), 104, 111; Faires, "Ethnicity in Evolution," 168.

89. Walsh, "Across 'The Big Wather,'" 105, 111.

90. Walsh, "Across 'The Big Wather,'" 13–14, 105, 111, 13 (quote).

91. Walsh, "Across 'The Big Wather,'" 82.

92. Walsh, "Across 'The Big Wather,'" 85.

93. Walsh, "Across 'The Big Wather,'" 109.

94. Walsh, "Across 'The Big Wather,'" 120–30.

95. Walsh, "Across 'The Big Wather,'" 117–18, 138–44; Nora Faires, "Immigrants and Industry: Peopling the 'Iron City,'" in Samuel P. Hays, *City at the Point*, 6.

96. Faires, "Ethnicity in Evolution," 94–95, 166–68.

97. Faires, "Ethnicity in Evolution," 182, 208, 213–20.

98. Faires, "Ethnicity in Evolution," 169–70, 213–16; Walsh, "Across 'The Big Wather,'" 118.

99. Joel A. Tarr, "The Omnibus, Commuter Railroad, and Horsecar: Walking City to Networked City," in Edward K. Muller and Joel A. Tarr, eds., *Making Industrial Pittsburgh Modern: Environment, Landscape, Transportation, Energy, and Planning* (Pittsburgh: University of Pittsburgh Press, 2019), 121–23; Baldwin, *Pittsburgh*, 228–30.

100. Will Carnegie, quoted in David Nasaw, *Andrew Carnegie* (New York: Penguin Press, 2006), 36; John J. Kudlik, "You Couldn't Keep an Iron Man Down: Rowing in Nineteenth Century Pittsburgh," *Pittsburgh History* 73, no. 2 (1990): 51–64.

101. Joel A. Tarr, "Infrastructure and City-Building in the Nineteenth and Twentieth Centuries," in Hays, *City at the Point*, 213–64. Allegheny City opened its wa-

terworks in 1849. Lisa A. Miles, *Resurrecting Allegheny City: The Land, Structures, and People of Pittsburgh's North Side* (Pittsburgh: self-published, 2007), 92.

102. Walsh, "Across 'The Big Wather,'" 145 (quote); *Centenary Edition of the Pittsburgh Catholic* (Pittsburgh, 1844), 39.

103. Walsh, "Across 'The Big Wather,'" 153.

104. Robert Kaplan, "The Know Nothings in Pittsburgh" (seminar paper, Department of History, University of Pittsburgh, 1977), 28–34.

105. Walsh, "Across 'The Big Wather,'" 148–51.

106. Kaplan, "Know Nothings," 9–10.

107. Walsh, "Across 'The Big Wather,'" 146.

108. *A Full Report of the Trial of Barker* (Pittsburgh: Kirkland & Sharp, 1849), 15, Barker File, Pennsylvania Room, Carnegie Library of Pittsburgh, Pittsburgh.

109. *Post*, November 20, 1849, quoted in Kaplan, "Know Nothings," 27.

110. *Post*, November 8, 1849.

111. Baldwin, *Pittsburgh*, 295–99; *Post*, November 20, 1849, cited in Kaplan, "Know Nothings," 27.

112. Holt, *Forging a Majority*; Kaplan, "Know Nothings," 15–18; Barker File, Pennsylvania Room, Carnegie Library of Pittsburgh.

113. *Post*, August 7, 1854.

114. Baldwin, *Pittsburgh*, 298–99; *Pittsburgh Gazette and Commercial Journal*, August 4, 1862, cited in Hal Kimmins, "Joseph Barker: Mayor of Pittsburgh 1850–51" (seminar paper, Department of History, University of Pittsburgh, 1963).

115. Walsh, "Across 'The Big Wather,'" 149–53.

116. Holt, *Forging a Majority*, 139–40.

117. *Gazette*, March 22, 1855; *Post*, April 3, 1855, quoted in Kaplan, "Know Nothings," 33.

118. Walsh, "Across 'The Big Wather,'" 159.

119. Dorothy Sterling, *The Making of an Afro-American: Martin Robison Delany, 1812–1885* (Boston: Da Capo Press, 1971), 3–5.

120. Sterling, *Making of an Afro-American*, 15–22.

121. J. Ernest Wright, "The Negro in Pittsburgh," 1940, microfilm of unpublished manuscript written for the Works Progress Administration, chap. 3, 52.

122. F. A. Rollin, *Life and Public Services of Martin R. Delany* (Boston: Lee and Shepard, 1868), 40–41. Rollin, who with Delany's assistance, wrote Delany's biography in 1868, is the first to make this point. Frank Rollin's real identity was Frances Rollin Whipper, a Santo Domingo–born woman who became a member of the black South Carolina elite. For information about Rollin, see Sterling, *Making of an Afro-American*, 279–80.

123. Sterling, *Making of an Afro-American*, 38–40; Laurence Glasco, "Double Burden: The Black Experience in Pittsburgh," in Hays, *City at the Point*, 71. Men and perhaps a few women of African origin were among the diverse groups of Europeans and Native Americans who passed through the region during the 1700s, but

their presence was minimal. More came following the British victory over France, as planters from Virginia and Maryland brought slaves with them when they settled in the Monongahela River Valley. Wright, "Negro in Pittsburgh," chap. 2, 2–8.

124. R. Eugene Harper, *The Transformation of Western Pennsylvania, 1770–1800* (Pittsburgh: University of Pittsburgh Press, 1991), 54–55, 264, 279–80; Wright, "Negro in Pittsburgh," chap. 2, 16–17; Ann G. Wilmouth, "Pittsburgh and the Blacks: A Short History, 1780–1875" (PhD diss., Pennsylvania State University, 1975), 7–8.

125. Wright, "Negro in Pittsburgh," chap. 2, 18–19; Harper, *Transformation of Western Pennsylvania*, 55; Robert W. Brewster, "The Rise of the Antislavery Movement in Southwestern Pennsylvania," *Western Pennsylvania Historical Magazine* 22, no. 1 (March 1939).

126. Brewster, "Rise of the Antislavery Movement," 1–2. Slave owners were required to register any slaves held at the time of the law's passage; failure to do so resulted in the slave's emancipation.

127. Wilmouth, "Pittsburgh and the Blacks," 17–18; Richard J. M. Blackett, "'... Freedom, or the Martyr's Grave': Black Pittsburgh's Aid to the Fugitive Slave," *Western Pennsylvania Historical Magazine* 61, no. 2 (1978).

April 1985): 117; Harper, *Transformation of Western Pennsylvania*, 280.

128. Wright, "Negro in Pittsburgh," chap. 3, 35, claims it was the first west of the mountains; Wilmouth, "Pittsburgh and the Blacks," 71.

129. Wright, "Negro in Pittsburgh," chap. 3, 35.

130. Sterling, *Making of an Afro-American*, 48–55.

131. Sterling, *Making of an Afro-American*, 62–74.

132. Blackett, "'... Freedom or the Martyr's Grave,'" 120; Wilmouth, "Pittsburgh and the Blacks," 1, table 1.

133. Blackett, "'... Freedom or the Martyr's Grave,'" 119; Rollin, *Life and Public Services*, 43.

134. Wilmouth, "Pittsburgh and the Blacks," 104–6, 120; Brewster, "Rise of the Antislavery Movement," 4–5.

135. Direct action and the use of the courts versus slave catchers became the norms after the 1847 passage of a state law barring the kidnapping of free African Americans. Rollin, *Life and Public Services*, 43; Blackett, "'... Freedom or the Martyr's Grave,'" 120–21.

136. Wilmouth, "Pittsburgh and the Blacks," 24–25; Glasco, "Double Burden," 73–74.

137. Wright, "Negro in Pittsburgh," chap. 3, 16–17; Joe W. Trotter and Eric Ledell Smith, *African Americans in Pennsylvania: Shifting Historical Perspectives* (University Park: Pennsylvania Historical and Museum Commission and Pennsylvania State University, 1997), 2.

138. Wilmouth, "Pittsburgh and the Blacks," 23; Ullman, *Martin R. Delany: The Beginnings of Black Nationalism* (Boston: Beacon Press, 1971), 29–31; Wright, "Negro in Pittsburgh," chap. 35, 63. Wright wrote that two children were killed in the

Hayti attack and that an Emancipation Day parade (no date) was stoned and marchers were beaten, with twenty injured. He also noted that a meeting hall and a church were set on fire (chap. 4, 22).

139. Philip S. Klein and Ari Hoogenboom, *A History of Pennsylvania* (New York: McGraw-Hill, 1973), 133; Sterling, *Making of an Afro-American*, 77; Glasco, "Double Burden," 72.

140. Sterling, *Making of an Afro-American*, 78, 81–83.

141. *Daily Commercial Journal*, September 7, 1846, cited in Wilmouth, "Pittsburgh and the Blacks," 23–25, 113–17; Rollins, *Life and Public Services*, 50–52.

142. Sterling, *Making of an Afro-American*, 92–117.

143. *Gazette*, September 30, 1850; Blackett, "' . . . Freedom or the Martyr's Grave,'" 126; Sterling, *Making of an Afro-American*, 119.

144. *Gazette*, September 30, 1850, see also October 1, 1850, and October 2, 1850; Blackett, "' . . . Freedom or the Martyr's Grave,'" 127–28, 130–34; Sterling, *Making of an Afro-American*, 119–20; Wright, "Negro in Pittsburgh," chap. 4, 64–66; *Gazette*, October 3, 1850.

145. Sterling, *Making of an Afro-American*, 122–35.

146. Sterling, *Making of an Afro-American*, 148–57. The pamphlet was titled *The Condition, Elevation, Emigration, and Destiny of the Colored People of the United States*.

147. Sterling, *Making of an Afro-American*, 219–53.

148. George L. Davis, "Pittsburgh's Negro Troops in the Civil War," *Western Pennsylvania Historical Magazine* 36 (1953): 101–13. Delany's father Samuel perished in a cholera epidemic before the war; his mother, Pati, died during the conflict at the age of 96.

149. Glasco, "Double Burden," 73.

FOUR: THE IRON CITY

1. Philip Foner, *The Great Labor Uprising of 1877* (New York: Monad Press, 1977); and Robert V. Bruce, *1877: Year of Violence* (Indianapolis: Bobbs-Merrill, 1959), are solid accounts of the 1877 conflicts. Estimates of property damage and the number killed and wounded vary greatly. Several of the people killed or wounded were taken from the scene and buried or treated privately.

2. Bruce, *1877*, 210.

3. Joseph Frazier Wall, *Andrew Carnegie* (Oxford: Oxford University Press, 1970; repr., Pittsburgh: University of Pittsburgh Press, 1989), 90–94.

4. Wall, *Andrew Carnegie*, 109, 115.

5. Wall, *Andrew Carnegie*, 124.

6. Wall, *Andrew Carnegie*, 119, 133–34 (quote).

7. Wall, *Andrew Carnegie*, 135.

8. David Nasaw, *Andrew Carnegie* (New York: Penguin Press, 2006), 60.

9. Wall, *Andrew Carnegie*, 143–44.

10. Wall, *Andrew Carnegie*, 146.

11. Wall, *Andrew Carnegie*, 100, 131.

12. Dr. Edward G. Everett, "Pennsylvania Raises an Army," *Western Pennsylvania Historical Magazine* 39 (May 1956): 89–99. J. Cutler Andrews uses this figure in Stefan Lorant, *Pittsburgh: The Story of an American City* (Garden City, NY: Doubleday, 1964), 137.

13. Wall, *Andrew Carnegie*, 159–71; Nasaw, *Andrew Carnegie*, 70–75.

14. Wall, *Andrew Carnegie*, 190.

15. Lorant, *Pittsburgh*, 126–41.

16. Francis G. Couvares, *The Remaking of Pittsburgh: Class and Culture in an Industrializing City, 1877–1919* (Albany: State University of New York Press, 1984), 10; James C. Holmberg, "The Industrializing Community: Pittsburgh, 1850–1880" (PhD diss., University of Pittsburgh, 1981).

17. David H. Wollman and Donald R. Inman, *Portraits in Steel: An Illustrated History of Jones & Laughlin Steel Corporation* (Kent, OH: Kent State University Press, 1999), 7–12; Glenn Porter and Harold C. Livesay, *Merchants and Manufacturers: Studies in the Changing Structure of Nineteenth-Century Marketing* (Baltimore: Johns Hopkins University Press, 1971), 65–69.

18. Wollman and Inman, *Portraits in Steel*, 12; Porter and Livesay, *Merchants and Manufacturers*, 55–61. For a broad overview of the iron industry, see Anne Kelly Knowles, *Mastering Iron: The Struggle to Modernize an American Industry, 1800–1868* (Chicago: University of Chicago Press, 2013).

19. Wollman and Inman, *Portraits in Steel*, 20–23.

20. George L. Davis, "Greater Pittsburgh's Commercial and Industrial Development 1850–1900 (with Emphasis on the Contributions of Technology)" (PhD diss., University of Pittsburgh, 1950), 61–69; Lorant, *Pittsburgh*, 132–37. Davis gives a figure of 2,038 canon and mortars for Fort Pitt.

21. Nasaw, *Andrew Carnegie*, 85–88; Wall, *Andrew Carnegie*, 239–51.

22. John N. Ingham, *Making Iron and Steel: Independent Mills in Pittsburgh, 1820–1920* (Columbus: Ohio State University Press, 1991), 51–56; Wollman and Inman, *Portraits in Steel*, 29; Nasaw, *Andrew Carnegie*, 98–99.

23. Kenneth J. Kobus, *City of Steel: How Pittsburgh Became the World's Steelmaking Capital during the Carnegie Era* (Lanham, MD: Rowman & Littlefield, 2015), 75–83; Kenneth Warren, *The American Steel Industry, 1850–1970: A Geographical Interpretation* (Oxford: Oxford University Press, 1973), 57–60; Kenneth Warren, *Wealth, Waste, and Alienation: Growth and Decline in the Connellsville Coke Industry* (Pittsburgh: University of Pittsburgh Press, 2001), 25–32.

24. Warren, *Wealth, Waste, and Alienation*, 15–16, 25–39; Kenneth Warren, *Triumphant Capitalism: Henry Clay Frick and the Industrial Transformation of America* (Pittsburgh: University of Pittsburgh Press, 1996), 11–19.

25. Nasaw, *Andrew Carnegie*, 110–12.

26. Ingham, *Making Iron and Steel*, 38–43.

27. Wollman and Inman, *Portraits in Steel*, 42–43; Wall, *Andrew Carnegie*, 307–14; Alfred D. Chandler Jr., *The Visible Hand: The Managerial Revolution in American Business* (Cambridge, MA: Harvard University Press, 1977), 259–60.

28. Jill Jonnes, *Empires of Light: Edison, Tesla, Westinghouse, and the Race to Electrify the World* (New York: Random House Trade Paperbacks, 2004), 118–19; *George Westinghouse, 1846–1914*, pamphlet (Pittsburgh: Westinghouse Electric Corporation, 1986), 7–15; Quentin R. Skrabec Jr., *George Westinghouse: Gentle Genius* (New York: Algora Press, 2007), 66–77.

29. Nasaw, *Andrew Carnegie*, 76–78.

30. Anne Madarasz, *Glass: Shattering Notions* (Pittsburgh: Historical Society of Western Pennsylvania, 1998), 43–50, 77–78; Naomi R. Lamoreaux and Kenneth L. Sokoloff, "Location and Technological Change in the American Glass Industry during the Late Nineteenth and Early Twentieth Centuries," Working Paper 5938, National Bureau of Economic Research, 1997; Couvares, *Remaking of Pittsburgh*, 10.

31. For 1880 Holmberg uses the boundaries of the City of Pittsburgh in 1909 to derive this figure and remain consistent with his earlier 1850 calculation. The date 1909 includes the annexation of Allegheny City and leaves out only a few small annexations after 1920. Holmberg, "Industrializing Community," chap. 8, 2.

32. Bernard J. Sauers, "A Political Process of Urban Growth: Consolidation of the South Side with the City of Pittsburgh, 1872," *Pennsylvania History* 1 (1974): 265–88; Lisa A. Miles, *Resurrecting Allegheny City: The Land, Structures & People of Pittsburgh's North Side* (Pittsburgh: by the author, 2007), 100, 131.

33. Joel A. Tarr with Thomas Finholt and David Goodman, "The City and the Telegraph: Urban Telecommunications in the Pre-Telephone Era," *Journal of Urban History* 14, no. 1 (1987): 38–80.

34. Walter C. Kidney, *Pittsburgh's Bridges: Architecture and Engineering* (Pittsburgh: Pittsburgh History & Landmarks Foundation, 1999), 54; Robert J. Gangewere, *The Bridges of Pittsburgh and Allegheny County* (Pittsburgh: Carnegie Library of Pittsburgh, 2001), 32.

35. Joel A. Tarr, "Omnibus, Railroad, and Horsecar: Walking City to Networked City," in Edward K. Muller and Joel A. Tarr, eds., *Making Industrial Pittsburgh Modern: Environment, Landscape, Transportation, Energy, and Planning* (Pittsburgh: University of Pittsburgh Press, 2019), 115–54.

36. Tarr, "Omnibus, Railroad, and Horsecar"; William Kenneth Schusler, "The Economic Position of Railroad Commuting Service in the Pittsburgh District—Its History, Present, and Future" (PhD diss., University of Pittsburgh, 1959).

37. Tarr, "Omnibus, Railroad, and Horsecar."

38. Tarr, "Omnibus, Railroad, and Horsecar," 10; Kidney, *Landmark Architecture*, 35–52.

39. Joel A. Tarr, "Infrastructure and City-Building in the Nineteenth and Twentieth Centuries," in Samuel P. Hays, ed., *City at the Point: Essays on the Social History of Pittsburgh* (Pittsburgh: University of Pittsburgh Press, 1989), 234–36; Miles, *Res-*

urrecting Allegheny City, 92, 95–98, 141; Joel A. Tarr, "Lighting the Streets, Alleys, and Parks of the Smoky City, 1816–1930," *Pennsylvania History* 86, no. 3 (2019): 315–34.

40. Anthony Trollope, *North America* (1862; New York: Knopf, 1951), quoted in Nasaw, *Andrew Carnegie*, 29. The three cities that Trollope mentioned are Swansea, Merthyr-Tydvil, and South Shields.

41. Joel A. Tarr, "The Horse Era in Pittsburgh," *Western Pennsylvania History* 92, no. 2 (2009): 28–40.

42. James J. Davis, *The Iron Puddler* (Indianapolis: Bobbs-Merrill, 1922), 87. C. L. Edson ghostwrote Davis's memoir.

43. Rob Ruck, Maggie Jones Patterson, and Michael P. Weber, *Rooney: A Sporting Life* (Lincoln: University of Nebraska Press, 2010), 1–9.

44. Davis, *Iron Puddler*, 57.

45. Davis, *Iron Puddler*, 63.

46. Davis, *Iron Puddler*, 75.

47. Davis, *Iron Puddler*, 73.

48. Davis, *Iron Puddler*, 85.

49. Davis, *Iron Puddler*, 91.

50. Hoe cakes are fried cornmeal batter.

51. Davis, *Iron Puddler*, 105.

52. Couvares, *Remaking of Pittsburgh*, 19.

53. Frederick W. Taylor, *The Principles of Scientific Management* (New York: W. W. Norton 1967), 31–32; David Montgomery, *Workers' Control in America* (Cambridge: Cambridge University Press, 1979), 13.

54. Davis, *Iron Puddler*, 134.

55. David Montgomery, *The Fall of the House of Labor* (Cambridge: Cambridge University Press, 1987), 17.

56. See especially David Montgomery, "Workers' Control of Machine Production," in his *Workers' Control in America*, 9–31; and Montgomery, "The Manager's Brains under the Workman's Cap," in his *Fall of the House of Labor*, 55–56.

57. Harry C. Mavrinac, "Labor Organization in the Iron and Steel Industry in the Pittsburgh District, 1870–1890, with Special Reference to William Martin" (master's thesis, University of Pittsburgh, 1956), 16–17. For the best account of the 1849–1850 strike, see James Linaberger, "The Rolling Mill Riots of 1850," *Western Pennsylvania Historical Magazine* 47, no. 1 (January 1964): 1–18.

58. Ingham, *Making Iron and Steel*, 102.

59. Ingham, *Making Iron and Steel*, 103.

60. Ingham, *Making Iron and Steel*, 102.

61. Mavrinac, "Labor Organization," 18, 22; Ingham, *Making Iron and Steel*, 102–4.

62. Couvares, *Remaking of Pittsburgh*, 24.

63. Couvares, *Remaking of Pittsburgh*, 15–17.

64. Ingham, *Making Iron and Steel*, 105–7; Dennis C. Dickerson, *Out of the Crucible: Black Steelworkers in Western Pennsylvania, 1875–1980* (Albany: State University of New York Press, 1986), 8.

65. Ingham, *Making Iron and Steel*, 104–7.

66. Ingham, *Making Iron and Steel*, 109.

67. Ingham, *Making Iron and Steel*, 107–8, 112–15.

68. Mavrinac, "Labor Organization," 20–25; Quote from Montgomery, *Fall of the House of Labor*, 23 (quote), 25.

69. Couvares, *Remaking of Pittsburgh*, 26–27. Couvares argues that "these craftsmen were not a small elite but a good portion of overall workforce, especially in iron and glass" (17).

70. Montgomery, *Fall of the House of Labor*, 27–28. Montgomery's calculations are based on statistics from John W. Bennett, "Iron Workers in Woods Run and Johnstown: The Union Era, 1865–1895" (PhD diss., University of Pittsburgh, 1977), 18; and David Brody, *Steelworkers in America: The Nonunion Era* (Cambridge, MA: Harvard University Press, 1960), 8–9.

71. Davis, *Iron Puddler*, 135; Couvares, *Remaking of Pittsburgh*, 28.

72. Couvares, *Remaking of Pittsburgh*, 31.

73. John Kudlik, "You Couldn't Keep an Iron Man Down: Rowing in Nineteenth Century Pittsburgh," *Pittsburgh History* 73, no. 2 (1990): 51–63.

74. *National Labor Tribune*, June 13, 1891, cited in Montgomery, *Fall of the House of Labor*, 33; Couvares, *Remaking of Pittsburgh*, 59–60.

75. Couvares, *Remaking of Pittsburgh*, 25–28. When Andrew Burtt ran for the state senate as a Labor Reform Party candidate, the indefatigable labor educator carried the iron- and glassworker wards on the South Side but lost the election.

76. Couvares, *Remaking of Pittsburgh*, 27.

77. Thomas Mellon, *Thomas Mellon and His Times* (Pittsburgh: University of Pittsburgh Press, 1994), 262. For more on the panic, see George L. Davis, "Greater Pittsburgh in the Panic of 1873" (master's thesis, University of Pittsburgh, 1948).

78. James A. Henretta, W. Elliot Brownlee, David Brody, and Susan Ware, *America's History*, vol. 2, *Since 1865* (New York: Worth, 1993), 547.

79. Burton J. Hendrick, *The Life of Andrew Carnegie* (Garden City, NY: Doubleday, Doran, 1932), 197.

80. *The Journal of Wilson Howell Carpenter*, November 7, 1875, 111, Senator John Heinz Pittsburgh Regional History Center, Pittsburgh.

81. Victor Anthony Walsh, "'Across the Big Wather': Irish Community Life in Pittsburgh and Allegheny City, 1850–1885" (PhD diss., University of Pittsburgh, 1983), 116–18; Bruce, *1877*, 120–22; James Caye Jr., "Violence in the Nineteenth Century Community: The Roundhouse Riot, Pittsburgh, 1877" (unpublished seminar paper, Department of History, University of Pittsburgh, 1969), 96–100.

82. *National Labor Tribune*, May 6, 1876. The *National Labor Tribune* debuted as the *Weekly Labor Tribune* on November 21, 1873.

83. *National Labor Tribune*, January 1, 1876.

84. *National Labor Tribune*, January 1, 1876.

85. Chandler, *Visible Hand*, 79–187.

86. Michael Fitzgibbon Holt, *Forging a Majority: The Formation of the Republican Party in Pittsburgh, 1848–1860* (New Haven, CT: Yale University Press, 1969), 16–17, 228–58.

87. *National Labor Tribune*, January 15, 1876.

88. Foner, *Great Labor Uprising*, 55.

89. *National Labor Tribune*, April 8, 1876.

90. *Pittsburgh Post*, July 6, 1877, quoted in Bruce, *1877*, 121.

91. Foner, *Great Labor Uprising*, 17–18, 55.

92. Foner, *Great Labor Uprising*, 34 (quote), also see 46–48.

93. Bruce, *1877*, 59–63; Foner, *Great Labor Uprising*, 29–32.

94. *Pittsburgh Dispatch*, July 20, 1877, quoted in Bruce, *1877*, 125, 126.

95. Douglas Mahrer, ed., "The Diary of Wilson Howell Carpenter," in William Trimble and John Kent Folmar, eds., *Forging a Society: Readings in the History of Western Pennsylvania* (Pittsburgh: Historical Society of Western Pennsylvania, 1983), 242–48.

96. Foner, *Great Labor Uprising*, 61.

97. Bruce, *1877*, 141.

98. Foner, *Great Labor Uprising*, 61–65; Bruce, *1877*, 143–47.

99. *National Labor Tribune*, July 28, 1877 (quote); Mahrer, "Diary of Wilson Howell Carpenter," 243.

100. *National Labor Tribune*, July 28, 1877.

101. Bruce, *1877*, 150; Mahrer, "Diary of Wilson Howell Carpenter," 245.

102. Bruce, *1877*, 155–56.

103. Bruce, *1877*, 175–76.

104. Mahrer, "Diary of Wilson Howell Carpenter," 244.

105. Mahrer, "Diary of Wilson Howell Carpenter," 244.

106. Couvares, *Remaking of Pittsburgh*, 7–8.

107. Foner, *Great Labor Uprising*, 64–66; Couvares, *Remaking of Pittsburgh*, 8; Mahrer, "Diary of Wilson Howell Carpenter," 245–46.

108. *Pittsburgh Evening Telegraph Daily*, July 23 through 26, 1877; Bruce, *1877*, 182–83.

109. *Pittsburgh Evening Telegraph Daily*, July 25, 1877; B. F. Jones, quoted in Ingham, *Making Iron and Steel*, 111.

110. Bennett, "Iron Workers," 68–69, 105–6; Couvares, *Remaking of Pittsburgh*, 8; Charles McCollester, *The Point of Pittsburgh: Production and Struggle at the Forks of the Ohio* (Pittsburgh: Battle of Homestead Foundation, 2008), 111–12.

111. *National Labor Tribune*, July 28, 1877.

112. Foner, *Great Labor Uprising*, 201.

113. Bruce, *1877*, 73, 195.

114. Bruce, *1877*, 301; Monte A. Calvert, "The Allegheny City Cotton Mill Riot of 1848," *Western Pennsylvania Historical Magazine* 46 (1946): 130–31.

115. *Pittsburgh Evening Telegraph Daily*, July 24, 1877.

116. Caye, "Violence in the Nineteenth Century Community," 60–70, 100.

117. Bruce, *1877*, 292.

118. Karl Marx to Friedrich Engels, July 24, 1877, quoted in Foner, *Great Labor Uprising*, 230.

119. Weeks from *Iron Age*, August 22, 1877, cited in Ingham, *Making Iron and Steel*, 116; *Boston Globe*, quoted in Bruce, *1877*, 164.

FIVE: SECOND INDUSTRIAL REVOLUTION, 1880 TO 1920

1. Helen Clay Frick, "Clayton Memoir," unpublished, 1950, The Frick Collection/Frick Art Reference Library Archives, New York.

2. Quentin R. Scrabec Jr., *The World's Richest Neighborhood: How Pittsburgh's East Enders Forged American Society* (New York: Algora, 2010), 10; David Cannadine, *Mellon: An American Life* (New York: Alfred A. Knopf, 2006), 106; Frick, "Clayton Memoir"; Dawn Brean, "Aluminum Leaf in the Gilded Age," in *Metal from Clay: Pittsburgh's Aluminum Stories* (Pittsburgh: University Art Gallery, University of Pittsburgh, 2019), 28.

3. John Blackridge, *The Complete Poker Player* (New York: Dick & Fitzgerald, 1880); W. J. Florence, *The Gentlemen's Hand-Book on Poker* (New York: George Routledge & Sons, 1892).

4. Edward K. Muller and John F. Bauman, "The Olmsteds in Pittsburgh: Landscaping the Private City," in Edward K. Muller and Joel A. Tarr, eds., *Making Industrial Pittsburgh Modern: Environment, Landscape, Transportation, Energy, and Planning* (Pittsburgh: University of Pittsburgh Press, 2019), 337.

5. Cannadine, *Mellon*, 106–8, 130–31, 142.

6. Email exchange with Pittsburgh chronicler of George Westinghouse, David Bear, December 27, 2021.

7. Mark David Samber. "Networks of Capital: Creating and Maintaining a Regional Industrial Economy in Pittsburgh, 1865–1919" (PhD diss., Carnegie Mellon University, 1995).

8. Alfred D. Chandler Jr., *The Visible Hand: The Managerial Revolution in American Business* (Cambridge, MA: Harvard University Press, 1977), 1–12.

9. Philip Scranton, *Endless Novelty: Specialty Production and American Industrialization, 1865–1925* (Princeton, NJ: Princeton University Press, 1997).

10. Henry Oliver Evans, *Iron Pioneer: Henry W. Oliver, 1840–1904* (New York: E. P. Dutton, 1942), 101.

11. John N. Ingham, *Making Iron and Steel: Independent Mills in Pittsburgh, 1820–1920* (Columbus: Ohio State University Press, 1991), 82. The innovative Clapp-Griffiths furnace produced a more malleable steel with a cheaper, high-phosphorous

pig iron than the Bessemer steel-making process did. It took a few years for Oliver to work out the problems with the new furnace. Evans, *Iron Pioneer*, 100–101.

12. *Gazette*, February 8, 1904, Scrapbook, Box 3, vol. 7, Oliver Iron and Steel Company, Pittsburgh, PA. Records, 1863–1930, 1959, AIS.1964.06, Archives Service Center, University of Pittsburgh (hereafter OISC Records).

13. The material drawn for this paragraph and the preceding two are from Evans, *Iron Pioneer*, 1–12.

14. Evans, *Iron Pioneer*, 28–32.

15. Evans, *Iron Pioneer*, 33–37.

16. Ingham, *Making Iron and Steel*, 80–82; Evans, *Iron Pioneer*, 22, 28–29, 33, 38–42. Lewis, Oliver, and Phillips flourished and reorganized in 1866 to take in Oliver's brothers, David B. and James B.

17. Evans, *Iron Pioneer*, 42, 55–94. Until 1911 Pittsburgh had a lower legislative chamber, the Common Council, and an upper chamber, the Select Council.

18. Ingham, *Making Iron and Steel*, 51–58, 76–82; David H. Wollman and Donald R. Inman, *Portraits in Steel: An Illustrated History of Jones & Laughlin Steel Corporation* (Kent, OH: Kent State University Press, 1999), 50.

19. Chandler, *Visible Hand*, 259–69. A detailed analysis of Carnegie's importance in developing mass-produced steel is found in Kenneth J. Kobus, *City of Steel: How Pittsburgh Became the World's Steelmaking Capital during the Carnegie Era* (New York: Rowman & Littlefield, 2015).

20. Ingham, *Making Iron and Steel*, 49.

21. Harold C. Livesay, *Andrew Carnegie and the Rise of Big Business* (Boston: Little, Brown, 1975), 93–106.

22. Ingham, *Making Iron and Steel*, 49; Joseph Frazier Wall, *Andrew Carnegie* (Oxford: Oxford University Press, 1970; repr. Pittsburgh: University of Pittsburgh Press, 1989), 307–29; Chandler, *Visible Hand*, 259–69. For many years Wall's superb biography of Carnegie was the standard work. Since then other authors have delved into Carnegie's long and rich career. The most recent full and excellent biography is by David Nasaw: *Andrew Carnegie* (New York: Penguin Press, 2006).

23. Ingham, *Making Iron and Steel*, 62–68; Wall, *Andrew Carnegie*, 474–76, 486–88; Livesay, *Andrew Carnegie and the Rise of Big Business*, 101–2.

24. Ingham, *Making Iron and Steel*, 68–72; Wall, *Andrew Carnegie*, 497–99.

25. Wall, *Andrew Carnegie*, 587.

26. Wall, *Andrew Carnegie*, 532; Livesay, *Andrew Carnegie and the Rise of Big Business*, 113.

27. Wall, *Andrew Carnegie*, 504–5; Livesay, *Andrew Carnegie and the Rise of Big Business*, 114–16; Paul F. Paskoff, ed., *Iron and Steel Industry in the Nineteenth Century* (New York: Facts on File, 1989), 265–67.

28. Kenneth Warren, *Wealth, Waste, and Alienation: Growth and Decline in the Connellsville Coke Industry* (Pittsburgh: University of Pittsburgh Press, 2001), 61; Wall, *Andrew Carnegie*, 483–85, 587.

29. Kenneth Warren, *Triumphant Capitalism: Henry Clay Frick and the Industrial Transformation of America* (Pittsburgh: University of Pittsburgh Press, 1996), 7–9; Warren, *Wealth, Waste, and Alienation*, 11–14.

30. Warren, *Triumphant Capitalism*, 10.

31. Warren, *Triumphant Capitalism*, 11–19; Warren, *Wealth, Waste. and Alienation*, 32; Martha Frick Symington Sanger, *Henry Clay Frick: An Intimate Portrait* (New York: Abbeville Press, 1998), 42–56.

32. Wall, *Andrew Carnegie*, 485.

33. Wall, *Andrew Carnegie*, 490–98; Livesay, *Andrew Carnegie and the Rise of Big Business*, 121–23, 132; Warren, *Triumphant Capitalism*, 43–49, 54–55.

34. Wall, *Andrew Carnegie*, 595–600, 614; Evans, *Iron Pioneer*, 204–11.

35. Wall, *Andrew Carnegie*, 619–20; Livesay, *Andrew Carnegie and the Rise of Big Business*, 160–63. First J. G. Leishman and then Charles M. Schwab replaced Frick as head of Carnegie Steel.

36. Evans, *Iron Pioneer*, 215–22; Wall, *Andrew Carnegie*, 613–20; Livesay, *Andrew Carnegie and the Rise of Big Business*, 152–54, 164–66. Prior to this time companies often relied on independent jobbers or wholesalers for sales.

37. Ingham, *Making Iron and Steel*, 72–75.

38. Evans, *Iron Pioneer*, 96–99; Ingham, *Making Iron and Steel*, 82.

39. Evans, *Iron Pioneer*, 100–108, 157–60; Ingham, *Making Iron and Steel*, 83. Oliver merged the Schoen Pressed Steel Car Company with an Illinois steel equipment manufacturer in 1899, moved it to Pittsburgh, and named the combined firm the Pressed Steel Car Company, soon to be embroiled in local labor disputes.

40. Evans, *Iron Pioneer*, 105–6, 153–60.

41. Evans, *Iron Pioneer*, 135–38, 193.

42. Evans, *Iron Pioneer*, 139–42. Oliver was named president of the new Pittsburgh and Western Railroad.

43. Writing a few years after Oliver's death, Herbert Casson characterized him: "His life was a series of magnificent climaxes, of startling successes and crashing failures. He packed the experiences of a half a dozen lifetimes into one. As a business man he was a marvel of force and elasticity. The harder he was thrown down, the higher he would rebound. His optimism was at all times invulnerable." Herbert N. Casson, *The Romance of Steel: The Story of a Thousand Millionaires* (New York: A. S. Barnes, 1907), 118.

44. Wollman and Inman, *Portraits in Steel*, 22–49, 59–83.

45. Ingham, *Making Iron and Steel*, 74–80, 55–91; Scranton, *Endless Novelty*.

46. Ingham, *Making Iron and Steel*, 151.

47. Ingham, *Making Iron and Steel*, 140–51.

48. Paskoff, *Iron and Steel Industry in the Nineteenth Century*, 146–47; Evans, *Iron Pioneer*, 265–67; Ingham, *Making Iron and Steel*, 83; *Pittsburgh Dispatch*, February 8, 1904, Scrapbook, Box 3, vol. 7, OISC Records.

49. Naomi R. Lamoreaux, *The Great Merger Movement in American Business, 1895–1904* (Cambridge: Cambridge University Press, 1985), 1–16, 56–59, 62–86.

50. Livesay, *Andrew Carnegie and the Rise of Big Business*, 183; Wall, *Andrew Carnegie*, 720.

51. Livesay, *Andrew Carnegie and the Rise of Big Business*, 184–86; Wall, *Andrew Carnegie*, 723–34, 765–93.

52. Ingham, *Making Iron and Steel*, 140–51; Samber, "Networks of Capital," 199–200. The headquarters of U.S. Steel was in New York until 1938 when Pittsburgh became the headquarters for production and sales, while financial matters remained in Wall Street at 71 Broadway. Kenneth Warren, *Big Steel: The First Century of the United States Steel Corporation, 1901–2001* (Pittsburgh: University of Pittsburgh Press, 2001), 148.

53. Evans, *Iron Pioneer*, 283–90; Warren, *Triumphant Capitalism*, 284–86; Wollman and Inman, *Portraits in Steel*, 62–82; Matthew S. Magda, *Monessen: Industrial Boomtown and Steel Community, 1898–1980* (Harrisburg: Pennsylvania Historical and Museum Commission, 1985), 3–9. The J&L works had blast furnaces, open-hearth furnaces, and rolling mills, with which it diversified into wire, tube, and tin products.

54. *A Company of Uncommon Enterprise: The Story of Dravo Corporation, 1891–1966, the First 75 Years* (Pittsburgh: Dravo Corporation, 1974). For an overview of the region's complex production system, see Edward K. Muller, "Industrial Suburbs and the Growth of Metropolitan Pittsburgh, 1870–1920," in Muller and Tarr, *Making Industrial Pittsburgh Modern*, 65–87.

55. Samber, "Networks of Capital," 50; *Pittsburgh* (New York: American Society of Mechanical Engineers, 1928), 91.

56. Patch town was the local name for small company coal towns.

57. Warren, *Wealth, Waste, and Alienation*, 25–156; Samber, "Networks of Capital," 53–56; Muriel Earley Sheppard, *Cloud by Day: A Story of Coal and Coke and People* (Chapel Hill: University of North Carolina Press, 1947).

58. Warren, *Wealth, Waste, and Alienation*, 157–94, 233–37; *Pittsburgh* (American Society of Mechanical Engineers), 102–8.

59. David Hounshell, Mark David Samber, and Joel A. Tarr, *Technology and Transformation: The Railroad as a Shaper of Regional Space, Natural Resources, Industrial Practice, and Economic Development in Pittsburgh, 1830s–1920* (unpublished report, Carnegie Mellon University, 1994); Samber, "Networks of Capital," 70.

60. Quentin R. Skrabec Jr., *George Westinghouse: Gentle Genius* (New York: Algora Press, 2007), 66–77; Samber, "Networks of Capital," 70–72, 79–100.

61. James E. MacCloskey Jr., *History of Harbison-Walker Refractories Company: From Star to Vega and Beyond* (Pittsburgh: Harbison-Walker Refractories Company, 1952).

62. Over many censuses the definition of what constitutes a metropolitan area has changed and consequently the calculation of their populations has also changed.

This calculation for 1920 uses counties, which may exaggerate the Pittsburgh metropolitan population. Regardless, the Pittsburgh area's rank ranged from sixth to at least tenth. In short, Pittsburgh was one of the nation's largest metropolitan areas.

63. Warren C. Scoville, *Revolution in Glassmaking* (1948; New York: Arno Press, 1972), 67–148; Anne Madarasz, *Glass: Shattering Notions* (Pittsburgh: Historical Society of Western Pennsylvania, 1998), 153–54; Richard John O'Connor, "Cinderheads and Iron Lungs: Window-Glass Craftsmen and the Transformation of Workers' Control, 1880–1905" (PhD diss., University of Pittsburgh, 1991), 226, 234; Charles Reinhard Fettke, *Glass Manufacture and the Glass Sand Industry of Pennsylvania* (Harrisburg, PA: J.L.L. Kuhn, 1919).

64. Samber, "Networks of Capital," 56–61; Brian C. Black, *Petrolia: The Landscape of America's First Oil Boom* (Baltimore: Johns Hopkins University Press, 2000).

65. Cannadine, *Mellon*, 99–101, 117–18.

66. Samber, "Networks of Capital," 201–5; Cannadine, *Mellon*, 177–80.

67. Joel A. Tarr and Karen Clay, "Pittsburgh as an Energy Capital: Perspectives on Coal and Natural Gas Transitions and the Environment," in Joseph A. Pratt, Martin V. Melosi, and Kathleen A. Brosnan, eds., *Energy Capitals: Local Impact, Global Influences* (Pittsburgh: University of Pittsburgh Press, 2014), 14–15; Joel A. Tarr and Karen Clay, "Boom and Bust in Pittsburgh Natural Gas History," in Muller and Tarr, *Making Industrial Pittsburgh Modern*, 250–68; Skrabec, *George Westinghouse*, 68–75; Henry G. Prout, *A Life of George Westinghouse* (New York: American Society of Mechanical Engineers, 1921), 224–32.

68. Skrabec, *George Westinghouse*, 66–68, 102–24, 138–46, 161–76. For an excellent narrative of the battle between Westinghouse and Thomas Edison, see Jill Jonnes, *Empires of Light: Edison, Tesla, Westinghouse and the Race to Electrify the World* (New York: Random House, 2003). For an example of the spread of electricity at the time, see Joel A. Tarr, "'Lighting the Streets, Alleys, and Parks of the Smoky City, 1816–1930," *Pennsylvania History* 86, no. 3 (2019): 315–34.

69. George David Smith, *From Monopoly to Competition: The Transformation of Alcoa, 1888–1986* (Cambridge: Cambridge University Press, 1988), 1–131.

70. Robert C. Alberts, *The Good Provider: H. J. Heinz and His 57 Varieties* (Boston: Houghton Mifflin, 1973).

71. Though some sectors showed considerable innovative energy, the region's economy remained generally overspecialized in its traditional iron and steel industries.

72. Samber, "Networks of Capital," 110–12. The G.C. Murphy company is an example of a local, integrated corporation not linked to the region's industrial complex. In 1899 George Clinton Murphy opened his first variety store in McKeesport, the center of the mid-Monongahela Valley, twelve miles from Pittsburgh. Imitating F. W. Woolworth's dime store chain, Murphy expanded to nearby towns in the Pittsburgh region, attracting Woolworth to buy his 14 stores in 1904. Two years later Murphy started a new chain of G.C. Murphy five and dime stores, with the first

one again in McKeesport. He expanded around the region until his sudden death in 1909 at the age of forty-one. John S. Mack bought the G.C. Murphy company and set out to revive the languishing firm. He had 30 stores in southwestern Pennsylvania, Ohio, and West Virginia by 1919, and bought other chains from Indiana to the East Coast. Managing, stocking, designing, building, and printing required integrating vertically with in-house capabilities for these functions. By the end of the 1920s the G.C. Murphy company operated 166 stores, with its headquarters in a seven-story building in McKeesport, taking its place in Pittsburgh's corporate community.

73. Cannadine, *Mellon*, 27–49. Sarah Jane Negley Mellon bore eight children, but Sarah Emma and Annie Rebecca both died young. Selwyn, the third-born of six sons, died when Andrew was seven.

74. Cannadine, *Mellon*, 44–49, 66, 82–88.

75. Samber, "Networks of Capital," 141–42, 179–93; Cannadine, *Mellon*, 79–80, 96. Chartered by Pennsylvania, trust companies had the authority to perform financial functions, especially dealing in stocks and bonds, that national and state banks were forbidden to do.

76. Samber, "Networks of Capital," 143–52, 179–93; Cannadine, *Mellon*, 118–20, 181.

77. Samber, "Networks of Capital," 193–99; Cannadine, *Mellon*, 135–38, 176.

78. Samber, "Networks of Capital," 207–20; Cannadine, *Mellon*, 138–39.

79. Cannadine, *Mellon*, 181.

80. "Henry W. Oliver Died at 2 O'Clock This Morning," *Pittsburgh Dispatch*, February 8, 1904; "Henry W. Oliver Died This Morning," *Pittsburgh Times*, February 8, 1904; "H. W. Oliver's Will Disposes of Millions," *Pittsburgh Post*, February 12, 1904; "Appraisers File Report," *Pittsburgh Post*, May 11, 1904, all in Scrapbook, Box 3, vol. 7, OISC Records. Also see Henry W. Oliver Papers, 1814–1915, MSS# 439, Senator John Heinz History Center, Pittsburgh.

81. Much of this section is drawn from Edward K. Muller, "Downtown Pittsburgh: Relentless Change," in Muller and Tarr, *Making Industrial Pittsburgh Modern*, 392–443.

82. Valerie S. Grash, "The Commercial Skyscrapers of Pittsburgh Industrialists and Financiers, 1885–1932" (PhD diss., Pennsylvania State University, 1998), 23–52. Jacob Jay Vandergrift also put up the seven-story Conestoga Building in 1893 on Water Street.

83. Grash, "The Commercial Skyscrapers of Pittsburgh," 76–160; Franklin Toker, *Pittsburgh: An Urban Portrait* (University Park: Pennsylvania State University Press, 1986), 19–78; Walter C. Kidney, *Landmark Architecture: Pittsburgh and Allegheny County* (Pittsburgh: Pittsburgh History & Landmarks Foundation, 1985), 135–72.

84. Grash, "Commercial Skyscrapers of Pittsburgh," 133–82; Toker, *Pittsburgh*, 47, 69–72; John F. Bauman and Edward K. Muller, *Before Renaissance: Planning in Pittsburgh, 1889–1943* (Pittsburgh: University of Pittsburgh Press, 2006), 90–91; Muller, "Downtown Pittsburgh," 404–12. The two eras are not directly comparable.

The number of new skyscrapers erected in the second half of the twentieth century was less than during the industrial era, but the square footage of the newer skyscrapers was much larger.

85. Samber, "Networks of Capital," 384–92; Cannadine, *Mellon*, 216–17.

86. Wollman and Inman, *Portrait in Steel*, 59–83.

87. Samber, "Networks of Capital," 446–48; Cannadine, *Mellon*, 219–20; Robert Lewis, *Chicago Made: Factory Networks in the Industrial Metropolis* (Chicago: University of Chicago Press, 2008).

SIX: COMING TO PITTSBURGH

1. Thomas Bell, *Out of This Furnace* (1941; repr., Pittsburgh: University of Pittsburgh Press, 1976), 3.

2. Agostino Carlino, unlike Kracha, was a real person.

3. Interviews by authors with Augustine Carlino (Agostino's grandson), March 4, March 30, and June 10, 1998, Pittsburgh.

4. The 1900 figure includes Allegheny City's population with that of Pittsburgh because Allegheny City was annexed by Pittsburgh before the 1910 US census. The 1920 figure for the region includes Allegheny County (including Pittsburgh) at 1,186,000 and three adjacent counties, Beaver, Washington, and Westmoreland. While such a figure includes considerable rural space, it also covers much of the industrial expansion beyond Allegheny County at the time. See Edward K. Muller, "Industrial Suburbs and the Growth of Metropolitan Pittsburgh, 1870–1920," in Edward K. Muller and Joel A. Tarr, eds., *Making Industrial Pittsburgh Modern: Environment, Landscape, Transportation, Energy, and Planning* (Pittsburgh: University of Pittsburgh Press, 2019), 65–87.

5. John Bodnar, Roger Simon, and Michael P. Weber, *Lives of Their Own: Blacks, Italians, and Poles in Pittsburgh, 1900–1960* (Urbana: University of Illinois Press, 1982), 30, table 2. These figures do not take into account earlier immigrants' children and grandchildren, who melded into the native-born white population.

6. Bodnar, Simon, and Weber, *Lives of Their Own*, 20, table 1, and 30, table 2; Richard Oestreicher, "Working-Class Formation, Development, and Consciousness in Pittsburgh, 1790–1960," in Samuel P. Hays, ed., *City at the Point: Essays on the Social History of Pittsburgh* (Pittsburgh: University of Pittsburgh Press, 1989), 130.

7. Bodnar, Simon, and Weber, *Lives of Their Own*, 69.

8. English workers in the Monongahela River Valley were sometimes called Johnny Bulls.

9. Karl Marx, *The Eighteenth Brumaire of Louis Bonaparte*, 1852, https://www.marxists.org/archive/marx/works/1852/18th-brumaire/ch01.htm.

10. Emancipation of the serfs in Russia was not complete until 1861. Ewa Morawska, *For Bread with Butter: The Life-Worlds of East Central Europeans in Johnstown, Pennsylvania, 1890–1940* (Cambridge: Cambridge University Press, 1985), 25; David Brody, *Steelworkers in America: The Nonunion Era* (New York: Harper &

Row, 1996), 96–97; Frank Huff Serene, "Immigrant Steelworkers in the Monongahela Valley: Their Communities and the Development of a Labor Class Consciousness" (PhD diss., University of Pittsburgh, 1979), 33–36, 41.

11. Morawska, *For Bread with Butter*, 28. These countries included Hungary, Slovakia, Poland, and much of the Ukraine, Transylvania, Croatia-Slavonia, Slovenia,
and Serbia.

12. Morawska, *For Bread with Butter*, 64.

13. Morawska, *For Bread with Butter*, 36.

14. Morawska, *For Bread with Butter*, 49, 53, 54.

15. Morawska, *For Bread with Butter*, 36. The overwhelming majority of overseas
migrants, including 85–95 percent of all eastern and central European migrants who
traveled overseas, went to the United States. Others left for Australia, Canada, and
Latin America.

16. Brody, *Steelworkers in America*, 96; Serene, "Immigrant Steelworkers," 99,
table 3.

17. Morawska, *For Bread with Butter*, 63.

18. William I. Thomas and Florian Znaniecki, *Polish Peasant in Europe and
America* (1918), cited in Morawska, *For Bread with Butter*, 70–71. These overseas
migrants probably had higher expectations than those who stayed within Europe.
The latter left for a season or two to make money; the former were more inclined to
seek fundamental change in their lives.

19. Bell, *Out of This Furnace*, 2–18; Brody, *Steelworkers in America*, 96; Morawska,
For Bread with Butter, 1, 39, 70–71.

20. Bell, *Out of This Furnace*, 2.

21. Bell, *Out of This Furnace*, 3–14.

22. Bell, *Out of This Furnace*, 11–18.

23. Bell, *Out of This Furnace*, 21–24.

24. Bell, *Out of This Furnace*, 25.

25. Bell, *Out of This Furnace*, 26–29.

26. Bodnar, Simon, and Weber, *Lives of Their Own*, 40–42, 62; Oestreicher,
"Working-Class Formation," 131n50; John Fitch, *The Steel Workers* (1911; repr.,
Pittsburgh: University of Pittsburgh Press, 1989), 147 (quote).

27. Bell, *Out of This Furnace*, 33–34.

28. Bell, *Out of This Furnace*, 44–45.

29. Many left dependents in Europe who had little recourse to seek compensation for company negligence. Even if the survivors resided in Pittsburgh, the laws
and their own lack of sophistication worked against their gaining more than a minimal settlement. Brody, *Steelworkers in America*, 101; Serene, "Immigrant Steelworkers," 150; Crystal Eastman, *Work, Accidents and the Law* (1910; repr., New York:
Arno Press, 1969), 14, 51, 132, 185.

30. Bell, *Out of This Furnace*, 47.

31. Bell, *Out of This Furnace*, 48; Serene, "Immigrant Steelworkers," 49.

32. Serene, "Immigrant Steelworkers," 39–40.

33. Bell, *Out of This Furnace*, 59–61.

34. Bell, *Out of This Furnace*, 68.

35. Bell, *Out of This Furnace*, 71–113; Brody, *Steelworkers in America*, 104.

36. Bell, *Out of This Furnace*, 35, 119; David P. Demarest Jr., afterword to Thomas Bell, *Out of This Furnace* (1941; repr., Pittsburgh: University of Pittsburgh Press, 1976), 417.

37. Bodnar, Simon, and Weber, *Lives of Their Own*, 240.

38. Bell, *Out of This Furnace*, 128, 147. Mary was an American, having been born in White Haven like Thomas Bell's mother.

39. Bell, *Out of This Furnace*, 136–37.

40. Bell, *Out of This Furnace*, 141, 184–85; Brody, *Steelworkers in America*, 104.

41. Serene, "Immigrant Steelworkers," 75–76.

42. Serene, "Immigrant Steelworkers," 67.

43. Arrangements varied. In some cases, a man paid a small fee for lodging and an equal share of the household food bill. Others paid a flat monthly rate. In households where each man, including the host, paid an equal share of the cost of meals, these payments covered the food eaten by the wife and the children. The boarders also paid a flat sum to cover the work a woman did cooking, cleaning, and washing clothes for them. Those fees defrayed much of the family's household budget. Brody, *Steelworkers in America*, 98; Serene, "Immigrant Steelworkers," 73–74.

44. Brody, *Steelworkers in America*, 105.

45. Brody, *Steelworkers in America*, 102; Serene, "Immigrant Steelworkers," 77–79; Margaret Byington, *Homestead: The Households of a Mill Town* (1910; repr., Pittsburgh: University of Pittsburgh Press, 1996), 160–61.

46. St. Michael's brought over Vincentian Sisters from Slovakia to teach religion, language, and culture for their parochial school and one in Homestead. Serene, "Immigrant Steelworkers," 77–81, 132–33.

47. Serene, "Immigrant Steelworkers," 150–51.

48. Brody, *Steelworkers in America*, 120; Francis G. Couvares, *The Remaking of Pittsburgh: Class and Culture in an Industrializing City, 1877–1919* (Albany: State University of New York Press, 1984).

49. S. J. Kleinberg, "Seeking the Meaning of Life: The Pittsburgh Survey and the Family," in Maurine W. Greenwald and Margo Anderson, eds., *Pittsburgh Surveyed: Social Science and Social Reform in the Early Twentieth Century* (Pittsburgh: University of Pittsburgh Press, 1996), 93–97.

50. Byington, *Homestead*, 14–15, 51, 145; Kleinberg, "Seeking the Meaning of Life," 93–97.

51. Paul Krause, *The Battle for Homestead, 1880–1892: Politics, Culture, and Steel* (Pittsburgh: University of Pittsburgh Press, 1992), 209–10.

52. Thomas Armstrong, "The Filthy Huns," *National Labor Tribune*, August 26, 1882, quoted in Krause, *Battle for Homestead*, 217,

53. *National Labor Tribune,* July 29, 1909, quoted in Brody, *Steelworkers in America,* 135.

54. Krause, *Battle for Homestead,* 215n14, 220.

55. Krause, *Battle for Homestead,* 213, 224.

56. David Demarest, ed., *The River Ran Red* (Pittsburgh: University of Pittsburgh Press, 1992).

57. Demarest, *River Ran Red,* 23, 316, 319–20.

58. Byington, *Homestead,* 175.

59. Byington, *Homestead,* 290. Krause points out that the Amalgamated Association was already "plagued by internal dissension and external assault" on the eve of the strike. It represented only one-fourth of those eligible for membership. By then some lodges accepted unskilled members, but the organization remained focused on the skilled. Moreover, Amalgamated had already embraced a far more conservative posture. Three of its key leaders had crossed over to management's side by 1891. Krause, *Battle for Homestead,* 289.

60. Byington, *Homestead,* 175.

61. David Brody, *Labor in Crisis: The Steel Strike of 1919* (Philadelphia: J. B. Lippincott, 1965), 40–41.

62. Margaret Byington reported in 1910 that slightly more than half of all Slavs in the Homestead mill were single. A report ten years later noted that about two-thirds of the foreign-born workers surveyed were married. Byington, *Homestead,* 140, quoted in Serene, "Immigrant Steelworkers," 185; Interchurch World Movement, *Report on the Steel Strike of 1919* (New York: Harcourt, Brace and Howe, 1920), 99–100.

63. Serene, "Immigrant Steelworkers," 101–2; Brody, *Steelworkers in America,* 123. In 1919 mill executives served as president of the Homestead borough council and burgesses in Munhall and Clairton, while the county sheriff and the Duquesne mayor were brothers of company men.

64. Byington, *Homestead,* 27–28, 92, 145.

65. Serene, "Immigrant Steelworkers," 22–23, 115–20.

66. Serene, "Immigrant Steelworkers," 110; Brody, *Steelworkers in America,* 166. The Homestead Works' visiting nurse reported forty-three widows of steelworkers with children on her list of clients. *Daily Messenger,* November 21, 1913, 1.

67. L. C. Gardner, "Community Athletic Recreation for Employees and Families" (Munhall, PA: Carnegie Steel, n.d.), eight-page typescript found in the Homestead Carnegie Library. For more on company-backed sport and recreation, see Rob Ruck, *Sandlot Seasons: Sport in Black Pittsburgh* (Champaign-Urbana: University of Illinois Press, 1987), chap. 1; Serene, "Immigrant Steelworkers," 22; Brody, *Steelworkers in America,* 169.

68. Serene, "Immigrant Steelworkers," 55, 150, 268, Bell, *Out of This Furnace,* 65–67, 124–25.

69. Bell, *Out of This Furnace,* 124–25.

70. Bell, *Out of This Furnace*, 147.

71. Bell, *Out of This Furnace*, 195.

72. Bell, *Out of This Furnace*, 185.

73. Bell, *Out of This Furnace*, 65–67.

74. Morawska, *For Bread and Butter*, 57–61; Bell, *Out of This Furnace*, 123; Brody, *Steelworkers in America*, 106. On their return to Europe, many of these workers shocked the gentry with their now less-than-deferential ways.

75. Fitch, *Steel Workers*, 216.

76. Oestreicher, "Working-Class Formation," 134; Bell, *Out of This Furnace*, 170; Richard Oestreicher, "The Spirit of '92: Popular Opposition in Homestead's Politics and Culture, 1892–1937," in Greenwald and Anderson, *Pittsburgh Surveyed*, 192. Eugene Debs was an actual politician mentioned in the novel. Debs's national vote was a skimpier 6 percent.

77. James R. Barrett, "Americanization from the Bottom Up: Immigration and the Remaking of the Working Class in the United States, 1880–1930," *Journal of American History* 79, no. 3 (December 1992): 997.

78. Brody, *Steelworkers in America*, 192–97.

79. Krause, *Battle for Homestead*, 24, 132, 150–51, 156, 158.

80. Brody, *Labor in Crisis*, 15.

81. David Montgomery, "'The New Unionism' and the Transformation of Workers' Consciousness in America, 1909–22," in his *Workers' Control in America: Studies in the History of Work, Technology, and Labor Struggles* (Cambridge: Cambridge University Press, 1979), is the definitive explanation of this labor upsurge.

82. John Ingham, "A Strike in the Progressive Era: McKees Rocks, 1909," *Pennsylvania Magazine of History and Biography* 90 (1966): 353–77; Patrick Lynch, "Pittsburgh, the I. W. W., and the Stogie Workers," in Joseph R. Conlin, ed., *At the Point of Production: The Local History of the I. W. W.* (Westport, CT: Greenwood Press, 1981), 79.

83. A.F. Toner, quoted in *Pittsburgh Leader*, re-quoted in Marylynne Pitz, "Pressed Steel Car Strike in McKees Rocks Reaches Centennial Anniversary," *Pittsburgh Post-Gazette*, August 16, 2009, https://www.post-gazette.com/business/businessnews/2009/08/16/Pressed-Steel-Car-strike-in-McKees-Rocks-reaches-centennial-anniversary/stories/200908160200.

84. Brody, *Steelworkers in America*, 138.

85. *Survey*, July 6 and August 3, 1912, cited in David Montgomery, *Fall of the House of Labor* (Cambridge: Cambridge University Press, 1987), 316.

86. The Turtle Creek valley, which cast 36 percent of its presidential votes for Eugene Debs in 1912, supported the workers.

87. Montgomery, *Workers' Control in America*, 91–112; Tom Price, "The Westinghouse Strikes of 1914 and 1916: Workers' Control in America" (unpublished seminar paper, Department of History, University of Pittsburgh, 1983), 20–23, 34–35, 39–40, 49; Dianne Kanitra, "The Westinghouse Strike of 1916," (unpublished semi-

nar paper, Department of History, University of Pittsburgh, 1971), 1, 11–18, 28–30. Though the Coal and Iron Police was created by the Pennsylvania General Assembly in 1865, it was a private police force paid for and directed by the coal and iron companies. Because it sought to intimidate workers and used violence to break strikes, the Coal and Iron Police was reviled in mining patches and mill towns.

88. Brody, *Labor in Crisis*, 8.

89. William Z. Foster, *The Great Steel Strike and Its Lessons* (New York: B. W. Huebsch, 1920), 17; Brody, *Labor in Crisis*, 45–46.

90. Brody, *Labor in Crisis*, 50, 70, 72–73.

91. Brody, *Labor in Crisis*, 62–66. The Mine, Mill, and Smelter Workers began as the Western Federation of Miners, a militant union.

92. Foster, *Great Steel Strike*, 94–95; Brody, *Labor in Crisis*, 100–102, 111. Foster claimed that about 98 percent of the votes cast favored a strike. The other demands were for the reinstatement of the men fired for organizing; an end to company unions and physical examinations for job applicants; a standard wage scale; double pay for overtime, holidays, and Sundays; and a dues checkoff, in which the company subtracted union membership dues from a worker's pay and handed that sum over to the union.

93. Foster, *Great Steel Strike*, 29; Brody, *Labor in Crisis*, 59–60, 69, 75–76.

94. Foster, *Great Steel Strike*, 50–52.

95. Foster, *Great Steel Strike*, 54–63, 90; Brody, *Labor in Crisis*, 77, 90–94.

96. Montgomery, *Workers' Control in America*, 97.

97. Brody, *Labor in Crisis*, 133; Foster, *Great Steel Strike*, 204.

98. Foster, *Great Steel Strike*, 96, 98–99; Brody, *Labor in Crisis*, 148–50.

99. This is according to John Fitch, introduction to Foster, *Great Steel Strike*, vii; see also 112, 115–18; Brody, *Labor in Crisis* 147, 155–61.

100. Foster, *Great Steel Strike*, 119–22, 129, 135.

101. Foster, *Great Steel Strike*, 168, 190–91.

102. Serene, "Immigrant Steelworkers," 212–14; Mary Heaton Vorse, "Aliens," *Outlook* (New York), May 5, 1920, 24.

103. Fitch, *Steel Workers*, 12.

104. Foster, *Great Steel Strike*, 196–99.

105. Foster, *Great Steel Strike*, 205–9; Brody, *Labor in Crisis*, 162.

106. Brody, *Labor in Crisis*, 174; Foster, *Great Steel Strike*, 235.

107. Bell, *Out of This Furnace*, 208–9.

108. Bell, *Out of This Furnace*, 210–12, 224–25.

SEVEN: ITALIANS AND AFRICAN AMERICANS IN PITTSBURGH

1. Interview by authors with Augustine Carlino, March 4, 1998. Agostino Carlino was born in 1868. He died in 1947 at the age of seventy-nine. Palmira Frazzini was born in 1869. She died in 1946 at the age of seventy-seven.

2. Soon after joining Luigi, Agostino celebrated his birthday on July 4. Luigi explained that because of his birthday, everybody would be off work that day. Agostino was apprehensive about losing a day's pay, but his brother responded there would be no work. "We're going to celebrate!" That night, as fireworks were exploding at a gathering of Italian and German workers, Agostino remarked, "This is a great country."

3. Robert F. Foerster, *The Italian Emigration of Our Times* (1919; repr., New York: Arno Press and New York Times, 1969), 38. Foerster offers figures for the number of immigrants from each province for most years from 1876 through 1913. Virginia Yans-McLaughlin, *Family and Community: Italian Immigrants in Buffalo, 1880–1930* (Ithaca, NY: Cornell University Press, 1971), 30–32.

4. Yans-McLaughlin, *Family and Community*, 27–33. For an overview of Italian workers' emigration, see Donna R. Gabaccia, *Italy's Many Diasporas* (Seattle: University of Washington Press, 2000).

5. John Bodnar, Roger Simon, and Michael P. Weber, *Lives of Their Own: Blacks, Italians, and Poles in Pittsburgh, 1900–1960* (Urbana: University of Illinois Press, 1982), 44; Federal Writers' Project, *The Italians of New York* (1938, repr., New York: Arno Press and New York Times, 1969), 36–45; Foerster, *Italian Emigration of Our Times*, 327. Foerster has separate chapters on Italian immigration to France, Germany, other European countries, and North Africa. In some years almost as many migrated to Argentina and Brazil as the United States. Ella Burns Myers, "Some Italian Groups in Pittsburgh" (MA thesis, Carnegie Technical Institute [now Carnegie Mellon University], 1920), 6.

6. Myers, "Some Italian Groups in Pittsburgh," 10.

7. Bodnar, Simon, and Weber, *Lives of Their Own*, 45.

8. Bodnar, Simon, and Weber, *Lives of Their Own*, 45. They cite interviews with Italian immigrants conducted in the 1970s, a half-century after many arrived, to support this point. Yans-McLaughlin, *Family and Community*, 27, 35.

9. Bodnar, Simon, and Weber, *Lives of Their Own*, 8. They indicate that "by 1910, unemployment was becoming a problem, and migration toward Europe exceeded that toward Pittsburgh."

10. Salvatore Migliore, "Half a Century of Italian Immigration into Pittsburgh and Allegheny County" (MA thesis, University of Pittsburgh, 1928), 8, 15. Migliore argues that Pittsburgh received a somewhat higher proportion of northern Italians than most cities. Peter J. DiNardo, "The Italians in Pittsburgh: A Family and Individual Struggle to Fuse Ancestral and American Values in a New Environment" (unpublished seminar paper, Department of History, University of Pittsburgh, 1989). Dinardo states that about 85 percent of the city's Italians were from southern Italy. He based his numbers on records from the Italian Sons and Daughters of America and the Mother of Good Counsel and Regina Coeli Catholic Churches, and includes Rome in the south. Bodnar, Simon, and Weber, *Lives of Their Own*, 20, table 1; Myers, "Some Italian Groups in Pittsburgh," 1–2.

11. Migliore, "Half a Century of Italian Immigration," 20–21. Myers, "Some Italian Groups in Pittsburgh," 10, cites one estimate of 30,000–40,000 Italians and Italian Americans in Pittsburgh in 1918. She gave the following population figures: East Liberty 7,000–8000; Bloomfield 5,000–6,600; Brushton 5,000; South Oakland/Hazelwood 2,000; downtown and the lower Hill 4,000; North Side 9,000; South Side 3,000; Manchester 1,000.

12. Bodnar, Simon, and Weber, *Lives of Their Own*, 48; Myers, "Some Italian Groups in Pittsburgh," 37.

13. Paul U. Kellogg, ed., *Wage-Earning Pittsburgh* (1914; repr., New York: Arno Press, 1974), 39. DiNardo, "Italians in Pittsburgh," 18, cites figures for the percentage of Italians working free from direct supervision from 1930–1960.

14. In 1928 a partial listing enumerated eighty different Italian contractors in the city. Bodnar, Simon, and Weber, *Lives of Their Own*, 64, table 4. These statistics are based on a selected sample and thus are only a partial record; Migliore, "Half a Century of Italian Immigration," 30.

15. Migliore, "Half a Century of Italian Immigration," 33, 71. Among these students were four of the school's thirty-six football players.

16. Bodnar, Simon, and Weber, *Lives of Their Own*, 58, 68.

17. Agostino's sons, who worked at Campbell-Horigan, also worked at Carlini Bros. Monuments in Greenfield. Carlino and Carlini were actually the surnames of the same family, resulting from the common misspellings that occurred in official records of the day; pers. comm., grandson Sam Carlino and great-grandson August Carlino.

18. Interview with Carlino, March 4, 1998; John F. Bauman and Edward K. Muller, *Before Renaissance: Planning in Pittsburgh, 1889–1943* (Pittsburgh: University of Pittsburgh Press, 2006), 90–91.

19. Interview with Carlino, March 4, 1998; Migliore, "Half a Century of Italian Immigration," 10–13.

20. Joel A. Tarr, "The Cable and Electric Streetcar Networks," in Edward K. Muller and Joel A. Tarr, eds., *Making Industrial Pittsburgh Modern: Environment, Landscape, Transportation, Energy, and Planning* (Pittsburgh: University of Pittsburgh Press, 2019), 146–47; interview with Carlino, March 4, 1998.

21. "Bloomfield Has the Disposition of Little Italy," *Tribune Review Focus*, September 11, 1994.

22. Florence Larrabee Lattimore, "Skunk Hollow: The Squatter," in *The Pittsburgh District: Civic Frontage*, ed. Paul Underwood Kellogg (1914; repr., New York: Arno Press, 1974), 124–30; Perry Bush, "A Neighborhood, a Hollow, and the Bloomfield Bridge: The Relationship between Community and Infrastructure," *Pittsburgh History* 74, no. 5 (1991): 160–72; Myers, "Some Italian Groups in Pittsburgh," 47. The bridge, completed in 1914, spanned the ravine between the Hill and Oakland.

23. *Pittsburgh Leader*, November 26, 1905, 7, quoted in Bodnar, Simon, and Weber, *Lives of Their Own*, 70.

24. Lattimore, "Skunk Hollow," 124–30. Myers visited 104 families in Bloomfield, East Liberty, and the Hill for her study "Some Italian Groups in Pittsburgh," 13–14; interview with Carlino, March 4, 1998 (quote).

25. Bodnar, Simon, and Weber, *Lives of Their Own*, 153–59, 179–80, 256, 180 (quote).

26. A gas furnace replaced the original coal furnace after World War II.

27. Wagner, the son of a German immigrant who entered the coal mines when he was twelve before finding his calling on the ballfield, joined Babe Ruth, Christy Mathewson, Ty Cobb, and Walter Johnson in the first class of inductees to the Baseball Hall of Fame.

28. Migliore, "Half a Century of Italian Immigration," 37–40, 47–50. When it was refurbished in 1960, Agostino's grandson, Augustine Jr., did much of the marble work. About 1939, when the refurbished chicken coop that served as a school for many Italian children was torn down, Father di Francesco went to Father Bauer at St. Joseph's to try to arrange for the sixty children under his care to temporarily continue their education there. Bauer allegedly gruffly denied their request. Interview with Carlino, March 4, 1998.

29. Migliore, "Half a Century of Italian Immigration," 56, 64–65. When Pittsburgh's Italian-born population began to shrink, Italian language papers printed in New York City replaced the local press.

30. Migliore, "Half a Century of Italian Immigration," 112.

31. Anna's parents were Giovanni (1878–1965) and Marietta Capretta (1885–1968).

32. For the festivals, see William Simon, Samuel Patti, and George Herrmann, "Bloomfield: An Italian Working Class Neighborhood," *Italian Americana* 7, no. 1 (1991): 110.

33. Joseph Carlino's sons, August and John, would one day provide similar leadership for the Castel di Sangro club.

34. "Declaration of Intention," US Department of Labor, January 14, 1914.

35. Paul U. Kellogg, ed., *Wage-Earning Pittsburgh* (1914; repr., New York: Arno Press, 1974), 56–57. Myers, found that 70 percent of those she studied had naturalized by 1919 and another 10 percent had taken out their first citizenship papers; Myers, "Some Italian Groups in Pittsburgh," 40.

36. Leonard W. Moss and Walter H. Thomson, "The South Italian Family: Literature and Observation," *Human Organization* 18 (1959): 38, quoted in Yans-McLaughlin, *Family and Community*, 84.

37. Bodnar, Simon, and Weber, *Lives of Their Own*, 98–99. That relative exclusion from the wage labor force held for all but African-American women in Pittsburgh in the late nineteenth century.

38. Bodnar, Simon, and Weber, *Lives of Their Own*, 100.

39. See Yans-McLaughlin, *Family and Community*, chap. 3, "Families on the

Move," for a fuller analysis and description of the Italian family's transition to the United States.

40. Bodnar, Simon, and Weber, *Lives of Their Own*, 209–10; DiNardo, "Italians in Pittsburgh," 9–10. Myers argues that between 1900 and1910, 43 percent of the increase in the number of Italians and Italian Americans in the city was due to children born in the United States. These neighborhoods became ethnic communities largely because of American-born members. In later years while several Italian neighborhoods either lost their Italian flavor or disappeared, Bloomfield flourished. Myers, "Some Italian Groups in Pittsburgh," 3.

41. Joe W. Trotter, "Reflections on the Great Migration to Western Pennsylvania," *Pittsburgh History* 78, no. 4, (1995/1996): 153–54.

42. Bodnar, Simon, and Weber, *Lives of Their Own*, 30; Peter Gottlieb, *Making Their Own Way: Southern Blacks' Migration to Pittsburgh, 1916–1930* (Urbana: University of Illinois Press, 1987), 65. In total, the number of black residents in Allegheny County (including Pittsburgh) grew by almost twenty thousand during the 1910s.

43. S. E. Tolnay and E. M. Beck, *Festival of Violence: An Analysis of Southern Lynchings, 1882–1930* (Champaign-Urbana, University of Illinois Press, 1995); *Chicago Defender*, quoted in Trotter, "Reflections on the Great Migration," 98.

44. Laurence Glasco, "Taking Care of Business: The Black Entrepreneurial Elite in Turn-of-the-Century Pittsburgh," *Pittsburgh History* 78, no. 4 (1995/1996): 179; Bodnar, Simon, and Weber, *Lives of Their Own*, 30.

45. Laurence Glasco, "High Culture and Black America: Pittsburgh, Pennsylvania, 1900–1920," unpublished paper, May 28, 1997, 3–4.

46. Glasco, "High Culture and Black America," 12, 41.

47. Glasco, "High Culture and Black America," 179.

48. Bodnar, Simon, and Weber, *Lives of Their Own*, 13; Dennis C. Dickerson, *Out of the Crucible: Black Steelworkers in Western Pennsylvania, 1875–1980* (Albany: State University of New York Press, 1986), 8–9, 20, 24; Trotter, "Reflections on the Great Migration," 154; Rob Ruck, *Sandlot Seasons: Sport in Black Pittsburgh* (Urbana: University of Illinois Press, 1987), 128–29. Dickerson cites several cases where black workers were brought in during strikes. Black puddlers from Richmond were recruited to break a puddlers' strike at the Pittsburgh Bolt Company in January 1875. At the Black Diamond Steel Works in 1875, another group of black workers were kept on after the strike. Other cases occurred at the Solar Iron Works 1887 and again in 1889, as well as at Homestead in 1892 and at the Pressed Steel Company in 1909 (two groups of strikebreakers were brought in on trains, one a racially mixed group of two hundred, the other an all-black group of fifty); There was also some violence from striking white workers directed at black workers brought in to break their walkout in Connellsville in 1907 at the Sligo Iron and Steel Mills.

49. Laurence Glasco, "Double Burden: The Black Experience in Pittsburgh," in

Samuel P. Hays, ed., *City at the Point: Essays on the Social History of Pittsburgh* (Pittsburgh: University of Pittsburgh Press, 1989), 74.

50. Glasco. "Double Burden," 69–70; Bodnar, Simons, and Weber, *Lives of Their Own*, 185–86.

51. Ernest J. Wright, "The Negro in Pittsburgh," unpublished typescript, Works Progress Administration, Washington, n.d., chap. 12, cited in Glasco, "Double Burden," 74.

52. Ruck, *Sandlot Seasons*, 151; "C. W. Posey Is Victim of Illness," *Pittsburgh Courier*, June 13, 1925; Wright, "Negro in Pittsburgh," chap. 11, 12; Glasco, "Taking Care of Business," 179.

53. Andrew Buni, *Robert L. Vann of the Pittsburgh Courier: Politics and Black Journalism* (Pittsburgh: University of Pittsburgh Press, 1974), 3, 30–33. Western University of Pittsburgh became the University of Pittsburgh in 1904.

54. Buni, *Robert L. Vann*, 36, 40, 42–43; Malvin R. Goode, "Let's Build a Monument to Two Giants," *New Pittsburgh Courier*, December 10, 1983. Mal Goode, who grew up on Hilltop, followed Vann to the University of Pittsburgh. He worked night shifts at the Homestead Steel Works while in college and after, later becoming the first African American national television correspondent in 1962.

55. Buni, *Robert L. Vann*, 44–47, 53, 54 (quote).

56. Buni, *Robert L. Vann*, 61–65, 74.

57. Glasco, "Double Burden," 74–75.

58. Abraham Epstein, *The Negro Migrant in Pittsburgh* (1918; repr., New York: Arno Press and New York Times, 1969), 7; Rob Ruck, *Sandlot Seasons*, 10.

59. Authors' interview with Harold Tinker, Pittsburgh, June 19, 1980. This and subsequent information and quotations were based on this interview.

60. Bodnar, Simon, and Weber, *Lives of Their Own*, 69–70.

61. Glasco, "Double Burden," 79–80; Ira DeA. Reid, "Social Conditions of the Negro in the Hill District of Pittsburgh" (Pittsburgh: General Committee on the Hill Survey, 1930), 38.

62. Scott Smith and Steven Manaker, with the assistance of Dean Chester and Tom Taylor, "Pittsburgh's African-American Neighborhoods, 1900–1920," *Pittsburgh History* 78, no. 4, (1995/1996): 159–62; Gottlieb, *Making Their Own Way*, 70; Bodnar, Simon, and Weber, *Lives of Their Own*, 196; Buni, *Robert L. Vann*, 62–65.

63. Gottlieb, *Making Their Own Way*, 23–25.

64. In 1917 one train brought 191 men recruited from Bessemer, Alabama, directly to Pittsburgh. Gottlieb, *Making Their Own Way*, 56–58, 78; Bodnar, Simon, and Weber, *Lives of Their Own*, 190–91.

65. Bodnar, Simon, and Weber, *Lives of Their Own*, 191–92; Gottlieb, *Making Their Own Way*, 126.

66. Gottlieb, *Making Their Own Way*, 67–70; Dickerson, *Out of the Crucible*, 57; Epstein, *Negro Migrant in Pittsburgh*, 14–16.

67. Dickerson, *Out of the Crucible*, 3; Gottlieb, *Making Their Own Way*, 90–94.

68. Gottlieb, *Making Their Own Way*, 79–81; Bodnar, Simon, and Weber, *Lives of Their Own*, 59.

69. Gottlieb, *Making Their Own Way*, 98–99.

70. Dickerson, *Out of the Crucible*, 8–17; Epstein, *Negro Migrant in Pittsburgh*, 36–42; Bodnar, Simon, and Weber, *Lives of Their Own*, 214. As late as 1940 a survey of fifty-three locals in Pittsburgh revealed that only five had black members.

71. Trotter, "Reflections on the Great Migration," 156; Dickerson, *Out of the Crucible*, 88–92. Some of the unions belonging to the coalition organizing steelworkers either formally or informally barred black members; others were indifferent to issues of concern to black workers.

72. Bodnar, Simon, and Weber, *Lives of Their Own*, 98–99; S. J. Kleinberg, *The Shadow of the Mills: Working-Class Families in Pittsburgh, 1870-1907* (Pittsburgh: University of Pittsburgh Press, 1989), 163; Rob Ruck and Christopher Fletcher, "Unequal Opportunity," *Pittsburgh Magazine*, September 1995, 80.

73. Bodnar, Simon, and Weber, *Lives of Their Own*, 63, 155, 159.

74. Bodnar, Simon, and Weber, *Lives of Their Own*, 188–96.

75. Bodnar, Simon, and Weber, *Lives of Their Own*, 188–90, 120–23. They determined that two of every three black Pittsburgh residents in 1910 were no longer in the city in 1920.

76. Glasco, "Double Burden," 88; Bodnar, Simon, and Weber, *Lives of Their Own*, 35–36.

77. Dickerson, *Out of the Crucible*, 101–2.

78. Gottlieb, *Making Their Own Way*, 23–25, 29–31, 90–93.

79. Gottlieb, *Making Their Own Way*, 129–30.

80. Ruck, *Sandlot Seasons*, 23–33.

81. Ruck, *Sandlot Seasons*, 28–38; Dickerson, *Out of the Crucible*, 104–17.

82. Buni, *Robert L. Vann*, 59–60; Dickerson, *Out of the Crucible*, 44.

83. Bodnar, Simon, and Weber, *Lives of Their Own*, 131–35, 142; Glasco, "Double Burden," 74, 83.

EIGHT: "LARGELY INEFFECTUAL"

1. James R. Barrett and David Roediger, "The Irish and the 'Americanization' of the 'New Immigrants,' 1900–1930," paper presented at "Rewriting Irish Histories," the Neale/Commonwealth Fund conference, University College, London, April 6, 2002.

2. James R. Barrett, "Irish Everywhere: Irish Americans and the Making of the Multicultural City," paper presented at Center for Advanced Study, University of Illinois at Urbana-Champaign, January 10, 2014, https://www.youtube.com/watch?v=wXWBsuwevoo.

3. Rob Ruck, Maggie Jones Patterson, and Michael P. Weber, *Rooney: The Sporting Life* (Lincoln: University of Nebraska Press, 2010), 1–20.

4. Ruck, Patterson, and Weber, *Rooney*, 298.

5. Ruck, Patterson, and Weber, *Rooney*, 59–60.

6. Joel Tarr, "Infrastructure and City Building in the Nineteenth and Twentieth Centuries," in Samuel P. Hays, ed., *City at the Point: Essays on the Social History of Pittsburgh* (Pittsburgh: University of Pittsburgh Press, 1989), 232–34.

7. Lincoln Steffens, *The Shame of Cities* (New York: McClure, Phillips, 1904), 153–54.

8. Ruck, Patterson, and Weber, *Rooney*, 62–63.

9. Michael P. Weber, *Don't Call Me Boss: David L. Lawrence, Pittsburgh's Renaissance Mayor* (Pittsburgh: University of Pittsburgh Press, 1988), 6–14.

10. Ruck, Patterson, and Weber, *Rooney*, 60–63.

11. Ruck, Patterson, and Weber, *Rooney*, 62–63.

12. Wikipedia, s.v. "Roman Catholic Diocese of Pittsburgh: Bishops of Pittsburgh," accessed October 15, 2022, https://en.wikipedia.org/wiki/Roman_Catholic_Diocese_of_Pittsburgh#Bishops_of_Pittsburgh.

13. Nora Faires, "Immigrants and Industry: Peopling the Iron City," in Hays, *City at the Point*, 7–8.

14. Robert C. Alberts, *The Good Provider: H. J. Heinz and 57 Varieties* (Boston: Houghton Mifflin, 1973).

15. "History," Buhl Foundation, accessed September 9, 2020, http://buhl foundation.org/history/; "Russell Boggs Funeral to Be Held Today at His Late Home," *Pittsburgh Press*, July 11, 1922, accessed September 9, 2020, http://www .newspapers.com/clip/15928604/the-pittsburgh-press; Paul S. Korol, "Boggs & Buhl Department Store, Once a North Side Institution," *Pittsburgh Senior News*, December 2004, accessed September 9, 2020, http://buhlplanetarium2.tripod.com /bio/boggsbuhl.htm; "Reporter Dispatch," *Allegheny City Society*, February 2003, http://alleghenycity.org/downloads/025%202003%2001%. Boggs died in 1922. A trusteeship of the Buhl Foundation operated the department store after Buhl's death until 1947 when it was sold to investors.

16. Jacob Feldman, *The Jewish Experience in Pennsylvania: A History, 1755–1945* (Pittsburgh: Historical Society of Western Pennsylvania, 1986), 14–25, 80–81, 91–106; Barbara S. Burstin, *Steel City Jews: A History of Pittsburgh and Its Jewish Community, 1840–1915* (Pittsburgh: Barbara S. Burstin Publisher, 2008), 14–27, 79–81.

17. This paragraph is by no means an exhaustive list of Pittsburgh's downtown department stores. Joseph Horne's store was the largest at the time. Burstin, *Steel City Jews*, 61–70.

18. Burstin, *Steel City Jews*, 143–44, 185, 193–97.

19. Burstin, *Steel City Jews*, 56–74.

20. Rob Ruck, "Sandlot Seasons: Sport in Black Pittsburgh" (PhD diss., University of Pittsburgh, 1983), 351–56.

21. Ruck, "Sandlot Seasons," 82–83, 356–57.

22. Margo Anderson and Maurine W. Greenwald, "Introduction: The Pittsburgh

Survey in Historical Perspective," in Maurine W. Greenwald and Margo Anderson, eds., *Pittsburgh Surveyed: Social Science and Social Reform in the Early Twentieth Century* (Pittsburgh: University of Pittsburgh Press, 1996), 1–8.

23. The early twentieth century witnessed the first of three swings in the political pendulum toward the left; the other two occurred in the 1930s and the 1960s. Each leftward veer was followed by one to the right that erased many of the changes they had brought about. But these leftward swings built on each other and changed how government and private forces addressed an array of issues. They made life more secure for working and poor people by expanding the role of government.

24. Linda K. Pritchard, "The Soul of the City: A Social History of Religion Pittsburgh," in Hays, *City at the Point*, 342.

25. Andrew Carnegie, *The Autobiography of Andrew Carnegie* (New York: Public Affairs, 2011), 331; Joseph Frazier Wall, *Andrew Carnegie* (Oxford: Oxford University Press, 1970; repr., Pittsburgh: University of Pittsburgh Press, 1989), 381–86 (quote); John White, "Andrew Carnegie and Herbert Spencer: A Special Relationship," *Journal of American Studies* 13, no. 1 (2009): 57–58, https://www.cambridge.org/core/journals/journal-of-american-studies/article/andrew-carnegie-and-herbert-spencer-a-special-relationship/8A43AE7E187B1D0876EED58D67D6DC5E.

26. John F. Bauman and Margaret Spratt, "Civic Leaders and Environmental Reform," in Greenwald and Anderson, *Pittsburgh Surveyed*, 153–54. Bauman and Spratt defined moral environmentalism as the belief that "an efficiently managed, clean, attractive, urban environment exerted a morally uplifting influence on a city's population." See also Jon A. Peterson, "The City Beautiful Movement: Forgotten Origins and Lost Meanings," in Donald A. Krueckeberg, ed., *Introduction to Planning History in the United States* (New Brunswick, NJ: Center for Urban Policy Research, Rutgers University, 1983), 53–54.

27. Roy Lubove, *Twentieth-Century Pittsburgh: Government, Business, and Environmental Change* (New York: John Wiley & Sons, 1969), 26–28; Lisa A. Miles, *Resurrecting Allegheny City: The Land, Structures, and People of Pittsburgh's North Side* (Pittsburgh: by the author, 2007), chap. 12. In 1900 Pittsburgh had a population of 321,616; Allegheny City's was 129,896.

28. Lubove, *Twentieth-Century Pittsburgh*, 55–57, 97–100; Tarr, "Infrastructure and City-Building," 233, 243–44; John F. Bauman and Edward K. Muller, *Before Renaissance: Planning in Pittsburgh from 1889 to 1943* (Pittsburgh: University of Pittsburgh Press, 2006), 86–101.

29. Tarr, "Infrastructure and City-Building," 213.

30. Tarr, "Infrastructure and City-Building," 235–38.

31. Tarr, "Infrastructure and City-Building," 215, 240–44.

32. David Schuyler, *The New Urban Landscape: The Redefinition of City Form in Nineteenth-Century America* (Baltimore: Johns Hopkins University Press, 1986), 2–8, 59–76; Bauman and Muller, *Before Renaissance*, 26–29; Barbara Judd, "Edward

M. Bigelow: Creator of Pittsburgh's Arcadian Parks," *Western Pennsylvania Historical Magazine* 58 (1975): 53–67.

33. Jake Oresick, "What's *in* a Namesake?" *Western Pennsylvania History* 98 (Fall 2015): 22–33.

34. Diana Nelson Jones, "City's First Ballpark Had View and Water Hazard," *Pittsburgh Post-Gazette*, July 10, 1998, https://old.post-gazette.com/regionstate /19980710bclose4.asp.

35. Daniel Bonk, "Ballpark Figures: The Story of Forbes Field," *Pittsburgh History* 76 (Summer 1993): 55–56.

36. For a more extended discussion of the development of Oakland as the city's civic center, see Bauman and Muller, *Before Renaissance*, 42–48, 59–62.

37. S. J. Kleinberg, *The Shadow of the Mills: Working-Class Families in Pittsburgh, 1870–1907* (Pittsburgh: University of Pittsburgh Press, 1989), 270–78; Lubove, *Twentieth Century Pittsburgh*, 25–26.

38. Jessie B. Ramey, "The Gendered Dimensions of Women's Philanthropy," in *A Gift of Belief: Philanthropy and the Forging of Pittsburgh*, Kathleen W. Buechel (Pittsburgh: University of Pittsburgh Press, 2021), 140–60. The Kingsley House was an institution offering educational, health, and social services for low-income residents of the lower Hill District.

39. Roy Lubove, "Iams, Lucy Virginia Dorsey," *Notable American Women, 1607–1950*, 3rd ed. (Cambridge, MA: Belknap Press of Harvard University Press, 1974), 249–51.

40. Lubove, *Twentieth-Century Pittsburgh*, 26 (quote); Ramey, "Gendered Dimensions," 151–55.

41. Lubove, *Twentieth-Century Pittsburgh*, 41–58.

42. Wall, *Andrew Carnegie*, 805–15 (quote); Robert Mitchell, "Andrew Carnegie Built 1,700 Public Libraries," *Washington Post*, April 9, 2018, https://www .washingtonpost.com/news/retropolis/wp/2018/04/09/andrew-carnegie-built -1700-public-libraries-but-some-towns-refused-the-steel-barons-money/.

43. Wall, *Andrew Carnegie*, 871–72, 882–83 (quotes); David Nasaw, *Andrew Carnegie* (New York: Penguin Press, 2006), 671–72.

44. Lubove, "Pittsburgh and the Uses of Social Welfare History," in Hays, *City at the Point*, 311–14; Wall, *Andrew Carnegie*, 796–884; Ramey, "Organized Philanthropy by and for Women," 7–15; Kenneth Warren, *Triumphant Capitalism: Henry Clay Frick and the Industrial Transformation of America* (Pittsburgh: University of Pittsburgh Press, 1996), 372.

45. The Buhl bequest is from "The Buhl Foundation: A Legacy for the Community," accessed September 9, 2020, http://buhlfoundation.org/history/.

46. Lubove, *Twentieth Century Pittsburgh*, 23 (quote); Lubove, "Pittsburgh and the Uses of Social Welfare History," 314.

AFTERMATH

1. For perspectives on the region's industrial growth between 1907 and the 1930s, see Glenn E. McLaughlin, *Growth of American Manufacturing Areas: A Comparative Analysis with Special Emphasis on Trends in the Pittsburgh District* (Pittsburgh: Bureau of Business Research, University of Pittsburgh, 1938); and Mark David Samber, "Networks of Capital: Creating and Maintaining a Regional Industrial Economy in Pittsburgh, 1865–1919" (PhD diss., Carnegie Mellon University, 1995).

2. Roy Lubove, *Twentieth Century Pittsburgh: Government, Business, and Environmental Change* (New York: John Wiley & Sons, 1969), 20–28, 57. John T. Cumbler defines this worldview as civic capitalism in *A Social History of Economic Decline: Business, Politics, and Work in Trenton* (New Brunswick, NJ: Rutgers University Press, 1989), 1–6. Sam B. Warner Jr. used the term "privatism" to describe the nineteenth-century city in his classic book on Philadelphia, *The Private City: Philadelphia in Three Periods of Its Growth* (Philadelphia: University of Pennsylvania Press, 1968), ix–xii. For a Pittsburgh example of civic deference to industrial priorities, see Edward K. Muller, "'In spite of a river ought to be a Pittsburgh town-slogan'; Riverfront Planning in Pittsburgh, 1900s–1970s," in Edward K. Muller and Joel A. Tarr, *Making Industrial Pittsburgh Modern: Environment, Landscape, Transportation, Energy, and Planning* (Pittsburgh: University of Pittsburgh Press, 2019), 363–91.

3. Neil Swanson, *The First Rebel: Being a Lost Chapter of Our History and a True Narrative of America's First Uprising Against English Military Authority* (New York: Farrar & Rinehart, 1937); R. L. Duffus, *New York Times*, July 25, 1937.

4. *Allegheny Uprising*, dir. William A. Seiter (RKO Radio Pictures, 1939). A segment in the PBS miniseries *The War That Made America* (Part One, "A Country Between," dir. Eric Strange, aired January 18, 2006), shows a dramatization of Smith running the Native American gauntlet following his capture in 1755.

5. *Pittsburgh*, dir. William Seiler (Universal Pictures, 1942); *The Quiet Man*, dir. John Ford (Argosy Pictures, 1952).

6. "Mike Fink Keel Boats," https://disney.fandom.com/wiki/Mike_Fink_Keel_Boats.

INDEX

Adams Express Company, 92
Adams, Henry, 36
AFL. *See* American Federation of Labor
African Americans, 4, 83, 186, 190;
    corporate welfare, 198–200; first
    wave of migration, 188–95;
    formation of Hannibal Guards, 93;
    joining in great northern migration,
    148; laborers, 93, 106, 148;
    migration to Pittsburgh, 85–87,
    150, 186–88; Old Pittsburghers,
    189, 190–93; second wave of
    migration, 195–96; William Tinker,
    177–78, 186, 187, 193–95, 198;
    women in labor market, 197; work
    and community, 198. *See also* black
    Pittsburgh; Great Migration;
    immigrants in Pittsburgh; Tinker,
    Carl; Tinker, Harold; Tinker, Leon;
    Tinker, Mamie Willhite Tinker;
    Vann, Robert L.
Aitkin, Anne, 73

Alcoa. *See* Aluminum Company of
    America
Alexander, Thomas, 141
Alleghenies baseball club, 210
Allegheny Arsenal in Lawrenceville, 95
Allegheny Bessemer Steel Company,
    124
Allegheny City, 100, 101, 218;
    annexation with Pittsburgh, 8–9,
    99, 117, 215, 252n31; Deutschtown,
    207; factories and workshops in,
    78–79, 91, 208; glassworks in, 138;
    population, 262n4; public park in,
    101
Allegheny Cotton Factory, 71
Allegheny County, 47, 93, 262n4; 1916
    presidential election in, 164; African
    Americans in, 187; CCAC, 217–18,
    219–20, 228; Italian migration to,
    180; laborer jobs at Carnegie Steel's
    mills in, 151; Pennsylvania Rail-
    road's suit against, 115–16

Pennsylvania Female College, 219

Pennsylvania Railroad Company (PRR), 91, 92, 93, 99, 110–11, 124, 130, 135; response to 1877 insurrection, 111–12, 114; suit against Allegheny County, 115–16

Pennsylvania Salt Manufacturing Company, 99

Pennsylvania State Constabulary, 173

Penn, William, 16

Peoples Natural Gas, 138

Pew, Joseph, 138

Philadelphia Company, 138

Phillips, John, 122–23

Phipps, Henry, 96, 125, 127, 132–33, 142

Pitcairn, John, 136

Pitcairn, Robert, 91, 112

Pittsburgh, 226

Pittsburgh Academy. *See* University of Pittsburgh

Pittsburgh and Connellsville Railroad, 99–100

Pittsburgh and Lake Erie Railroad (P&LE), 129–30, 135

Pittsburgh Bessemer Steel Company, 124

Pittsburgh Bolt Company, 106

Pittsburgh Catholic, 206

Pittsburgh Chamber of Commerce, 214, 220; and CCAC, 217–18; Greater Pittsburgh, 214–15

Pittsburgh Coal Company, 142

Pittsburgh Council of Social Services Among Negroes, 200

Pittsburgh Courier, 187, 188, 191, 192–93

Pittsburgh Daily Gazette, 63, 67, 70, 82, 86

Pittsburgh Directory, 59

Pittsburgh Dispatch, 132, 142

Pittsburgh Gazette, iii, 47

Pittsburgh Leader, 167, 181

Pittsburgh Locomotive Works, 135

Pittsburgh Morning Post, 63, 69, 70

Pittsburgh, Pennsylvania: 1848 textile strike, 67–72; anti-Catholicism in, 79–82; and Black Boys, 34–35; black migrants in, 82–87; class and cultural differences in immigrants, 4–5; craftsmen's contribution to, 101–6; definition of metropolitan area, 259–60n62; dependence of regional economy, 120; impact of dynamism of industrial capitalism, 223–24; economic collapse, 60–61; economy in transition, 64–65; ethnic, religious, and racial diversity, 7–8; financial panic in, 109–10; free market ideology, 6; as Gateway to West, 52–55; German immigrants in Pittsburgh, 76–79, 201–2, 207–12; Great Railroad Strike in, 89–91, 109, 111–16; growth of industrial metropolis, 8–10; industrial and economic development of, 4, 5–6, 98–101; industrial opportunities, 55–57, 61, 64–66; Irish immigrants in Pittsburgh, 76–81, 201–6; legacies of reformers, 225–30; O'Hara and Fink's role in trade development, 50–52; Pennsylvania's claim on, 32–34; plebeian culture in, 107–9; proprietorship of, 35–37; puddler's strike (1867), 106–7; Renaissance I redevelopment program, 10; role of industrial elites in, 117–20; Scottish immigrants to, 72–76; skilled settlers in, 4; social and cultural development, 6–7; Steel Strike (1919) in, 170–74; transformation into Iron City, 91, 94–98; transition to industrially based economy, 88; as urban frontier, 57–60; Virginia *vs.* Pennsylvania's claim on, 32–34; Whiskey Rebellion, 39–49; working classes in, 65–67. *See also* Progressivism in Pittsburgh; Second Industrial Revolution of Pittsburgh

Pittsburgh Plate Glass Company (PPG), 136

Pittsburgh Post, 111

Pittsburgh Post-Gazette, 227

Pittsburgh Reduction Company. *See* Aluminum Company of America (Alcoa)

Pittsburgh Steamship Company, 130